UNCOVERED

Uncovered

Women's Roles, Mitzvot, and Sexuality in Jewish Law

Nechama Goldman Barash

Urim Publications
Jerusalem · New York

Uncovered:
Women's Roles, Mitzvot, and Sexuality in Jewish Law

by Nechama Goldman Barash

Copyright © 2024 Nechama Goldman Barash

All rights reserved
No part of this book may be used
or reproduced in any manner whatsoever without
written permission from the copyright owner,
except in the case of brief quotations
embodied in reviews and articles.

Typeset by Juliet Tresgallo

Printed in Israel

First Edition

ISBN 978-965-524-375-8

Front cover art: Eden Wolfgor
Cover design by the Virtual Paintbrush

Urim Publications
P.O. Box 52287
Jerusalem 9152102 Israel
www.UrimPublications.com

Cataloging-in-Publication data is available from the Library of Congress.

Dedication

by Debra Gerber

I feel privileged to have the opportunity to dedicate this book to the memory of my mother, Ursula ("Ulla") Breuer Merkin.

My mother was born in 1919 in Frankfurt am Main, where she lived until 1936 when, together with her parents and four siblings, she moved to the Land of Israel. She moved to New York in 1947 following her father's death, married my father, Hermann Merkin, in 1949, and died in 2006.

Her father, Isaac Breuer, a lawyer, philosopher, and Orthodox Jewish communal leader in both Frankfurt and Jerusalem, did not believe that women should study Talmud and did not permit her to study at the Hebrew University, whether for ideological or political reasons. My grandfather did, however, devote hours to studying with my mother with the result that, as a high school student in New York in the late 1960s, I sensed that I was perhaps the only student whose mother was entirely at home with Rashi, Ibn Ezra, and Ramban.

She taught Chumash at the Horev School during the 1940s. She also taught English and for years following my *aliyah* in 1983, former students of hers, discovering that I was Ulla Breuer's daughter, would enthuse over how she had taught English through songs which they still remembered 40 years later.

My mother emerged as a strong-willed person but remained forever loyal to and loving of her father. Looking backwards over the years when I have studied at Matan and Pardes, I sensed that my mother felt that she had "missed the boat" regarding women's Torah studies.

What my mother did have and passed on to me was enormous respect for education – both the art of teaching and the dedication of teachers to their students. In that sense, she was very much a product of her parents' home as well as the Jewish community and communal traditions of Frankfurt. She shared that with my father, Hermann Merkin, who revered no less the world of Jewish learning and scholarship.

I have attended Nechama Barash's classes for five years, even if mostly as a backbencher. She is a master teacher who loves her work and the world of rabbinic scholarship. By virtue of her skills as both scholar and educator, Nechama quietly commands the respect of her students. Hopefully this book will bring her teaching to a much broader audience.

In closing, I think of a possible variation of Robert Frost's poem, "The Road Not Taken" – the road not yet open. The world of תורה שבעל פה or women's learning was not open to my mother, a function of both time and circumstance. I believe enthusiastically and without reservation that she would have been equally pleased to facilitate bringing Nechama's teaching to a broader audience and to have sat next to me in her classes.

Contents

Introduction	13
Chapter One	
Does Gender Matter?	23
Time-Caused *Mitzvot* and the Status of Women	25
What Is Classified as a Time-Caused *Mitzvah*?	26
What Are Some Examples of Time-Caused *Mitzvot*?	29
Time-Caused *Mitzvot* Related to the Jewish Cycle of Festivals	31
Many Exceptions to the Rules	34
One Does Not Learn from General Principles	36
Can and Should Women Wear *Tzitzit*?	38
Should Women Don *Tefillin*?	41
Tefillin – For Those Who are Obligated to Study Torah	42
Women and *Shema*	47
Kiddush on Shabbat	55
Summary	59
Attitudes Toward Women in Rabbinic Literature	60
Infusing Theological Meaning into the Gender Gap	63
Feminist Scholars in the Twentieth Century	68
Suggestions for Moving Forward	71
Final Words	78

Chapter Two
Women and Torah Study – A Beit Midrash of Their Own   **81**

   Teach Your Sons and Not Your Daughters   83
   The Next Stage: Maimonides and Sefer Hassidim   93
   Should Women Learn Talmud?   104
   Can Women Become Halakhic Authorities?   111
   Women as Judges   112
   King but Not Queen: Women in Positions of Authority   116
   Deborah: Judge and Prophetess   117
   The Contemporary Picture   119
   Leadership and Professional Training Programs on the Path to Ordination   122
   One Last Note about Ordination (*Semikhah*)   128
   Women's Voices   129

Chapter Three
Ervah   **135**

   Biblical Sources   139
   Ervah as a Deterrent to Prayer and Blessing   142
   Covered but Uncovered   145
   Three Sources of *Ervah*   150
   The Jerusalem Talmud Parallel   152
   Follow-up in Berakhot   153
   Post-Talmudic Discussion of the Berakhot Text   155
   Summary   163

Contents

Chapter Four
Wearing Pants in the Community — **165**

   The Prohibition Against Women Wearing Men's Apparel — 166

   Summary — 176

   Trousers as Women's Apparel — 176

   The Rabbinic Reaction — 177

   Female Respectability — 192

   Concluding Thoughts — 195

Chapter Five
The Voice of a Woman — **199**

   Samuel's Statement: Three Citations — 199

   A Ban on Song — 203

   Post-Talmudic Interpretation — 207

   From the Shulhan Arukh Until Today — 215

   Modernity and Kol Isha — 217

Chapter Six
Women and Hair Covering – *Dat Yehudit* — **231**

   Mishnah Ketubot: *Dat Moshe* and *Dat Yehudit* — 232

   Going Out With a Bared Head — 236

   The *Sotah* Ritual — 239

   Summary — 241

   The Babylonian Talmud — 242

   And in a Woman's Courtyard? — 249

   Is the Basket Enough? — 250

   Types of Head Covering — 251

   Going Out on Shabbat — 252

Head Covering Practices in the Rabbinic Era	254
Head Covering for Unmarried Women	255
Conclusions	256

Chapter Seven
Women and Hair Covering – *Ervah* — 259

Introducing Kimhit and the Zohar	260
The Responsa of Maharam Alshakar	263
Conclusion	282
Modern Practice and Interpretation	282

Chapter Eight
Part One – Sexual Intimacy — 293

The Laws of Family Purity	293
The Biblical Laws of *Niddah*	296
Sexually Prohibited Relationships	296
Niddah and the Laws of Impurity (*Tumah*)	298
Birth	299
Seminal Emissions and Uterine Bleeding	301
The Unification of *Niddah* and *Zavah*	305
Shifting Attitudes Toward *Niddah* Laws	309
Modern Challenges to *Niddah*	312

Part Two – Behavior When the Couple is Prohibited by Laws of *Niddah* — 317

The Perpetual Honeymoon?	317
Forbidden Touch – Biblical or Rabbinic?	322
Ordinary Interaction and Touch	328
Touch or Die?	331

Contents

Caring for an Ill Husband	333
Caring for a Wife When She Is Ill	333
Support During the Birthing Process	336
Mental Illness	338
Emotional Touch	341
Further Halakhic Safeguards – *Harkhakot*	343
Desexualizing the Most Sexual Space: The Bedroom	348
Eating Together	349
Passing from Hand to Hand	351
Finding the Right Balance	354

Chapter Nine
Premarital Relationships — 357

Introduction	**357**
Forbidden Touch	358
Do Not Come Near	358
Emotional Touch	360
The Halakhic Prohibitions Relating to Non-Marital Sexual Relations	**361**
Kadesh/Kadeshah	361
The *Niddah* Prohibition and Single Women Using the *Mikvah*	364
Summary of Opinions about Non-Marital Sexual Relations	369
Other Aspects of Non-Marital Sexuality	**369**
Expectations of Virginity	369
Fear of *Mamzerut*	370

Masturbation	371
Unsanctioned Sexual Urges	372
Sex Education	**377**
Crossing the *Shomer Negiah* Threshold	377
Formulating a Jewish Sexual Ethic?	379
An Imperfect World: How Should We Be Educating?	380
Appendix	**383**
Bibliography	**388**
About the Author	**392**

Introduction

EVERY YEAR ON Simchat Torah, my parents and I walked from my grandparents' home in Sheepshead Bay to the ultra-Orthodox community of Boro Park in order to see the vibrant *hakafot* (dancing with the Torah scrolls) that are central to the holiday's celebration. I loved the long walk down Ocean Parkway as we stopped off at different places, packed in among the hundreds of people who had come together to joyously celebrate the culmination of reading the Torah before starting to read it all over again. There was stuffed cabbage, kugel, sponge cake, and candy, and for the adults, toasts of l'chaim over whiskey and wine. We would go to enormous men's *yeshivot* like Mir and Chaim Berlin as well as smaller spaces known as *shteibelach*. In all of them, the fervent excitement translated into dancing with the Torah on the men's side of the *mechitza* while enthusiastic women crowded in to watch from behind the curtain. For many years, observing such fervor was enough to inspire me; I felt that the men's dancing was an embodiment of my own spiritual expression.

One year, when I was 15, I unexpectedly began to wonder why I was relegated to watching. I walked away from the little window that was my peephole into the men's world and pondered why I was watching and not dancing. In retrospect, it was the beginning of my exploring the role gender plays in observant Jewish spaces. While I am still inspired by the passionate dancing of the men on Simchat Torah, it is no longer enough for me. I continue to search for spiritual outlets for myself as a woman, challenging the social religious structures that sometimes act as a barrier to my spiritual growth.

This book is the result of decades of immersion in the vast sea of Torah and Talmud texts as an observant Jewish woman, gradually moving from frustration to acceptance to empowerment by finding a "seat at the table," so to speak, of halakhic discourse. Coming of age in the second half of the twentieth century, I am acutely aware of the enormous privilege I have enjoyed with opportunities to learn Torah as a woman available at every stage I sought them out.[1] This book is the answer to my daughters and to my students who often ask me why I stay committed to Orthodoxy. As an Orthodox woman and a feminist, my values are based on intellectual critique and religious belief, coupled with halakhic practice. In essence, my dedication to halakhic observance is informed by the questions I ask and the answers I seek.

The first chapter looks at women's exemption from Time-Caused mitzvot as creating a foundation for a gender binary in which men and women are unequally obligated in mitzvot. Chapter Two explores women's exemption from Torah study and the effect it has on Orthodox society. In chapters three through seven, the halakhic practices of women's attire, public singing, and hair covering are examined, presenting traditional texts along with an analysis of their impact considering modern attitudes toward these topics. The laws restricting sexual behavior, often referred to as Family Purity Law, are addressed in two parts in Chapter Eight. Part One gives an overview of the halakhic structure with emphasis on the evolution in halakhic practice from the post-Second Temple period onward. Part Two examines the impact these halakhot have on a couple's intimacy

---

1. In 2019, I published an article in *Tradition* titled *A Rupture of Her Own*, reflecting on my journey into the study of rabbinic and halakhic texts. It appears in excerpted form as an Appendix to this volume and serves as personal background, presenting inner thoughts regarding key issues that will be developed and analyzed in the course of the book.

Introduction

both when sexually permitted and prohibited. Chapter Nine explores halakhic and social issues around non-marital sexuality given the modern dating reality in which men and women come of age sexually many years before they marry.

The topics in this book are based on the curricula of various Women and *Halakhah* courses that I have taught over the years. At times I have called the course "Permitted but Prohibited," reflecting the ambivalence within the halakhic discourse around women's status in society. These topics cover some of the most "popular" issues that have engaged women as they try to understand the context of a religious system of legislation that is 3,000 years old, developed in a world where women's roles were vastly different. My approach involves historical and textual contextualization as I trace the evolution of each specific topic from the earliest to the most contemporary of sources. As with any interpretive book, the presentation and analysis of halakhic sources reflects my own trajectory of study and most notably my perception of where things stand today.

About Translations in This Book

Special thanks to the incredible Sefaria database which made looking for rabbinic texts in general very efficient and accessible. This book would have taken even longer without this incredible resource.

Translations of biblical texts are based on *The Contemporary Torah: A Gender-Sensitive Adaptation of the JPS Translation*, Jewish Publication Society, 2006, found on Sefaria. Any adjustments of that translation are at the author's discretion.

Translations of Babylonian Talmud texts are based on the William Davidson Talmud, a free digital edition with parallel translations of rabbinic text. The William Davidson Talmud includes Rabbi Adin Even-Israel Steinsaltz's complete Modern Hebrew and English translations of the Talmud. Any adjustments of that translation were made at the author's discretion.

Translations of the Jerusalem Talmud are based on the translation and commentary by Heinrich W. Guggenheimer, Berlin, De Gruyter, 1999–2015, with adjustments at the author's discretion.

Regarding other rabbinic texts found throughout the book whose translations are not specifically cited, they were translated at the author's discretion.

Acknowledgments

I would be remiss not to thank the many people who helped me on my journey.

I had the honor to study at three wonderful institutions of higher Torah study for women. At Stern College, I had the privilege to study with Rabbi Moshe Kahn *z"l*. I was completely unprepared for his advanced class, but I worked hard and consider that to be one of my most formative educational experiences, one that helped direct me down the path that led to writing this book.

I came to Nishmat in the summer of 1991 to study Talmud with Rabbi Yair Kahn, who initiated me into the world of women's Talmud study in Israel that continued for the next two decades. Twenty years later, I entered the Yoatzot Halacha program with great trepidation. To my delight, these were two of the most astonishing years I had intellectually and religiously, pushing me to master an enormous amount of material and fostering engaging, interesting, and multilayered conversations on all matters having to do with women's bodies, sexuality, and fertility. My role as *yoetzet* has given me the opportunity to counsel and help women and couples from very diverse communities across the religious spectrum as well as outside of the observant community. The women and couples I counsel in areas of intimacy and *halakhah* are the impetus for the two chapters in this book on laws of *niddah*.

Matan Jerusalem is my spiritual home. Any time I walk into the building I feel a lightening of whatever load I am carrying. It is a place where everybody knows my name. I began studying at Matan in winter 1991 thanks to the kindness of Malka Bina, who allowed me to study at no cost as long as I committed to a certain number of hours. As a young *olah* living on very little, it was the only way I could afford to immerse myself in the world of advanced Talmud study. I never really left. Every time I was ready for more intensity,

Introduction

Matan welcomed me into another program. I studied in the Advanced Talmud Institute for three years while I completed a Master's degree in Talmud at Bar Ilan University.[2] Years later I returned to study in Matan's Hilkhata program. I am now proud to be on the faculty of Matan, teaching Torah in the *beit midrash* that gave me so many years of nourishment. I am humbled by my fellow Matan colleagues who have gone on to create a world of Talmud and *halakhah* study for women that has no precedent.

When David Bernstein, former dean of Pardes Institute, heard me teach at an open house at Matan, he invited me to substitute teach at Pardes. From there, I began a long process of teaching in virtually every program Pardes has to offer before making my way onto the full-time faculty. It was in the Pardes summer program that I began developing the source material and the methodology for the content of this book. My students at Pardes over the years pushed me to think and re-think the presentation of sources and challenged me to articulate an understanding of the broader meta-*halakhah* in light of today's social realities both inside and outside of Orthodox Judaism.

Midreshet Torah V'Avodah hired me in its founding year, 2014, and I have been an essential part of the faculty ever since. From the beginning, MTVA has acknowledged the importance of my voice as halakhically committed coupled with critical thinking within the educational vision for our students. I feel completely supported and respected by the faculty and staff, many of whom have become close friends and beloved colleagues along the way.

My community in Elazar, where I have lived for 27 years, was a place where I found my communal voice, helping shape women's religious life through establishing a women's *megillah* reading and Simchat Torah program, working to make the local *mikvah* a more user-friendly environment, and teaching Torah classes on a regular basis to men and women. Several of them reflected a slow, gradual process of growth and communal acceptance, and I refer to a number of these initiatives in the book as representative of changes taking

---

2. My dissertation was on the beautiful captive woman in Deuteronomy 21.

place in religious communities. Special thanks to Ronni Richter who was my partner in these enterprises. Gush Etzion in general is a place where women's Torah scholarship has flourished, and I have found many kindred spirits in the broader Gush community. Thank you as well to the incredible friend group too numerous to name who have helped me maximize my abilities in studying and teaching Talmud and *halakhah* by seeing the value and impact my scholarship has had on their own lives.

One of the last things my mother, Risa Ebert Goldman, said to me before she died was, "You can do this, Nechama." My mother was not an enthusiastic cheerleader who believed her children could do anything. She saw our flaws and encouraged us to nonetheless push past them to be our best selves. She died at the beginning of my teaching career, something that saddens me always, but especially after a wonderful class that I would have liked to share with her. She did, however, know that she was a role model to me as an educator and teacher, who deeply cared about the texts that she taught and even more so about her students. Her words of encouragement have become a mantra that I hear in my head whenever I feel self-doubt.

My father, Professor Steven Goldman, shaped my academic rigor as well as my ability to read texts both critically and with sensitivity. He always respectfully considered my questions and encouraged me to look for answers both inside and outside the world of the Beit Midrash. His enthusiasm was heartening, particularly in the early drafts of the book, which he and his wife, Phoebe Weisbrot, read and commented on. Some of those drafts were written up at their home in Monticello sitting by Sackett Lake where they made sure I had no responsibilities and was free to write. I thank them both for their continued support.

I have been blessed with four daughters, Talya, Chagit, Eden, and Ayala, who teach me firsthand the complexity of raising young women committed to Jewish tradition in a modern world. They (often) remind me that I am their mother first and foremost. For them (and for me), everything else in my life is of less significance. I thank them (mostly) for their love and patience, and I feel incredibly

Introduction

fortunate that I have raised four independent and talented young women with whom I remain close. Special thanks to my daughter Eden for designing the book's beautiful cover, capturing the spirit that I wished to convey in the design.

I feel special gratitude and affection for my siblings Dov, Miryam, and Yedida. They are an inextricable part of my childhood, and the hours we spend laughing and reminiscing about the years growing up together are priceless echoes of the love, values, and upbringing we all share. Whatever happens, I know I can continue to lean on them, and with them I am simply the oldest sibling. My brother, Dov, inhabits a different religious space than I do. We have engaged in endless debates about issues that relate to the topic of this book. I have no doubt that our at times heated discussions have made this a better book. With him in mind, I have tried to present material in a way that will be more acceptable to those who have different religious viewpoints than I.

Family lore has it that I taught my cousin Jodi Wachspress about the birds and the bees when I was eight and she was six. Perhaps that is the reason that both of us ended up in similar fields helping people create healthy intimacy. She is not only my cousin but remains a close friend and colleague. I have discussed many of the book's topics with her, particularly those dealing with sexuality. Her husband, Josh *z"l*, was a brother with whom I never fought, and his recent loss has opened an enormous hole in our lives that it is hard to imagine will ever be filled.

My in-laws and their families have been endlessly supportive and proud of my professional endeavors. Jerry Barach, my father-in-law, has been an indefatigable champion of my Torah study since I married into the family, coming to my weekly classes and regularly clipping newspaper articles of interest in my field.

There are many friends who over the years have pushed me to write this book. Some of them deserve special mention for urging me to keep going, particularly when I considered giving up. They include Rachel Furst, who explained to me why my first attempt at a draft needed some major rethinking and greater focus; Ruthie

Amaru and Laurie Kossowsky, who in every conversation over the last five years have asked when the book will be coming out; my oldest friends, Aviva Aharon, Ruthie Fuld, Lisa Saffran, and Margi Saks, who have been on this journey with me since the Beth Jacob years; and Sara Feigelson, Elisheva Gordon, Ariella Kasovitz, and Jeremy Simon, whom I first met while in Stern College. They have all actively supported me during the years it took to write this book, never doubting that I would finish it. It is an enormous gift to have so many friends who have known me practically from childhood and can contain my angst so effortlessly.

Yael Ziegler is my oldest friend, dating back to seventh grade in Torah Academy. It is actually astonishing that both of us ended up in higher Torah education for women. I am grateful for the many things that we share and discuss: our love for Torah study, our passion to teach and inspire through Torah text, and our commiseration over some of the religious challenges faced by our generation.

My students at the many programs I have taught on over the years, but notably those at MTVA, Matan, and Pardes, have been eagerly awaiting this book. I hope that it justifies their excitement. Special thanks to MTVA alumna Maya Hoff who served as my intern, copyediting an early version of the manuscript. When she told me that she could hear my voice in the words of the book as she read it, I knew I had to continue. Special thanks to Ariella Kasovitz and Aviva Aharon for reading and commenting on drafts of the manuscript. My thanks as well to Yocheved Hartman and Neshoma Lustig for reading and commenting on the last chapter.

Joshua Amaru and Shalom Berger of Academic Language Experts deserve special commendation for the attention spent on preparing this manuscript for publication. Josh, who is also a good friend, went above and beyond the time allotted for the job to carefully read and comment on every aspect of the manuscript. He gave me the confidence to feel that the text was ready and worthy of publication. Thanks as well to Sharon Meyer at Urim Publications who copyedited the manuscript one last time before publication. Additional thanks to Tzvi Mauer, publisher of Urim Publications, for taking interest in

Introduction

this book when it was still in the manuscript stage and bringing it to publication.

Debra Gerber came to me five years ago to ask if I had a project that she could sponsor in memory of her dear mother, Ursula. We came up with the idea for this book, which I naively thought would take only two years even as I continued to teach full-time. Thanks to Debra and Louis's generous sponsorship and incredible patience, this book is finally being published. May the memory of Debra's mother, Ursula Merkin, to whom this book is dedicated, indeed be blessed by the Torah learned in her memory by all those who read the content of these pages.

There are not enough words with which I can thank my husband, Dan. He believed in this project and in my ability to complete it, and he spent endless hours reviewing, editing, and pushing me to continue working. In Genesis Rabbah it is written: *It is not good that a man should be alone: It was taught: He who has no wife dwells without good, without help, without joy, without blessing, and without atonement.* It has been my own experience after many years of marriage that indeed, my marital partnership brings me: good, help, joy, blessing, and at times, atonement. I offer us a shared blessing of continuing to experience many more years of happiness together.

Lastly, to the Holy One who has fashioned me in the Divine Image with a soul striving to connect and inspiring within me a never-ending ability to feel simultaneously challenged and moved by the Torah that I learn and teach.

Coda:

It is impossible to ignore the change in circumstances that have taken place in Israel as this book was going to press. War broke out on October 7, 2023. As a country we are struggling to contain the trauma and agony over losing men, women, and children who were massacred and kidnapped by those who came solely to unleash evil and horror in our midst, along with the rising toll of soldiers dying on the battlefield as fighting continues. Around the world there has been an unprecedented rise in Jew-hatred as hundreds of thousands of people chant calls for genocide of the Jews. And yet, the Jewish people are strong and have united against a common enemy despite the months of divisiveness that pervaded Israel prior to the war. There has been an incredible outpouring of support both from within and without as people rush to volunteer time and resources to refugees, farmers, and soldiers. We are in a period of darkness punctuated by moments of incredible light as we witness the kindness, courage, and strength of good people.

With a prayer that by the time this book is published, there will be an end to the fighting and all of the hostages will have come home.

Nechama Goldman Barash
May 2024

Chapter One

Does Gender Matter?

Before approaching the topic of women and their obligation in *mitzvot*, particularly in contrast to the obligation of men, let us first ask ourselves a broader question: does gender matter in our lives? There is no doubt that biology matters in determining certain fundamental differences between men and women. Common sense, along with many academic studies, indicate that men and women feel and think differently, experience events and relationships differently, and learn differently. Whether these differences are the result of the influence of nature, nurture, or a combination of the two, it is reasonable to conclude that men and women differ not only physiologically but psychologically, intellectually, and emotionally as well.

Nonetheless, in the Western world, most people, particularly young people, acknowledge that in their "secular" lives, the significance of gender is limited mostly to dating and building personal relationships. Equality between the sexes is something they have been educated toward all of their lives. Their teachers and professors are both men and women. Their fellow students or colleagues are both male and female. Many have male and female employers or supervisors and co-workers of all genders. At least formally, men and women have equal educational and professional opportunities. While women are still underpaid in some professions in comparison to men – and are greatly underrepresented in some key areas like government and C-level positions – they have the opportunity to study and work in fields that are meaningful, interesting, and financially lucrative. In marriage, men and women create partnerships and divisions of labor regarding household and child-rearing responsibilities that are not automatically based on gender. Scheduling is often based on who has the greater flexibility and on external childcare arrangements.[1] This is becoming the case even in the more traditional ultra-Orthodox communities where the women are increasingly the breadwinners and the men as a result have become more involved in running the household and caring for the children while nonetheless dedicating much of their day to learning Torah.

In contrast, gender matters greatly in Orthodox Jewish practice and theology. Men have far more religious obligations than women on a daily, weekly, monthly, and annual basis. A quorum of 10 men is required for a prayer service to take place. Only men lead services, read Torah, and generally oversee the functioning of the synagogue. If there are nine men, a boy under bar mitzva can be brought to hold a Torah and serve as the tenth man (but not a grown woman). Men alone are deemed fit to serve as witnesses (with a few exceptions) and religious judges, most significantly in areas of marriage, divorce, and conversion. Professionally, men are circumcisers, ritual slaughterers, *kashrut* supervisors, rabbis, and cantors.[2] While this may seem onerous to some, it also confers privileges. For along with obligations, men have greater legal weight in determining *halakhah*. Until recently, all

---

1. It would be grossly inaccurate to portray modern society as fully egalitarian in nature. There are still many gender biases in place that hurt men and women with preconceptions of innate capabilities based on biology. With enough willpower, however, men and women can often push past such stereotypes and fight, if necessary, legally, for entry into gender-specific spaces.

2. From a halakhic perspective, women can ritually slaughter, circumcise, and act as *kashrut* supervisors although throughout history it has not been traditionally done. The purpose of such a list is to show that professionally, beyond teaching, women have very few leadership or professional roles in Orthodox Judaism. One obvious exception is *mikvah* attendants; however, in many cases men are paid to oversee the mechanical workings of the mikvah. More on this will be addressed in chapter 2.

halakhic questions were directed to men only. Furthermore, halakhic rules, categories, and precedents were constructed and applied without the participation of women even though they were directly addressed in laws having to do with marriage, divorce, sexuality, and more.

Time-Caused *Mitzvot* and the Status of Women[3]

One of the major halakhic distinctions between the genders is women's exemption from positive time-caused *mitzvot* (such as *tzitzit, tefillin, sukkah, lulav,* and *shofar*). To a young woman growing up in the Orthodox world, this reality is often presented definitively as the seminal proof that men and women are intended by God to fulfill dissimilar roles. I would go as far as to suggest that the foundation of gender separation rests greatly, though not exclusively, on this distinction.

In modern times, two reasons are often taught as the explanations for this gender division:

Women are more spiritual than men and as a result "need" fewer *mitzvot*.[4] This is understood to be the innate wisdom of the Torah, which recognizes that men and women cannot be religiously fulfilled in the same way. Men are more at risk and thus require more structure and boundaries to pursue a covenantal relationship with God.

Women are the primary caretakers of young children and therefore cannot possibly be obligated in time-caused *mitzvot* that would keep them from focusing on this essential role.

As will be explained below, the concept of "time-caused" defies a uniform designation, which complicates the attempt to neatly explain women's exemption from this category of *mitzvot*. There is also debate regarding which *mitzvot* are time-caused and which, while clearly

---

3. Thanks to Rabbi Scott Kahn for the suggestion to translate אמרג ומז more accurately as time-caused rather than time-bound.

4. This approach first appears in Maharal, *Sifrei Maharal* (Jerusalem:1971), *Be'er HaGola* 27a, and later in R. Samson Raphael Hirsch, *Commentary to Leviticus* (New York: 1971), 23:43.

time-caused, nonetheless obligate women. Furthermore, the Talmud brings no explanation for the above distinction.

Over the centuries, different attempts to explain women's exemption from time-caused mitzvot have been brought to suggest fundamental character differences between the sexes. An analysis of rabbinic sources will be presented along with a critical examination of how textual interpretations evolve and shape gender identity.

What Is Classified as a Time-Caused *Mitzvah*?

The primary source for women's exemption from time-caused *mitzvot* is in a Mishnah in Tractate Kiddushin:

Mishnah Kiddushin 1:7	משנה מסכת קידושין פרק א משנה ז
All of the *mitzvot* that a father is commanded to do for his son, women are exempt from, and all of the *mitzvot* the son is commanded to do for the father, both women and men are equally obligated. And all of the positive time-caused commandments, men are obligated and women are exempt. And all of the positive non-time-caused commandments, both women and men are obligated. And all of the negative commandments, whether time-caused or not, both men and women are obligated except for the prohibition to shave one's sideburns or beard with a razor and for priests (male) not to incur impurity of the dead.	כל מצות הבן על האב אנשים חייבין ונשים פטורות וכל מצות האב על הבן אחד אנשים ואחד נשים חייבין וכל מצות עשה שהזמן גרמה אנשים חייבין ונשים פטורות וכל מצות עשה שלא הזמן גרמה אחד אנשים ואחד נשים חייבין וכל מצות לא תעשה בין שהזמן גרמה בין שלא הזמן גרמה אחד אנשים ואחד נשים חייבין חוץ מבל תשחית ובל תקיף ובל תטמא למתים:

Does Gender Matter?

There are four categories of *mitzvot* presented in this Mishnah: positive time-caused, positive non-time-caused, negative time-caused, and negative non-time-caused. Women are obligated in three of the categories and exempted from *mitzvot* defined as positive time-caused. No explanation is given and there is no clarity as to what time-caused means or how to define the concept of time in this regard. Furthermore, the distinction between time-caused and non-time-caused *mitzvot* appears in the Talmud only in this context to emphasize the difference in *mitzvah* obligation between women and men. It serves no other function in the Talmudic discourse[5] and contributes to the overall impression that women have less religious responsibility.

Although no explicit reason is given in the Talmud for this time-caused exemption, I would suggest that the context in which it is introduced in Tractate Kiddushin more than hints at the reason. Historically and halakhically, when a woman marries, she transitions from her father's authority (*reshut*) to her husband's.[6] The implication is that her commitment to serve her husband preempts her commitment to serve her father. One could reasonably understand the Mishnah's presentation of a woman's exemption in a similar way: her commitment to her husband exempts any time-caused commitment to her Father in Heaven. This is best illustrated in a parallel text which presents a detailed explanation of the obligation incumbent upon a son when honoring his father:

---

5. Judith Hauptman, *Rereading the Rabbis*, p. 226.
6. Ideally a father would accept *kiddushin* on behalf of a daughter under 12.5 years of age even if the young couple did not formally begin to live together. Until that age a father had legal rights over his daughter and could marry her off even against her will (in Mishnaic and Talmudic times). After this age, the girl becomes a bogeret or legal adult. She could not be married against her will and her father did not have legal authority over her, although presumably, if she was living at home, her father would be heavily involved in her choice to marry.

Tosefta Kiddushin 1:11	תוספתא מסכת קידושין פרק א הלכה יא
What is a *mitzvah* that a son has towards his father – to feed, give to drink, dress and cover, bring him outside and bring him inside, wash his face, hands, and feet. The same applies to both men and women but the man is able to perform this *mitzvah* while the woman is unable to do so for the authority of others is upon her.	אי זו היא מצות הבן על האב מאכיל ומשקה מלביש ומכסה מוציא ומכניס ומרחיץ את פניו ידיו ורגליו אחד האיש ואחד האשה אלא שהאיש ספיקה בו לעשות והאשה אין ספק בידה לעשות מפני שיש רשות אחרים עליה.

To clarify the above text, men and women are equally obligated in the fifth commandment to honor one's parents. The cited Mishnah above states that women are obligated together with men in the fidelity of son to father or, more broadly, children to parents. However, married women are not free to fulfill this obligation because they require the permission of their husbands to do so, states the Tosefta. Due to the marital relationship, they are released from their filial obligations according to *halakhah* (although they are not exempted)[7] and no biblical verses are cited to justify such a move. The message is clear: a married woman will not be free to perform this *mitzvah* in the same way as a man.[8] In the Middle Ages, the presumed time

---

7. This is codified in Maimonides and Shulhan Arukh.
8. It must be noted that while a husband has the ability to prevent his wife from caring for her parents, if a man continuously prevents his wife from seeing her parents, it is grounds for divorce with a *ketubah*. The language in the Mishnah (Ketubot 7:4) is forceful:
One who vows his wife not to go to her father's house, when [he] is with her in the city, one month, he may maintain her as his wife. If the vow is for two months, he must divorce her and give her her marriage contract. And when her father is in a different city, from one Festival, i.e., until the next Festival, he may maintain her as his wife. For three Festivals, however, he must divorce her and give her her marriage contract.

restrictions that burden married women will become a more broadly used justification for why women are overall exempted from positive time-caused *mitzvot*, as suggested above.

Nonetheless, in the case of filial obligations, both the Jerusalem Talmud and the Babylonian Talmud add a caveat that if a woman becomes widowed or divorced, she resumes her full obligation to honor her parents.[9] In contrast to a blanket exemption from positive time-caused *mitzvot*, this temporary exemption is only for the duration of a marriage. It is interesting that such a distinction – between married and unmarried women – did not emerge with regard to exemptions from other *mitzvot*, reinforcing the unknowability behind the general principle.

Finally, husbands could always grant their wives permission to fulfill the commandment to honor their parents. In the seventeenth century, a prominent commentary on the Shulhan Arukh known as Shakh (*Siftei Kohen* by Shabtai Ben Meir HaKohen) notes that if a husband is not insistent that she give up her obligation, a married woman remains fully duty bound to honor her parents. In the modern era, it is largely assumed by both husband and wife that a woman will continue to actively honor and respect her parents for the duration of her marriage.

What Are Some Examples of Time-Caused *Mitzvot*?

B. Talmud Kiddushin 33b–34a	תלמוד בבלי מסכת קידושין דף לג עמ' ב – לד עמ' א
The Sages taught: What is a positive, time-caused *mitzvah*? Sukkah, lulav, shofar, ritual fringes (*tzitzit*), and phylacteries (*tefillin*).	כל מצות עשה שהזמן גרמא וכו': ת"ר איזוהי מצות עשה שהזמן גרמא? סוכה ולולב שופר וציצית ותפילין.

---

9. J. Talmud Kiddushin 1:7, 61a; B. Talmud Kiddushin 30b.

Uncovered

| And what is a positive *mitzvah* that is not time-caused? A mezuzah, a parapet on a roof, returning a lost item, and the release of the mother bird from the nest, [the *mitzvah* of sending away a mother bird when one finds it sitting on chicks or eggs]. | ואיזוהי מצות עשה שלא הזמן גרמא מזוזה מעקה אבידה ושילוח הקן. |

In the lengthy Talmudic discussion that is excerpted above and continues for several pages in the Talmud, there is an attempt to analyze the classification of positive time-caused *mitzvot* from which women are exempt. Several examples are given and include the following: *sukkah, lulav, shofar, tzitzit,* and *tefillin*. These *mitzvot* can be grouped into two categories, although it is difficult to establish a unifying thread between the two.

1. *Sukkah, lulav,* and *shofar* are time-caused because they can only be fulfilled on specific days of the year. No one disagrees with the time-caused nature of these *mitzvot*, as their performance is meaningless once the holiday passes. There is a uniform acceptance of these specific *mitzvot* (*shofar, sukkah, lulav*) as both time-caused and exempting women. Accordingly, it would be logical for this exemption status to apply to all positive commandments on holy days that are calendar dependent including Shabbat and Passover, but ultimately it does not.

2. *Tefillin* and *tzitzit* are ritual objects that are to be worn all day every day (in Talmudic times) and are certainly distinct from the previous time-caused examples of once a year *mitzvot*.[10] Neither of these examples are uniformly accepted in the Talmud as time-caused, as will be explained below. This category of *mitzvah* is

---

10. In the time of the Talmud, *tefillin* were worn all day, every day (except for Shabbat although even that was not unanimously agreed upon) The Talmudic Tractate Berakhot Chapter 3 has numerous discussions of how to bring *tefillin* into the bathroom. At a certain point in the post-Talmudic period, there was a move to limit wearing *tefillin* to the morning in conjunction with prayer.

qualitatively different than the previous one and will require a different interpretive lens.

3. *Shema*, which is said every day, once in the morning and once in the evening without exception, does not appear in the list of exemptions in the Kiddushin text although it is unquestionably the quintessential example of a positive time-caused *mitzvah* from which women are exempted. Regarding its time-caused nature, it more closely resembles the daily *mitzvot* of *tefillin* and *tzitzit*, but it is even broader because it is an obligation both day and night. This *mitzvah* will be thoroughly addressed after analyzing the Kiddushin source.

Time-Caused *Mitzvot* Related to the Jewish Cycle of Festivals

Women's exemption from sitting in a *sukkah* provides an opportunity to analyze the principle of women's exemption from time-caused *mitzvot*. Although it is clear from the outset that women will be exempted, since this is an explicit example given in the *beraita* quoted above, the Talmud offers equally valid interpretive arguments through which women could have been obligated not only in *sukkah* but in all positive time-caused *mitzvot*. An excerpt from the discussion appears below:

B. Talmud Kiddushin 34a	תלמוד בבלי מסכת קידושין לד עמ' א
But what of *sukkah* which is a positive, time-caused *mitzvah*, as it is written, *you shall dwell in booths seven days*, yet the reason [of women's exemption] is that Scripture wrote *ha-ezrah* or *the citizen*[11] to exclude women, otherwise women would be obligated!	והרי סוכה דמצות עשה שהזמן גרמא, דכתיב: בסוכות תשבו שבעת ימים. טעמא דכתב רחמנא האזרח, להוציא את הנשים, הא לאו הכי נשים חייבות!

---

11. The verse in Leviticus 23:42: "All **the citizens** in Israel shall dwell in *sukkot*." The definite article "the" is an exclusion [the verse could have been "all citizens in Israel"]

Said Abaye, It is necessary: I would have thought, since it is written *you shall dwell in booths seven days, you shall dwell* [meaning] even as you [normally] dwell [in a house]: just as [normal] dwelling [implies] a husband and wife [together], so must the *sukkah* be [inhabited by] husband and wife! But Raba said it is necessary: I might have though we derive *fifteen* here and in connection with Passover[12]: just as there women are liable [to eat *matzah*], so here too. Hence it is necessary.	אמר אביי: איצטריך. סלקא דעתך אמינא הואיל דכתיב: בסוכות תשבו, תשבו – כעין תדורו. מה דירה - איש ואשתו, אף סוכה - איש ואשתו. ורבא אמר: איצטריך. סד"א נילף חמשה עשר חמשה עשר מחג המצות, מה להלן נשים חייבות אף כאן נשים חייבות, צריכא.

There are compelling reasons, both methodological and practical, to obligate women in the *mitzvah* of *sukkah*. Abaye notes that if the *mitzvah* on Sukkot is to "dwell" in the *sukkah*, it should include women. Otherwise, men will be obligated to eat their meals and sleep inside the *sukkah* while their wives and daughters eat and sleep inside the home, though Sukkot is a holiday in which families are commanded to rejoice together, as explicitly stated in the biblical text cited below.

Deuteronomy 15: 13–15	דברים טו
After the ingathering from your threshing floor and your vat, you shall hold the Feast of Booths for seven days.	יג חַג הַסֻּכֹּת תַּעֲשֶׂה לְךָ, שִׁבְעַת יָמִים: בְּאָסְפְּךָ- מִגָּרְנְךָ, וּמִיִּקְבֶךָ.

---

and serves to exclude the women ... were not for the specific exclusion, explains the Talmud, women would be obligated.

12. The verbal analogy is built on the following two verses: "On the **fifteenth** day of this seventh month is the festival of Sukkot" (Leviticus 23:34) together with "And on the **fifteenth** day of the same month is the festival of Passover" (Leviticus 23:6).

Does Gender Matter?

You shall rejoice in your festival, with your son and daughter, your male and female slave, the Levite, the stranger, the fatherless, and the widow in your communities. You shall hold a festival for the Lord your God seven days, in the place that the Lord will choose; for the Lord your God will bless all your crops and all your undertakings, and you shall have nothing but joy.	יד וְשָׂמַחְתָּ בְּחַגֶּךָ: אַתָּה וּבִנְךָ וּבִתֶּךָ, וְעַבְדְּךָ וַאֲמָתֶךָ, וְהַלֵּוִי וְהַגֵּר וְהַיָּתוֹם וְהָאַלְמָנָה, אֲשֶׁר בִּשְׁעָרֶיךָ. טו שִׁבְעַת יָמִים, תָּחֹג לַיהוָה אֱלֹהֶיךָ, בַּמָּקוֹם אֲשֶׁר-יִבְחַר יְהוָה: כִּי יְבָרֶכְךָ יְהוָה אֱלֹהֶיךָ, בְּכֹל תְּבוּאָתְךָ וּבְכֹל מַעֲשֵׂה יָדֶיךָ, וְהָיִיתָ אַךְ שָׂמֵחַ.

In a different vein, Rava argues that Sukkot could be equated to Passover, based on an exegetical tool known as *gezerah shavah*, meaning the same biblical language is used in both cases. This exegesis allows the laws of one to be imposed onto the other. As they each fall on the 15th of the month, the word "fifteen" serves as the exegetical link. Since women are obligated to bring the Passover offering and to eat *matzah* on Passover – even though they are time-caused *mitzvot* – this could serve as a precedent to obligate women in *sukkah* which falls on the same date of a different month. At the end of this passage, the Talmud concludes that the article "the," which in Hebrew is one extra letter, is inserted in the text to clarify that women are exempt despite interpretive arguments that could determine otherwise:

Leviticus 23:42	ויקרא כג
You shall live in booths seven days; all the citizens in Israel shall live in booths.	מב בַּסֻּכֹּת תֵּשְׁבוּ, שִׁבְעַת יָמִים; כָּל-הָאֶזְרָח בְּיִשְׂרָאֵל, יֵשְׁבוּ בַּסֻּכֹּת.

In a parallel Talmudic text in Tractate Sukkah,[13] where the discussion

---

13. B. Talmud Sukkah 28a–b.

about women's exemption from *sukkah* is directly relevant to the material in the tractate, the Talmud does not engage in textual analysis of any sort. Rather, it introduces an irrefutable proof for women's exemption: *hilkhata*, meaning it is an oral tradition received from Sinai. The exemption can conclusively be established based on a tradition passed down from Sinai rather than an exegetical proof from within the biblical text. This bars any sort of future consideration for women's possible obligation.

To summarize, the Talmud in Kiddushin is unequivocal in its ruling that women are exempt from the *mitzvah* of *sukkah* despite the textual arguments by Abaye and Rava from within the Torah text that suggest the possibility of obligation. In Tractate Sukkah, a simpler, more authoritative proof is used: *hilkhata*. It is a tradition dating back to Sinai, and textual arguments are irrelevant.

Many Exceptions to the Rules

The Mishnah established a principle in which women are exempt from time-caused *mitzvot* that take place at a specific time or on a specific day of the year. At the same time, the Mishnah states explicitly that women are obligated in all non-time-caused *mitzvot*. Yet, the Talmud brings several significant examples where women are obligated in positive time-caused commandments and exempt from non-time-caused positive ones:

B. Talmud Kiddushin 33b	תלמוד בבלי מסכת קידושין לג עמ' ב
Is this in fact a rule? What about *matzah*, joy on holidays, and *hakhel*, the public reading the Torah every seven years, which are all time-caused positive commandments and women are obligated?	וכללא הוא? הרי מצה שמחה הקהל דמצות עשה שהזמן גרמא ונשים חייבות!

Does Gender Matter?

Plus, what about learning Torah, procreation, and redeeming one's firstborn son, which are not time-caused positive commandments, and women are exempt? Rabbi Yohanan says: One does not deduce practical *halakhot* from general principles, even in a place where it says: "except," to exclude a specific matter.	ותו, והרי תלמוד תורה פריה ורביה ופדיון הבן דלאו מצות עשה שהזמן גרמא הוא, ונשים פטורות! אמר רבי יוחנן: אין למדין מן הכללות ואפילו במקום שנאמר בו חוץ.

In this piece of Talmud, we are taught that women are obligated in eating *matzah*, rejoicing on the holidays, and gathering to hear the king read the Torah every seven years. This passage also acknowledges that women are exempt from several key non-time-caused positive *mitzvot*, notably Torah study, procreation,[14] and redeeming one's firstborn son.[15] In short, the Mishnaic statement in which women are exempt from positive time-caused *mitzvot* and obligated in positive non-time-caused *mitzvot* is by no means clear-cut since there are many exceptions to both rules. As Rabbi Yohanan states, we do not make deductions from general principles. This raises the question of why such a principle exists in the first place and what role it plays in shaping the binary gender arrangement. It is difficult to avoid the sense that the exemption of women from certain mitzvot is somehow

---

14. Procreation is an enormous topic that is beyond the scope of this book as it touches on fertility, sexuality, and contraception. It must be noted that a man cannot perform this *mitzvah* without a woman! According to the letter of the law, if a wife cannot fulfill the *mitzvah* or is put at risk by pregnancy, then a man must take another wife. If the sons or daughters die, which was very common in the ancient world, the man must continue to procreate. On the other hand, a woman may remain unmarried, marry a man known to be sterile, and use certain devices to prevent pregnancy because she is not biblically commanded to procreate, allowing her some latitude in protecting herself from becoming pregnant.

15. Women's exemptions from redeeming the firstborn son, circumcising their sons, or teaching their sons Torah all are based on the same principle. Since women themselves are not obligated to be redeemed, circumcised, or learn Torah, they cannot be obligated to facilitate the obligation for their sons.

arbitrary, yet the general statement in the Mishnah must hold true in at least some cases or it would be rendered meaningless.

One Does Not Learn from General Principles
R' Yohanan said: One does not learn from general principles, even in a place where it says "except" (i.e., when the general principle is explicitly stated with its exceptions...)

The Talmud's response to so many exceptions to the principle stated in the Mishnah is to conclude with the statement of the early and very important *amora*, Rabbi Yohanan, that general principles are rules of thumb, not hard and fast rules. In other words, although the Mishnah seems to be codifying a straightforward legal principle, the role of the stated principle is to be examined, assessed, diminished, or broadened even if it lessens the accuracy of the statement. This analysis of the principle ultimately shows that when there are well-established practices for certain *mitzvot*, they cannot be overturned by the application of a principle. Maimonides in his commentary to the Mishnah in Kiddushin expresses this dichotomy between the rule and the applied practice:

Maimonides Commentary to Kiddushin 1:7	פירוש המשנה להרמב"ם מסכת קידושין פרק א משנה ז
And a positive time-caused commandment is one where the obligation must be carried out at a set time, and when that time passes, the obligation does not take effect, as with *sukkah, lulav, shofar, tefillin,* and *tzitzit* because their obligation is in the day and not the night. And all others like them.	ומצות עשה שהזמן גרמא - הן מצות שאדם חייב לעשותם בזמן מוגבל, וכשלא יהיה זה - הזמן נתבטל חיובם, כמו הסוכה והלולב שופר תפילין וציצית שהם מחוייבין ביום ולא בלילה, וכל מה שדומה לזה.

Does Gender Matter?

And positive non-time-caused *mitzvot* are those whose obligation takes place regardless of time such as *mezuzah*, building a parapet, and charity. You already know that we have a principle that one does not learn from (heuristic) rules, and the term "all" [in the statements about women and positive commandments] truly means "most." But there is no general rule regarding the positive commandments in which women are obligated or exempted, rather they are passed on orally and are matters received by tradition. Is it not the case that eating *matzah* on the first night of Pesah, rejoicing on the festivals, *Hakhel*, the public reading of the Torah every seven years, *tefillah*, reading of the *megillah*, lighting Hanukkah candles, lighting Shabbat candles, and reciting *kiddush* are all positive time-caused commandments and for each of them a woman's obligation is the same as a man's obligation. Furthermore, the *mitzvah* of procreation, learning Torah, redeeming the firstborn, and the war with Amalek, each are non-time-caused positive commandments and yet women are not obligated in them. All are passed on by tradition as was explained.	ומצות עשה שלא הזמן גרמא - הם המצות המחוייבות בכל הזמנים, כגון מזוזה, ומעקה והצדקה. וכבר ידעת שהעיקר אצלנו אין למדין מן הכללות, ומה שנאמר כל אמנם רוצה לומר הרוב, ואמנם מה שהנשים מחוייבות ממצות עשה ומה שאינן מחוייבות ממה שמגיע אליהן אינו תלוי בכלל, ואמנם נמסרים על פה והם דברים שבאו בקבלה. הלא ידעת, שאכילת מצה בלילי פסחים ושמחה במועדים והקהל ותפילה ומקרא מגילה ונר חנוכה ונר שבת וקידוש היום, אלו כולם מצות עשה שהזמן גרמא, וכל אחד מהם מחייבות על הנשים כמו שהם מחייבות לאנשים. וכמו כן מצות פריה ורביה ותלמוד תורה ופדיון הבן, כל אחד מהם מצות עשה שלא הזמן גרמא, ואף על פי כן אין הנשים חייבות בהן. ואמנם נמסרים על פה כמו שזכרנו.

Maimonides acknowledges that the rule exempting women from

37

time-caused *mitzvot* is not comprehensive since there are too many exceptions. He concludes that the classifications of *mitzvot* from which women are exempt do not follow any legal reasoning or logic, but rather are passed on by tradition. This is similar to the argument brought in Tractate Sukkah exempting women from the *mitzvah* based on a longstanding tradition from Sinai. Nonetheless, both medieval and contemporary commentaries have attempted to interpret the principle as the Torah's response to something ingrained in female "nature," sometimes suggesting that women are seen as spiritually deficient, while other times suggesting they are spiritually superior. We will examine some of these explanations later in this chapter.

Can and Should Women Wear *Tzitzit*?

As noted above, there are two parallel categories of *mitzvot* defined as time-caused in the Mishnah. The first is *mitzvot* that occur at a certain time or on a certain day of the year. The second includes *tefillin* and *tzitzit* which are *mitzvot* worn on the body every day (except for *tefillin* on Shabbat and holidays).[16] While there seems to be uniformity in the Talmud around the exemptions for *shofar*, *lulav*, and *sukkah*, there is disagreement with regard to *tzitzit* and *tefillin*. Why should these *mitzvot* fall into the category of time-caused and why were women exempted from wearing them?

Tosefta Kiddushin Chapter 1, Halakhah 10	תוספתא מסכת קידושין פרק א (ליברמן) הלכה י
What is a positive time-caused commandment? *Sukkah*, *lulav*, and *tefillin*. What is a positive non-time-caused commandment? Returning a lost object,	אי זו היא מצות עשה שהזמן גרמא? כגון סוכה לולב ותפלין. אי זו היא מצות עשה שלא הזמן

---

16. The *halakhah* is that *tefillin* are not worn on Shabbat or holidays, which makes it time-caused. However, this decision was not accepted by all Tannaitic Sages. Hence the debate as to whether *tefillin* is a time-caused *mitzvah* or not.

sending away a mother bird from the nest, building a parapet, and *tzitzit*. Rabbi Shimon exempts women from *tzitzit* because it is a positive time-caused commandment.	גרמא? כגון אבידה ושלוח הקן מעקה וציצית. ר' שמעון פוטר את הנשים מן הציצית מפני שהיא מצות עשה שהזמן גרמא.
J. Talmud Kiddushin 61c	תלמוד ירושלמי מסכת קידושין דף סא טור ג
What is a positive time-caused commandment? *Sukkah, shofar, lulav,* and *tefillin*. What is a positive non-time-caused commandment? Returning a lost object, sending away a mother bird from the nest, building a parapet, and *tzitzit*. Rabbi Shimon exempts women from *tzitzit* because it is a positive time-caused commandment. Rabbi Shimon said to them (the Sages) do you not agree with me that *tzitzit* is a positive time-caused *mitzvah* since night clothing (pajamas) is exempt from *tzitzit*? Rabbi Hila said: the reason the rabbis included women in *tzitzit* is if a person had clothing that he wore both day and night they would be obligated in *tzitzit* (and thus, the *mitzvah* on this particular item of clothing would not have a time-caused quality since a person would wear it day and night).	אי זו היא מצות עשה שלא הזמן גרמא? כגון אבידה ושילוח הקן ומעקה וציצית. ר"ש פוטר הנשים מן הציצית שהיא מ"ע שהזמן גרמא. אמר להן ר' שמעון אין אתם מודין לי שהיא מצות עשה שהזמן גרמא? אמר להן ר' שמעון אין אתם מודין לי שהיא מצות עשה שהזמן גרמא? שהרי כסות לילה פטור מן הציצית! אמר ר' הילא טעמון דרבנין שכן אם היו מיוחדות לו ליום ולילה שהיא חייבת בציצית.

There is a known disagreement between the Sages and the Tanna Rabbi Shimon. This is repeated in multiple Tannaitic sources with the Tanna Kamma (the majority opinion) ruling that women are obligated in *tzitzit* because it is not a time-caused *mitzvah*. The obligation is determined by the four-cornered nature of the garment, rather than time. Rabbi Shimon disagrees and claims that it is a time-caused *mitzvah*. In the Jerusalem Talmud brought above (and in a parallel discussion in the Babylonian Talmud Tractate Menakhot 43a–b), Rabbi Shimon asks his colleagues why they disagree with him given that a night garment is exempt from *tzitzit* because the fringes cannot be seen and the biblical verse commands *and you shall see them*. In his mind, a daytime *mitzvah* that is not also a nighttime *mitzvah* becomes time-caused. In both Talmuds, the counter-argument to Rabbi Shimon is that a garment worn both night and day is obligated in *tzitzit* because the *mitzvah* is not time-caused but determined by the type of clothing.

It is significant, although not surprising, that when the Babylonian Talmud quotes the Tosefta in Kiddushin it leaves out the argument between the Sages and Rabbi Shimon, creating the impression of halakhic uniformity by placing *tzitzit* in the category of time-caused *mitzvot*. Rabbi Shimon's opinion becomes normative and the only opinion passed on,[17] although two anecdotes about Amoraim indicate that there were women who wore *tzitzit* based on the halakhic position that it is not time-caused and thus obligatory well after the Tannaitic period.[18] In later halakhic literature, *tzitzit* became a *mitzvah* from which women are not merely exempt but actively discouraged and even prevented from performing.[19]

---

17. This is not unusual, as the Babylonian Talmud does this countless times in order to condense certain conversations.

18. Bavli Sukkah 11a and Bavli Menahot 43a. Rabbi Amram the Pious and Rav Yehudah attached *tzitzit* to their wives' garments. See Rashi and Tosafot there.

19. Maimonides in the Laws of *Tzitzit* 3:9 writes explicitly that women may wrap themselves in *tzitzit* (without reciting a blessing), and the Shulhan Arukh codifies it simply as a positive time-caused *mitzvah* from which women are exempt. The Rema, after acknowledging this truth, nonetheless defines it as an act of conceit should women choose to perform this *mitzvah*.

Does Gender Matter?

Should Women Don *Tefillin*?

Like *tzitzit*, the time-caused nature of *tefillin* is not without dissent in the Talmud.

B. Talmud Eruvin 96b	תלמוד בבלי מסכת עירובין דף צו עמ' ב
As is written in a *Beraita*: He who finds *tefillin* on Shabbat brings them indoors by wearing them one pair at a time – this applies to both men and women, to new and old *tefillin* – these are the words of Rabbi Meir. Rabbi Yehuda forbids it in the case of new *tefillin* but permits it in the case of old ones. Rabbi Meir and Rabbi Yehuda disagree only regarding new and old, but they agree regarding women. Learn from this that *tefillin* must be a positive commandment without a fixed time and women are obligated to perform all such commandments.	דתניא: המוצא תפילין מכניסן זוג זוג אחד האיש ואחד האשה אחד חדשות ואחד ישנות דברי ר"מ. ר' יהודה אוסר בחדשות ומתיר בישנות. ע"כ לא פליגי אלא בחדשות וישנות אבל באשה לא פליגי. שמע מינה מצות עשה שלא הזמן גרמא הוא וכל מצות עשה שאין הזמן גרמא נשים חייבות.

This source in Eruvin is interesting because it cites several major Tannaim who rule that women are obligated in *tefillin* since it is not a time-caused *mitzvah*. Like *tzitzit*, there is a lack of uniformity in the Talmudic discussion with regard to women's exemption or obligation in these *mitzvot*. Such disparity is never mentioned in modern conversations about women wearing *tefillin* and *tzitzit* since the final halakhic consensus – even in the Talmud – veered steeply and absolutely away from considering such a possibility. For instance, a Tannaitic midrash considers *tefillin* the very prototype of positive time-caused *mitzvot*.

Uncovered

Mekhilta DeRabbi Shimon Bar Yochai Chapter 13	מכילתא דרבי שמעון בר יוחאי פרק יג
Another interpretation: "In order that the teaching of the Lord's Torah be in your mouth" (Exodus 13:9) – to exclude women. Just as *tefillin* are distinctive insofar as they are a positive time-caused commandment from which women are exempt, so too are women exempt from all time-caused positive commandments.	ד"א למען תהיה תורת ה' בפיך להוציא את הנשים. מה תפילין מיוחדות מצות עשה שהזמן גרמה נשים פטורות כך כל מצות עשה שהזמן גרמה נשים פטורות.

This midrash ties the *mitzvah* of *tefillin* to the obligation to constantly study Torah; women are exempt because they are exempt from studying Torah. The next line then integrates the presentation of *tefillin* as a time-caused *mitzvah* to women's overall exemption from time-caused *mitzvot*.

The discussion of women and *tefillin* is not exhausted by the question of its inclusion or exclusion from the time-caused category. Ultimately, *tefillin*, even if not time-caused, is also connected to Torah study since it contains within its parchment the text of the *Shema* within which lies the central commandment to study Torah.

Tefillin – For Those Who are Obligated to Study Torah

Mekhilta D'Rabbi Yishmael Bo Chapter 13	מכילתא דרבי ישמעאל בא מסכתא דפסחא פרשה יג
"In order that the teaching of the Lord's Torah be in your mouth" (Exodus 13:9). Why was this said? Since it says [about *tefillin*] "And it shall be a sign," I understand that even women should be	למען תהיה תורת ה' בפיך למה נאמר? לפי שנאמר והיה לך לאות, שומע אני אף נשים במשמע. והדין

Does Gender Matter?

obligated. This makes sense since *mezuzah* is a positive *mitzvah* and *tefillin* is a positive *mitzvah*; if you learn from *mezuzah* which is practiced by men and women, you might think *tefillin* also should be practiced by women as well as men. The Torah then says, "In order that the teaching of the Lord's Torah be in your mouth" (Exodus 13:9). I only meant this for one who is obligated in learning Torah. From here it is learned that all are obligated in *tefillin* except for women and slaves. Michal the daughter of Kush would put on *tefillin*, the wife of Jonah would go on pilgrimage during the three festivals, Tabi the slave of Rabban Gamliel would put on *tefillin*.	נותן, הואיל ומזוזה מצות עשה ותפילין מצות עשה, אם למדת על מזוזה שהיא נוהגת בנשים כבאנשים, יכול אף תפילין נהגו בנשים כבאנשים – תלמוד לומר למען תהיה תורת ה' בפיך, לא אמרתי אלא במי שהוא חייב בתלמוד תורה. מכאן אמרו הכל חייבין (בתלמוד תורה) [בתפלין] חוץ מנשים ועבדים. מיכל בת כושי היתה מנחת תפלי. אשתו של יונה היתה עולה לרגלים. טבי עבדו של רבן גמליאל היה מניח תפילין.

The Mekhilta asks a pointed question: why is an exegetical connection not made between *tefillin* and *mezuzah*? Women are obligated in *mezuzah* since it is a *mitzvah* determined by a structure (the house) and not by time or through learning Torah. As both *mitzvot* appear in the *Shema* text and both involve *Shema* written on parchment, one could ask why not obligate women in *tefillin* because of *mezuzah*? The midrash clarifies that *tefillin* are directly connected to an obligation to learn Torah. Women are exempt from this obligation of Torah study (although it is positive non-time-caused) and thus are exempt from *tefillin*. It concludes with two illustrations of exempted parties – Michal, a woman, and Tabi, a slave – who nonetheless put on *tefillin*, suggesting that exemption does not equal prohibition.[20]

---

20. In the parallel citation of this source in the Jerusalem Talmud, the discussion goes in a different direction and actually serves to work against the possibility of women performing similar *mitzvot*, specifically *tefillin*.

Uncovered

According to both Mekhilta texts cited, the exemption of women from *tefillin* is connected to Torah study and/or time-caused *mitzvot*. This then establishes an integral relationship between the exemption from learning Torah with the exemption from time-caused *mitzvot*. The logic seems to proceed as follows: since women are exempt from the obligation to study Torah, they are exempt from *tefillin*, and since *tefillin* is a time-caused *mitzvah*, women are exempt from all time-caused *mitzvot*.

The Babylonian Talmud offers similar logic:

B. Talmud Kiddushin 34a	תלמוד בבלי מסכת קידושין לד עמ' א
And women are exempted from positive time-caused commandments. From where do we derive this? It is derived from the *mitzvah* of *tefillin*: just as women are exempt from donning *tefillin*, so too women are exempt from	ומצות עשה שהזמן גרמא נשים פטורות. מנלן? גמר מתפילין. מה תפילין נשים פטורות אף כל מצות עשה שהזמן

J. Talmud Berakhot Chapter 2

We have learned elsewhere: Women and bondsmen are exempt from reciting the *Shema* and from *tefillin*. This ruling is questioned: did not Michal the daughter of Kushi don *tefillin* and did not Jonah's wife go up for the pilgrimage festivals and the Sages did not object? R. Hizkiah answered in the name of R. Abbahu, "Jonah's wife was turned back, and the Sages did object to Michal, the daughter of Kushi." In contrast, the Babylonian Talmud presents the opinion that women can perform optional *mitzvot* despite their exemption.

B. Talmud Eruvin 96a.

We have learned: Michal the daughter of Kushi used to don *tefillin* and the Sages did not object; Jonah's wife would go up for the pilgrimage festivals and the Sages did not object. We must infer that these are regarded as positive *mitzvot* not dependent upon a set time. Or perhaps the teaching is in accord with the view of Rabbi Yose who says that women may opt to lay their hands on an offering (*semicha*). If you do not say so, why did the Sages not object to Jonah's wife going up for the pilgrimage festivals? Can anyone maintain that going up for the pilgrimage festivals is not a positive *mitzvah* dependent upon a set time? We must conclude that this teaching is in accord with the view that these *mitzvot* are optional for women.

all positive time-caused *mitzvot*. And tefillin is learned from Torah study. Just as women are exempt from Torah study, so too women are exempt from donning phylacteries.	גרמא נשים פטורות. ותפילין גמר לה מתלמוד תורה. מה תלמוד תורה נשים פטורות אף תפילין נשים פטורות.

B. Talmud Kiddushin 34a	תלמוד בבלי מסכת קידושין דף לד עמ, א
And let us say the opposite and juxtapose *tefillin* to *mezuzah*. *Tefillin* are juxtaposed to Torah study in both the first paragraph and in the second paragraph of *Shema*, whereas *tefillin* are not juxtaposed to *mezuzah* in the second paragraph. But if so, let us juxtapose *mezuzah* to Torah study and exempt women. This could not enter your mind as it is written [with regard to the *mitzvah* of *mezuzah*:] "That your days may be multiplied." Can it be said that men need life but women do not need life?	ונקיש תפילין למזוזה? תפילין לתלמוד תורה איתקיש בין בפרשה ראשונה בין בפרשה שניה. תפילין למזוזה בפרשה שניה לא איתקיש. ונקיש מזוזה לתלמוד תורה? לא סלקא דעתך. דכתיב: למען ירבו ימיכם - גברי בעי חיי נשי לא בעי חיי?!

The Talmudic analysis used here is based on a methodological principle called *hekesh* or juxtaposition. To understand the analysis, it is necessary to see the contrasting order of the relevant *mitzvot* in the first two paragraphs of *Shema*:

Deuteronomy 6 (First paragraph)	דברים ו ואהבת
Teach them repeatedly to your children. Bind them as a sign to your hand and they shall be an emblem between your eyes.	ושננתם לבנך ודברת בם בשבתך בביתך ובלכתך בדרך ובשכבך ובקומך

Teach them repeatedly to your children. Bind them as a sign to your hand and they shall be an emblem between your eyes. Write them on the doorposts of your house and gates.	וקשרתם לאות על ידיך והיו לטטפות בין עניך וכתבתם על מזוזות ביתך ובשערך
Deuteronomy 11 (Second paragraph)	דברים יא והיה אם שמע
Bind them as a sign on your hand and they shall be an emblem between your eyes. Teach them to your children…. Write them on the doorposts of your house and gates.	וקשרתם אותם לאות על ידיכם והיו לטופות בן עיניכם ולמדתם אתם את בניכם לדבר בם בשבתך בביתך ובלכתך בדרך ובשכבך ובקומך וכתבתם על מזוזות ביתך ובשערך

In short, the Talmud essentially claims that while the biblical verse on *tefillin* is adjacent to the verse on *mezuzah* in the first paragraph of *Shema*, it is not adjacent to *mezuzah* in the second paragraph. Meanwhile, the commandment to don *tefillin* is adjacent to the verses about teaching Torah to one's children in both paragraphs of *Shema*. For this reason, *tefillin* must be classified as similar to Torah study, from which women are exempt, rather than similar to *mezuzah*, in which women are obligated. It goes through a similar process with *mezuzah*, suggesting that women could be exempted from *mezuzah*, which is not a time-caused *mitzvah*, because of its textual juxtaposition to the verse *teach it to your children* which obligates sons and not daughters in the *mitzvah* to study Torah.[21] The conclusion of the Talmud is that in the second paragraph of *Shema*, the text following the command to *write them on the doorposts of your house* promises *so that you will enjoy long life*" and men and women both need long life.

---

21. See Chapter Two for an in-depth analysis of women's exemption from Torah study.

Does Gender Matter?

Women and *Shema*

In the Kiddushin text brought above, the *mitzvah* of *Shema* is not addressed. It comes up peripherally in the context of *mitzvot* that are mentioned in the text of *Shema*, such as *tefillin*, *mezuzah*, and Torah study. Women's explicit exemption from this *mitzvah* appears in a Mishnah in Tractate Berakhot 19a–b that states that women, slaves, and minors are exempt from *Shema* and *tefillin* and obligated in prayer, *mezuzah*, and Grace after Meals. The ensuing Talmudic discussion regarding this Mishnah assumes an awareness of the Mishnah in *Kiddushin* exempting women from time-caused *mitzvot* as follows:

B. Talmud Berakhot 20a	תלמוד בבלי מסכת ברכות דף כ עמ' א
Mishnah: Women, slaves and minors are exempt from reciting the *Shema* and putting on *tefillin*, but are obligated for prayer, *mezuzah*, and Grace after Meals (*Birkat Hamazon*). Gemara: (Regarding *Shema*) That is obvious, as *Shema* is a positive time-caused *mitzvah*, and the halakhic principle is: Women are exempt from any positive time-caused *mitzvah*. Lest you say: Since *Shema* includes accepting the kingdom of Heaven, perhaps women are obligated in its recitation despite the fact that it is a time-caused, positive *mitzvah*. Therefore, the Mishnah teaches us that, nevertheless, women are exempt. We also learned in the Mishnah that women are exempt from *tefillin*. That is obvious as well. Lest you say: Since the *mitzvah* of *tefillin* is juxtaposed in the Torah to the *mitzvah* of *mezuzah*, therefore, the Mishnah teaches us that	משנה: נשים ועבדים וקטנים פטורין מקריאת שמע ומן התפלין, וחייבין בתפלה ובמזוזה ובברכת המזון. גמרא: קריאת שמע - פשיטא! מצות עשה שהזמן גרמא הוא וכל מצות עשה שהזמן גרמא נשים פטורות! מהו דתימא עשה שהזמן גרמא נשים פטורות! מהו דתימא הואיל ואית בה מלכות שמים קא משמע לן. ומן התפלין - פשיטא! מהו דתימא הואיל ואתקש למזוזה קא משמע לן.

nevertheless, women are exempt. We also learned in the Mishnah that women, slaves, and children are obligated in prayer.

Although the *mitzvah* of prayer is only in effect at particular times, which would lead to the conclusion that women are exempt, nevertheless, since prayer is supplication for mercy and women also require divine mercy, they are obligated. However, lest you say: Since regarding prayer it is written: "Evening and morning and afternoon I pray and cry aloud and He hears my voice" (Psalms 55:18), perhaps prayer should be considered a positive time-caused *mitzvah* and women would be exempt, the Mishnah teaches us.

And *mezuzah*. The Gemara asks: That too is obvious. Lest you say: Since the *mitzvah* of *mezuzah* is juxtaposed in the Torah to the *mitzvah* of Torah study, just as women are exempt from Torah study, so too they are exempt from the *mitzvah* of *mezuzah*. Therefore, the Mishnah explicitly teaches us that they are obligated.

And Grace after Meals. The Gemara asks: That too is obvious. The Gemara replies: Lest you say: Since it is written: "When the Lord shall give you meat to eat in the evening and bread in the morning to the full," it is considered a positive time-caused *mitzvah*, exempting women. Therefore, the Mishnah teaches us that women are obligated.

וחייבין בתפלה ‑ דרחמי נינהו. מהו דתימא הואיל וכתיב בה: ערב ובקר וצהרים כמצות עשה שהזמן גרמא דמי, קא משמע לן.

ובמזוזה ‑ פשיטא! מהו דתימא הואיל ואתקש לתלמוד תורה, קמשמע לן

ובברכת המזון ‑ פשיטא! מהו דתימא הואיל וכתיב: בתת ה' לכם בערב בשר לאכל ולחם בבקר לשבע, כמצות עשה שהזמן גרמא דמי, קא משמע לן.

Does Gender Matter?

In the Mishnah, women are grouped with minors and Canaanite slaves. However, the focus of the ensuing Talmudic discussion is limited to women.

The Talmudic discussion reexamines every *mitzvah* specified in the Mishnah, essentially asking why the gender distinction exists for each of these *mitzvot*. Two thousand years later, it is striking to read the point-counterpoint in which the inclusion of women, counter to the Mishnah's ruling, is considered for each *mitzvah* and justified before ultimately accepting the Mishnah's position. The structure of the discussion introduces each *mitzvah* with the obvious reason for its exemption and then embarks on a methodology known as *you might have thought*, followed by an excellent argument for women's inclusion (or exemption) from the particular *mitzvah* before ending with *thus it teaches us* to justify the need for specification in the Mishnah. This lends itself to the impression that the determination of legal principle could have gone in a different direction while remaining equally compatible with the interpretation of Torah and law. I have found myself wanting to hit pause after the *you might have thought...* specifically with regard to *Shema* and *tefillin*, wondering what the religious world of women would have looked like had we been obligated from the outset in these two central *mitzvot*.

Women's blanket exemption from *Shema* certainly provokes curiosity since the *Shema* is a liturgical affirmation of the key doctrinal commitments underlying rabbinic Judaism (belief in one God and dedication to God through performance of the commandments),[22] and the Talmudic discourse wonders whether they might have been obligated because of *Shema*'s theological significance. Since the Mishnah exempts women from *Shema*, such an argument is ultimately rejected. The reason brought for the exemption from *Shema* is based on the verse that is traditionally used to exempt women from learning Torah, which perhaps serves a more compelling reason for the exemption:

---

22. Elizabeth Shanks Alexander, *Gender and Timebound Commandments in Judaism*, Cambridge University Press, 2013, p. 137.

J. Talmud Berakhot Chapter 3 Halakhah 3	תלמוד ירושלמי, מסכת ברכות פרק ג הלכה ג (וילנא)
Mishnah: Women, slaves, and minors are exempt from reciting the *Shema* and putting on *tefillin* but are obligated for prayer, *mezuzah*, and *Birkat Hamazon*. **Gemara:** Where do we learn that women are exempt from the obligation to recite the *Shema*? From the verse *and you shall teach them to your sons*. To your sons and not to your daughters.	משנה: נשים ועבדים וקטנים פטורין מק"ש ומן התפילין וחייבין בתפלה ובמזוזה ובה"מ. גמרא: נשים מניין? ולמדתם אותם את בניכם [דברים יא יט] את בניכם ולא את בנותיכם.

Rather than utilize the principle of time-caused *mitzvot* to exempt women from *Shema* (which has always seemed weaker to me given that *Shema* is said every single day and night), it derives the exemption directly from a verse which is part of the *Shema* passage, *and you shall teach it to your children*. This verse is traditionally interpreted by the Sages to refer to the obligation to teach one's sons Torah to the exclusion of daughters. As seen regarding *tefillin* above, the *mitzvah* of reciting the *Shema* straddles two possible interpretive positions to explain women's exemption. Despite the dual nature of the *mitzvah* (time-caused and/or part of Torah study) which seems to exempt women simultaneously from both directions, there are still rabbinic voices that disagree and obligate women in *Shema*. One such dissent is found in the minor Talmudic tractate of *Sofrim*/Scribes:

Minor Tractate Sofrim 18:4	מסכתות קטנות מסכת סופרים פרק יח הלכה ד
Some [congregations] read the Book of Lamentations in the evening of the Ninth of Ab, while others postpone it to	יש שקורין ספר קינות בערב. יש מאחרין עד הבקר לאחר קריאת תורה

Does Gender Matter?

the [following] morning after the reading of the Torah, when the reader stands up, his head covered with ashes, his clothes torn, and reads it with weeping and lamentation. If he is able to translate it, well and good; but if he is unable he entrusts it to one who knows how to translate properly and [that person] does the translation, so that the rest of the people, the women and children may understand it; in that women are obliged to listen to the reading of the Book, how much more so does it apply to men. Women have similarly an obligation in reading the *Shema*, prayer, the Grace after Meals, and affixing a *mezuzah*. But if they are not acquainted with the holy tongue they are to be taught [to say them] in any language which they can understand and master. From this it was deduced that the man who recites the benedictions must raise his voice for the benefit of his young sons, his wife, and daughters.	שלאחר קריאת תורה עומד וראשו מתפלש באפר ובגדיו מפולשין וקורא בבכיה ויללה. אם יודע הוא לתרגמו מוטב ואם לאו נותנו למי שיודע לתרגם בטוב ומתרגם לפי שיבינו בו שאר העם והנשים ותינוקות שהנשים חייבות לשמוע קריאת ספר כאנשים וכ"ש זכרים. וכן חמה חייבות בקריאת שמע בתפלה ובברכת מזון ובמזוזה. ואם אינן יודעות בלשון הקדש מלמדין אותן בכל לשון שהן יכולות לשמוע וללמד. מכאן אמרו המברך צריך שיגביה קולו משום בניו הקטנים ואשתו ובנותיו.

In this rabbinic text, women are obligated to hear the reading of the Book (Torah), and they are also obligated in *Shema*, prayer, Grace after Meals, and *mezuzah*. Furthermore, if they do not know Hebrew, they are taught to say the prayers in any language that they can understand. Therefore, a man must raise his voice so that his minor sons, wife, and daughters can hear and be included when he recites blessings. While this text is singular in obligating women in *Shema*, it emphasizes the lack of uniformity on the subject of women's obligation in *mitzvot* by directly contradicting the Berakhot text which assumes absolute exemption from *Shema*.

In contrast to *Shema*, women are obligated in prayer. However, prayer poses a significant internal contradiction to the time-caused exemption since prayer in the Talmud usually refers to the *Amidah* prayer, which must be said three times a day. The Talmud itself acknowledges that prayer is time-caused, citing a verse from Psalms:

> **B. Talmud Berakhot 20a**
>
> Gemara: Obligated in prayer.
> Because [prayer] is supplication for mercy and women also require divine mercy, they are obligated. Lest you say: Since regarding prayer it is written: "Evening and morning and afternoon I pray and cry aloud and He hears my voice" (Psalms 55:18), perhaps prayer should be considered a time-caused, positive *mitzvah* and women would be exempt, the Mishnah teaches us.

In addressing the latent inconsistency in obligating women in prayer while exempting them from *Shema*, the Talmud explains that all human beings need mercy extended to them by God. Attempts to resolve the obligation to pray with the exemption from time-caused commandments is dealt with by medieval and modern commentaries alike. It is universally accepted that women have an obligation to pray. However, there are different suggested requirements, from a minimal acknowledgment of God's role in the world and thanks to God (which alleviates some of the dissonance around women's obligation in prayer and its time-caused nature) to an obligation to say the *Amidah* both morning and afternoon. Ironically, in modernity, many religious women are confident that they are exempted from prayer because of its time-caused nature. How then can they be obligated in something as time-consuming as prayer?

The last *mitzvah* mentioned in the Mishnah in Berakhot, in which women are obligated, is Grace after Meals. As with the other *mitzvot*, the Talmud debates the inclusion of women in what seems to be a positive time-caused commandment.

> **B. Talmud Berakhot 20a**
>
> Grace after Meals. That too is obvious. Lest you say: Since it is written: "When the Lord shall give you meat to eat in the evening and bread in the morning to the full" (Exodus 16:8), it is considered a positive time-caused *mitzvah*, exempting women from its recitation. Therefore, the Mishnah teaches us that women are obligated.

The Talmud brings a verse in which it is written that God gave the children of Israel meat at night and bread in the morning. Here too, the Talmud explains, one might assume that women should be exempt because of the time-caused nature of meals attested to in the Torah. Nonetheless, it concludes they are obligated to give thanks to God after eating. In an adjacent piece of Talmud, the discussion continues wondering whether a woman can recite the Grace for a man. This builds on a principle brought below that if two people are both equally obligated, they can fulfill the other's *mitzvah* obligation by reciting the text or blessing for the other:

B. Talmud Berakhot 20a	תלמוד בבלי מסכת ברכות כ
Ravina said to Rava: We learned in the Mishnah that women are obligated in the *mitzvah* of Grace after Meals. However, are they obligated by Torah law or merely by rabbinic law? What difference does it make? The difference is regarding her ability to fulfill the obligation of others when reciting the blessing on their behalf. Granted, if you say that their obligation is by Torah law,	אָמַר לֵיהּ רָבִינָא לְרָבָא: נָשִׁים בְּבִרְכַּת הַמָּזוֹן, דְּאוֹרָיְיתָא אוֹ דְּרַבָּנַן? לְמַאי נָפְקָא מִינַּהּ – לְאַפּוֹקֵי רַבִּים יְדֵי חוֹבָתָן. אִי אָמְרַתְּ בִּשְׁלָמָא דְּאוֹרָיְיתָא, אָתֵי דְּאוֹרָיְיתָא וּמַפֵּיק דְּאוֹרָיְיתָא. אֶלָּא אִי אָמְרַתְּ

53

one whose obligation is by Torah law can come and fulfill the obligation of others who are obligated by Torah law. However, if you say that their obligation is by rabbinic law, then from the perspective of Torah law, women are considered to be one who is not obligated, and the general principle is that one who is not obligated to fulfill a particular *mitzvah* cannot fulfill the obligations of the many in that *mitzvah*.	דְּרַבָּנַן, הָוֵי "שֶׁאֵינוֹ מְחוּיָּיב בַּדָּבָר", וְכָל שֶׁאֵינוֹ מְחוּיָּיב בַּדָּבָר אֵינוֹ מוֹצִיא אֶת הָרַבִּים יְדֵי חוֹבָתָן.

In the following text the Talmud brings unequivocal condemnation of men who allow their wives or minor children to say the Grace after Meals for them. Interestingly, Grace after Meals remains an unresolved point of halakhic contention regarding the degree of obligation and whether women are obligated biblically or rabbinically.

B. Talmud Berakhot 20a	תלמוד בבלי מסכת ברכות כ
Come and hear from what was taught in a *beraita*: Actually they said that a son may recite a blessing on behalf of his father, and a slave may recite a blessing on behalf of his master, and a woman may recite a blessing on behalf of her husband, but the Sages said: May a curse come to a man who, due to his ignorance, requires his wife and children to recite a blessing on his behalf.	תָּא שְׁמַע: בֶּאֱמֶת אָמְרוּ בֵּן מְבָרֵךְ לְאָבִיו וְעֶבֶד מְבָרֵךְ לְרַבּוֹ וְאִשָּׁה מְבָרֶכֶת לְבַעֲלָהּ, אֲבָל אָמְרוּ חֲכָמִים: תָּבֹא מְאֵרָה לְאָדָם שֶׁאִשְׁתּוֹ וּבָנָיו מְבָרְכִין לוֹ.

This kind of automatic rejection of women (equated here with children) fulfilling men's *mitzvah* obligations will permeate the entire discussion brought below even when men and women are equally obligated. There is a reflexive dismissal of women being able to fulfill men's *mitzvah* obligations, as if this diminishes somehow the religious role of men as the more active sex in practice and ritual.

Kiddush on Shabbat

The continuation of the Talmudic discussion in Berakhot looks at another exception to the rule of women's exemption from time-caused *mitzvot*. As noted above in the Kiddushin text, eating *matzah*, rejoicing on festivals, and gathering to hear the Torah read every seven years are exceptions to the principle of exemption. The text in Berakhot discusses women's obligation in the *mitzvah* of reciting *kiddush* over wine at the beginning of Shabbat, further widening the gap between the principle and its application by using an exegetical methodology that is supported by the biblical text.

B. Talmud Berakhot 20b	תלמוד בבלי מסכת ברכות דף כ' עמ' ב
Rav Adda bar Ahava said: Women are obligated to recite the sanctification of the Shabbat day [*kiddush*] by Torah law. Why? *Kiddush* is a positive time-caused *mitzvah*, and women are exempt from all positive time-caused *mitzvot*. Abaye said: by rabbinic, law. Rava said to Abaye: First, Rav Adda bar Ahava said that women are obligated to recite *kiddush* by Torah law, and, furthermore, let us obligate them to fulfill all positive time-caused *mitzvot* by rabbinic law, even though they are exempt by Torah law (which the rabbis did not do). Rather, Rava said: In the Book of Exodus, the verse said: "Remember Shabbat and sanctify it" (Exodus 20:8), while in the Book of Deuteronomy it is	אמר רב אדא בר אהבה נשים חייבות בקדוש היום דבר תורה. אמאי? מצות עשה שהזמן גרמא הוא וכל מצות עשה שהזמן גרמא נשים פטורות! אמר אביי מדרבנן. א"ל רבא והא דבר תורה קאמר! ועוד כל מצות עשה נחייבינהו מדרבנן! אלא אמר רבא אמר קרא (שמות כ, ז) זכור (דברים ה, יא) ושמור.

| said: "Observe Shabbat and sanctify it" (Deuteronomy 5:12). Anyone included in the obligation to observe Shabbat by avoiding its desecration, is also included in the *mitzvah* to remember Shabbat by reciting *kiddush*. Since these women are included in the *mitzvah* to observe Shabbat, so too are they included in the *mitzvah* of remembering Shabbat. | כל שישנו בשמירה ישנו בזכירה. והני נשי הואיל ואיתנהו בשמירה איתנהו בזכירה. |

The structure of the Talmudic passage continues to frame the obligation or exemption of women from specific commandments through the lens of the time-caused principle. It starts off with Rav Adda stating that women are obligated in *kiddush*, meaning the nighttime *kiddush* that sanctifies the beginning of Shabbat. The Talmud then asks why this should be so since *kiddush* is a *mitzvah* that is applicable only once a week, on Shabbat, and women are exempt from time-caused *mitzvot*.

Abaye suggests that perhaps their obligation is rabbinic rather than biblical. Accordingly, women and men have unequal obligations, with men being biblically commanded and women only rabbinically commanded. This solution upholds the principle of time-caused exemption, while also allowing for women's (lesser) obligation. Rava rejects this suggestion based on a literal reading of Rav Adda, who stated explicitly that the obligation was based on a law of the Torah. Furthermore, Rava notes, if that were so, women should have been rabbinically obligated in all time-caused *mitzvot*, which is not the case.

Rava then employs a classic exegetical methodology: two similar verses command the observance of Shabbat. The first states: **Remember** (*zakhor*) the Sabbath day to keep it holy. "Remember" is understood to mean actively remembering the Shabbat through the recitation of *kiddush* and other rituals commanded on Shabbat. The second verse has a one-word variation: **Guard** (*shamor*) the Sabbath day to keep it holy. One must refrain from transgressing on the Sabbath in order to maintain its holiness.

Does Gender Matter?

Since women are obligated in the guarding of Shabbat (*shamor*), asserts Rava, they must be obligated in the remembering of Shabbat (*zakhor*) which includes *kiddush*.[23] This ultimately turns into a halakhic blueprint for other *mitzvot* involving Shabbat such as *hamotzi* (blessing over two *hallot*), the requirement to eat three meals, and *havdala* (the ceremony to conclude Shabbat). This principle, along with a specific reference to *kiddush*, is stated clearly in Shulhan Arukh.

Shulhan Arukh Orah Hayyim 271	שולחן ערוך אורח חיים סי' רעא
Women are obligated in *kiddush*, even though it is a positive, time-caused commandment, because *zakhor* is compared to *shamor*. And these women, since they are included in guarding [the Sabbath], they are included in remembering it. And they can discharge men [from their obligation] since they are obligated biblically, like them.	נשים חייבות בקידוש אף על פי שהוא מצות עשה שהזמן גרמא, משום דאיתקש זכור לשמור, והני נשי הואיל ואיתנהו בשמירה איתנהו בזכירה ומוציאות את האנשים הואיל וחייבות מן התורה כמותם.

To summarize the Talmudic discussions, most of which appear in Kiddushin and Berakhot, the list of obligations and exemptions for women regarding the time-caused *mitzvot* principle is presented below:

---

23. The same methodology is used for the obligation of women to eat *matzah* on the first night of Passover. Since the prohibition on owning or eating *hametz* appears next to the commandment to eat matzah on Passover in several places in the Torah, a logical extension is used to connect the positive and negative commandments. Women are prohibited from *hametz* so they must be obligated to eat *matzah*. This logic is used to obligate them in both the negative and positive *mitzvot* when fasting on Yom Kippur. Since it is prohibited for them to eat, they must be positively commanded to fast, even though it is time-caused.

Exemptions from positive time-caused *mitzvot*	Obligations in *mitzvot* despite their time-caused nature	Exemptions from positive non-time-caused *mitzvot*
Shema	*Kiddush*	Learning/Teaching Torah
Tefillin (difference of opinion)	Grace after Meals (possibly rabbinic)	Procreation
Tzitzit (difference of opinion)	*Tefillah* (possibly rabbinic)	Redeeming the Firstborn
Sukkah	*Matzah*	Circumcision of a son
Lulav	*Hakhel* - (Hearing the king read the Torah once every seven years)	Honoring father and mother once married
Shofar	*Simhah* – (Joy on holidays)	Laying hands on a sacrificial animal
Pilgrimage on festivals	Paschal Offering	Donating a half-shekel to the Temple
	Destroying *Hametz*	
	Fasting on Yom Kippur (positive and negative)	

The following is a list of rabbinic time-caused *mitzvot* and women's obligations and exemptions that appear in discussions scattered across the Talmud:

Rabbinic Positive Time-Caused *Mitzvot*	
Women are obligated: Hannukah candles *Megillah* and other Purim *mitzvot* *Bedikat Hametz* (difference of opinion whether they can perform the *mitzvah* or must have it performed for them)	**Women are exempt:** Counting of the *Omer* (Majority opinion deems it is rabbinic but Maimonides counts it as biblical)

Four cups of wine and all Passover *mitzvot* *Hallel* on the night of Pesach *Lehem Mishneh* (the obligation to have two loaves of bread at the first two and preferably third Shabbat meal) Lighting Shabbat candles *Havdalah* *Eruv Tavshilin*	*Hallel* (rabbinic)

Summary

The Mishnah states that women are exempt from positive time-caused *mitzvot* and obligated in all non-time-caused *mitzvot*. It gives no reason for this differentiation. There are so many exceptions to this rule – both to obligate women in time-caused *mitzvot* and to exempt them from non-time-caused ones – that the Talmud quotes Rabbi Yohanan's dictum that we do not truly learn from "principles" in the Mishnah. In the course of much of the Talmudic discussions, a parallel path is set forth in which the reader can imagine "the road not taken" toward greater gender equality in *mitzvah* obligation based on different textual analysis. Over and over, the possibility of equality in *mitzvot* is rejected and that of gender differentiation is sustained. Yet, simultaneously and at times surprisingly, women are exempted from only a handful of positive time-caused *mitzvot*.

Despite the principle of exemption, women are obligated in all the positive time-caused *mitzvot* having to do with Shabbat, Passover, and Yom HaKippurim. They are obligated in daily prayer (although they do not count in a *minyan*). In addition, women are fully obligated in the four *mitzvot* of Purim and must light candles on Hannukah (once married, their husbands can light for them).[24] In fact, there are almost

---

24. With regard to some of the rabbinic time-caused *mitzvot* in which women are obligated, such as those associated with Hannukah and Purim, as well as rabbinic Passover *mitzvot*, Rabbi Yehoshua ben Levi (a first generation *amora* and thus someone who lived close to the period of the *tannaim*) suggests as an explanation

no rabbinically mandated time-caused *mitzvot* from which they are exempt, with the possible exception of counting the *omer*, whose origins are biblical, and reciting *Hallel* on festivals, which is based on Temple practice (from which women were almost entirely exempted).

Attitudes Toward Women in Rabbinic Literature

A quick survey of rabbinic sources about women shows that they can be divided into three main categories. The first category treats women as "Other." Here, women are portrayed as temptresses and pollutants. They are seen as lightheaded and liable to misconstrue information. According to several midrashim, even God was unable to control Woman's nature. In some midrashic narratives, God tries to create Woman as docile and submissive by creating her out of the most hidden part of man's body.[25] Ultimately, He fails and Woman is described as haughty, inquisitive, loquacious, jealous, and more. In one particularly difficult text, the Talmud quotes: "A woman is essentially a flask full of feces and her mouth is full of blood, [a reference to menstruation], yet men are not deterred and they all run after her with desire."[26] These sources show a distinct suspicion toward and bias against women, who are portrayed as strange beings in comparison to men.

In contrast, another category of sources describes the Jewish wife and mother in overwhelmingly positive terms and acknowledges the tremendous influence and impact women have on the family.[27]

---

that they were part of the miracle and that is the reason that women were included in these obligations.

25. See Genesis Rabbah 18: 2 and Deuteronomy Rabbah Parasha 6:11.

26. Bavli Shabbat 152a. (Text translations are generally taken from Sefaria.org, with minor edits, as necessary.)

27. See Shemot Rabbah 28:1 and B. Talmud Berakhot 17a. In both of these sources women are rewarded for taking their children and husbands to the house of study and waiting for them to return. In Shemot Rabbah, God tells Moses that if He makes the mistake of speaking to the men first, as He did in Eden with Adam, the women will make the Torah void, so great is their influence. As a result, God

Does Gender Matter?

Without women's commitment to God's covenant, the men, who are obligated to pass on the Torah, would not have the temerity or discipline to fulfill their duties.[28] Women as wives are thus central partners in the perpetuation of the covenant. Their importance and stature in this group of Talmudic texts are defined by their position as mothers, passing on religious resonance to their offspring, nurturing them as young children, and providing a warm home for the family. The Jewish nation could not survive without Jewish women, both figuratively and literally, given that Judaism is passed on matrilineally. The Talmud takes pains to legally protect the most vulnerable women in society. If a man or a woman needs to be supported financially, a community with limited resources should first act to protect its women, in order to shield them from a life of debauchery and prostitution.[29] Unmarried female orphans are entitled to support from their father's estate even though it essentially undermines their brothers' biblical right to solely inherit.[30] Married women have rights

---

    addresses the House of Jacob (interpreted as the women) before the Sons of Israel (the community of men).

28. See Genesis Rabbah 17:2, 7 and others in that chapter.
29. B. Talmud Horayot 13a. As is often the case with rabbinic sources it is not unusual to find contradictory positions regarding a given situation. While there is often a protective attitude towards vulnerable women in rabbinic literature, we find a rabbinic decree requiring a woman who is pregnant or has recently given birth to wait 18–24 months before remarrying, ostensibly for the protection of the child (see B. Talmud Ketubot 59b–61a, B. Talmud Yevamot 42a–b, Shulhan Arukh Even HaEzer 13:11). Over the centuries, women widowed or divorced by their husbands were desperately seeking to remarry in order to have a source of sustenance. Some of the women were faced with prostitution in order to feed their children and asked the courts permission to remarry. Yet in some of these cases the rabbinic authorities would still not allow them to remarry. See Responsa Mahari Mintz #5, Responsa Hatam Sofer (Even HaEzer 1), Section 3:30 and for contemporary discussion see Igrot Moshe Even HaEzer Section 4:49–50. The halakhic sources show a curious reluctance to override this particular rabbinic decree despite the vulnerability of the women and children in these cases.
30. Tosefta Ketubot 6:8, Mishna Ketubot 13:3.

to food, clothing, and sexual relations and can petition the court if their husbands are not fulfilling their marital obligations.

Finally, the third category of sources presents the halakhic status and obligations of women in distinction to men. Here the imbalance between the sexes is clear. Women are not equal to men. This is especially reflected in the entire structure of marriage and divorce. In Jewish marriage, a man exclusively acquires the sexual rights of his wife. There is no way to soften this legal reality. For this reason, Jewish divorce requires the husband to willingly release his wife from this contract of marriage by saying, "You are now permitted to any man." Furthermore, for similar reasons, only married women are charged with committing halakhic adultery; married Jewish men are not considered to be halakhically adulterous or implicated in the conception of a *mamzer* if they are unfaithful, as long as their sexual partners are unmarried. The Jewish divorce laws have become perhaps the most dissonant aspect of the gendered structure of traditional Judaism, for it leaves women completely at the mercy of men in acrimonious cases, stranded for years in limbo, forced to cede money or property in order to be freed of a toxic marriage. This effectively creates a moral Achilles heel for a religion that believes that halakhic practice simultaneously leads to greater ethical behavior, particularly in contrast to other cultures and religions.

Circling back to the general topic of this chapter ,since men have more *mitzvot*, their lives are actually worth more qualitatively. Thus, if the terrible choice must be made to save the life of a man or a woman, the man's life is given priority.[31] This outlook can be seen as a direct reflection of the Torah itself since passages in Leviticus dictate a differing monetary valuation for men and women (when an individual wants to donate a person's value to the Temple), with men having greater value.[32] While many commentaries try to explain

---

31. B. Talmud Horayot 13a.
    In case of rescue or returning a lost item, the man precedes the woman. With regard to clothing (a garment) or release from captivity, the woman precedes the man.

32. See Leviticus Ch. 27.

that the difference in valuation between the genders is based on the market price for male versus female slaves and not as a measure of spiritual or communal worth, it has importance as a source in the Torah where a gender hierarchy and value differentiation is present.

As was illustrated in the chart brought above, women are obligated in many *mitzvot*. They are obviously expected to have competency regarding those areas of *halakhah* for which women are traditionally responsible in a Jewish home, e.g., the laws of *kashrut*, Shabbat, and sexual intimacy. However, there is a hierarchy that directly stems from the imbalance in *mitzvot* obligation and is well reflected in a daily blessing brought by Rabbi Meir in the Talmud: "It was taught: R. Meir says: A person must say three benedictions every day and these are they: who has made me an Israelite; who has not made me a woman; who has not made me an ignoramus...."[33]

In modernity this blessing has come under sharp criticism from Orthodox feminists for its perceived misogyny. In response, Moshe Meiselman in his book *Jewish Women in Jewish Law*, "acknowledges that the role differentiation implicit in her exemption from certain mitzvot is part of the overall divine plan for the world, whose justification lies in the will and wisdom of God."[34] In other words, the smaller number of *mitzvot* incumbent upon women is no less according to God's will than the greater number obligating men. Women's status of holiness might be seen as inferior or superior to men (depending on the historical period) because of this differentiation in *mitzvah* obligation.

Infusing Theological Meaning into the Gender Gap

After studying the rabbinic sources and the ensuing analysis, it is clear that the exemption from time-caused *mitzvot* does not functionally create an absolute binary gender distinction since women are obligated

---

33. B. Talmud Menakhot 43b. See Rabbi Daniel Sperber's excellent analysis of the difference in blessings for men and women, *On Changes in Jewish Liturgy: Options and Limitations*, Urim Publications, 2010, pp. 33–40.

34. Moshe Meiselman, *Jewish Women in Jewish Law*, New York, 1978, pp. 49–51.

in many *mitzvot* and can voluntarily take on others. Conceptually, however, it remains at the heart of gender differentiation in Orthodox Judaism, serving as the foundation for the "separate but equal" philosophy. This distinction has turned into a platform highlighting the differences in character between men and women in traditional Orthodoxy, which, in turn, transmits the sentiment that if men and women have such vastly different religious dispositions – and especially if this can be attributed to God's will – then it is natural for women to be limited in religious participation.

Although contemporary explanations for why women are exempt from specific *mitzvot* by God and/or *Hazal* attribute it to heightened spirituality or time restraints while taking care of children, medieval explanations focus on a wife's subordination to her husband and the spiritual inferiority of women. The discrepancy between past and present justifications, along with absolute silence from the Mishnah itself, reinforces the sense that the explanations are generally a result of a fluid social reality.

Both Jacob ben Abba Mari Anatoli in thirteenth-century southern France and David Abudraham in fourteenth- century Spain attribute women's exemption from positive time-caused *mitzvot* to the tension it would cause in the household, forcing a woman to choose between God and her husband:

Abudraham, Section III (translation: Rabbi Mendell Lewittes[35])	Malmad HaTalmidim, *Parashat Lekh Lekha* (translation: Rabbi Mendell Lewittes[36])
A woman is exempt from positive precepts dependent upon a set time because she is bound to her husband, to	The sign of the covenant [circumcision] is rightly limited to the male, seeing that the female's role is that of

---

35. English taken from Getsel Ellinson, *Woman and the Mitzvot, Vol. 1, Serving the Creator*, 1986, p. 40.

36. Ibid., p. 39.

attend to his needs. Were a woman obliged to perform such *mitzvot*, her husband might bid her to do something at the precise moment that she is fulfilling one of these *mitzvot*. Should she fulfill the bidding of her Creator and neglect her husband's demands, she faces her husband's wrath. On the other hand, should she fulfill her husband's demands and neglect the bidding of her Creator, she faces the wrath of her Creator. Consequently, the Creator exempted her from these obligations in order to promote harmony between husband and wife.

Do we not find that even the Great Name written in sanctity and purity is effaced in order to promote harmony between husband and wife?

help-mate to the male. It is said, *Yet, your urge shall be for your husband, and he shall dominate you* (Gen. 3:16), implying that her husband will lead her and direct her in his ways, and that she act in accordance with his instructions.

For this same reason, women are exempt from all positive precepts dependent on a set time. Were she bound to observe these *mitzvot* at the set time, her husband would then be left without help at such times. This would lead to discord between them and undermine his authority, which was designed to benefit both husband and wife.

Both of these sources present the principle of exemption as an absolute statement although they obviously know that women remain obligated in many positive time-caused *mitzvot*. What is interesting is the attempt to explain the exemption in light of women's character and role in society. Women are meant to be wives, and wives are subject to the will of their husbands. This is very much in line with the approach brought in Tosefta Kiddushin (cited above) explaining that a married woman is exempted from honoring her parents since she is subordinate to her husband. These authorities suggest that without a clear exemption, women would be caught between Creator and husband. Each would be vying for her absolute fidelity and neither God nor husband would understand her forsaking one for the other.

In order to have harmony in the home, God exempted her from certain obligations.

A different approach emerges in Rabbi Yehoshua Ibn Shuaib, from fourteenth-century Spain, who suggests that a man should bless God every day that "He has not made him a woman" since women's souls are lesser. Just as the souls of Israelite men are holier than those of non-Jews and Canaanite slaves, so too they are holier than women's souls, even though women are included in the covenant.

Drashot R. Yehoshua Ibn Shuaib, Tazria-Metzora	דרשות ר״י אבן שועיב, תזריע-מצורע
Therefore, men bless every day that *He has not made me a non-Jew, that He has not made a slave and that He has not made me a woman...* for the souls of Israel are holier than that of the other nations, and from the lowly Canaanite slaves and even from women, and even if they are obligated in *mitzvot* and they are from Israelite seed, their souls are not like the souls of men who are connected to Torah and all of the *mitzvot*, both positive and negative.	ולכן אנו מברכין בכל יום שלא עשאני גוי ושלא עשאני עבד ושלא עשאני אשה... כי נשמתן של ישראל הן קדושות יותר מן האומות ומן העבדים הבנעניים הפחותים ואפילו מן הנשים, ואם הם שייכי במצות והן מזרע ישראל אין נשמתן כנשמת הזכר השייך בתורה ובכל המצות.

This is radically different from the more widely known approach in modernity that appears in the sixteenth century, in the commentary of Judah Loew ben Bezalel, known famously as the Maharal of Prague, in which women are presented as spiritually superior and thus, less in need of *mitzvot*.[37] The Maharal was inspired by a famous midrash that states that God gave the Torah first to women and only afterwards to men. This midrash reflects a sentiment that is prevalent in rabbinic literature as reflective of the second category of sources about wife and

---

37. Maharal of Prague, *Be'er HaGolah* 27a.

mother presented above. It is understood that wives and mothers have tremendous influence over husbands and sons in the home, so their inclusion at Sinai, while not explicitly stated, needs to be read into the biblical text. Without the initial enthusiastic acceptance of women, men would never have been able to commit to Torah and *mitzvot*.[38]

Since the main duty of women in this worldview is to enable and inspire men's religious observance, this evolved into a more positive commentary on the imbalance in *mitzvah* observance as seen in the Maharal. Several hundred years later, Rabbi Samson Rafael Hirsch explains that the Torah exempted women because time-caused *mitzvot* are unnecessary for their religious commitment in contrast to men who need constant and daily reminders.

> R. Samson Rafael Hirsch (nineteenth-century Germany), *Commentary to Torah*, Leviticus 23:43 (translation: Rabbi Mendel Lewittes)[39]:
>
> Clearly, women's exemption from positive time-caused *mitzvot* is not a consequence of their diminished worth; nor is it because the Torah found them unfit, as it were, to fulfill these *mitzvot*. *Rather, it seems to me, it is because the Torah understood that women are not in need of these mitzvot.* The Torah affirms that our women are imbued with a great love and a holy enthusiasm for their role in Divine worship, exceeding that of men. The trials men undergo in their professional activities jeopardize their fidelity to Torah and therefore, they require, from time to time, reminders and warnings in the form of time-related precepts. Women, whose lifestyle does not subject them to comparable trials and hazards, have no need for such periodic reminders.

---

38. Pirkei D'Rabbi Eliezer – Horeb.
    Rabbi Pinchas says: On the eve of Sabbath, Israel stood at Sinai, the men prepared alone and the women alone. God said to Moses: Go inquire of the daughters of Israel whether they want to receive the Torah. And why were the women asked? For it is the way of men to follow the opinion of women, as it is written "thus shall you say to the house of Jacob," these are the women, and "tell the children of Israel," these are the men.

39. Ellenson, p. 41.

Upon reading Rabbi Hirsch, one cannot help but ponder his last sentence. In the past, women may not have been subject to comparable trials and hazards as men, but what would he say of a society in which men and women interact regularly in the same challenging external environments? Given that he greatly contextualizes his explanation to a reality that no longer exists, would he argue that now women should be equally obligated?

The Maharal and Rabbi Hirsch reframed some of the earlier speculations on women's character (inferior to men) and women's role (subservient to husband), into a more female-positive outlook in which women are spiritually superior and thus in need of fewer *mitzvot*.

In short, the two meta-halakhic explanations that became dominant in the twentieth century were women's innate spirituality leading to less existential necessity for *mitzvot* and the reinforcement of the woman's central role as wife and mother, rather than submission to her husband. For Orthodox and non-Orthodox feminists alike, this differentiation, which results in gender bifurcation and more obligations for men, can seem apologetic and even demeaning. Despite the traditional religious narrative that women are given equal bidding to fulfill the will of God *in their own way*, it justifies a hierarchy that ultimately translates into exclusive male authority.

Feminist Scholars in the Twentieth Century
In the late twentieth century, female Talmud scholars began to read the sources that presented the differences in obligation and religious participation between men and women critically. Many felt that the overall gender differentiation was not mandated by God, but largely based on interpretation of texts reflecting traditional behavior in a patriarchal society. These women scholars confronted the traditional approach which sought to justify a gender binary.

Judith Plaskow, in her seminal book *Standing Again at Sinai*, wrote that "any *halakha* that is part of a feminist Judaism would have to look very different from *halakha* as it has been....it would begin with the assumption of women's equality and humanity and legislate only on that basis."[40] More recently, Elizabeth Shanks Alexander wrote an entire book on gender and time-caused commandments in Judaism, suggesting that we learn more "about the rule's role in structuring gender when we focus on women's exemption from a discrete subset of time-caused, positive commandments than when we focus on women's exemptions from the category as a whole.....undergirding the rule is an assumption that women are not central actors in the creation and perpetuation of the covenantal community."[41] Throughout her book she focuses mostly on the exemptions from *Shema*, *tefillin*, and *tzitzit* as representative of women's exemption from Torah study, an exemption which goes the furthest in creating a hierarchy between men and women.

Orthodox women were also not immune to feminist scholarship and discourse with a focus on the undergirding of rabbinic Judaism regarding gender. In an essay titled "The Jew Who Wasn't There: Halacha and the Jewish Woman,"[42] Rachel Adler wrote movingly about the hierarchy that emerges when women have fewer *mitzvot* than men:

> Make no mistake; for centuries, the lot of the Jewish woman was infinitely better than that of her non-Jewish counterpart. She had rights which other women lacked until a century ago...the problem is that very little has been done since then (1000 CE) to ameliorate the position of Jewish women in observant society. All of this can quickly be rectified if one steps outside of Jewish tradition and Halacha. The problem is how to attain some justice and some growing room for the Jewish woman if one is committed to remaining within Halacha. Some of these problems are more easily solved than others. For example, there is ample precedent for decisions permitting women to study Talmud, and it should become the policy of Jewish day schools

---

40. Judith Plaskow, *Standing Again at Sinai*, HarperCollins, 1991, p. 72.

41. Alexander, pp. 236–37.

42. Jewish Women's Archive. "The Jew Who Wasn't There: Halacha and the Jewish Woman," by Rachel Adler, 1973. <https://jwa.org/media/jew-who-wasnt-there-halacha-and-jewish-woman>.

> to teach their girls Talmud. It would not be difficult to find a basis for giving women aliyot to the Torah. Moreover, it is both feasible and desirable for the community to begin educating women to take on the positive time-caused mitzvot from which they are now excused; in which case, those mitzvot would eventually become incumbent upon women.

It is not surprising that in his *Jewish Women in Jewish Law*, a book that conforms to a traditionalist approach, Moshe Meiselman strongly attacks Adler for having no respect or appreciation for a system that he perceives as respecting and valuing women because of the very distinction in obligation that she was critiquing. "What can be done," he asks, "if it is God's will that men and women serve their Creator differently?"

Many in Orthodoxy today continue to echo Meiselman, affirming the gender distinction as handed down from God to Moses at Sinai and thus, inviolate. The question that many Orthodox feminists return to over and over again is whether, in fact, God willed it that men and women serve different religious roles, or if the evolving structure of *halakhah* had, at its outset, a clear social hierarchy in which men and women could not be equal. Tamar Ross, in her book on gender and religious practice, dedicates a section to examining women's unequal obligation to perform *mitzvot*. Ross, who is a committed Orthodox Jew, a retired professor of Jewish Thought at Bar-Ilan University, and a senior faculty member at the renowned Lindenbaum Seminary for women in Jerusalem, generated much controversy when she published her book, *Expanding the Palace of Torah*, in the 1990s. In the citation below she specifically refers to the hierarchy that emerges from the difference in *mitzvah* obligation between men and women.[43]

> As further examples will demonstrate, men's greater religious obligations, whether or not they are actually fulfilled, confer other

---

43. Tamar Ross, *Expanding the Palace of Torah*, Brandeis University Press, 2004, p. 38.

> legal privileges. By the same token, women's lesser obligations
> disenfranchise them in many areas. As in the case of other classes
> situated on the hierarchical scale, difference in religious responsibility
> then serves as rationale for women's diminished valuation. Under
> certain circumstances, the legal repercussions are significant indeed.
> Because greater obligation to *mitzvoth* is translated in halakhic
> terms as greater worth, the Mishnah rules that a man's right to life
> precedes that of a woman's in most life-threatening situations. This
> consideration is explicitly stated in some sources as justification for
> the ruling that if a man and a woman are drowning, the man should
> be saved first.
> Of particular significance is also the fact that women are exempt
> (and according to dominant traditional position, even deliberately
> distanced) from the central religious activity of studying Torah,
> despite the fact that this activity is not classified as time-caused. As a
> result, although there is no ban in principle on women functioning
> as halakhic authorities, in practice they have had no official part to
> play in the tradition's legislative and interpretive process. Because of
> their lack of proficiency in the Oral Law, women have been virtually
> excluded from any participation in halakhic discussion and its
> formulation.

It was one thing for non-Orthodox scholars like Plaskow and Hauptman to write feminist critiques of rabbinic sources. It was another thing entirely for Orthodox Jews like Rachel Adler (who at the time was Orthodox), Tamar Ross, and Blu Greenberg to do the same with the sharp focus of scholarship, textual acuity, and insider knowledge, along with an appreciation for, and commitment to, *halakhah*. As a result of the raised glass ceiling resulting in greater educational opportunities for women in Torah and Talmud scholarship, women for the first time began adding their own voices to the reading of rabbinic texts, questioning some of the basic premises behind the narrative of "equal but different" gender roles.

Suggestions for Moving Forward
Questions surrounding women's status in traditional Jewish *halakhah* and community have become among the most pressing questions

of the day, theologically, sociologically, and halakhically. These issues unleash questions about modernity, morality, the evolution of *halakhah*, and rabbinic authority. It has become challenging for open-minded Orthodox Jews to articulate a rational justification for the widening gap between the roles that women play in their secular lives as compared to their Jewish lives. Women's lesser obligation in *mitzvot* and in the central obligation of Torah study and segregation in the synagogue have impacted women's ability to be visible and participate fully in central parts of Jewish life. For some women, there is a sense of religious marginalization particularly when the romanticization of the male-female partnership is simultaneously reaffirmed as justification for this necessary bifurcation. The traditional, and to my mind, apologetic explanations continue to be used in defense of these differences.

Perpetuating the *mitzvah* disparity can cause some (although not all) women to feel alienated and estranged from commitment to performance of *mitzvot*. This in turn can lead to women disparaging what is actually incumbent upon them, such as prayer and Grace after Meals, wrongly concluding that they must be exempt. If more women would recite *kiddush* and bless the *hallah* in their homes or at communal events, it would visibly remind us that women have an equal obligation in many of the time-caused *mitzvot* and that men and women can and should share these religious responsibilities, especially when their lives outside of the religious space are decidedly egalitarian.

To further this sense of dissonance, the classic justifications based on women's roles in hearth and home apply much less than before. Most women marry later than they did in the past. Thus, for many years after women become obligated in *mitzvot* at the age of 12, they are often busy pursuing education and professional opportunities rather than marrying and raising children. In addition, women have many years of healthy living after their responsibilities for child-rearing and housekeeping have diminished. Furthermore, women are certainly subject to many of the same spiritual and religious challenges faced by men in modernity as well as the particular questions raised by feminism, which begs the question whether women should be exempted from any time-caused *mitzvot*. One could argue that given the change in their social reality, women should be obligated in all *mitzvot* and only exempted when family circumstances require it.

A way in which feminist critique might inspire us to more thoughtfully look at gender roles of *mitzvah* performance is to focus on *mitzvot* in which women are clearly obligated (*kiddush*, *megillah* reading, etc.) despite the time-caused nature of the *mitzvah*, and remove the gender bias favoring men.

Strengthening this suggestion, it is noteworthy that even though they are formally exempt, women in many Orthodox communities are educated from a young age to recite the *Shema*, hear the *shofar* on Rosh Hashana, sit in a *sukkah*, bless the four species, and say Hallel on holidays as if they were obligated. In other words, the inconsistencies that emerged in the analysis above as to what is a time-caused *mitzvah* and why women are exempt from some and not others, are exacerbated when we look at those optional *mitzvot* that have come to be treated as pivotal and quasi, if not fully, binding. Perhaps it is time to recognize the origins of the positive time-caused *mitzvot* exemption and its implications, and remove it from the equation altogether!

Likewise, the need for thoughtful change leading to greater connection and engagement by women in perpetuating the religious covenant goes beyond the positive time-caused *mitzvah* platform. Unfortunately, there is a "permitted but prohibited" attitude that has infiltrated halakhic discourse that discourages people from deviating from the *mesorah* even when there is room in *halakhah* to thoughtfully reconsider.

In other words, social norms are more compelling than actual halakhic determination, turning something permitted into a virtual prohibition. To illustrate, at times people who visit my home are uncomfortable with my making the blessing over *hallah* although halakhically both men and women are equally obligated in the *mitzvah*. When my brother asked a prominent Orthodox rabbi about this practice, he was told that while a woman *could* perform this ritual, she should not do so, since it goes against the *mesorah*, meaning tradition. Thus, women are discouraged from active participation, even concerning *mitzvot* in which they are obligated!

In another instance, a former student of mine arrived at her single brother's home for dinner on Friday night. While the meal had not yet begun, they had already made *kiddush*. She asked for a cup of wine so that she could make *kiddush* and one of the male guests offered to make it for her. She politely refused and asked for wine so that she could make *kiddush* herself. He again offered to make *kiddush* for her more aggressively, insisting that women cannot make *kiddush*. Halakhically this is inaccurate. Women and men are equally obligated in *kiddush*, as was presented earlier in the chapter! Given that the men had already fulfilled their obligation, it was actually preferable for my student to make her own *kiddush*! This kind of scene repeats itself regularly throughout the Orthodox world as it is automatically assumed that women are exempted from most rituals or dependent on men to fulfill them.

Furthermore, the traditionalist approach, that women should not perform certain *mitzvot* because of *mesorah*, creates dissonance for the not insignificant population of men and women who remain single well into adulthood, as well as those who divorce and become widowed/widowered. This reality has forced them to uncomfortably assume rituals for themselves and/or their children from which they thought they were exempt or feel awkward performing. A colleague recently told me that she had grown up with a very traditional attitude toward religious gender roles, ironically even as she was studying to become a Talmud teacher. When she was divorced, she reluctantly began to make *kiddush*, bless the *hallah*, and make *havdalah* for herself and her children. Upon remarrying, she assumed she and her husband would each resume their respective gendered rituals since he had been lighting the Shabbat candles for his family after his wife died. To her surprise, her new husband encouraged her to continue making *kiddush* because he preferred not to for dietary reasons. And in a lovely twist, they each decided to continue lighting Shabbat candles for their respective families. Once the boundary between gender roles had to be removed for halakhic reasons (they were each the only head of their household), this couple saw the potential in reexamining the performance of *mitzvot* outside of gendered social norms. Perhaps others could begin to do the same from the outset.

In a similar vein to what was suggested above, some examples of things *permitted yet prohibited* will be brought below with directed suggestions about rethinking women's presence in public ritualistic spaces.

a. Women have traditionally had little to no presence in the synagogue and women's sections in the synagogue were small, if they existed at all, with little concern for their seeing or hearing the service on the men's side. In contrast, today, most Orthodox communities invest thought and resources when building a women's section to ensure that it be easily accessible and provide women with the ability to see and hear the entire service. This consideration, in and of itself, reflects a change in the way synagogue is experienced by women, essentially representing a break from tradition. However, very few Orthodox synagogues allow the Torah to be passed through the women's section although all authorities agree that a woman can touch a Torah without concern for menstrual impurity.[44] This has become a flash point in Orthodox services on some college campuses. The irony that this happens in a progressive environment where female and male students are treated equally further underscores the gap for women between their secular and religious lives. It serves as an excellent illustration of a non-halakhic issue carrying within it the meta-halakhic anxiety around changing the natural order of gender differentiation in any way that differs from what it was in the past. It seems to me that in Modern Orthodoxy, passing women the Sefer Torah should not be a cause of fear but rather a natural and organic way of sending women the message that the Torah belongs to them too.

---

44. A Torah scroll cannot contract impurity. Even if a dead body were to fall on it, it would remain pure due to the stringent requirements that go into the material used to construct the Torah.

b. Similarly, women dancing with a Torah on Simhat Torah is a heated issue that continues to divide congregations in most Modern Orthodox communities. It is hard to understand how in the twenty-first century, women dancing with the Torah has led to verbal and, at times, even physical violence. The disproportionate inequality in the experience of young boys and men who are actively engaged in reading Torah and dancing with the scrolls compared to that of the women who passively watch from the side, often talking during the long stretches of dancing, is not only painful to experience but seems to be a breach in religious values. One wonders how women, who today are actively engaged in the study of Torah, could possibly threaten the natural order by showing their passion and love for Torah in the manner that men do on the holiday meant to celebrate such passion.

c. Women saying *kaddish* after losing a parent has gained traction in the last thirty years as women look to incorporate a ritual that traditionally reflects the ongoing year of mourning for parents. This practice reflects growing literacy and activism on the part of observant women who seek greater involvement within the halakhic framework. While this has slowly earned acceptance, it sadly remains a struggle, as if hearing the voices of women chanting a prayer will violate the sacredness of the prayer space and harm the congregation's ability to express devotion to God. Perhaps it would be less jarring to hear women's voices if they were obligated to attend prayer services on a regular basis. Then they would have a more equal footing when discussing the women's section and active roles women could potentially play during or after the services. Enacting such changes as passing the Torah over to the women's side, allowing women to dance with the Torah on Simhat Torah, and supporting women saying *kaddish*, none of which are prohibited, would help to remove the overwhelming sense of imbalance that characterizes the synagogue experience even as women's presence is taken for granted in Orthodox synagogues, in itself a break from tradition.

d. Finding ways for women to participate in the Jewish marriage ceremony. Traditionally, there has been no role for women to play in any part of the ceremony. The bride is passive, holding out her finger to accept the ring, but having no active role beyond the Ashkenazic custom of circling her husband seven times before taking her place next to him. In the last decade, there have been increasing attempts within the halakhic framework to turn the *huppah* into a more partnered space. These range from allowing women to read the *sheva berakhot* in translation or say a personal blessing under the *huppah*, and in singular cases, allowing women to say some of the *sheva berakhot*.[45] In Israel, in some circles, it is not uncommon for women in leadership positions (myself included) to read the *ketubah*. To quote a prominent head rabbi of Yeshiva University (Rabbi Hershel Schachter), "a monkey could also read the *ketubah*" as the reading has no legal or ritual significance. It is thus disappointing that many Orthodox rabbis/communities vociferously prevent women from playing even a non-halakhically significant role in the marriage ceremony. Some rabbinic authorities have found halakhically appropriate ways for the wife to give a ring to the husband by clearly distinguishing it from the act of *kiddushin* when the husband gives the ring to the wife. All of these attempts have been met with resistance in the majority of Orthodox communities. Nonetheless, simultaneously there is growing acceptance in some communities, particularly in some of the more liberal national religious communities in Israel. The persistence of couples insistent on finding ways of making the marriage ceremony more interactive and equitable, along with the rabbinic authorities and communities willing to make such a move, has started a sea change that I can only hope will evolve into wider, more mainstream acceptance.

---

45. A lovely and less controversial practice is for a woman to recite an eighth blessing authored by Rabbi Amram Gaon (ninth century), which is a beautiful blessing not part of the *sheva berakhot* that brings an ancient Jewish wedding prayer into the ceremony.

Final Words

One fear that has been articulated when the question of greater gender equality specifically in *mitzvot* arises is that any change in the traditional structure will lead to women demanding complete equality, which goes against thousands of years of worship and practice. This concern will be addressed in the chapter exploring the world of women's Torah study which has led to a petition for female ordination. While there is some truth to this concern, the use of the "slippery slope" argument seems to be an avoidance of looking critically at the religious social reality, shutting down further discussion and limiting the possibility of developing meaningful approaches to these issues.

Another, more legitimate fear, to my mind, is that increasing women's roles could potentially lead to a decrease in men's participation in Jewish life. In other words, will we gain the women only to lose the men? In egalitarian spaces, it is not uncommon to find more women attending prayer services and more women registered for rabbinical school than men. One could ask in response whether better education and religious direction could preempt such a decline. After all, men have not stopped becoming doctors and lawyers even as women are working alongside them and vying for the same jobs in many fields!

* * *

A final anecdote: My grandmother, one of 13 children in Williamsburg, Brooklyn, never sat in a *sukkah* growing up because there was only room for her father and brothers. Since women were not obligated in this *mitzvah*, she, her sisters, and her mother sat in the kitchen. In contrast, my mother, who did not consider herself a Jewish feminist in any way, took upon herself the *mitzvah* of sitting in the *sukkah* as an absolute requirement. Even when there was no room, she insisted on being allowed to eat in the *sukkah* to the acute annoyance of men who had to crowd even more to let her in, grumbling because she really wasn't obligated. She also scrupulously blessed the *lulav* and *etrog* each day of Sukkot and prayed twice a day, not just the mandatory *Shemoneh Esrei*, but the full morning and afternoon prayers that included *Shema* and *Hallel* when relevant (which she sang loudly), both prayers from which she was exempt. She was careful to hear *shofar* every year of her life regardless of the age of her children, hiring babysitters when necessary. Nonetheless, she did not have an agenda to fulfill all voluntary *mitzvot*. She was not interested in making *kiddush* or blessing the *hallah* on Shabbat (unless my father was away and then, interestingly, she did make *kiddush* even when my brother was around, as the acting head of the household). She never wanted to read Torah or wear *tefillin*. She committed to "extra" *mitzvot* that to her were an obvious conduit to spiritual growth.

For my mother, it was unthinkable that the *mitzvot* that she had taken upon herself should not be fully binding. Otherwise, where was the religious commitment? Her approach had nothing to do with seeking equality. It was an organic extension of her ongoing relationship with Torah and *mitzvot* and her recognition that rituals create profound depth and meaning stemming from unyielding commitment to their performance. While at times I was annoyed with her, I began to admire how she saw the *mitzvot* as directly connected to her service of God, making no distinction between those that formally obligated her and those that she had taken upon herself.

It is my ardent hope that the upcoming generations will work together to create more partnerships in religious spaces and think creatively about increased *mitzvah* obligation for women, rather than automatically falling back on the traditional structure as the default. Lack of education, apathy, and fear, however, continue to make this an uphill struggle.

Chapter Two

Women and Torah Study – A Beit Midrash of Their Own

When Rabbi Meir Shapiro instituted *Daf Yomi* (daily study of one page of Talmud) in 1923 as a means of connecting Jews through Torah study in which every Jew would be on the same page,[1] he could not have conceived of a world in which women study Talmud, let alone study *Daf Yomi*. And yet, when the fourteenth cycle ended in January 2020, there were a significant number of women around the world who joined in the celebrations as active participants.

Watching women take the stage at a women's *Siyyum HaShas* (celebration of the completion of the Talmud) held at the Jerusalem Convention Center in January 2020, some of them women who had founded advanced programs of study in Talmud and *halakhah*, filled me with awestruck recognition that at some point in the last 35 years, a historical process had been set into motion that I was privileged to

---

1. Rabbi Meir Shapiro said at the first general assembly of Agudat Israel in 1923: "What a great thing! A Jew travels by boat and takes gemara Berakhot under his arm. He travels for 15 days from Eretz Yisrael to America, and each day he learns the *daf*. When he arrives in America, he enters a *beis medrash* (house of study) in New York and finds Jews learning the very same *daf* that he studied on that day, and he gladly joins them. Another Jew leaves the States and travels to Brazil or Japan, and he first goes to the *beis medrash*, where he finds everyone learning the same *daf* that he himself learned that day. Could there be greater unity of hearts than this?"

witness and take part in. There is a moving passage describing Rabbi Akiba's small group of students who restored the Torah in a vast wasteland following the destruction of the Second Temple:

B. Talmud Yevamot 62b	תלמוד בבלי מסכת יבמות סב
The world was barren until Rabbi Akiva came to our teachers in the South and taught them: Rabbi Meir, Rabbi Yehudah, Rabbi Yose, Rabbi Shimon, and Rabbi Elazar ben Shamua. And it was they who revived the Torah at that time.	וְהָיָה הָעוֹלָם שָׁמֵם, עַד שֶׁבָּא רַבִּי עֲקִיבָא אֵצֶל רַבּוֹתֵינוּ שֶׁבַּדָּרוֹם וּשְׁנָאָהּ לָהֶם: רַבִּי מֵאִיר, וְרַבִּי יְהוּדָה, וְרַבִּי יוֹסֵי, וְרַבִּי שִׁמְעוֹן, וְרַבִּי אֶלְעָזָר בֶּן שַׁמּוּעַ, וְהֵם הֵם הֶעֱמִידוּ תוֹרָה אוֹתָהּ שָׁעָה

On that day in Jerusalem in 2020, it felt as if the Talmud had been restored for all women by this core group in a formerly barren desert, motivating young and old alike to find themselves in the vast sea of pages of the Talmud.

Nonetheless, despite major advances in education and knowledge, there are Modern Orthodox communities that do not allow women to teach Torah, Talmud, or *halakhah* to mixed classes of men and women and certainly not to men alone. In the post-high school world of seminaries and *yeshivot*, this is even more apparent. Male rabbis teach young women, often making up a large percentage of a seminary's faculty, but there are no all-male *yeshivot* that employ women to teach Torah classes to their student body. This gives a two-fold negative message, implying that women are less qualified to teach Torah, Talmud, and *halakhah*, and insinuating that women who teach Torah will somehow introduce a sexual stimulus into the Beit Midrash.

In this chapter, I will present and briefly analyze sources about women and Torah study as well as sources about women holding positions of authority in Orthodox Jewish institutions. The chapter will conclude with a contemporary discussion about women and rabbinic ordination in Orthodox society.

Teach Your Sons and Not Your Daughters

Deuteronomy 11:19–21	דברים יא
And teach them to your sons (*beneichem*) – to recite them when you stay at home and when you are away, when you lie down and when you get up; And inscribe them on the doorposts of your house and on your gates – So that you and your children (*beneichem*) may live a long life in the land that the LORD swore to your fathers to give to them, for as long as there is a heaven over earth.	יט וְלִמַּדְתֶּם אֹתָם אֶת בְּנֵיכֶם לְדַבֵּר בָּם בְּשִׁבְתְּךָ בְּבֵיתֶךָ וּבְלֶכְתְּךָ בַדֶּרֶךְ וּבְשָׁכְבְּךָ וּבְקוּמֶךָ. כ וּכְתַבְתָּם עַל מְזוּזוֹת בֵּיתֶךָ וּבִשְׁעָרֶיךָ. כא לְמַעַן יִרְבּוּ יְמֵיכֶם וִימֵי בְנֵיכֶם עַל הָאֲדָמָה אֲשֶׁר נִשְׁבַּע ד' לַאֲבֹתֵיכֶם לָתֵת לָהֶם כִּימֵי הַשָּׁמַיִם עַל הָאָרֶץ.

This biblical passage, which makes up the second paragraph of the *Shema* prayer, mentions an obligation to teach these words to *beneichem*, a conjugation of the Hebrew word *ben*, which is translated as "your sons." The overwhelming majority of biblical references to *ben*, or *banim* in plural, refer to a son or sons, although there are a small number of instances in which the plural *banim* refers to all children. One of those instances is verse 21 cited above in this same passage: *so that you and your children may live a long life*, where the word *beneichem* appears to be referring to all descendants, male and female.[2] Returning to our verse and the obligation to teach *beneichem*, the *midrash halakhah* cited below interprets the clause to indicate a

---

2. BDB Dictionary, p. 120, Genesis 21:7, Exodus 21:5.

father's responsibility to teach his son Torah from a young age. By association, it implies unequivocally that the verse excludes daughters:

Sifrei Deuteronomy Piska 46	ספרי דברים פרשת עקב פיסקא מו
"And you shall teach them to *beneichem*." Your sons and not your daughters, so taught R. Yose b. Akiva. Hence the Sages have said: Once an infant begins to talk, his father should converse with him in the holy tongue and should teach him Torah, and if he does not teach him Torah, it is as if he buries him (the son).	"ולמדתם אותם את בניכם" בניכם ולא בנותיכם. דברי רבי יוסי בן עקיבה. מיכן אמרו כשהתינוק מתחיל לדבר אביו מדבר עמו בלשון הקודש ומלמדו תורה ואם אין מדבר עמו בלשון קודש ואינו מלמדו תורה ראוי לו כאילו קוברו.

The *midrash* introduces two important points that are incorporated into practical *halakhah*. First, the word "them," in the verse *you shall teach them*, refers to all of Torah and not just to the words of *Shema*. Second, daughters are excluded, as the biblical verse is narrowly interpreted to include only sons. It is surprising on some level that the midrashic interpretation took such pains to emphasize that the verse itself excludes daughters. As noted above, the word *ben* usually refers to sons. However, the *midrash* is certainly aware that in other instances Talmudic exegesis understood this word to include daughters, even when the text could easily be understood as referring only to sons. Perhaps the most prominent example occurs in Deuteronomy 25:5, where the law of *yibum*, levirate marriage, is described. If a man dies without a *ben* (which could be translated as either "child" or "son"), his widow has an obligation to wed her deceased husband's brother (normally a forbidden relationship), in order to bear a child to commemorate the deceased.[3] One might intuitively assume that

---

3. Deuteronomy 25: 5–10.

Women and Torah Study – A Beit Midrash of Their Own

ben in this context refers to a male child who will carry on the dead man's name and inherit his property. Midrash Tannaim[4] interprets the biblical passage to mean that any progeny left by the deceased, male or female – including a grandchild born to the son or daughter who is no longer alive – fulfills the Torah's mandate. This is also the unanimous conclusion of the Talmud; *yibum* is mandated only when a man dies without any children, sons or daughters. Here we have an example where the simple meaning of the text is replaced with a broader meaning that deliberately includes daughters, which results in a greater limitation on the practice of *yibum*.

Returning to the question of women's lack of obligation in Torah study: in Tractate Kiddushin, the Talmud concludes that women are exempt from the obligation to teach their sons Torah because they are exempt from study themselves, based on the Sifrei's exegesis that men are commanded to teach their sons and not their daughters. However, the Sifrei's interpretation only exempted women from studying or teaching Torah. It did not prevent or prohibit women from such study. A much bigger obstacle, and the main deterrent to women's Torah study over the last two thousand years, is to be found in Mishnah Sotah 3:4:

Mishnah Sotah 3:4 (Sefaria translation and commentary)	משנה מסכת סוטה פרק ג משנה ד
When a guilty woman drinks she does not manage to finish drinking before her face turns green and her eyes bulge, and her skin becomes full of protruding veins, and the people standing in the Temple say: Remove her, so that she does not render the Temple courtyard impure.	אינה מספקת לשתות עד שפניה מוריקות ועיניה בולטות והיא מתמלאת גידין. והם אומרים הוציאוה הוציאוה שלא תטמא העזרה.

---

4. Midrash Tannaim 25:5.

| If she has merit, it delays punishment for her. There is a merit that delays one year, there is merit that delays two years, and there is a merit that delays for three years. From here Ben Azzai states: A person is obligated to teach his daughter Torah, so that if she drinks, she will know that merit delayed punishment for her.
Rabbi Eliezer says: Anyone who teaches his daughter Torah is teaching her promiscuity [*tiflut*].
Rabbi Yehoshua says: A woman desires to receive the amount of a *kav* of food and a sexual relationship [*tiflut*] rather than to receive nine *kav* of food and abstinence. | אם יש לה זכות היתה תולה לה. יש זכות תולה שנה אחת, יש זכות תולה שתי שנים, יש זכות תולה שלש שנים. מכאן אומר בן עזאי: חייב אדם ללמד את בתו תורה שאם תשתה תדע שהזכות תולה לה.
רבי אליעזר אומר: כל המלמד בתו תורה כאילו לומדה תפלות. |

The predicament of a *sotah* woman is described in the Torah, Numbers Chapter 5. According to the Torah, when a man suspects his wife of adultery but there were no witnesses, ordinary legal action is impossible. In lieu of a trial, the suspected adulteress, known colloquially in rabbinic texts as a *sotah*, meaning one who went astray, must drink water mixed with earth from the floor of the Temple courtyard and with rubbings resulting from erasing a passage in a scroll that includes God's name. If she is guilty, "her belly will swell and her thigh will sag" (Numbers 5:27), suggesting impairment of fertility and/or sexuality. The Mishnah in Tractate Sotah cited above describes what will befall a woman who is guilty of adultery after she drinks the *sotah* water.[5]

---

5. While the biblical text does not explicitly qualify when a jealous husband is entitled to subject his wife to the *sotah* ordeal, the oral law as expressed in the Mishnah limits the *sotah* ordeal to a situation where the husband has explicitly warned his wife before witnesses not to seclude herself with a particular man and she nevertheless is found to have done so in front of witnesses.

By the time the woman is brought to the High Priest for the ritual which will prove her guilt or innocence, she has definitively secluded herself with a man. The Mishnah, in far greater detail than the biblical text, describes a graphically violent

Women and Torah Study – A Beit Midrash of Their Own

Earlier in the Mishnaic text (not cited), various steps were added to the Bible's protocol. Among these was a stipulation that merely being suspicious of your wife is not cause enough to initiate the *sotah* proceedings. Instead, witnesses must come to testify that they saw her secluding with another man. In other words, there must be strong grounds for suspicion regarding her guilt. Only a lack of witnesses to the actual act of fornication spares her from court proceedings and the death penalty. It should be noted that by the Mishnaic period, the institution of *sotah* had long been abolished[6] so that the discussion is purely theoretical. This historical fact will be helpful in understanding some of the discussion below having to do with the connection between *sotah* and Torah study for women.

The Mishnah presents a description of a dramatic physical outcome if she had indeed committed adultery. The *water that brings the curse* causes her eyes to bulge and her veins to swell, resulting in her almost immediate death. What happens, wonders the Mishnah, if, despite her alleged guilt, there are no repercussions after she drinks the potion? Will this cause people to doubt the power of God's word?

The answer given is that merit can suspend the punishment; she will not die immediately, and the punishment may be delayed for up to three years. The type of merit that can suspend such punishment, however, remains undefined. This will be explored in the Talmud by several generations of Babylonian Talmudic Sages.[7]

Returning to the Mishnaic text cited above, Ben Azzai infers that a man is obligated to teach his daughter Torah as a way of accruing

---

ritual, including the ripping of her clothing to expose her breasts and the uncovering and disheveling of her hair. See Ishay Rosen-Zvi, *The Mishnaic Sotah Ritual*.

6. Mishnah Sotah 9:9. The move to abolish the *sotah* ordeal is attributed to Rabbi Yohanan Ben Zakai who lived at the end of the Second Temple period.

7. B. Talmud Sotah 21a. Rav Yosef states that performing *mitzvot* only provides protection in the moment that the *mitzvah* is performed. It has no long-term, lasting effect that would protect from punishment or from sin. Learning Torah on the other hand does have such an effect and "protects people from punishment and saves them [from sinning]." Later, Amora Rava suggested that *mitzvot* can protect a person from punishment long-term.

merit from the learning of Torah and to ensure that she understands that it is due to that merit that she does not die immediately.

To the modern reader, Ben Azzai aligns with the outlook that education empowers. By teaching women to understand the underpinnings of the *sotah* structure, they can navigate the system without the crippling fear of the unknown. I would even suggest that within the words of the text there emerges an educational philosophy that is preemptive. By educating her toward accruing merit, she may no longer have the desire or time to engage in an adulterous relationship.

The problem, as the Talmud is quick to point out, is that according to the Sifrei brought above, women are not obligated to study Torah. How then can the merit of Torah study provide protection from punishment if they have no *mitzvah* to do so? The answer given by the late Amora Ravina is that women do not accrue such merit from their own learning, and can only do so, *by making their sons read and study and waiting for their husbands until they come home from the study hall*.[8] This position greatly dilutes the impact of Ben Azzai's statement and denudes it of practical application with regard to female Torah study.

Rabbi Eliezer, in sharp contrast to Ben Azzai, sees the education of women as dangerous and contributory to sexual licentiousness in society. The Amora Rabbi Abahu explains Rabbi Eliezer's reasoning as follows: if women study Torah, they will learn deceit.[9] In other words, if women know how to navigate the halakhic system, they will do so and thus avoid consequence or punishment for promiscuous behavior. It suggests that keeping women ignorant and afraid of punishment is imperative in promoting the sexual mores of monogamy and faithful marriage.

The overarching conclusion in the Talmudic passage[10] is that the study of Torah protects men from transgression, and in particular,

---

8. B. Talmud Sotah 21a.

9. Ibid., 21b.

10. Ibid., 21a–b.

Women and Torah Study – A Beit Midrash of Their Own

from the evil inclination which is a euphemism for sexual desire. In stark contrast, it is assumed that women will misuse their knowledge to throw off the shackles of rabbinic authority and societal convention, leading to greater sexual promiscuity. Perhaps there was also an underlying concern that a woman who learns Torah could "become like a man" in her intellectual and religious accomplishments, inserting a sexually threatening and emasculating scenario into the exclusively androcentric world of the rabbinic academy. The Jerusalem Talmud cites a heated conversation between a wealthy woman and the Tanna Rabbi Eliezer ben Hyrcanus. The matron asks a question about the story of the Golden Calf in Exodus and Rabbi Eliezer, instead of answering her, retorts: *May the words of Torah be burned and not given to a woman!*[11] He refuses to answer a question that would involve explaining the words of Torah to a woman.

Although Ben Azzai and Rabbi Eliezer are quoted side by side in the Mishnah, it is solely the opinion of Rabbi Eliezer that is discussed in the Babylonian Talmud and in all subsequent commentary. In effect, Ben Azzai is erased from all halakhic discourse, since his statement is not addressed at all in the Babylonian Talmud's analysis of the Mishnah and does not appear in the Geonim and Rishonim.[12] Rabbi Eliezer's opinion is exclusively cited as authoritative *halakhah*, thereby justifying the denial of access to Torah study for women.

There are, however, some interesting parallel early rabbinic sources that remained largely unexplored until the twentieth century when women's Torah education became a central issue.

---

11. Mishnah Sotah 3:18.

12. In the J. Talmud Sotah 3:18, the Talmud asks Rabbi Elazar ben Azaryah to explain the commandment of *hakhel*, the septennial reading of the Torah to the entire people by the king described in Deuteronomy 31:10–13. In that verse it is explicitly stated that men, women, and children are obligated to hear the Torah being read. Rabbi Eliezer explains that men come to learn, women to hear, and children to give reward to those who bring them. The Talmud suggests that Ben Azzai would explain women's *mitzvah* not as listening but as learning, given his approach in the Mishnah. This is significant because in contrast to the Babylonian Talmud, the Jerusalem Talmud retains Ben Azzai's opinion as a legitimate option.

Uncovered

In Tosefta Berakhot there is a fascinating text that discusses whether men and women in different states of *tum'ah* (ritual impurity) are permitted to read Torah and study religious texts. The only category of impurity completely excluded from such pursuits involves men who have experienced a seminal emission:

Tosefta Berakhot Chapter 2:12	תוספתא מסכת ברכות (ליברמן) פרק ב הלכה יב
Zavim, Zavot, Niddot, and women who gave birth are permitted to read the Torah and to learn Mishnah, *Midrash*, laws, and *Aggadot*. And men who had a seminal emission (*Baalei Kerayim*) are forbidden in all of them. Rabbi Yossi says, "He can learn the laws that he is familiar with, as long as he does not arrange the Mishnah."	הזבין והזבות והנדות והיולדות מותרין לקרות בתורה בנביאים ובכתובים ולשנות במשנה במדרש בהלכות ובאגדות, ובעלי קריין אסורין בכולן. ר' יוסה אומר אבל שונה הוא בהלכות הרגילות ובלבד שלא יציע את המשנה.

Seminal emission is the most common and easily rectified state of ritual impurity. It requires immersing in a ritual bath soon after the emission.[13] At a certain point in the early rabbinic period, it was decided that all men experiencing a seminal emission should refrain from prayer or Torah study until immersing in a ritual bath. It appears that men were encouraged to minimize seminal emissions, even as it would be impossible to eliminate such a bodily function completely due to a man's obligation to procreate and engage in sexual relations with his wife. It is startling to discover, however, a text that casually references women reading Torah and learning Mishnah, *midrash*, *halakhah*, and *aggadah*! Furthermore, this text is

---

13. For a *kohen*, there is an additional requirement to wait until after sunset before consuming sacrifices and tithes, all of which must be eaten in a state of ritual purity. See the opening pages of B. Talmud Tractate Berakhot.

Women and Torah Study – A Beit Midrash of Their Own

repeated almost verbatim in the Jerusalem Talmud.[14] In his twentieth-century *responsum*, Rabbi Eliezer Waldenberg[15] cites the Tosefta and Jerusalem Talmud to acknowledge that a different, more permissive, and legitimate approach to women reading and studying Torah, Oral Law (Mishnah, *halakhah*, *aggadah*) was extant in central rabbinic texts.

A similar theme appears in the Babylonian Talmud but with significant emendation:

B. Talmud Berakhot 22a	תלמוד בבלי מסכת ברכות דף כב עמ' א
As it was taught in a *beraita*: "And you shall impart them to your children and your children's children" (Deuteronomy 4:9), and it is written thereafter: "The day that you stood before the LORD your God at Horeb" (Deuteronomy 4:10). Just as below, the Revelation at Sinai was in reverence, fear, quaking, and trembling, so too here, in every generation, Torah must be studied with a sense of reverence, fear, quaking, and trembling. From here the Sages stated: *Zavim*, lepers, and those who engaged in intercourse with menstruating women, despite their severe impurity, are permitted to read the Torah, Prophets, and Writings, and to study Mishnah and Gemara and *halakhot* and *aggadah*.	דתניא: "והודעתם לבניך ולבני בניך," וכתיב בתריה "יום אשר עמדת לפני ה' אלהיך בחורב," מה להלן באימה וביראה וברתת ובזיע אף כאן באימה וביראה וברתת ובזיע. מכאן אמרו: הזבים והמצורעים ובאין על נדות – מותרים לקרות בתורה ובנביאים ובכתובים, לשנות במשנה וגמרא ובהלכות ובאגדות,

---

14. J. Talmud Berakhot 3:4.
15. Tzitz Eliezer 9:3.

91

However, those who experienced a seminal emission are prohibited from doing so. Rabbi Yosei says: One who experiences a seminal emission studies *mishnayot* that he is accustomed to study, as long as he does not expound upon a new Mishnah to study it in depth.	אבל בעלי קריין אסורים. רבי יוסי אומר: שונה הוא ברגיליות ובלבד שלא יציע את המשנה.

The text is very similar to the text in the Tosefta and Jerusalem Talmud. There is, however, a major modification. Women who were featured prominently in the Tosefta as having the ability to read and learn Torah, are absent. In the Babylonian Talmud, women who experience uterine bleeding (menstrual, uterine, parturient), are replaced by a new persona, a man who has relations with a *niddah*. Despite this ritual impurity, he can nonetheless read and study Torah.[16]

Just as Ben Azzai disappears from the Babylonian Talmudic discourse on teaching daughters Torah, the women who read and studied Torah in Tosefta are edited out of the Babylonian Talmud. One singular exception is the Tannaitic figure Beruriah, the purported wife of Rabbi Meir who is described as a learned woman.[17]

---

16. Saul Lieberman in his commentary to the Tosefta writes, "The Munich manuscript (of the Babylonian Talmud) is suspicious in my eyes for it seems that they deliberately removed the women and replaced them with men, meaning that only men are allowed to participate in these rituals and Torah study. See Tosefta Kifshuta, Zeraim Part 1, p. 20, footnote 10. I could not find one B. Talmud manuscript or early print edition that did not have this emendation to the text. The emendation is significant, however, as it had tremendous impact on the future halakhic process regarding the question of women learning and reading Torah."

17. There are many excellent academic articles questioning the historical accuracy of Beruriah as Rabbi Meir's wife. See David Goodblatt, "The Beruriah Traditions," *Journal of Jewish Studies* 26: 68–86, 1975; Rachel Adler, "The Virgin in the Brothel and Other Anomalies: Character and Context in the Legend of Beruriah," *Tikkun* 3, 1988; Daniel Boyarin, *Carnal Israel*, University of California Press, pp.181–196, 1993; and most recently, Etam Henkin's excellent analysis of all of the rabbinic sources in "The Mysterious 'Bruriah' Episode," *Studies in Halakha and Rabbinic History*, Maggid, 2021, pp. 102–127.

Women and Torah Study – A Beit Midrash of Their Own

Unfortunately, it is beyond the scope of this chapter to fully analyze the Beruriah stories, fascinating as they are. Furthermore, she never served as a model for emulation until the modern era and had no impact on the attitude toward women's education in classic rabbinic and post-rabbinic sources. If anything, the legend recorded in Rashi's commentary that explains that Beruriah was seduced by her husband Rabbi Meir's student (at his insistence) because she mocked the rabbis for considering women lightheaded, stands as a stark lesson against educating women in Torah.[18] By ignoring Ben Azzai, the question of women's education in Torah study lay largely dormant until the nineteenth century.

The Next Stage: Maimonides and Sefer Hassidim

Maimonides is nuanced in his analysis of women and Torah study. Most startlingly, he allows that women who study Torah do indeed receive a reward despite the passage in Sotah cited earlier which rejects this possibility. In this manner, Maimonides perhaps retains something of the spirit of Ben Azzai. He also was the first to differentiate between women studying the Written Torah and the Oral Torah. This distinction will remain an important marker in the evolution of women's Torah study when school curricula begin to emerge in the nineteenth century onward.

---

18. See Rashi on B. Talmud Avodah Zarah 18b *ikka d'amri*. In recent years, academic scholarship has tried to verify the source of the difficult sordid story brought in Rashi. At the very least, there is a parallel ending found in Rabbeinu Nissim of Kiron from the tenth century in his book *Yafeh Min Hayehsua* where he brings the story about the rescue of the sister of Beruriah and the danger that was caused to Rabbi Meir as a result of this act. He ends by stating simply that Rabbi Meir went and took his wife and all that he had and moved to Iraq (*Bavel*). For an academic analysis with important conclusions essentially arguing that the text found in Rashi was not brought by Rashi, see Etam Henkin's chapter on Beruriah cited above in the previous footnote.

Maimonides Mishneh Torah Laws of Talmud Torah 1:13	רמב״ם משנה תורה הלכות תלמוד תורה פרק א הלכה יג
A woman who studies Torah has a reward but not like the reward of a man because she is not commanded and anyone who does something that is not commanded on him to do so – his reward is not like the reward of the one who is commanded but rather less. Even though she has a reward, the rabbis commanded that a man should not teach his daughter Torah because most women's minds are not directed towards study. Rather they misinterpret, rendering the text irrational because of their poor minds. The rabbis said, "Anyone who teaches his daughter Torah, it is as if he taught her *tiflut*." What are we talking about? Oral Torah. However, Written Torah one should not teach her *ab initio*, but if he taught her, it is not as if he taught her *tiflut*.	אשה שלמדה תורה יש לה שכר אבל אינו כשכר האיש מפני שלא נצטוית, וכל העושה דבר שאינו מצווה עליו לעשותו אין שכרו כשכר המצווה שעשה אלא פחות ממנו. ואע״פ שיש לה שכר צוו חכמים שלא ילמד אדם את בתו תורה מפני שרוב הנשים אין דעתם מכוונת להתלמד אלא הן מוציאות דברי תורה לדברי הבאי לפי עניות דעתן. אמרו חכמים: כל המלמד את בתו תורה כאילו למדה תפלות. במה דברים אמורים? בתורה שבעל פה. אבל תורה שבכתב לא ילמד אותה לכתחלה, ואם למדה אינו כמלמדה תפלות.

There are several points to note in this quote from Maimonides:

- Women receive a reward when they study Torah although not equal to the reward of men. This is in line with the overall Talmudic approach that those who are exempt from a *mitzvah* but nonetheless perform it receive less reward than those obligated.
- *Tiflut* or licentiousness could only come from women studying Oral Torah (although women would still receive a reward for such study).

Women and Torah Study – A Beit Midrash of Their Own

- Written Torah cannot be associated with *tiflut*. Nonetheless, a father should not teach it to his daughter *ab initio*.

Maimonides presumes that R. Eliezer's reasoning as to why women should not be taught is because women are mentally inferior to men. This concept was not unique to Maimonides. It is simply reflective of the prevailing philosophical and medical theories of the day. What is interesting is that Maimonides emphasizes that Torah study for women is no different than any other *mitzvah* performed voluntarily for which the person receives reward. Maimonides believed that Torah study, which represented intellectual achievement in pursuit of closeness to God, was the purpose of the very existence of mankind, particularly of the Jewish people. Perhaps that is why he saw it as a worthy activity even for women.

At around the same time, in Germany, women's education was addressed in *Sefer Hasidim*, an important collection of laws, customs, ethical exhortations, and spiritual practices attributed to Rabbi Judah the Hasid (1150–1217). In it, fathers are commanded to teach their daughters *mitzvot* so that they know what to do when overseeing a Jewish home:

Sefer Hasidim 313	ספר חסידים סימן שי"ג
Everyone must teach his daughters the *mitzvot*. The Talmudic statement that he who teaches his daughter Torah is as if he taught her *tiflut* refers only to the profundities and rationale of the *mitzvot* and the mysteries of the Torah; these are not taught to a woman or to a minor. However, a woman should be taught how to observe the *mitzvot*, for if she does not know the laws of Shabbat, how can she observe Shabbat, and this applies to all similar *mitzvot*.	חייב אדם ללמוד לבנותיו המצות כגון פסקי הלכות. ומה שאמרו שהמלמד לאשה תורה כאלו מלמדה תיפלות זהו עומק תלמוד וטעמי המצות וסודי התורה אותן אין מלמדין לאשה ולקטן. אבל הלכות מצות ילמד לה, שאם לא תדע הלכות שבת איך תשמור שבת? וכן כל

| Indeed, in the days of Hizkiyahu, king of Judea, men and women, old and young were familiar with the laws of purity and sacrifices. | מצות כדי לעשות להזהר במצות. שהרי בימי חזקיהו מלך יהודה אנשים ונשים גדולים וקטנים ידעו אפילו טהרות וקדשים. |

Sefer Hasidim rules that a man is obligated to teach his daughter practical *halakhah*. While the author does not reject Rabbi Eliezer's prohibition, he restricts it to refer only to the deep study of Talmud or to the *mysteries of the Torah*. A father must teach his daughter about the *mitzvot* so that she knows how to perform them properly. In essence, by limiting Rabbi Eliezer to the profundities of Torah, *Sefer Hasidim* provides a rather broad framework for some form of education. Together with Maimonides, this includes the possibility that such learning has merit for the women who engage in it – and for the men who teach them.

The positions of Maimonides and *Sefer Hasidim* are essentially the only texts through which the discourse evolves. Both positions become codified into Shulhan Arukh and Rema respectively.[19] During the late Middle Ages, the Sages of France and Germany accepted both approaches, the distinction between Oral and Written Torah as codified by Maimonides (limiting women to Written Torah) along with the need to teach daughters, indicating that women should be educated at home in basic Jewish texts and rituals.[20] Furthermore, there are credible accounts of outstanding educated women who served as religious leaders and scholars at this time.[21] In the Cairo Geniza, for example, there are descriptions of elementary schools in which girls and young women studied, as well as schools in which both men and women served as teachers. Overall, however, few women

---

19. Shulhan Arukh Yoreh Deah 246:6 and Rema ad loc.
20. Avraham Grossman, *Pious and Rebellious: Jewish Women in Medieval Europe*, p. 161.
21. See Grossman, pp. 162–63; David Golinkin, *The Status of Women in Jewish Law: Responsa*, Schechter Institute of Jewish Studies, 2012, p. 365.

had any comprehensive Jewish education, despite the softening of Rabbi Eliezer's position.

The next section in this chapter will examine some of the changes that began to take place in parts of Europe in the nineteenth century regarding the education of girls in Jewish sacred texts. The discourse documented in some of the *responsa* and historical documents from that time reflects both urgency and hesitation, qualities that will continue to be pronounced into the twentieth-first century as the glass ceiling restricting women's education incrementally and then exponentially rises.

Progress on the issue of women was achieved in the late eighteenth century when the call for women's general education began to grow dramatically in Germany as a result of the Enlightenment. In 1827 the first Orthodox elementary school in Germany established to combine secular and religious subjects opened its doors to young women. It was in this era that Rabbi Esriel Hildesheimer and Rabbi Samson Rafael Hirsch began to advance formal schooling for females. Rabbi Hirsch felt that the purpose of Jewish learning was not purely academic; rather the goal was religious instruction designed to motivate the student to act.

> No less should Israel's daughters learn the content of the Written Law and the duties which they have to perform in their lifetime as a daughter and young woman, as mother and housewife. Many times have Israel's daughters saved the purity of the Jewish life and spirit. The deliverance from Egypt itself was won by the women; and it is by the pious and virtuous women of Israel that the Jewish spirit and Jewish life can and will again be revived.[22]

The urgency to educate Jewish girls stemmed from the exigency to reinforce their traditional role as wives and mothers. Hirsch reiterated the position taken by *Sefer Hasidim* but in the context of a broader

---

22 R. Shimshon Raphael Hirsch: *Horeb*, Part II, The Soncino Press, London, 1962, p. 371. See also Hirsch's commentary to Deuteronomy 11:19.

educational effort outside of the home and with a modern framing. In his book *Horeb*, he set forth the curriculum necessary to educate girls[23]: Hebrew language, vernacular, Torah, Prophets and Writings, Science, History, Teaching of Duties, Writing, and Arithmetic. While boys would be taught the theoretical instruction of the law, girls would be prevented from acquiring such information. Nonetheless, Hirsch strongly felt that learning "our sacred literature" was essential in order to teach conscientious fulfillment of duty and execution of the tasks one is obligated to perform.[24] This is probably the first time that text-based education for women is openly connected to deeper engagement and commitment to ritual and practice.

Another German rabbi who was also involved in furthering educational opportunities for girls at that time was Rabbi Esriel Hildesheimer. An admirer of Hirsch, he felt that "if it is true that knowledge is power, then the Jewish knowledge of our wives and young ladies will contribute to an invincible Jewish power; in the home, in Jewish family life and to a priceless influence in the area of the education of our sons."[25]

The forces of assimilation, along with the position and role of

---

23. Ibid., pp. 411–412.

24. "ולמדתם The term לימוד is more comprehensive than שינון. We believe that it is for this reason that the *Halakhah* bases its statement בניכם ולא בנותיכם limiting the commandment to teach the Torah to the instruction of our sons exclusive of our daughters on the sentence למדתם אותם את בניכם and not וששנתם לבניך. **The fact is while women are not to be exposed to specialized Torah study or theoretical knowledge of the Law, which are reserved for the Jewish man,** such understanding of our sacred literature as can teach the fear of the Lord and the conscientious fulfillment of our duty, and all such knowledge which is essential to the adequate execution of our tasks should indeed form part of the mental and spiritual training not only of our sons but of our daughters as well." R. Shimshon Raphael Hirsch, R. Shimshon Raphael, *Siddur Tefillot Yisrael*, Mossad HaRav Kook, Jerusalem, p. 70.

25. David Ellenson, "German Orthodox Rabbinical Writings on the Jewish Textual Education of Women: The Views of Rabbi Samson Raphael Hirsch and Rabbi Esriel Hildesheimer" in *Gender and Jewish History*, eds. M. A. Kaplan and D. Moore, p. 167.

women in German society, worked in their favor, highlighting the need for an institutional framework. Rabbis Hirsch and Hildesheimer believed that their innovative approach was necessary for the preservation of the Jewish family. While their stances represented a departure from the traditional Jewish communal norm that denied women formal educational access to all classical textual learning, neither Hirsch nor Hildesheimer permitted female students to study Talmud or the Codes of Jewish Law. The primary responsibility for these young, educated women would be to serve as an anchor for Jewish tradition and practice within the home, inspiring their husbands and children. Individual growth and development were surely not the focus.

The trend in Germany did not automatically spread to Eastern Europe. In Poland, the situation was such that precious communal resources invariably went to financing schools for boys to study Torah. A Compulsory Education Law was passed in the Hapsburg Empire requiring all children between 6 and 14 to attend public schools. In an attempt to shield their sons from that requirement, Orthodox families deliberately sent their daughters to public schools to fill school quotas with girls. The daughters, rather than the sons, were thus exposed to the external and seductive forces of the gentile world, resulting in young observant women assimilating at astonishing rates. Paradoxically, the rabbinic leaders were reluctant and, in many cases, forcefully resistant, to opening Jewish schools for girls because it went against tradition. A generation of girls grew up identifying as Poles in language, thought, and culture and were completely mismatched with yeshiva-educated boys. The Orthodox press cried out against their defection from Orthodoxy, but the trend continued. In some extreme cases, women converted to Christianity to marry non-Jewish lovers although more often it was to escape arranged marriages and the repression of their restrictive religious home environments![26]

There had already been suggestions put forth to open Jewish

---

26. Naomi Seidman, *Sarah Schenirer and the Bais Yaakov Movement*, Littman, 2019, pp. 19–20.

schools for girls in Galicia but they had been rejected, partially on the grounds of the ban by Rabbi Eliezer. At a rabbinical conference in Krakow in 1903, the idea was reintroduced. One rabbi pleaded that all girls be educated in the knowledge of Torah "since so many of them are already far from their people and Jewish spirit."[27] Another proposed the establishment of an afternoon Talmud Torah for girls to learn prayers, blessings, and laws. In response, one of the dissenters proclaimed, "Even this custom they wish to bring to Israel – Talmud Torahs for women! God Forbid! Such a thing will not be!"[28] The conference ended in a stalemate. While it was recognized that there was a growing crisis among young Orthodox women, it was determined that rejecting tradition in such a fashion would flagrantly defy rabbinic authority and be perceived as a capitulation to modernity.

The situation only began to change during World War I, when rabbis from Germany who had graduated from Hildesheimer's rabbinical seminary in Berlin began to arrive in communities in Warsaw (Poland) and Kovno (Lithuania). Responding to the vital need, they set up Jewish gymnasia for boys and girls and began to offer popular religious talks to older girls and women.[29] This followed the trend that had begun in Germany decades earlier and reflected an organic evolution in Jewish pedagogy, encouraging both boys and girls to gain fluency in sacred texts alongside secular subjects.

In Krakow, however, the strong Hasidic leadership utterly opposed Jewish education for girls, even though it was in that city where the most famous defections of Hasidic girls to convents took place. Against this backdrop, it is all the more remarkable that Sarah Schenirer succeeded in her endeavors. She faced an uphill battle when she embarked on her journey to develop and implement a system of learning for girls in more traditional religious communities

---

27. Ibid., p. 22.

28. Ibid.

29. Rachel Manekin, *The Rebellion of the Daughters: Jewish Women Runaways in Habsburg Galicia*, pp. 186–192.

than those established by the Hirsch and Hildesheimer graduates. It is noteworthy that shortly before she opened the first Beis Yaakov school, Rabbi Yisrael Meir Kagan, known as the Chofetz Chaim, acknowledged the dire need for such schools in a commentary to Tractate Sotah:

> **Chofetz Chaim, Likutei Halakhot, Sotah 21b (translation Rabbi Mendell Lewittes)[30]**
>
> "He who teaches his daughter Torah." Evidently, this was so only in previous times, when family tradition was strong enough for everyone to emulate his parents as indicated in the verse, *Ask your father and he will tell you* (Deuteronomy 32:7). We could say that a girl should not be taught to learn Torah but rather model her conduct on that of her righteous parents. Now, however, our sins being many, parental tradition has weakened very much and frequently the daughters even leave home. Specifically, for those who regularly study gentile languages, it is surely a great *mitzvah* to teach them – Chumash and the Prophets and the Writings and the moral instruction of the Sages such as Ethics of our Fathers and Menorat ha-Ma'or so as to strengthen within them our holy faith. If not, they are liable to completely stray far from the path of the Lord and transgress all the principles of our religion, God forbid.

Although Rabbi Kagan acknowledged Rabbi Eliezer's ban, the current state of affairs had so drastically eroded any formerly accepted model that daughters were rejecting tradition and leaving home. It was now a *mitzvah* to teach them the contents of Jewish sacred texts lest they completely stray and transgress. Despite the acknowledged necessity, he did not actively pursue the establishment of a school system for girls. It was into this breach that Sarah Schenirer stepped. Born in Krakow in 1883 to a Hasidic family, Schenirer was a seamstress who

---

30   Translation taken from Getsel Ellinson, *Women and the Mitzvot, Vol. I, Serving the Creator*, World Zionist Organization, 1986, p. 263.

spent every evening studying Torah.[31] After she heard Rabbi Dr. Moshe David Flesch in Vienna call for the spiritual rejuvenation of Judaism through greater devotion and commitment to Torah study on the part of the Jewish woman,[32] she began to implement her plan to teach Jewish texts. In 1917, she gathered 40 women and girls for a study session. The older girls mocked her, but the women enjoyed her lecture. She realized then that she was going to have to start with younger students and in a more systematic way, reflecting the process toward elementary education described in the Talmudic Tractate Bava Batra.[33] Amid growing controversy, she sought to consult with the Belzer Rebbe, who wrote "blessings and success" on a piece of paper that he gave to her brother, thus approving of her initiative, even as he refrained from allowing his Hasidim to send their daughters to her school.[34] Nonetheless, the numbers of enrolled students grew exponentially, and a few years later the Orthodox Agudah organization took over the running of the schools.

What was particularly noteworthy about Sarah Schenirer's life work was not just the school system for young students that she established, but the teacher training college that she founded which provided a strong foundation in belief and practice for the young women who became teachers dedicated to inspiring their students.[35] While the goal

---

31. Deborah Weissman, "Bais Ya'acov: A Historical Model for Jewish Feminists," in *The Jewish Woman: New Perspectives*, ed. E. Koltun, p. 141.

32. Ibid.

33. B. Talmud Bava Batra 21a. The Talmud relates that schools were first opened for older boys of 16 and 17 years of age before it became clear that such boys were intractable. The revamped education system began with boys of six and seven.

34. There is a well-known letter written in 1933 by Rabbi Kagan (Chofetz Chaim) in which he gave his stamp of approval to Bais Yaakov. The letter was actually solicited by Aggudah (not by Sarah Schenirer) to counter opposition in Frysztak to the opening of a Bais Yaakov. In it, he urged all men who fear God to send their daughters to study in this school, while categorically rejecting the concern for the prohibition to teach daughters Torah. He concluded by calling it a *mitzvah* to educate young women in Bais Yaakov.

35. My own grandmother was a student in one of the first Bais Yaakov classes in

Women and Torah Study – A Beit Midrash of Their Own

of both the college and the school system was to reinforce observance, it did so through encouraging religious enthusiasm and fervor, using informal educational methods such as songs, dances, plays, and trips.[36] Religious piety and ideological commitment were the mission and highest achievement for Orthodox Jewish women. This was meant to extinguish any desire they may have felt for advanced secular education.[37] For this reason, the schools did not provide a strong foundation in Hebrew text study beyond traditional Yiddish texts that were universally approved of, so that the girls learned sacred texts based on Yiddish translation and commentaries intended for lay people rather than in the original Hebrew.[38] Yiddish was touted as a holy language and complete immersion in it was meant to counter attraction to Polish language and culture. This was in contradistinction to the Hirsch-Hildesheimer gymnasia which were interested in inculcating a Torah with *Derekh Eretz* ideology that allowed for secular studies, as well.

Even within the most conservative and resistant ultra-Orthodox communities, the Bais Yaakov school system has proven the remarkable impact education can have in engaging and connecting young women to their religious heritage and halakhic practice. Indeed, the tide was already turning in all parts of the Jewish world as schools were being established with a focus on a modern education system for both girls and boys, integrating a strong commitment to religious observance with secular subjects necessary for building a

---

Williamsburg, New York. One of 13 children, born to a very religious family, she went to public school according to American compulsory education laws, but attended afternoon classes at Bais Yaakov in an after-school program. It had an enormous impact on her, and for my entire life I heard her talk about the influence of Rebbetzin Vichna Kaplan, who inspired her students to constantly think about their relationship to God and have their love for Him reflected in everything they did. Regarding text study, however, she was largely ignorant.

36. Manekin, pp. 234–235.
37. Ibid.
38. Ibid.

sustainable life in contemporary society. Today it appears obvious that every community builds their own school systems for girls that reflect its own ideologies, customs, and interpretations. From the most extreme Hasidic sects to the most liberal Orthodox, children of both sexes in observant communities attend Jewish schools that tailor their curricular offerings to reflect religious ideology regarding the world of Torah study as well as the secular world.

Should Women Learn Talmud?

As educational opportunities for women increased in the mid-to-late twentieth century and the feminist movement demanded equal educational, professional, social, and economic opportunities for women, it was to be expected that the question of Talmud study for women would come to the fore. In 1937, even before feminism actively took root in the Orthodox community, Rabbi Joseph Dov Soloveitchik and his wife Tonya founded the Maimonides School in Boston that offered girls and boys equal educational opportunities, including the study of Talmud. Still, it remained outside of the Orthodox mainstream school curricula for many decades.[39] In the 1970s Rabbi Moshe Feinstein was asked about teaching Mishnah in Bais Yaakov schools. He answered briefly but emphatically in the negative:

Igrot Moshe	איגרות משה, יו"ד ג, פז
In the Bais Yaakov schools for girls, teachers want to teach mishnayot. Maimonides ruled like Rabbi Eliezer that this should not be taught.	בבתי הספר לנערות בית יעקב רוצים המורים ללמוד עמהן משניות. רמב"ם פסק כרבי אליעזר שאין ללמד.

---

39. As a result, Rabbi Soloveitchik's students went on to argue for and against the practice. See Seth Farber, *An Orthodox American Dreamer*, Chapter 4, Brandeis University Press, 2003, pp. 68–87.

| Mishnah is Oral Law and therefore it should be prevented. Only Pirkei Avot should be taught in order to awaken in them love for Torah and good values but not the rest of the tractates. Since the matter is simple/clear, I will remain concise. | משניות הוא תורה שבעל פה, ולכן צריך למונעם. רק פרקי אבות (יש ללמד) בהסבר לעוררן לאהבת תורה ולמידות טובות, אבל לא שאר המסכתות, ומתוך פשיטות אקצר. |

At the same time, in Israel, *responsa* by ultra-Orthodox rabbis like Bentzion Feurer and Moshe Malka endorsed nuanced and moderate positions with regard to integrating Oral Law (Mishnah and Talmud) into the curricula for girls. Rabbi Feurer was asked whether it is permissible to teach both Written and Oral Torah to girls. His response, published in the religious education journal *No'am*, explicitly concluded that the teaching of Mishnah was permitted and to be regarded as positive, particularly in schools where students were going to be taught real *tiflut*, i.e., secular studies.

Rabbi Benzion Fuerer, *Noam*, Volume 3 (translation Rabbi Mendell Lewittes)[40]

But today a daughter who does not study Torah studies actual *tiflut* instead, and surely if we must choose between actual *tiflut* and "as if" *tiflut*, we prefer the latter. In our times, the argument for Torah study by women outweighs by far the argument against; for in place of the perfect faith diffused by the Torah, young women are fed meaningless notions of *tiflut* and objectionable ideas found in secular irreligious literature. A single Torah text book might well eradicate the impact of many volumes of *tiflut* study. Whether we like it or not, the traditional *melamed* has been replaced by the lady-teacher who transmits the Torah to boys and girls in elementary school. If

---

40   Translation taken from Getsel Ellinson, *Women and the Mitzvot, Vol. I, Serving the Creator*, World Zionist Organization, 1986, pp. 266–268.

> girls do not learn Torah in school, the irreligious teacher will replace the religious teacher and transmit to the children in elementary school their own spurious version of Torah…evidently this induced the eminent Torah scholars of the past two generations to approve teaching Torah to girls — both Written and Oral Torah, e.g., Mishnah, Codes, etc. I wish that all Jewish girls would study Torah and not expose their hearts to the *tiflut* of this permissive generation.

Rabbi Moshe Malka, an eminent rabbinic authority from Morocco who became the rabbi of Petah Tikva, went even further in acknowledging the need to increase Torah study for women to keep up with the educational challenges provided by advanced secular education. He suggested that R. Eliezer would surely waive his ban in light of the contemporary educational reality.

While in practice no ultra-Orthodox schools formally teach their female students Talmud, the explanations given by these rabbinic authorities further illuminate the contemporary discourse on the topic. In addition to Rabbi Malka, a number of rabbinic authorities, including the Lubavitcher Rebbe, recognized the dissonance in limiting women from studying the Oral Law while allowing them to study secular subjects at the highest academic levels.

> Menachem Mendel Schneerson, Sichot, Part III, Parashat Emor 5750, p. 171
>
> In the generations preceding us, there did not exist educational institutions for girls…every daughter received [the traditions] from her mother and the older women [in the community], etc. Nonetheless, in the last few generations, the great rabbis established educational institutions for girls, seeing it as an exigency of the hour, since without question they leave their homes and are influenced by what they see outside, etc., and thus, it is a necessity to establish for them educational institutions in which they will receive proper and approved religious education.

Women and Torah Study – A Beit Midrash of Their Own

> And this then applies to the study of the Oral Torah (beyond the study of *halakhot* that apply directly to them). Since nonetheless, women and girls learn a variety of disciplines through which cunning enters into them. Thus, it is not just permissible for women to study the Oral Law, but beyond this, according to the very reasoning of the *halakhah* itself, it is necessary to teach them Oral Torah. Not just to learn the halakhic decisions without their reasons, but also to teach them the reasons behind the laws, including the fine dialectical arguments that are found in the Torah. For it is in human nature, male and female, to desire and take pleasure even more in this kind of study. Through this there will be in them a development of the senses and of the connections infused with the spirit of our Holy Torah.

Rabbi Schneerson recognized the disparity that restrictions on women in the world of Torah study created in comparison with their access to secular knowledge. In addition, he astutely noted that women of today, just like men, crave the intellectual stimulation provided by dialectical Talmud study. This acknowledgment undercut the coherency of the fragile construct that from the time of Maimonides had attempted to uphold some semblance of Rabbi Eliezer's statement by differentiating between Written and Oral Torah, giving legitimacy for women to learn Written Torah while maintaining clear boundaries to avoid their learning Oral Torah.

Nonetheless, as with the Belzer Rebbe who approved Sarah Schenirer's initiative but not for his own community, the Lubavitch school system for girls has never included Oral Torah study in its curriculum. Although halakhically permissible, communities that reinforce strong gender differentiation in all aspects of communal structure and society still prefer educational frameworks that continue to distinguish between boys' and girls' curricula of study. This is especially manifest with regard to Talmud study which is taught only to boys and men.

In the 1970s, women slowly began studying Talmud in organized settings. Rabbi David Silber, who was a student of Rabbi Soloveitchik, established Drisha, a women's yeshiva, in New York City. Likewise, in Israel, Rabbi Chaim Brovender established a yeshiva for women,

Beruria (now Midreshet Lindenbaum), known fondly as "Brovender's" for many years. Stern College opened a Talmud class for women in 1977. Before that time, the students had access to Talmudic texts as primary sources used in preparation for classes in Jewish history, law, and biblical exegesis. This was the first time a course aimed at students' gaining independent skills in Talmud was offered. To reinforce its legitimacy and importance to Yeshiva University, Rabbi Joseph Dov Soloveitchik taught the inaugural class. At the end of his lecture, he expounded on the importance of both men and women studying Oral Torah [41]:

> Without *Torah She-Ba'al Peh* (Oral Torah), there is no Judaism. Any talk about Judaism minus *Torah She-Ba'al Peh* is just meaningless and absurd. Like if one never studied physics and writes the philosophy of nature. It's ridiculous, you can't write the philosophy of nature before you are acquainted with physics, so you cannot write about Judaism if you are not acquainted with *Torah She-Ba'al Peh*. It's important that not only boys should be acquainted, but girls, as well. I'll support you as far as education is concerned. If you have problems come to me, I'll fight your battles.

From the late 1980s onward, more and more opportunities arose for women in Modern Orthodoxy to study Talmud. The discourse of *bedieved* – as something permitted after-the-fact – which justified such studies in the 1970s, gave way to a discourse of *lechathila*, in which Talmud study for women was seen as an organic continuation of the obligation to teach girls Torah that had begun in the nineteenth century.

The passage in *Shema* which was interpreted by the *Sifrei* as *and teach it to your sons*, had been tacitly reinterpreted as *and teach it to your children* by the twentieth century, in order to justify and reinforce the need to allocate communal resources to educating girls

---

41. Saul Berman, *Forty Years Later: The Rav's Opening Shiur at the Stern Beit Midrash For Women*, Lehrhaus, October 9, 2017.

in parallel to boys. It was no longer understood to be particularly about fathers and sons but about parents and children. By the late twentieth century, many Modern Orthodox high schools had begun to incorporate Talmud into their curricula for girls. Many *midrashot* (post-high-school Torah study programs) offer some Talmud, varying from minimal exposure to a significant number of hours spent studying Talmud text.

On a more advanced level, in 1990, Matan opened an Advanced Talmud Institute (from which I graduated) which provided stipends for women to study full-time for three years, together with a schedule that allowed for daycare pick-up time. Nishmat and Midreshet Lindenbaum's Beruria Scholars program offered similar opportunities. Alumnae of those programs began to open *midrashot* for Israelis and/or Americans with an emphasis on Talmud study. Yeshiva University eventually opened GPATS, a graduate program in advanced Talmud studies. Most recently, Drisha "made *aliyah*" and opened the first yeshiva (rather than a *midrasha*/seminary) for women run by a cadre of women who have been studying and teaching Talmud for decades and who have implemented a yeshiva-style curriculum. There has been awe-inspiring progress in making the Talmud accessible to a critical mass of women of all ages who now have the tools to engage with a text that is central to Jewish and religious identity and practice. This, in turn, has allowed women to access the page as active learners rather than passive listeners, joining the echoing voices raised in Torah study dating back to Sinai.

This progress might translate into a false sense of complacency. While there are, indeed, opportunities for women to advance in their study of Talmud, it is important not to romanticize the current reality. Despite Rabbi Soloveitchik's clear support, there have been misgivings expressed about where this kind of study will lead, and suspicion that as a result of their study women will be unsatisfied with the traditional gendered structure of Orthodoxy. Thirty-five years after he served as the first Talmud instructor at Stern, Rabbi Mordechai Willig publicly stated that the phenomenon of women's Talmud study must be reevaluated because of the subsequent rumblings caused by such learning[42]:

> The inclusion of Talmud in curricula for all women in Modern Orthodox schools needs to be reevaluated. While the *gedolim* of the twentieth century saw Torah study to be a way to keep women close to our *mesorah*, an egalitarian attitude has colored some women's study of Talmud and led them to embrace and advocate egalitarian ideas and practices which are unacceptable to those very *gedolim*.

In practice, relatively few female students take intensive Talmud classes. Furthermore, there is a considerable imbalance between the worlds of Torah study for men and for women that is unlikely to change in the near future. This imbalance is radically different than anything in the academic and professional worlds in which standards and expectations are the same for men and women. Stern College, for instance, offers advanced Talmud classes that require the small number of students who register to prepare for six hours a week and attend a two-hour *shiur*. In contrast, men at Yeshiva College enrolled in the Beit Midrash program, which makes up about half of the student body, devote 24 hours a week to Talmud study over and above their regular college course load.

The contrast is equally striking in the Israeli seminary/yeshiva world. Women's gap year seminary programs in Israel which schedule 6 to 10 hours of Talmud a week are considered "heavy" on Talmud study. Parallel programs for young men expect their students to study six to eight hours of Talmud a day. This has led to criticism both from the young women seeking more rigorous studies and from the male yeshiva world which – at times mockingly – finds women's programs lacking.

The underlying explanation behind the disparity is that men have a *mitzvah* to study Torah – meaning Talmud – throughout their lives. Thus, considerable support, resources, passion, and even pressure are

---

42. http://www.torahweb.org/torah/2015/parsha/rwil_ekev.html

Women and Torah Study – A Beit Midrash of Their Own

put on men in religious society to ensure that the hallowed study halls known as *Batei Midrash* are filled. Since women are not traditionally viewed as being obligated to study Torah for Torah's sake and the question of necessity to educate women in Talmud remains an open one, there is no corresponding social or financial structure to support such intensive study. Furthermore, many women's programs pedagogically endorse a more diverse program of study, offering not only Talmud and *halakhah* but also serious classes in Bible and Jewish philosophy. This broadening of access to a more diverse course of study of Torah beyond Talmud can be seen as an advantage to women's education compared to the traditionally rigid structure of men's *yeshivot*. Still, from within the world of *yeshivot*, it is more likely to be perceived as inferior.

Although it is unanimously accepted that parents are obligated to educate both sons and daughters in Torah, this does not translate into an equally perceived lifelong obligation to study daily. Once a woman marries and has children, child-rearing and household duties are seen as women's religious obligations, parallel to Torah study for men. I have heard lectures in which leading rabbinic authorities express the opinion already articulated in Tractates Sotah and Berakhot (cited earlier in this chapter), that for a woman, the laundry, child-rearing, and housekeeping duties that allow her husband to study Talmud bring her merit as if she studied Talmud herself. Nonetheless, it must be acknowledged that there is a proliferation of Torah study classes regularly available to women in all Modern Orthodox and ultra-Orthodox communities, reinforcing the greater communal acceptance that Torah study in its many forms is the most central way to ensure and inspire connection and dedication to a life of religious practice.

Can Women Become Halakhic Authorities?

The advent of women's Talmud study qualified women to take up leadership roles in communities based on their Talmudic and halakhic expertise. This ultimately led to the debate about whether it is appropriate to appoint women to leadership positions within the Orthodox Jewish community.

Uncovered

There are three considerations regarding the greater topic of women and positions of authority that need to be evaluated from a halakhic standpoint. Each one of these considerations will be examined textually below.

- Women's testimony is not accepted by rabbinic courts except under very specific circumstances. The Mishnah states that those who are not fit to serve as witnesses are barred from serving as judges as well.

- The Torah states that should the people of Israel desire it, they shall appoint a king. *Midrash halakhah* explains that the Torah explicitly specifies a king and not a queen. Based on this interpretation, Maimonides stipulates that only men may be appointed to positions of communal authority.

- Women are considered a source of sexual distraction in *halakhah*. This point is not directly addressed in the sources about religious leadership, but it hovers in the background of all conversations having to do with women interacting with men. It is a topic that is addressed broadly throughout this book, particularly in the upcoming chapters on *ervah*.

Women as Judges

Deuteronomy 19:15–17	דברים יט
A single witness may not confirm a person's guilt or blame for any transgression or sin; a case can be ruled valid only on the testimony of two witnesses or more.	טו לֹא-יָקוּם עֵד אֶחָד בְּאִישׁ, לְכָל-עָוֹן וּלְכָל-חַטָּאת, בְּכָל-חֵטְא, אֲשֶׁר יֶחֱטָא: עַל-פִּי שְׁנֵי עֵדִים, אוֹ עַל-פִּי שְׁלֹשָׁה-עֵדִים—יָקוּם דָּבָר.

Women and Torah Study – A Beit Midrash of Their Own

If a man appears against another to testify maliciously The two men in dispute shall appear before the LORD, before the priests or magistrates in authority in that time.	טז כִּי-יָקוּם עֵד-חָמָס, בְּאִישׁ, לַעֲנוֹת בּוֹ, סָרָה. יז וְעָמְדוּ שְׁנֵי-הָאֲנָשִׁים אֲשֶׁר-לָהֶם הָרִיב, לִפְנֵי יְהוָה, לִפְנֵי הַכֹּהֲנִים וְהַשֹּׁפְטִים, אֲשֶׁר יִהְיוּ בַּיָּמִים הָהֵם.

The biblical text makes clear that two witnesses are necessary to establish the guilt or innocence of a defendant. The text also relates to false testimony, establishing that disputes should be brought before God, represented by the priests or the judges/magistrates who hold authority at the time. The following verse, not cited, is the command and obligation for the judge or priest to investigate the matter thoroughly before ruling. The following *midrash halakhah*, based on the verses above, serves as the source for the Talmudic exclusion of women as witnesses:

Sifrei Devarim Shoftim 190	ספרי דברים פרשת שופטים פיסקא קץ
"And they will stand" (Deuteronomy 19:17). It is incumbent that those being judged should stand. "Two men." I only know thus that this is when there are two men. A man and a woman or a woman and a man or two women one against the other, how do I know they too stand in judgment? The Torah says: "who have a dispute." Any people (male or female) in any kind of dispute.	ועמדו. מצוה בנדונים שיעמדו. שני האנשים. אין לי אלא בזמן שהם שני אנשים איש עם אשה ואשה עם איש שתי נשים זו עם זו מנין? תלמוד לומר: אשר להם הריב. מכל מקום.

| Could this mean then that a woman can stand as witness? It says here "two" and it says there (Deuteronomy 19:15) "two" [witnesses]. Just as here it means men to the exclusion of women, so too there it means men to the exclusion of women. | יכול אף אשה תהא כשירה לעדות? נאמר כאן: שני, ונאמר להלן: שני. מה שני האמור כאן אנשים ולא נשים אף שני האמור להלן אנשים ולא נשים. |

The exegesis in the Sifrei proceeds as follows:

In verse 15, we have the word *shenei* (two) in the masculine that describes the need for two or more witnesses. In verse 17 we have the word *shenei* (two) followed by the noun "men" to describe two people in a dispute. This rendering of "two men" in verse 17 is understood also as an elucidation of the same noun "two" in verse 15, clarifying that it, too, refers to two men, to the exclusion of women as witnesses. Paradoxically, the exegesis in the same *midrash* of verse 17 is that the term "two men" is non-gendered and denotes both men and women as litigants!

As noted above, this type of exegesis in which the usage of masculine pronouns or the use of the word "men" or "sons" to exclude women is prevalent in rabbinic interpretation. However, it is notable that in this case, women are excluded as witnesses based on the explicit noun "men" in verse 17, while they are included in the justice system as litigants, despite the use of the explicit noun "men" in the same exact verse. Such inconsistency can be jarring, but it is ubiquitous in the unfolding of *halakhah* from the outset.

A Mishnah in Tractate Niddah further states that those who cannot serve as witnesses cannot serve as judges.

Mishnah Niddah 6:4	משנה מסכת נדה פרק ו משנה ד
Whoever is eligible to act as a judge in a capital case can serve as a judge in a	כל הראוי לדון דיני נפשות ראוי לדון דיני ממונות.

Women and Torah Study – A Beit Midrash of Their Own

monetary case and there are those who are eligible to serve as judges in a monetary case but not serve on a capital case. Whoever is eligible to act as a judge is eligible to act as a witness but one may be eligible to act as a witness and not as a judge.	ויש שראוי לדון דיני ממונות ואינו ראוי לדון דיני נפשות. כל הכשר לדון כשר להעיד. ויש שכשר להעיד ואינו כשר לדון:

To summarize, women cannot act as witnesses, and they cannot serve as judges since one who cannot witness cannot judge. Nowhere in the rabbinic conversation is any attempt made to rationalize the exclusion of women, e.g., due to a flaw in women's character. The oft-heard claim that women cannot be witnesses because they do not have the ability to remain objective due to their emotional tendencies has no basis in the Talmud.[43] In practice, women can actually testify in many important areas of law. These include testimony regarding the state of affairs between a husband and wife, whether a woman is a virgin (including her own virginity), establishing that a captive woman was not raped and is subsequently permitted to marry a priest, and her own or another woman's personal status which would permit or prohibit her/them from marrying.

Furthermore, women can testify in monetary cases in which a single witness is sufficient such as issues of *kashrut*, separating *hallah*, checking for *hametz*, and menstrual purity and impurity.[44]

---

43. Rabbinic sources recognized that under certain circumstances we cannot assume that men are objective witnesses, and various professions, such as gambling, moneylending with interest, and even shepherding disqualify men. See Mishnah Rosh Hashanah 1:5 and B. Talmud Sanhedrin 25b. Family members are automatically disqualified from testifying about one another. Blind, deaf mute, mentally ill, and minor males are all disqualified, not only as witnesses but also as litigants.

44. Rabbi Daniel Sperber concludes that in all of these areas it would follow that if a woman can testify, she can also serve as a judge. While his position is singular, it is the logical extension of the process that unfolded regarding women and serving as a witness in court. If women can, in fact, offer testimony even in limited cases, they should logically be able to issue judicial rulings in those cases. See Daniel Sperber,

The exclusion of women from testifying in court cases where only two male witnesses are accepted is treated as an apodictic statement, existing without explanation or contextualization.[45] There are also many exceptions to the rule.

King but Not Queen: Women in Positions of Authority

Deuteronomy 17:15	דברים י"ז
You shall appoint a king over yourself, one chosen by the LORD your God. Appoint a king of your own people; you must not appoint a foreigner over you, one who is not your kinsman.	טו שׂוֹם תָּשִׂים עָלֶיךָ מֶלֶךְ, אֲשֶׁר יִבְחַר יְהוָה אֱלֹהֶיךָ בּוֹ. מִקֶּרֶב אַחֶיךָ, תָּשִׂים עָלֶיךָ מֶלֶךְ—לֹא תוּכַל לָתֵת עָלֶיךָ אִישׁ נָכְרִי, אֲשֶׁר לֹא-אָחִיךָ הוּא.
Sifrei Devarim 157:2, 8–10	ספרי דברים קנ"ז:ב', ח'-י'
(2) "A king": and not a queen. (8–10) Another thing: "You shall appoint a king." This is a positive commandment.	ב מלך. ולא מלכה. ח-י דבר אחר. שום תשים עליך מלך. מצות עשה.

Rabba, Maharat, Rabbanit, Rebbetzin: Women with Leadership Authority According to Halachah, Urim Publications, 2020, p. 27.

45. In a strident defense of the traditional approach to women's roles in Orthodoxy, Moshe Meiselman admits that the disqualification of women as witnesses might be completely arbitrary with no rational explanation. He writes, "There are many possible reasons for the technical disqualification of women and no one really knows for sure. The only clear facts are that the ability to testify is neither a right nor a privilege but an obligation from which women have been excused. This disqualification of women is a technical rule rather than an expression of lack of credibility. Thus, women's statements are acceptable whenever credibility is required rather than witnessed testimony. Women's statements are not considered witnessed testimony. Nonetheless, a woman's oath is acceptable in court as is the oath of any credible person." See Moshe Meiselman, *Jewish Women in Jewish Law*, Ktav, 1978, p. 79.

Women and Torah Study – A Beit Midrash of Their Own

"You cannot appoint a foreigner." This is a negative commandment. From here it was said that a man should be appointed to be a communal leader, and a woman should not be appointed to be a communal leader.	לא תוכל לתת עליך איש נכרי. מצות לא תעשה. איש נכרי. מיכן אמרו: האיש ממנים פרנס על הציבור ואין ממנים האשה פרנסת על הצבור.

The verse in Deuteronomy commands the nation of Israel to appoint a king when they enter the Land of Israel. The *midrash halakhah* limits the concept of monarchy to men. In a subsequent (less known) clause, the *midrash* adds a statement that only men can serve as communal leaders.

Maimonides famously incorporated this restriction from the *midrash halakhah* into the Mishneh Torah, where he extended the limitation on communal leadership to all positions of authority. This became known in the halakhic discourse as *serarah,* or power of authority – a catchword for the prohibition against women serving in positions of authority.

Maimonides Mishneh Torah Laws of Kings 1:5	רמב"ם משנה תורה הלכות מלכים פרק א הלכה ה
A woman should not be appointed king as it is written in the Torah, "appoint a king" and not a queen. This principle also applies to all other positions of authority within Israel. Only men should be appointed to fill them.	אין מעמידין אשה במלכות שנאמר: עליך מלך, ולא מלכה. וכן כל משימות שבישראל אין ממנים בהם אלא איש.

Deborah: Judge and Prophetess

The judge and prophetess Deborah served as an ancient precedent for a wise woman's ability to act as both a political and religious authority, posing a challenge to the later disqualification of women as rabbinic court judges (or rabbis).

Judges 4:4–5	שופטים ד
Deborah, wife of Lapidot, was a prophetess; she led Israel at that time. …and the Israelites would come to her for judgment.	ד וּדְבוֹרָה אִשָּׁה נְבִיאָה אֵשֶׁת לַפִּידוֹת—הִיא שֹׁפְטָה אֶת-יִשְׂרָאֵל בָּעֵת הַהִיא. ה...וַיַּעֲלוּ אֵלֶיהָ בְּנֵי יִשְׂרָאֵל לַמִּשְׁפָּט.

How could Deborah, a woman who is prohibited by Oral Law from serving as a judge, serve as judge and leader? The Babylonian Talmud does not address this specific question. Many Talmudic commentaries, however, are bothered by this discrepancy and attempt to come up with an approach that maintains the integrity of both Oral Law and the biblical story.

Two common answers are commonly given to solve this conundrum. The first, prevalent in the school of Tosafot,[46] is that Deborah taught the relevant laws for the disputed case but did not actually judge. A variation on this is found in Sefer HaHinukh which referred to "wise women fit to render halakhic decisions."[47] Both acknowledge women's ability to master halakhic material, although Tosafot limited the application of this knowledge to an educational, rather than leadership, role. In a slight variation, Nahmanides writes that the community was guided by her leadership in the manner of a queen guiding her populace.[48] She was not appointed judge (or queen) but she was treated with the veneration and authority given to a leader.

A second approach, brought by several rishonim,[49] is that she was appointed to be a judge by the community. Since the people

---

46. Tosafot Nidda 50a.

47. Sefer HaHinukh, *Mitzvah* 152.

48. Nahmanides commentary to B. Talmud Shavuot 30a.

49. See Talmudic commentaries Rashba and Ran to B. Talmud Shavuot 30a.

voluntarily accepted her authority, she served as a judge by the will of the people and not through halakhic fiat. There is actually a well-established rule originating in a Mishnah found in Tractate Sanhedrin 24a that litigants can agree to be judged by anyone, even individuals who would ordinarily be precluded from serving as judges, such as relatives.[50]

In short, not everyone agreed with Maimonides that women were automatically barred from serving in positions of leadership. Major medieval authorities such as Nahmanides, Rashba, and Ritva understood that Deborah could serve as a precedent for women in positions of political authority if they achieved communal acceptance. Ritva's position is particularly interesting because while he agreed with Maimonides that the prohibition of *serarah* barred women from all communal positions, he contended that if there was communal acceptance, there was no *serarah*.[51] According to this approach, Deborah *de facto* served as [rabbinic] judge and political leader since the people chose to accept her authority and unanimously submitted to her. A community can therefore appoint a woman as their political, communal, or religious leader without violating the tenet of *serarah*.

The Contemporary Picture

The question of women and positions of authority was almost completely theoretical until the twentieth century. Over 100 years ago, on the eve of the first election in Mandatory Palestine, the issue of women's suffrage and participation in public life was a contentious one in Israel. It came before Rabbi Abraham Isaac Kook, Chief Ashkenazi Rabbi, and Rabbi Ben Zion Meir Uziel, Chief Sephardi Rabbi, for resolution.[52]

---

50. See also Shulhan Arukh, Choshen Mishpat 21:1–3.

51. Ritva commentary to B. Talmud Shavuot 30a.

52. Abraham Isaac Kook, "On the Election of Women," September 1919, and "On Women's Voting," April 1920, Jerusalem, translation Zvi Zohar; and Uziel Ben Zion, *Mishpetei Uziel* 44, translation Zvi Zohar, published in *The Edah Journal* in The Halakhic Debate of Women in Public Life, 2001.

Rabbi Kook prohibited both possibilities, stating that women must be prevented from occupying any positions of office as well as those involving judgment and testimony. He further wrote that the idea of women engaging in public life perverts the ideals that Torah represents for a just and moral society that guards and protects the holy and pure nature of the wife and mother in the home. Another concern related to the possible promiscuity and immodesty that could ensue should women leave the home to enter the voting booth, let alone if they were to work alongside men in mixed venues. Rabbi Uziel completely disagreed. He held that women in his day could engage in public life and hold positions in public office, viewing men and women as equally capable and finding no compelling halakhic reason to prevent it.

> **Rabbi Ben Zion Uziel, Mishpetei Uziel 44 (translation Zvi Zohar)**
>
> This ruling of the Rambam only refers to an appointment by the Sanhedrin. But when the appointment is by the consent of the community, where through a majority vote the public voices its opinion, the agreement and trust of the public in its appointees, who will be supervising their communal affairs – in such a case even he would agree that there is no hint of a prohibition [i.e., for a woman to serve].
> …It is common sense that in any serious meeting and meaningful conversation there is no question of lack of modesty….And sitting in the proximity [of women] when involved in communal affairs, which is work of holiness, does not lead to lightheartedness. For all Israel are holy people, and her women are holy and are not to be suspect of breach of modesty and morality.

In addition to invoking the approach that communal appointment is not the *serarah* prohibited by Maimonides, he concludes that the concern for sexual immodesty is unfounded. Women and men can respectfully interact in professional environments without concern for immorality.

While women were given the vote and the ability to run for office by

Women and Torah Study – A Beit Midrash of Their Own

the state, controversy erupted around the question of women serving on religious councils in Israel and as synagogue presidents in the United States. In Israel, in 1987, Leah Shakdiel made headlines when she turned to the High Court after the Attorney General barred her from serving on a religious council because of the halakhic restriction of *serarah*. The court overturned the Attorney General's ruling, and in 2016 the Attorney General's office ruled that all religious councils must be comprised of 30 percent women. In practice, it is difficult to find enough women to serve on such councils. One might conclude that this difficulty stems from the fact that these positions were previously closed to them for religious reasons, even though legal and halakhic allowances are now being made. It is equally possible that women feel uncomfortable forcing the hands of religious leaders based on a secular court decision. On the other hand, it is also possible that women are simply disinterested in serving on religious councils for other reasons, having more to do with time constraints and general apathy about religious affairs.

In the United States, the National Council of Young Israel, which mostly caters to a Modern Orthodox population, does not allow women to serve as president of their synagogues due to *serarah*. Recently someone suggested to me that *serarah* might only be a pretext for preventing what is often a fairly intense working relationship between rabbi and president to develop between the rabbi and a female president, an observation worth considering. *Serarah* was also invoked in a famous two-part *responsum* written by Rabbi Moshe Feinstein, who was asked whether a widow could be appointed as *kashrut* supervisor in place of her dead husband in order to support herself and her son. After explaining why a woman could serve in this capacity due to the many *rishonim* who disagreed with Maimonides on *serarah*, he concludes that he feels it advisable to uphold Maimonides' ruling. Instead, he suggested a compromise: a rabbi would formally hold the title of *kashrut* supervisor while the widow would be hired to do the supervising.[53] Even today, *serarah* remains one of the focal

---

53. Igrot Moshe, Yoreh Deah, Part 2, 44–45. The debate over women working as *kashrut*

points of all questions regarding women and communal authority, despite near halakhic consensus that communal acceptance obviates the halakhic issues.

Leadership and Professional Training Programs on the Path to Ordination

By the early 1990s, Talmud study programs began to act to advance their graduates beyond the walls of the Beit Midrash. In Israel, Midreshet Lindenbaum opened a program to train women to serve as rabbinic advocates in the rabbinic divorce courts. For the first time, women were intensively studying the halakhic laws of divorce in depth and taking rigorous exams to qualify for jobs that had previously been available only to learned men. Eventually, some of their graduates began to work in the rabbinic courts, arguing difficult and complex cases before the judges.[54]

In 1997, Nishmat opened its halakhic advisors or Yoatzot Halacha program to train women in the intricate and sensitive laws of *niddah*, to enable them to respond to *niddah* and sexuality questions. In

---

supervisors became politicized in Israel when the women's organization Emunah petitioned the supreme court in 2013 to allow them to apply for jobs that were exclusively held by men, as long as they passed the requisite exams. Most recently, the rabbinic organization Tzohar teamed up with Emunah to provide courses for female *kashrut* supervisors. In practice, however, there are few women in the field.

54. Two well-known graduates are Dr. Rachel Levmore and Rabbanit Rivka Lubitch. As a consequence of her work with *agunot*, meaning "chained" women who are unable to get Jewish divorces, Levmore composed two halakhic prenuptial agreements intended to prevent or circumvent drawn out and embittered divorce situations. Lubitch, who has worked tirelessly to expose the complex reality of children labeled as *mamzerim* in Israel, has experienced much backlash and personal attacks for her work. She has also written a painful and devastating account of her 20 years working as a rabbinic advocate in the rabbinic divorce courts. It must be noted that the last 30 years have seen some critical advances (not enough, but still, some progress) made in the rabbinic courts in trying to find broader solutions for women trapped and unable to obtain divorces. These changes have come as the result of collaborations between learned women and men, who, together with female lawyers, professional feminist advocates, and the assistance of public pressure, have presented these matters as central, critical issues in our time.

Women and Torah Study – A Beit Midrash of Their Own

addition to the intense halakhic training (which rivals parallel all-male training programs), Nishmat includes hundreds of hours of supplementary information in gynecology, sexuality, fertility, and intimacy. The Nishmat hotline has answered over 250,000 questions to date, in addition to the hundreds and thousands of questions fielded by women not working on the hotline who are graduates of Nishmat and similar training programs. This "breaking of silence" suggests an enormous need that was simply waiting to be met. I field multiple calls and questions weekly from women who thank me for my sensitivity and availability, admitting that they would never call a male rabbi with such personal questions. During the recent corona virus outbreak, Yoatzot Halacha and Nishmat were at the forefront of ensuring *mikvah* safety throughout the crisis, along with the Jerusalem-based Eden Center staffed entirely by women and committed to safe and meaningful *mikvah* practice.

The Yoatzot Halacha program is not without critics. There are prominent right-wing Orthodox communities in the Diaspora where rabbinic leaders have fought to prevent a *yoetzet* from establishing herself in the community and have actively discouraged women from going to them for answers. In the Fall 2019 issue of the ultra-Orthodox journal *Dialogue*, Rabbi Aharon Feldman, the head of the prestigious Ner Israel Yeshiva in Baltimore and a senior member of Agudas Israel, the largest ultra-Orthodox rabbinic council in America, wrote an article titled "*Yoatzot Halakhah* – Are They Good for Jews?" In it, he disparaged the training of women to answer halakhic questions in the laws of *niddah*, and more to the point, critiqued this phenomenon as a terrible distortion of the tradition in which rabbis were the only address for such questions. He wrote that the increased observance by women of these laws does not justify the ensuring harm to the integrity of Torah:

> As such, the introduction of *yoatzot halakhah* into the synagogue must be resisted. We cannot permit a movement which strives to uproot *Halakhah* – which is the goal of many of those who would

> introduce female rabbis – to take the slightest hold in our Shuls. Even if it is true that *yoatzot halakhah* will contribute to greater observance of *taharas ha-mishpacha* (family purity), winning the battle for increased observance of this Mitzva is not worth losing the war for the integrity of the entire Torah.[55]

Rabbi Feldman was attacking what the *yoatzot* represent, a fundamental shift in how halakhic questions are answered and the role women play in leadership and community. To Rabbi Feldman, Orthodox feminism, fueled by learning programs such as the Yoatzot Halacha program, has paved the way for a break with tradition by giving women legitimacy as communal leaders with rabbinic authority. In the second decade of the twentieth-first century, a number of programs began teaching women the basic curriculum for ordination. As these programs gained traction and began graduating students, the topic of ordaining women in the Orthodox community which had previously seemed theoretical and even impossible, became an increasingly controversial reality as the possibility arose of women taking a seat at the rabbinic table. Programs launched in Israel at Matan, Midreshet Lindenbaum, Beit Morasha, Harel, and Yeshivat Maharat in New York, educate women in laws of Shabbat, *kashrut*, marriage, conversion, mourning, and *niddah*, with rigorous exams given after each unit of study. All bestow titles upon their graduates but most avoid the controversial usage of the title Rabbi. Instead, the titles range from those incorporating the Hebrew word for teacher into the title such as *Heter Hora'ah* (literally, permission to instruct) and *Morat Halakhah* (teachers of *halakhah*), which mirrored earlier approaches found in Tosafot, for example, allowing women to teach *halakhah*,[56] to the more controversial *Rabba* (an invented female version of the word *Rav* or Rabbi in Hebrew) and finally, *Maharat*, a Hebrew acronym for the words *Manhiga Hilkhatit Rukhanit Toranit*

---

55. Aharon Feldman, "*Yoatzot Halakah* – Are They Good for Jews?" *Dialogue*, Fall 2019.

56. Tosafot Nidda 50a. See earlier discussion around the prophetess Deborah teaching *halakhah*.

Women and Torah Study – A Beit Midrash of Their Own

denoting a female "leader of Jewish law spirituality and Torah." It seems to me that in the United States, the topic remains more politicized than in Israel both because of the concern for appearing to resemble non-Orthodox denominations which have been ordaining women for decades[57] and because of the professional status and job market for rabbis, which differs considerably from what exists in Israel.

Rabbis Feldman and Willig rightly perceived that opening the pages of Talmud to women was the beginning of an increasingly slippery slope, as women push for more access to the most central Jewish texts located at the foundation of observance and ritual. As Rabbi Willig also anticipated, the synagogue has become a flashpoint for reconsideration of gender roles, first with women's *tefillah* groups,[58] followed by women's *megillah* readings and partnership prayer groups

---

57. Ordaining women in the other denominations of Judaism caused tremendous internal fighting and strife until the inevitable happened. Some of the rhetoric protesting ordination of women within those denominations strongly resembled the arguments used in Orthodoxy. It is difficult to ignore, however, that sharing the profession with women means sharing professional opportunities and the power base that the rabbinic community confers upon its members. One of the results has been that in non-Orthodox settings more women are in rabbinical school than men. This is also seen in egalitarian prayer spaces where I have observed that there are more women than men. As I often note in my lectures, I do not want to lose the men to gain the women. It will require a concerted educational effort on the part of both genders to create shared and respectful environments in which men and women seek out equal opportunities without feeling threatened by the shared space.

58. Women's *tefillah* groups began in the late 1980s in an attempt to create meaningful prayer spaces for women without challenging the gender imbalance within the traditional synagogue. Rabbi Avi Weiss wrote a halakhic analysis in his book *Women at Prayer: A Halakhic Analysis of Women's Prayer Groups*, Ktav, 1988 (revised 2001). The idea was to allow women to pray together and read from the Torah with *aliyot* without including the category of prayer defined as *devarim she'bikedusha*, prayers requiring a *minyan* of men, specifically *kaddish* and *kedushah*. These were considered flashpoints of controversy with many rabbis publicly denouncing and coming out aggressively against them. In the end, they largely have faded away in favor of partnership *minyanim* which involve men and women, a *mehitzah*, and women only participating in the parts of the service that do not require a *minyan*. In this case, the presence of men allows the participants to include all prayers in the service.

in which women can actively lead some (but not all) of the service, including reading the Torah. This has disturbed the equilibrium of tradition, *mesorah*, a concept that will be elaborated on below.

As with all issues of a gendered nature, concerns for the impact of such a move on the broader religious structure are paramount. The Orthodox and ultra-Orthodox rabbinical institutions responded accordingly to the idea of women being ordained. The following statement was issued by the Moetzes Gedolei HaTorah of America on February 25, 2010[59]:

> These developments represent a radical and dangerous departure from Jewish tradition and the *mesoras haTorah* and must be condemned in the strongest terms. Any congregation with a woman in a rabbinical position of any sort cannot be considered Orthodox.

The Rabbinical Council of America (RCA), which, as a body, has supported women's Torah study, was more nuanced in its rejection:[60]

> In light of the opportunity created by advanced women's learning, the Rabbinical Council of America encourages a diversity of halakhically and communally appropriate professional opportunities for learned, committed women, in the service of our collective mission to preserve and transmit our heritage. Due to our aforesaid commitment to sacred continuity, however, we cannot accept either the ordination of women or the recognition of women as members of the Orthodox rabbinate, regardless of title. Young Orthodox women are now being reared, educated and inspired by mothers, teachers, and mentors who are themselves beneficiaries of advanced women's Torah education.

---

59. Can be found in torahmusings.com/2010/02/moetzes-condemns-ordination-of-women/.

60. Resolution on Women's Communal Roles in Orthodox Jewish Life Adopted Without Dissent by the 51st Convention of the Rabinical Council of America, April 27, 2010. See www.rabbis.org/news/article.cfm?id=105551.

Women and Torah Study – A Beit Midrash of Their Own

> As members of the new generation rise to positions of influence and stature, we pray that they will contribute to an ever-broadening and ever-deepening wellspring of *Talmud Torah*, *yir'at Shamayim* and *dikduk be-mitzvot*.

In 2015, the RCA publicized a resolution on its "policy concerning women rabbis" in which they reasserted that female rabbis are a violation of the *mesorah* and stated that RCA members may not ordain women, hire women in rabbinic positions, or allow a title implying ordination to be used by a teacher of Torah studies in an Orthodox institution.[61] In 2020 in Israel, a group of observant and learned women who had already passed private ordination exams petitioned the High Court demanding to take official rabbinate ordination exams that would recognize their level of knowledge on par with that of men and grant them equal pay and professional status. After the High Court ruled in their favor, the response on the part of the rabbinate was similar to that put out by the RCA:

> In accordance with the halakhic position of the council of the chief rabbinate, that reflects the traditional-halakhic position that has existed for many generations in the Orthodox world, it is impossible to ordain women into rabbinic positions.[62]

The common denominator of all these statements is the preservation of heritage and tradition, known as *mesorah* in halakhic literature. While questions of ordaining outstanding minors arose from the fourteenth century onward, there was absolute silence concerning the ordination of women (who are often grouped with minors in rabbinic literature).

---

61. The emphasis on the word "Orthodox" in each of these responses seems to be a direct reference to the fact that ordination of women has been a flagship issue differentiating Orthodoxy from Conservative and Reform Judaism in the twentieth century. This denotes a political concern and reticence from conceding on an issue that has served as a defining disagreement between the denominations.

62. https://www.ynet.co.il/judaism/article/H111F65O0U (Hebrew).

This is hardly surprising given that women were not systematically educated, certainly not in the nuances and intricacies of Jewish law. There was no possible opportunity for a *mesorah* of women rabbis to be established. Educating women on an institutional level was itself born out of a breach in the *mesorah* that eventually led to widespread institutionalized education of young women across the spectrum, as described earlier in this chapter.

One Last Note about Ordination (*Semikhah*)
Another argument that has been presented against offering ordination to women is their inability to be conferred with classic *semikhah*. This term refers to a specific type of ordination that existed in ancient times and has not been bestowed for over 1,000 years, but remains a benchmark for determining who can be ordained, even in the diminished format that is conferred today. In other words, since women were never conferred with the ancient and now obsolete form of *semikhah*, they are not eligible for present-day ordination. Theoretically, this argument should apply to male converts as well since early rabbinic and halakhic texts exclude male converts from positions of religious authority including judging, witnessing, and communal authority in a manner similar to the exclusion of women described above. Nonetheless, learned male converts are permitted to serve as synagogue rabbis (a decision dating back hundreds of years), and there seems to be no concern that they will somehow forget the halakhically imposed restrictions on their leadership.[63]

Rabbi Eliyahu Bakshi-Doron, former Chief Sephardic Rabbi of

---

63. Michael J. Broyde and Shlomo Brody, "Orthodox Women Rabbis? Tentative Thoughts that Distinguish Between the Timely and Timeless," *Hakirah*, Vol. 11. To highlight the distinction between women and male converts, they describe a conversation with a senior administrator at a universally respected yeshiva that ordains rabbis and was planning to issue it to a convert as a sign of his accomplishments in learning, even though he understood that he would be unable to serve on a rabbinic court. He was given permission to act as synagogue rabbi because this was not deemed *serarah* but *avdut*, i.e., servitude, because of the nature and pressures of communal service and the reality in which rabbis are subservient to the synagogue board.

Women and Torah Study – A Beit Midrash of Their Own

Israel, is the only authority that I am familiar with who equates the ability of converts to hold positions of leadership – including Torah leadership – with that of women:[64]

> ...It appears that a woman (and a convert) can serve in leadership positions...A woman (and convert) can serve as decision-makers and teach Torah and halakhic rulings...They can judge without coercion. There is some question whether they can be appointed to positions of authority through a democratic vote, whose halakhic status is comparable to their being accepted by the congregation. In the opinion of many authorities, this is permitted. Therefore, in the case of a woman, one should rule leniently in this direction, since the actual prohibition is the subject of controversy among the Rishonim. In all such positions, one must make a clear distinction between the power of authority and the power of leadership.

Not surprisingly, he nonetheless affirmed that he would not support ordaining women, seeing it as a Reform innovation.[65] As with Feldman and his opposition to the *yoatzot*, we see the push-pull motion that has defined the movement of women advancing in Torah study from the outset. Women can teach and answer halakhic questions. They can even judge without coercion, according to Rabbi Bakshi-Doron. However, they cannot become rabbis.

Women's Voices

Until now, women have been conspicuously absent from halakhic discourse. That too is beginning to change. In *Expanding the Palace of Torah: Orthodoxy and Feminism*, Tamar Ross writes, "It is likely that women entering into the halakhic discussion will contribute their unique perspective, impacting on any given topic. Taking into

---

64. Eliyahu Bakshi-Doron, *Binyan Av*, 65:5, Jerusalem, 1982, p. 287.
65. In a letter written by Rabbi Bakshi-Doron to the RCA on June 26, 2015, he strongly rejected the notion of women rabbis although he admitted that women can function as *poskot*, i.e., halakhic authorities, but not on an official communal level. See Marc B. Shapiro's article in the *Seforim* blog from February 9, 2016, p. 6 for more details.

consideration different concerns can bring about different conclusions regarding the law." A decade later, Rabbanit Dr. Michal Tikochinsky wrote an article in which she noted that Ross' words have been found to be accurate,[66] citing several examples that illustrate the need for female voices. One was the role of women in a given congregation. This includes sensitivity to the height and transparency of the *mehitzah* (although sometimes, it is actually women who prefer a more opaque divider) and ways of making women feel included in the congregation, which is made up primarily of men. Another was the immersion of women for conversion in the presence of a *beit din*. A third was the voice of women in answering questions around menstruation and *mikvah* as well as expanding the role of women in Jewish marriage ceremonies in the manner of reading *ketubah* or acting as a master of ceremonies. One of the most welcome changes in the last decade has been the increased publication of halakhic articles and *responsa* by learned women. This is an important advancement in disseminating the years of scholarship, research, and interpretation that have been going on in the women's *yeshivot*.

Another issue that has come to the fore in the last few decades has been the recitation of *kaddish* by women during services. Although Rabbi Moshe Feinstin wrote that "throughout the generations it was customary that from time to time, a female mourner would enter the synagogue to say kaddish,"[67] women were more often told that they could not say *kaddish* in the synagogue or that they could do so only with men accompanying them, which caused pain and humiliation for a growing number of women. Those who had no brothers were told to hire strangers in their stead to fulfill their duty toward the memory of a parent or spouse or child. The push to allow women to say *kaddish* in synagogue has been driven by knowledgeable women

---

66. Tikochinsky's article, "Women in Positions of Halachic Leadership," appears as the Afterword in Daniel Sperber's *Rabba, Maharat, Rabbanit, Rebbetzin: Women with Leadership Authority According to Halachah*, Urim Publications, 2020.

67. *Responsa Igrot Moshe* OH 5:12.

Women and Torah Study – A Beit Midrash of Their Own

who make use of halakhic sources to argue for its legitimacy.[68] While recitation of *kaddish* by women has become more acceptable, there are still many communities in which it is seen as suspicious and controversial. Only recently, I found myself in two prayer quorums in which I was discouraged from saying *kaddish* out loud. While allowing women to lecture on Torah after services has also become more accepted, many communities will still not allow a woman to speak in the main sanctuary or in the middle of services. It appears that there is a desire to keep women in some (lesser) undefined role rather than blur any gender boundaries that would allow for religious female leadership roles.

Let me describe one more situation, with which I have been personally involved, that reflects the advancement in scholarship and ownership over halakhic sources by religious women. Over the last 900 years, tradition required a *mikvah* attendant to oversee a woman's immersion in the ritual bath. This requirement does not appear in the Talmud and Geonim and is first cited in literature from the twelfth century. Until then, it seems likely that women went together to immerse, if only for reasons of safety, because of the requirement to immerse after dark and the frequent location of *mikvaot* on the outskirts of town.

Shulhan Arukh cites two halakhic positions which he presents as being equally halakhically valid in Beit Yosef, his commentary to the Tur.[69] In the first, he cites the position of Rabbeinu Asher, known as Rosh, who writes that a woman over 12 years old should stand over the immersing woman to make sure that none of her hair protrudes from the water, which would invalidate the immersion. The second position brought in Shulhan Arukh and cited in the name of the

---

68. For an excellent source analysis, see Rahel Berkovits, *A Daughter's Recitation of Mourner's Kaddish*, JOFA, 2011. See also Michal Smart and Barbara Ashkenas, *Kaddish: Women's Voices*, Urim Publications, 2013. My own essay on saying *kaddish* for my mother can be found on p. 124.

69. Beit Yosef 198:40.

medieval authority Raavad is that when a woman immerses alone, she should gather her hair into a loose hair net to avoid this problem.

Shulhan Arukh Yoreh Deah 198:40	שולחן ערוך יורה דעה הלכות נדה סימן קצח סעיף מ
A Jewish woman older than 12 years and one day must stand over her when she immerses to ensure that not one hair of her head floats above the water. If there is no one to stand above her, or it is nighttime, she should tie her hair in with threads made of hair that are not a barrier [from contact with water] or with woolen threads or a hairband on her head, as long as it is loosened or with a hairnet or she should tie a loose garment on top of her hair.	צריך להעמיד על גבה יהודית גדולה יותר מי"ב שנה ויום אחד בשעה שהיא טובלת שתראה שלא ישאר משער ראשה צף על פני המים. ואם אין לה מי שתעמוד על גבה, או שהוא בלילה, תכרוך שערה על ראשה בחוטי שער שאינם חוצצים או בחוטי צמר או ברצועה שבראשה, ובלבד שתרפם או בשרשרות של חוטים חלולות או קושרת בגד רפוי על שערותיה:

By the twentieth century, it was unthinkable that women would immerse alone. However, in the wake of feminism and the rise in sexual harassment, women have been encouraged to express feelings of discomfort or coercion with regard to their sense of agency over their own bodies. Some began to ask why they could not immerse unattended since it was their personal *mitzvah*. After learning halakhic sources, women discovered that the *mikvah* attendant was not halakhically mandated to ensure their preparedness for immersion. In addition, with *mikvaot* that are indoors and well lit, it is easy to discern whether the entire body along with every hair on the head has gone under the water. Stories of aggressive intervention by *mikvah* attendants who insisted on checking women head to toe before allowing them to immerse began to circulate, but even those who had no complaints wondered why they were obligated to have someone else observing them in this most vulnerable state of nakedness.

Several years ago, a woman came to the *mikvah* where I volunteer. She told me she hated the *mikvah* because she disliked having another woman present. I offered her the option of going in alone. When she emerged, she said it was the first time after many years of marriage that she had actually enjoyed the experience of ritual immersion. It was the first of several similar stories I heard over a short period of time. I immediately called two rabbis to relay this information and discuss future steps. The first was the rabbi of my community who responded that if it was important to them, we should allow women to immerse alone as a policy. From that time on, the *mikvah* in my hometown allows women to choose whether to have an attendant present. As with that first woman I encountered, some share that it is the first time they feel comfortable with this *mitzvah*. Others ask that the attendant come in only once they are in the water to supervise the actual immersion, asking them to leave before they emerge from the water. In this model, there is a sense of supervision but without a feeling of uncomfortable exposure. For all of the women I have spoken to about this approach, a sense of choice as how they want to perform the *mitzvah* provides increased agency over their bodies which has enhanced the meaningfulness of the *mitzvah* for them.

The second conversation was with one of the rabbinic founders of the Yoatzot Halacha program. After I shared some of these stories with him, he paused and said something extraordinary: "Nechama, this is why we need women to answer questions in this area of *halakhah*. It would never have occurred to me or to my colleagues that a woman would have a problem with another woman being present."[70] Women's voices expressing discomfort with a practice that is not a halakhic necessity has allowed the opening of spaces that are compatible with both *halakhah* and the needs of women today. Nonetheless, this break from tradition became a point of contention in *mikvaot* across Israel.

---

70. Private conversation with Rabbi Yaakov Warhaftig, 2013.

Eventually, a group of women petitioned the Israeli High Court, arguing that *mikvah* was their private *mitzvah* and it was no one's concern to ensure proper compliance or observance. They expanded their argument to push back against the standard practice of asking women if they were married, arguing that even if single or gay women immersed, it in no way invalidated the waters of the *mikvah* and thus, was an infraction of civil liberties in a publicly funded institution. The Ministry of Religious Affairs fought back fiercely, as did many *mikvah* attendants who felt that the feminist movement was unreasonably threatening to erode something foundational about *mikvah* practice.

In the end, the Israeli Supreme Court ruled in favor of the petitioners. It was a significant moment historically because it was born out of the years of advanced Torah scholarship for women and pushed forward by women who felt their voices were significant in this conversation. The success of these arguments is changing the way *mikvah* is practiced within the halakhic structure, giving full agency to the women who are obligated in the *mitzvah*. This initiative has not been welcomed everywhere. Within Israel there are rabbis who continue to instruct women that the only proper way to immerse is with a *mikvah* attendant and in many *mikvaot* outside of Israel, the *mesorah* of the attendant is not only maintained but strictly enforced. Whereas in Israel *mikvaot* are run by a government ministry and therefore subject to court rulings, outside of Israel, *mikvaot* are privately funded by the community and as a result, the local rabbinic authority has the final and sometimes the only word.

Chapter Three

Ervah

WALKING INTO AN observant Jewish community, one of the first things that an insider will notice is how women dress, since this often reflects the religious tenor of observance and commitment among its members. Sleeve length, skirt length, pants versus skirts, and the amount of hair covered/uncovered, as well as the choice of head covering, are the assumed measures of a women's religious identity more than any other ritual practice or commitment. In essence, to someone who has grown up in the religious community, it is assumed that dress choices implicitly represent greater or lesser commitment to *halakhah*.

For that reason, conversations around women's dress are rarely neutral. For those who accept religious clothing guidelines determined by their community as the correct way to dress, there is a sense that anything less is a violation of the word of God. Women who become more rigorously observant will often manifest their increased commitment by lengthened sleeve, hemline, and different thickness of stocking. Their external clothing is meant to reflect a deep internalization of covenantal affiliation with Torah and *mitzvot*.

In contrast, in Modern Orthodox communities and among women who leave ultra-Orthodoxy, one can find women who describe the years of "skirting" (checking the length of a student's skirt) and dress coding in Orthodox educational institutions as oppressive and coercive. For some of them, the scar tissue over the open wounds around their bodies and clothing has hardly healed, and they struggle to listen to any defense of religious expectations of dress. There is a sense that the idea that women are told how to dress at all serves as a fundamental violation of their agency and seems to them hardly relevant to their religious commitment or identity. This is supported by the modern, liberal, feminist discourse in which women seek to claim ownership over dress choices and body image. Many view the *halakhot* that restrict them as dating back to an era in which women and their bodies were largely seen as triggers for male sexual desire. What further increases the contentiousness of the dialogue is that there are almost no parallel dress restrictions on men,[1] nor is there any concern for female sexual arousal that occurs in the context of interaction between the sexes. This feeling is reinforced by the perception in greater secular society that respectful gender interaction is possible even when women are not following religious dress codes.

When the relevant texts are presented to justify the halakhic framework, they are rejected as unsatisfying as grounds for continued practice. As we will see below, critical examination of these texts raises many questions that cannot be easily answered. Women, particularly young women, want to learn the halakhic sources and judge for themselves the authenticity of the textual basis for a religious dress code. I often hear the following questions asked:

- Is there is a requirement stemming from the Torah for women to cover their bodies?

- Since the sources related to women and dress reflect the need to protect men from sexual desire, why is the obligation incumbent upon women?

---

1. This is only relevant with regard to the Modern Orthodox community where men are expected to dress in a respectable manner in school and synagogue but guidelines for covering their bodies do not include covering elbows and knees. In the ultra-Orthodox community, men wear dark pants and white shirts with jackets and hats. In the Hassidic community, each community has its own "uniform" of dress for men which involves several layers of clothing.

Ervah

- Can't men control themselves?
- If the dress code is designed to differentiate religious Jewish women from their counterparts and safeguard them from secular promiscuous society, where did the particulars around knees and elbows come from?
- If it is a Jewish societal norm, who determines the code of dress?
- Why is the skirt elevated to the level of a ritual object like a *kippah* and *tzitzit* for women when it is simply a neutral garment worn by Jews and non Jews alike?

Orthodox educators have generally refrained from advising that these strictures be revised. Instead, they have suggested a variety of justifications for these practices and have developed relevant educational approaches in response.

Most centrally, women continue to be taught that their religious duty includes modest (as defined by the religious community) clothing choices in their ongoing service to God.

A prevailing explanation for this duty is that a woman should proudly view herself as a protector, helping men avoid unwanted and uncontrollable sexual thoughts. In this way, women are active partners in the continuous drive toward holiness, sanctity, and service to God in the family, community, and greater society. This approach works more organically in right-wing, ultra-Orthodox sectors where feminist ideology advocating full gender equality is often rejected as alien to the core beliefs of Torah and rabbinic authority.

Nonetheless, this conservative approach is also presented in Modern Orthodox schools, with much greater dissonance, where it is frequently disregarded or considered offensive and irrelevant by female students (and their mothers) who flout the dress code outside of school (and sometimes in school). The dissonance is even more pronounced when students note that their fathers and brothers are able to concentrate and work in environments where women are immodestly dressed without needing special protection.

Another educational approach seeks to empower women to dress modestly as part of their ongoing engagement with God's presence in their lives.[2] This ideology shifts the focus away from the male gaze and concerns for male sexual desire, placing it in the realm of women's religious identity, which should be externally reflected in their clothing choices along with all other aspects of their religious lives.[3] Here the spirit of the law is compelling but when translated into the applied letter of the law it loses ground. Students feel alienated by the textual material which focuses on the degree to which the body should be covered (knees, elbows, etc.) and the emphasis on skirts (versus pants/leggings). Part of this dissonance is because modest dress was the societal norm throughout history and therefore was not a topic that needed to be addressed in *halakhah*. There is not a rich textual history through which to trace the halakhic development requiring women to dress a certain way. Thus, the source for a dress code for women is derived from early halakhic discussions in Tractate Berakhot that relate to the prohibition on men worshipping God or engaging in Torah study in the presence of *ervah* (to be defined below, but literally meaning "nakedness") and which define the presence of a woman as one of the sources of this *ervah*. In modern times, these Talmudic guidelines have become the foundation for the required dress code for a religious woman at all times, even outside the walls of the synagogue and religious study hall. Therefore, understanding the definition of *ervah* in rabbinic and halakhic literature is central to engaging in any conversation about women and dress in religious society.

In this and the following chapters, the topic of women and *ervah* will be examined through an analysis of the relevant primary texts. The halakhic discussions around *ervah* touch on the issue of male

---

2. See Lea Taragin-Zeller, "Modesty for Heaven's Sake: Authority and Creativity Among Female Ultra-Orthodox Teenagers in Israel", Nashim 26, pp. 75–96.

3. Oriya Mevorach, *What Are You Asking?* Maggid, 2020 (Hebrew). Mevorach uses this approach to redirect the misogyny latent in the rabbinic texts toward an empowering feminist outlook that upholds the letter of the law but reinterprets the spirit behind it.

Ervah

sexual desire and the struggle to control it when in the physical proximity of women. Reflected therein is a strong aspiration to build a society focused on sanctity and Godliness, protected from sexual distractions that result from the intermingling of men and women. While Judaism embraces sexuality as divinely sanctioned within marriage, it is acutely aware of the corrosive character of sexuality embedded therein, particularly in the context of male sexual desire.

Unfortunately, textual analysis on these sensitive topics is often glossed over in favor of glib pronouncements regarding halakhic prohibitions and male sexual desire. These reflect either patronizing oversimplification or coercive rigidity that precludes any sort of productive discussion and provides little room for nuanced approaches or the questioning of a particularly biased reading.

My aim is to approach the topic with a critical yet respectful outlook, evaluating the textual sources in the Torah, Talmud, and later rabbinic writings enabling the reader to engage in the ongoing religious conversations around gender, dress, and sexuality in Judaism as an educated participant. As the key rabbinic texts are presented, each relevant concept will be assessed and its original context examined. The next step will be to see how the earliest commentators on the Talmud, known as *rishonim* (1000–1500 CE), relate to the Talmudic material. Understanding how earlier sources evolved over time into later presentations of the topic is essential in order to appreciate contemporary approaches. Finally, a look at some of the more recent halakhic material will be necessary to gain perspective on the current situation. In the next four chapters, the topics of *ervah*, women wearing pants, singing publicly, and covering their hair will be analyzed independently and in terms of their relationship to the concept of *ervah*, along with other practical halakhic considerations.

Biblical Sources

The concept of *ervah* appears in the Torah in different contexts. The first reference is in Exodus 28:42, requiring a *kohen* to wear an undergarment as part of the priestly vestments to cover his genitalia or, literally, *ervah*. In chapters 18 and 20 of Leviticus, the term *ervah* appears repeatedly in the context of sexual prohibitions, in reference to the genitalia of women who are sexually forbidden. Exposing a woman's *ervah* is a euphemism for illicit sexual intercourse in the Torah. The language is directed toward the Israelite male as he is told repeatedly that he is prohibited to expose the *ervah* of his father's wife, his brother's wife, his sister, or of a menstruating woman. This collection of prohibitions is referred to as *gilui arayot*, literally exposing the *ervah* of prohibited women. Violation of these commandments leads to an absence of *kedushah* or sanctity. God threatens to expel the nation of Israel from its land for violating these laws, which are central to maintaining a relationship of holiness with God who is holy.

Two references to *ervah* are also found in Deuteronomy, but with a different textual presentation than seen previously in Exodus and Leviticus. The phrase *ervat davar* (literally, a "matter of nakedness") appears first in Deuteronomy 23:15 where it states:

Deuteronomy 23:15	דברים כג
The Lord your God walks in the midst of your camp… therefore shall your camp be holy; that He see no matter of nakedness (ערות דבר) in you and turn away from you.	טו כִּי ה' אֱלֹקֶיךָ מִתְהַלֵּךְ בְּקֶרֶב מַחֲנֶךָ ... וְהָיָה מַחֲנֶיךָ קָדוֹשׁ וְלֹא יִרְאֶה בְךָ עֶרְוַת דָּבָר וְשָׁב מֵאַחֲרֶיךָ.

As we learned in Leviticus with regard to the character of the Land of Israel, holiness is possible only when *gilui arayot* – the exposing of prohibited sexual nakedness (i.e., prohibited sexual relations) – is controlled. In Deuteronomy, this idea is expanded beyond prohibited sexual acts to refer something more conceptual.[4] Many translators translate *ervat davar* as "offensive" or "inappropriate behavior," not

---

4. While the earliest rabbinic interpretation of this verse interjects the Leviticus sources into the Deuteronomy verse by explaining that "sexually prohibited behavior removes the Divine Presence" (see Sifrei Deuteronomy Chapter 258), a plain reading of the text seems to go beyond Leviticus.

Ervah

limited only to sexual promiscuity. *Ervat davar* must be removed or controlled if God is to be present in the camp of the Israelites when they go out to war against their enemies. This verse commands holiness even during wartime, an environment where Godliness would seem to be most absent. It is juxtaposed to the previous passages in which men are commanded to leave the camp to purify themselves in water following a seminal emission and to carry a spike with their gear in order to bury excrement in a designated area outside of the camp. The Torah suggests that *ervat davar* relates not only to limits on sexual behavior found in Leviticus but also about something broader – the concept of muting the physical in deference to the spiritual. While bodily wastes are a normal part of the human condition and cannot be prevented, discretion must be shown in the surreal world of war where the physical is often far more manifest than the spiritual.

The laws of Israelite military encampments were not practically relevant for thousands of years (until recently), yet these guiding concepts of discretion regarding bodily function remained resonant in the rabbinic period and onward. *Ervah* and *ervat davar* – defined as sexual promiscuity, bodily nakedness, and the unseemly (i.e., human waste) – must be absent for holiness to exist.

The final biblical reference to *ervah* is in Deuteronomy 24:1 where the term *ervat davar* is used to explain the reason that a man might divorce his wife:

Deuteronomy 24:1 (translation Robert Alter)	דברים כד
When a man takes a wife and beds her, it shall be, if she does not find favor in his eyes because he finds in her some shamefully exposed thing, and he writes her a document of divorce and puts it in her hand and sends her away from his house.	א כִּי יִקַּח אִישׁ אִשָּׁה וּבְעָלָהּ וְהָיָה אִם לֹא תִמְצָא חֵן בְּעֵינָיו כִּי מָצָא בָהּ עֶרְוַת דָּבָר וְכָתַב לָהּ סֵפֶר כְּרִיתֻת וְנָתַן בְּיָדָהּ וְשִׁלְּחָהּ מִבֵּיתוֹ.

The biblical text presents a case where a man decides to send away his wife after finding an *ervat davar* in her. In Mishnah Gittin 9:10, based on the biblical phrase *ervat davar*, Beit Shammai suggests that the divorce is based on "a matter of *ervah*" or prohibited sexual behavior. Beit Hillel broadens the interpretation and reads it as an "*ervah*-like matter" or something unseemly or indecent that gives the man grounds for divorce, even something as mundane as intentionally "spoiling his soup." Sexual infidelity is, perhaps, the most obvious expression of *ervat davar*, but it can include other inappropriate behavior as well. The linguistic connection between the two verses in Deuteronomy suggests that just as *ervat davar* inhibits God's presence in the military camp, *ervat davar* can cause a man to divorce his wife.

In summary, *ervat davar* expands the definition of *ervah* from a specific bodily area (genitalia) that must be covered, to a broader concept of some form of indecent behavior (even involuntary) that, if unchecked, inhibits God's presence or leads, in the case of marriage, to divorce. In Talmudic and post-Talmudic discourse, it appears that *ervah* and *ervat davar* blend together so that once definitions of *ervah* are established, they expand to encompass far more than the simple covering of female nakedness.

Ervah as a Deterrent to Prayer and Blessing

The central starting point for a halakhic discussion regarding religious dress codes for women is a text that appears in the third chapter of Tractate Berakhot in the Babylonian Talmud. It is here that several rabbinic statements about women and *ervah* are arranged into a scripted discussion about an exposed thigh, uncovered hair, or hearing a woman's voice.

Before examining that text, a general introduction to the Talmudic chapter in which it is found will help frame its analysis. Throughout the vast corpus of Talmudic literature, *ervah* often refers to a woman who is sexually prohibited to a man based on either familial relationship or her marital status, as per Leviticus 18. In Tractate Berakhot, however, the term *ervah* is used to refer to those parts of the body that cannot be

Ervah

exposed during prayer or Torah study.[5] The topic of the third chapter of Berakhot focuses on the correct way to recite the *Shema*, a prayer whose focus is the fundamental acceptance of God's presence, referred to as "the Kingdom of Heaven," which requires utmost concentration and discipline. The chapter examines distractions that interfere with men's ability to say *Shema* properly. These include seminal emissions, nakedness, bodily waste, and sexual arousal.[6]

In the page of Talmud that immediately precedes the text about women as sources of *ervah*, the following scenarios are presented and discussed:

a. A married couple lying in bed. The Talmud assumes that people sleep naked and the proximity of *ervah* is inevitable even when covered with a sheet or coverlet. Where can the man store his *tefillin* safely to protect them from theft or from mice while treating them respectfully? The text does not directly refer to *ervah* but there is nakedness and the potential for sexual relations.

b. Two traveling men are sleeping naked in bed covered by a sheet. How should they recite the *Shema*? Although the Talmud does not suggest there is any sexual impropriety in this scenario, male nakedness is *ervah* and thus an impediment to engaging with God's presence through recitation of the *Shema*. This would be the case even if a man were alone.

c. The Talmud asks about a husband and wife naked in bed together. The man is obligated to recite the *Shema* while the woman is not. Her body is familiar *ervah*, which suggests that he may be able to recite *Shema* without distraction; however, there is still

---

5. Yehuda Henkin, *Understanding Tzniut: Modern Controversies in the Jewish Community*, Urim Publications, 2008. See Rabbi Henkin's analysis, pp. 11–29. See also Getsel Ellinson, *The Modest Way*, The World Zionist Organization, 1992, pp. 170–173.

6. A woman cannot perform religious duties in the presence of *ervah* either, but they are not the focus of discussion and there are some clear biological distinctions specific to men.

a possibility that the man will experience sexual desire. Can he say *Shema* in such a case?

Different resolutions are offered in each of these cases:

In the first case, the *tefillin* preferably should be tied in a knot within the coverlet beside his head. They can remain there even when the couple has sexual relations.

In the second case, the two men, who are ostensibly lying side by side, should turn their heads away from each other's *ervah*. They can even lie backside to backside as they turn away from one another since buttocks do not, according to Rav Huna, constitute halakhic *ervah*.[7]

Female nakedness is then addressed by quoting a Mishnah from Tractate Hallah. The Mishnah states that a woman, when alone, can make the blessing over *hallah* while naked for she can squat and cover her *ervah*.[8] A man, however, cannot, because his *ervah* cannot be flattened against the ground or hidden by crouching. In the case of the man and woman, it is left as a Tannaitic debate whether he can say *Shema* while lying naked in bed with his wife. Later, Maimonides will rule that a spouse can lie naked in bed next to her husband even with their bodies touching as he says *Shema* without any barrier between them based on the criteria of familiarity.[9] In other words, his ongoing familiarity with her body in bed neutralizes the sense of *ervah* if they are lying passively next to one another. Shulhan Arukh will rule similarly although he brings an opposing opinion which forbids such contact and writes that it is best to heed his words.[10]

Returning to the Talmudic text in Berakhot, a scenario is described where a father is naked in bed with his small children. At what point do their sexual organs become *ervah* and prevent him from saying

---

7. Nonetheless, the *halakhah* is that two men must have a garment separating their bodies, preventing their loins from touching even back to back. See footnotes below.

8. Mishnah Hallah 2:3.

9. Mishneh Torah, Laws of *Shema*, 3:18

10. Shulhan Arukh Orah Hayyim 73:1–2.

Ervah

Shema? The Talmud suggests that the age of the child will determine the answer to this question.

Immediately before the textual unit that serves as the cornerstone for halakhic rulings regarding women's dress we learn: a question is asked by Rav Mari to Rav Pappa: "What if you see your pubic hair poking out of a garment just as you want to say *Shema*?" Pubic hair is the quintessential Talmudic indicator of sexual maturity for males and females. Does seeing a hair distract or prevent you from saying *Shema*? Rav Pappa answers that it is just hair and nothing more. Even though pubic hair is a sign of sexual maturity, its appearance outside of actual exposed nakedness is not a cause for distraction. Not everything associated with sexual organs is viewed as unseemly or *ervat davar*!

To summarize: *ervah* in all of these passages is the actual exposure of sexual organs. The halakhic concern is the prohibition of saying prayers in the presence of uncovered genitalia of both men and women. Nudity is not regarded as disturbing in itself, to the extent that the Talmud calmly discusses a naked woman separating *hallah* and does not regard her as posing a danger to the religious integrity of society. The Talmud is merely inquiring – does her nakedness preclude her from making the blessing invoking God's name? The surprising answer is that as long as her genitalia are covered, she may make the blessing while naked.

Covered but Uncovered

We now arrive at the series of statements that serve as a foundation for the halakhic discourse on women's dress. They appear as a unit only once in the entire Babylonian Talmud, woven together from statements made by Amoraim living between 200–300 CE; the context where each statement was originally made is unclear.[11]

---

11. This *sugya* appears only once in the entire Babylonian Talmud. It appears in a truncated form in the Jerusalem Talmud in the Tractate of Hallah. One of the statements in the *sugya* appears in the Tractate of Kiddushin 70a on its own. It is the statement of Shmuel that the voice of a woman is *ervah* – understood to mean even the speaking voice of a woman rather than the widely understood singing

Uncovered

Due to its centrality, this brief unit, whose statements largely stand on their own without elaboration or discussion, will be analyzed in its entirety. In the previous section we learned that *ervah* referred to the nakedness of genitalia. This textual unit transcends the confines of the previous pages of Talmud in which *ervah* had a very well-defined boundary. Here there are no exposed or semi-exposed genitalia. Nonetheless, the Sages quoted posit that exposure of other parts of a women's body – or even her voice – are defined as *ervah,* even though no actual physical *ervah* is present:

B. Talmud Berakhot 24a	תלמוד בבלי מסכת ברכות כד
R. Yitzhak said: A *tefah* (handsbreadth)[12] in a woman constitutes *ervah*. How so? If one gazes at it?! *But has not* R. Sheshet [already] said: Why did Scripture enumerate the ornaments worn outside the clothes with those worn inside?[13] To tell you that if one gazes at the little finger of a woman, it is as if he gazed at her secret place! No, he was referring to one's own wife, and only when he recites the *Shema*. Rav Hisda said: A thigh in a woman is *ervah*, as it is written (Isaiah 47:2), "Bare your *shok*, wade through the rivers," and it is written (ibid., v. 3), "Your *ervah* shall be uncovered and your shame shall be exposed."	אָמַר ר' יִצְחָק: טֶפַח בָּאִשָּׁה עֶרְוָה. לְמַאי? אִילֵימָא לְאִסְתַּכּוֹלֵי בַּהּ, וְהָא אָמַר רַב שֵׁשֶׁת: לָמָּה מָנָה הַכָּתוּב תַּכְשִׁיטִין שֶׁבַּחוּץ עִם תַּכְשִׁיטִין שֶׁבִּפְנִים — לוֹמַר לָךְ כָּל הַמִּסְתַּכֵּל בְּאֶצְבַּע קְטַנָּה שֶׁל אִשָּׁה, כְּאִילוּ מִסְתַּכֵּל בִּמְקוֹם הַתּוֹרֶף. אֶלָּא בְּאִשְׁתּוֹ וְלִקְרִיאַת שְׁמַע. אָמַר רַב חִסְדָּא: שׁוֹק בָּאִשָּׁה עֶרְוָה, שֶׁנֶּאֱמַר: "גַּלִּי שׁוֹק עִבְרִי נְהָרוֹת", וּכְתִיב: "תִּגָּל עֶרְוָתֵךְ וְגַם תֵּרָאֶה חֶרְפָּתֵךְ".

---

voice of a woman. The topic of women and singing will be addressed in a different chapter.

12. A *tefah* is a standard unit of measurement found in the Talmud, equal to 7–9 centimeters.

13. This statement is referring to a verse in Numbers 31:50: "So we have brought as

146

Ervah

Shmuel said: A woman's voice is *ervah*, as it is written (Song of Songs 2:14), "For your voice is sweet and your appearance is comely." Rav Sheshet said: Hair in a woman is *ervah*, as it is written (ibid., 4:1), "Your hair is like a flock of goats."	אָמַר שְׁמוּאֵל: קוֹל בָּאִשָּׁה — עֶרְוָה, שֶׁנֶּאֱמַר: "כִּי קוֹלֵךְ עָרֵב וּמַרְאֵיךְ נָאוֶה". אָמַר רַב שֵׁשֶׁת: שֵׂעָר בָּאִשָּׁה עֶרְוָה, שֶׁנֶּאֱמַר: "שַׂעְרֵךְ כְּעֵדֶר הָעִזִּים".

The Talmud cites the opinions of four Sages[14] in the context of the greater overall theme of the chapter which, as noted, examines types of *ervah* that lead to an inability to say *Shema*. What is unique is that they are no longer about literal nakedness. It is entirely possible that each of these statements was originally part of a discussion expressing concern for sexual arousal in the presence of females, independent of reciting the *Shema*. There are many such statements in the Talmud regarding the seductive power a woman's presence might have and how merely gazing at her may distract and derail men from a religious focus.[15] It was understood then, as it is now, that religious society is best protected when male sexual desire is contained.

---

an offering to the LORD such articles of gold as each of us came upon: armlets, bracelets, signet rings, earrings, and pendants, that expiation may be made for our persons before the LORD." The last ornament in Hebrew is called כומז or gold ornament according to biblical dictionaries. However, the *midrash* interprets it to mean an internal piercing of the pudendum, reflecting on the sensitivity of male desire which can be equally inflamed by ornaments both external and internal.

14. The statements do not appear in chronological order although three out of four of them lived in the second and third generation of Amoraim, between 200–300 CE. Rabbi Isaac was an Amora in the Land of Israel in the second and third generation. Rav Sheshet lived in the second and third generation of Amoraim in Babylonia. Rav Hisda also lived in the second and third generation in Babylonia. He was a student of Rav and a contemporary of Rav Sheshet. Shmuel is the earliest of the four. He is a first generation Amora in Babylonia and a partner to Rav with whom he usually disagrees.

15. See B. Talmud Avodah Zarah 20a, Nedarim 20a, Berakhot 61a, among others. For example, in Nedarim 20a: Rabbi Aḥa, son of Rabbi Yoshiya, says: Anyone who watches women will ultimately come to sin, and anyone who looks at the heel/buttocks of a woman will have indecent children as a punishment. Rav Yosef

Uncovered

If the first statement in the *sugya* above, made by Rabbi Yitzhak, defining the uncovered *tefah* or handsbreadth of a woman as being *ervah* is taken at face value, its implications are far-reaching. It would essentially equate the uncovering of any body part more than a *tefah* with *ervah*, whether it is the face, hands, or naked genitalia. Consequently, interaction between men and women would be nearly impossible. The casualness of the previous page of Talmudic discussion regarding male and female nakedness in bed, and buttocks that might not be *ervah*, provides a jarring contrast to Rabbi Yitzhak's statement that a generic uncovered *tefah* is *ervah*.

Following Rabbi Yitzhak's statement, the Talmud brings Rav Sheshet's midrashic interpretation comparing the temptation of seemingly innocuous outer ornaments like bracelets to an inner ornament that comes into contact with the female sexual organ. Rav Sheshet uses this juxtaposition to state that one who gazes at a woman's little finger might as well be looking at her actual genitalia (the absolute definition of *ervah*).[16] In essence, if a man gazes lustfully even at a most innocuous part of a woman's body like her pinky, it has the power to arouse him both sexually and spiritually. His interpretation acknowledges the sexual power that the covered and, obviously, uncovered female body has to arouse men. This too provides a sharp, even uncomfortable, contrast to the earlier scenarios where a couple naked in bed simply turned back-to-back so that the man could recite *Shema* despite the actual presence of revealed *ervah*.

The question posed by the text for the reader is how is this passage meant to be understood? There are two suggested answers to that question:

---

said: And this relates to all women, including his wife when she has the status of a menstruating woman. Rabbi Shimon ben Lakish said: The heel of a woman that is mentioned is not the heel of the foot, but the place of uncleanliness, i.e., the genitalia, and it is called a heel as a euphemism, as it is situated opposite the heel.

16. It is certainly noteworthy that Rav Sheshet, who leads a discussion here on the male gaze and pointing to the little finger of a woman as a possible source of visual sexual arousal, himself was blind.

Ervah

1. Rabbi Yitzhak and Rav Sheshet are both talking about *Shema* since that is the theme of the chapter, and the entire unit is structured around sexual distraction when a man is reciting this important prayer. All of the subsequent statements are meant to be understood within the context of the laws of *Shema*. Distractions can be very subjective, and their purpose is to illustrate this point.

2. After previously discussing *ervah* with regard to the laws of *Shema*, the Talmud has moved into a more general discussion about the male gaze and the power of sexual desire that can be triggered at all times simply by the presence of a woman. The additional three statements about the thigh, voice, and hair of a woman would then constitute advice about spiritually dangerous situations rather than a definition of applied *halakhah*.

Whatever the original intent was, the fact that they are positioned by the Talmud within the discourse about reciting the *Shema* has halakhic implications. Nonetheless, Rabbi Yitzhak's statement – that the *tefah* of a woman is *ervah* – has become an important source for halakhic consideration beyond the laws of *Shema* (as will be examined in the next four chapters) and into broader applications regarding women's presence and impact on men in religious society.

In contrast, the teaching brought in the name of Rav Sheshet remains outside any clearly defined applied *halakhah* on matters of dress and *ervah*, since no one expects women to cover their little finger at all times. It indicates the awareness that a man's intrinsically carnal nature could lead him to have intense sexual thoughts even while gazing at something as innocuous as a woman's little finger. Rav Sheshet's statement is not directly tied to laws of *Shema* in any practical or applied sense. He is pointing out that the valence of the male gaze is not a feature of its object but of the subjective experience of the gazer. If he is looking at the woman sexually, it does not matter if he is even looking at something as innocuous as her little finger. His comment can be seen as rhetorical hyperbole which serves as a cautionary assertion about unseemly behavior which could be tied to *ervat davar*, precluding God's presence from residing within sacred space. In other words, sacred space can only be maintained when man's behavior including his thoughts are appropriately directed toward heaven.

Following Rav Sheshet, three additional statements about *ervah* have an associative quality linking one to the other. No further analytical discussion takes place after these statements. Their halakhic importance and practical application are unclear in the Talmudic context and left open to further evaluation in the post-Talmudic era:

Three Sources of *Ervah*

B. Talmud Berakhot 24a	תלמוד בבלי מסכת ברכות כד.
Rav Hisda said: A thigh in a woman is *ervah*, as it is written (Isaiah 47:2), "Bare your *shok*, wade through the rivers," and it is written (ibid., v. 3), "Your *ervah* shall be uncovered and your shame shall be exposed." Shmuel said: A woman's voice is *ervah*, as it is written (Song of Songs 2:14), "For your voice is sweet and your appearance is comely." Rav Sheshet said: Hair in a woman is *ervah*, as it is written (ibid., 4:1), "Your hair is like a flock of goats."	אָמַר רַב חִסְדָּא: שׁוֹק בָּאִשָּׁה עֶרְוָה, שֶׁנֶּאֱמַר: "גַּלִּי שׁוֹק עִבְרִי נְהָרוֹת", וּכְתִיב: "תִּגַּל עֶרְוָתֵךְ וְגַם תֵּרָאֶה חֶרְפָּתֵךְ". אָמַר שְׁמוּאֵל: קוֹל בָּאִשָּׁה — עֶרְוָה, שֶׁנֶּאֱמַר: "כִּי קוֹלֵךְ עָרֵב וּמַרְאֵיךְ נָאוֶה". אָמַר רַב שֵׁשֶׁת: שֵׂעָר בָּאִשָּׁה עֶרְוָה, שֶׁנֶּאֱמַר: "שַׂעְרֵךְ כְּעֵדֶר הָעִזִּים".

After Rav Sheshet's statement about the pinky, it would seem that the next three statements are redundant. However, the Talmud now brings three specific examples of qualities in a woman that have erotic potential. Each is illustrated by an associative biblical verse, for support. The first statement in this section is made by Rav Hisda, who declares that the thigh of the woman is *ervah*, quoting a source

Ervah

in Isaiah.[17] The use of sources from the Prophets reinforces the impression that such statements were made in the context of moral guidance to avoid possible triggers for male sexual arousal, possibly during the recitation of *Shema*, but not necessarily.

The second statement is made by Shmuel. He declares that the voice of a woman is ervah.[18] Shmuel seems to be referring to the voice of a woman in all settings and at all times, including a woman's conversational voice. This reading is upheld by other references to Shmuel's position. In Kiddushin 70a, a student of Shmuel uses this precise statement to explain the rabbinic prohibition of sending regards to a woman through her husband. The premise is that verbal interaction with women opens the door to *ervah* itself or more concretely, it expresses a concern for interaction that will lead to the uncovering of nakedness through acts of *gilui arayot*, and should be avoided as much as possible.

If we were to read Shmuel's statement along with that of Rabbi Yitzhak who stated that even a handsbreadth of a woman is *ervah* and Rav Sheshet that a woman's pinky can be a source of sexual arousal, and impose them as obligations upon women, then our conclusion must be that women be completely covered from head to toe and silent in order to remove any semblance of *ervah*. This has no basis in Jewish societal reality. Evidently these statements were directed at men, not women, warning them that in the imagination, improper thoughts can be sparked by even the smallest stimulation, essentially making it the equivalent of actually viewing *ervah*.

The final statement in the unit is also offered by Rav Sheshet who was cited earlier in the text. In line with the previous statements, he brings another source of *ervah* – the hair of a woman – framed by a

---

17. Verses from prophetic teachings like Isaiah are not ordinarily presented as sources for *halakhah*; neither are verses from biblical poetry like the Song of Songs which serve as the primary texts supporting the next two statements. The reason for acknowledging this is because later in modernity these statements are treated as *halakhot* and given either a biblical or quasi biblical status.

18. See Chapter Five in which Samuel's statement is extensively analyzed.

quote from the *Song of Songs*. This statement becomes central to the discussion of hair covering as it unfolds in the post-Talmudic era.

The Jerusalem Talmud Parallel

A parallel text in the Jerusalem Talmud reinforces the assumption that the statements in our unit were not intended as practical prohibitions of physical exposure in women, but rather purity of thoughts in men, at least in the time of the Talmud. The following source (mentioned earlier in the chapter) appears in Tractate Hallah around the scenario referenced earlier in Berakhot:

Mishnah Hallah 2:3	משנה חלה ב:ג
A woman sits and separates *hallah* while naked because she can cover herself. A man cannot.	הָאִשָּׁה יוֹשֶׁבֶת וְקוֹצָה חַלָּתָהּ עֲרֻמָּה, מִפְּנֵי שֶׁהִיא יְכוֹלָה לְכַסּוֹת עַצְמָהּ, אֲבָל לֹא הָאִישׁ.

J. Talmud Hallah 2:1[19]	תלמוד ירושלמי מסכת חלה ב:א
Is it to say that the buttocks do not fall under the category of *ervah*? That is indeed the case for saying a blessing. But as to looking at them even for a second, that is forbidden. As it is taught in a *Beraita*: He who stares at a woman's heel/buttocks is as if he stared at the womb. He who stares at the womb, it is as if he had sexual relations with her.	הָדָא אָמְרָה עֲגָבוֹת אֵין בָּהֶן מִשּׁוּם עֶרְוָה. הָדָא דְּאַתְּ אָמַר לִבְרָכָה אֲבָל לְהַבִּיט אֲפִילוּ כָּל־שֶׁהוּא אָסוּר. כְּהָדָא דְּתָנֵי הַמִּסְתַּכֵּל בַּעֲקֵיבָהּ שֶׁל אִשָּׁה כְּמִסְתַּכֵּל בְּבֵית הָרֶחֶם. וְהַמִּסְתַּכֵּל בְּבֵית הָרֶחֶם כְּאִלּוּ בָּא עָלֶיהָ.

---

19. Translation: Jacob Neusner, *The Talmud of the Land of Israel*, Volume 9, Hallah, The University of Chicago Press, 1991, p 67.

Ervah

Shmuel said, hearing the voice of a woman is forbidden on grounds of *ervah*. What is the source? "Because of the sound of her harlotry, she polluted the land, committing adultery with stone and tree" (Jeremiah 3:9).	שְׁמוּאֵל אָמַר קוֹל בְּאִשָּׁה עֶרְוָה מַה טַעַם וְהָיָה מִקוֹל זְנוּתָהּ וַתֶּחֱנַף הָאָרֶץ וְגוֹ׳.

This passage is important for two reasons. First, it presents the practical application that blessings may, in fact, be said in the presence of buttocks because they are not strictly speaking *ervah*. However, gazing sexually at buttocks is identical to looking at the womb, or more practically, at genitalia. And looking at a woman's genitalia is akin to having sexual relations with her, presumably because of its stimulating effect on the male viewer. It is obvious that this statement is meant to be hyperbolic; the author of the passage does not equate looking as actually doing. It is, however, understood that such a strong stimulus is likely to lead to prohibited sexual behavior. While there may not actually be *ervah* present, since strictly speaking only genitalia and not buttocks fit the technical definition, there is definitely *ervat davar* even if not specifically referenced by that terminology. Samuel's statement that aural stimulus can lead to sexual promiscuity appears for a third time in the Talmudic corpus.

Follow-up in Berakhot

Before we continue to examine the halakhic boundaries of *ervah*, a brief summary of how the tractate continues is in order. There is no follow-up or in-depth discussion about any of the statements regarding women and *ervah*. Nothing is clarified or categorized, and no practical application is sought. Instead, the Talmud picks up the thread of a previously asked question about *tefillin* and how and where to place them when exposed to excrement in the context of an outhouse. It then moves on to other topics such as belching, passing gas, and sneezing during prayer. The occurrence of bodily waste and related topics are addressed before coming back to reconsider male nakedness. A question is asked about male genitalia that can be seen behind something transparent, like glass. In contrast, excrement behind glass can be present even during *Shema*. What seemingly causes it to be a distraction is its smell or the possibility of stepping on it. Once it is covered with a glass receptacle, it is no longer problematic even though it can still be seen because its polluting quality – smell – has been minimized. This is not the case regarding human nakedness about which the Torah writes "that He see no matter of nakedness – *ervat davar* in you" (Deuteronomy 23:15). The Talmud concludes that although the sexual organ is covered by something transparent, it is still visible to the eye and considered exposed despite a covering. It is thus prohibited during *Shema*.[20] Its visual presence is enough to deflect the possibility of a direct engagement with God through blessings, prayer, and Torah study. One final note about male *ervah*: it is completely limited to genitalia.[21] Nothing else about the man is defined as such, which brings our analysis into much sharper relief. Understandably, exposed genitalia are objectively inappropriate when one is aspiring for a spiritual connection through prayer and other related activities. This applies to both male and female genitalia regardless of whether the person reciting the *Shema* is male or female. A second issue that is connected to *ervah* involves distraction due to sexual arousal. This aspect is more subjective and specific to men since they might be aroused by the sight or sound of women. In consequence, the broader concept of *ervah* goes far beyond the first aspect which is really about actual nakedness, so that a woman's voice, hair, or pinky have the power to distract a man sexually and must be contained, explicitly in the context of *Shema*.

---

20. Berakhot 25b.

21. This is summarized succinctly and clearly in the Arukh HaShulhan in the laws of Kriat *Shema*, Orah Hayyim 75:1. "Although for a man only the genitals constitute indecent exposure, it is not so regarding a woman…"

Ervah

Post-Talmudic Discussion of the Berakhot Text

After the Talmud was redacted, the rabbinic authorities known as *ge'onim* interpreted the text, producing some of the earliest works of Talmudic synthesis and interpretation. They proposed a sharp distinction between *halakhah* and *aggadah*, which are often found side by side in Talmudic discussion. *Halakhah*, the straightforward legal discourse in the Talmud, was regarded as authoritative, legal, and significant. *Aggadah*, the lessons learned from rabbinic stories and homiletical interpretations of biblical text, had a lesser status to their mind, at least with regard to practical halakhic application. They also distinguished between rulings that could be accepted as practiced law and the vast Talmudic literature of give-and-take. Essentially, they sought to winnow the Talmudic dialogue down to its legal conclusions, separating rabbinic speculation, philosophy, and other teachings from legally binding rules.[22]

The book *Halakhot Gedolot* from the ge'onic period refers briefly to the statements in Berakhot about subjective *ervah*, but only within the context of the *Shema*; they serve no other applied purpose.[23] In a similar vein, the Ge'on Rav Hai is cited in *Otzar Gaonim* as follows:[24]

And so Rabbeinu Hai wrote that the law prohibits a man to say *Shema* in front of a woman who uncovers a handsbreadth that is normally covered, for a *tefah* of a woman is *ervah*. And additionally, he should not recite *Shema* when she is singing, for the voice of a woman is *ervah*, but opposite her face or opposite an area of her body normally covered or while she is talking	וכתב רבינו האי גאון ז"ל דהוא הדין לכל אשה שמגלה טפח במקום מכוסה שאסור לקרוא כנגדה דטפח באשה ערוה. וכן אין לו לקרות בשעה שמנגנת דקול באשה ערוה אבל כנגד פניה או כנגד מקום שאין דרך

---

22. Chaim N. Saiman, *Halakhah: The Rabbinic Idea of Law*, Princeton University Press, New Jersey, 2018, pp. 146–147.

23. Sefer Halakhot Gedolot, Hilkhot Berakhot, Chapter Three, p. 44.

24. Berakhot, p. 30, section 102.

| normally it is permitted and even when she is singing, it is permitted if he can concentrate on his prayer ....and does not pay attention to her song, and .... (even) when a handsbreadth is uncovered, it is not prohibited (to say *Shema*) unless he gazes at it but casual looking is permitted. | לכסות או בשעה שמדברת כדרכה מותר ואפילו בשעה שמנגנת אם יכול לכון בלבו לתפלתו בענין שאינו שומע אותה ואינו משים לבו אליה מותר ואין לו להפסיק קריאתו וכן שמגולה טפח אינו אסור אלא כשמסתכל בה אבל בראיה בעלמא מותר. |

Rav Hai Gaon permits a man to look at a woman when saying *Shema* as long as he does not gaze intently at parts of her body that are normally covered. He even allows for her to be singing or partially uncovered if the man can concentrate on *Shema*. It is the man's thoughts or response to a woman that distracts him, not her presence. When he is not reciting *Shema*, presumably, there is no immediate concern for such distraction.

In the period of Talmudic interpretation and rabbinic authority known as *rishonim (*1000–1500), we find a number of different approaches regarding the application of the statements in Berakhot that extend beyond the contours of saying *Shema* into the broader questions around the effect of women's presence on men. The earliest, however, completely ignores the *ervah* statements even with regard to *Shema*. Rabbi Isaac Alfasi of Fez, known as the Rif (1013–1103), authored a comprehensive halakhic work*, Sefer HaHalakhot*, in which he quotes all of the passages of halakhic relevance from the Talmud and states a halakhic ruling. When redacting the relevant page in Berakhot, he omits the *ervah* statements about thigh, hair, and voice, giving them no halakhic weight.

Subsequently, Maimonides (1135–1204) writes in the laws of *Shema* that the entire body of a woman is considered *ervah* if a man

Ervah

is gazing at her during his recitation of *Shema*.[25] Moreover, even if a woman has one *tefah* exposed, a man cannot recite *Shema* regardless of his intent or thoughts:

Maimonides Mishneh Torah Laws of Kriat *Shema* 3:16	רמב״ם משנה תורה הלכות קריאת שמע ג:טז
Just as the *Shema* may not be read in a place where there is ordure or urine till he has moved away [to a distance of at least four cubits], so it is forbidden to read the *Shema* in the presence of any person, even a gentile or child, whose privy parts are exposed, even though a glass partition separates him from them, unless he turns away his face. Since he is able to see, he may not read the *Shema*, unless he turns away his face. Any part of a woman's body is *ervah*. Hence, while reading the *Shema*, one must not gaze at a woman's body, even if she is his wife. And if a handsbreadth of a part of her body is exposed, he must not read the *Shema* while facing it.	כְּשֵׁם שֶׁאָסוּר לִקְרוֹת כְּנֶגֶד צוֹאָה וּמֵי רַגְלַיִם עַד שֶׁיַּרְחִיק כָּךְ אָסוּר לִקְרוֹת כְּנֶגֶד הָעֶרְוָה עַד שֶׁיַּחֲזִיר פָּנָיו. אֲפִלּוּ כּוּתִי אוֹ קָטָן לֹא יִקְרָא כְּנֶגֶד עֶרְוָתָן אֲפִלּוּ מְחִצָּה שֶׁל זְכוּכִית מַפְסֶקֶת הוֹאִיל וְהוּא רוֹאֶה אוֹתָהּ אָסוּר לִקְרוֹת עַד שֶׁיַּחֲזִיר פָּנָיו. וְכָל גּוּף הָאִשָּׁה עֶרְוָה לְפִיכָךְ לֹא יִסְתַּכֵּל בְּגוּף הָאִשָּׁה כְּשֶׁהוּא קוֹרֵא וַאֲפִלּוּ אִשְׁתּוֹ. וְאִם הָיָה מְגֻלֶּה טֶפַח מִגּוּפָהּ לֹא יִקְרָא כְּנֶגְדָּהּ:

Like Rav Hai, Maimonides uses the verb להסתכל to define the male gaze (i.e., with sexual imagination) that is a deterrent to saying *Shema*. In contrast, he extends it to include the entire body of the woman, covered or uncovered, since the body of a woman is *ervah* (his words). In other words, while Rav Hai specifically prohibits gazing at an uncovered *tefah* normally covered while saying *Shema*, Maimonides

---

25. Shalom Berger pointed out to me that Maimonides uses different verbs to describe the act of looking. In this passage the word used is להסתכל which he suggested means to gaze with intent. It would not prevent a man from noticing the presence of a woman. I am interested in the idea that the entire body of a woman, even when covered, is *ervah* if a man intentionally gazes at her.

expands this to include any and all gazing at a woman. This is further qualified by the next line in which he clarifies that if there is an uncovered *tefah* (normally covered), a man cannot say *Shema* at all in its presence. To compare, Rav Hai allowed *Shema* to be said in the presence of an uncovered *tefah* if there was no intentional gaze. Even for Maimonides, however, the mere presence of a (covered) woman need not be avoided when saying *Shema* if she is dressed properly and he has no intent to stare.

In his "Laws of Prohibited Sexual Relations," Maimonides forbids any sort of intimacy between men and women prohibited to one another:

Maimonides Mishneh Torah Laws of Prohibited Sexual Relations 21:2	רמב״ם משנה תורה הלכות איסורי ביאה כא:ב
One who engages in these behaviors is suspected of committing *arayot*. And it's forbidden for a person to intimate with his hands or feet or to hint with his eyes to any woman forbidden to him (*arayot*) or to laugh with her or to engage in light-headedness. And even to smell her perfume or to gaze at her beauty is forbidden. And one who engages in this deliberately receives lashes of rebelliousness. And one who gazes even at the little finger of a woman intending to derive sexual pleasure is comparable to one who looks at her genitalia. And even to hear the voice of an *ervah* or to look at her hair is forbidden.	הָעוֹשֶׂה דָּבָר מֵחֲקוֹת אֵלּוּ הֲרֵי הוּא חָשׁוּד עַל הָעֲרָיוֹת. וְאָסוּר לְאָדָם לִקְרֹץ בְּיָדָיו וּבְרַגְלָיו אוֹ לִרְמֹז בְּעֵינָיו לְאַחַת מִן הָעֲרָיוֹת אוֹ לִשְׂחֹק עִמָּהּ אוֹ לְהָקֵל רֹאשׁ. וַאֲפִלּוּ לְהָרִיחַ בַּשְּׂמִים שֶׁעָלֶיהָ אוֹ לְהַבִּיט בְּיָפְיָהּ אָסוּר. וּמַכִּין לַמִּתְכַּוֵּן לְדָבָר זֶה מַכַּת מַרְדּוּת. וְהַמִּסְתַּכֵּל אֲפִלּוּ בְּאֶצְבַּע קְטַנָּה שֶׁל אִשָּׁה וְנִתְכַּוֵּן לֵהָנוֹת כְּמִי שֶׁנִּסְתַּכֵּל בִּמְקוֹם הַתֹּרֶף. וַאֲפִלּוּ לִשְׁמֹעַ קוֹל הָעֶרְוָה אוֹ לִרְאוֹת שְׂעָרָהּ אָסוּר:

By referencing the Talmudic statements on *ervah* regarding the little finger, hair, and voice into his laws of forbidden sexual relations,

Ervah

Maimonides extends the applied boundaries of *ervah* beyond the narrow contours of the laws of *Shema*. In all interactions with women, a man must assess whether he intends to "derive sexual benefit." On one hand, Maimonides seems to endorse restricted interaction between men and women. On the other hand, the parameter of intent allows men to engage with women when necessary, even outside the family unit, but places on the man the burden to be honestly aware of his feelings.

A similar approach emerges in the commentary of Rashba (Rabbi Solomon ben Aderet, 1235–1310) on Berakhot. Rashba focuses on habituation in the interactions between men and women as the determining factor of what constitutes a trigger for sexual arousal, beyond the specific paradigm of a man saying *Shema*. While he takes the expectation of modest dress for granted, he believes that the aspects of a woman's body that are regarded as *ervah* can change based on societal norms of dress. He clarifies that the handsbreadth that is considered *ervah* in the Talmud (Rabbi Yitzhak) refers to an uncovered handsbreadth in a normally covered and thus, sexually suggestive area of the body. While Maimonides seemed to understand that with intent any part of a woman's body could become *ervah*, Rashba defines it more narrowly as only the areas of the body normally covered have that potential:

Commentary of Rashba on Berakhot 24a	חידושי הרשב"א מסכת ברכות דף כד עמוד א
Rav Hisda said the *shok* of a woman is *ervah*. And specifically for others and for men and because of sexual thoughts but not for herself, since it is taught a woman can sit and take the dough portion while naked. And what Rav Yitzhak said, that a handsbreadth in a woman is nakedness,	אמר רב חסדא שוק באשה ערוה, ודוקא לאחרים ולאנשים ומשום הרהור אבל לעצמה לא דהא קתני האשה יושבת וקוצה לה חלתה ערומה. והא דאמר רב יצחק טפח באשה ערוה ואוקימנא

and established with regard to his wife and *Shema*, Raavad interpreted that it is specifically the handsbreadth from a normally covered part of her body. And on this Rav Hisda stated that the *shok* (thigh) of a woman is a hidden place and it is *ervah* and even with regard to her husband, even though the same place is not hidden for the man. However, her face, hands, feet, and her speaking voice that is not a singing voice and her hair outside of her veil which is not covered causes no concern (for sexual thoughts) because he is accustomed to them and is not distracted, and in another woman it is prohibited to look at any area of her, including her little finger and her hair and it is prohibited to hear her speaking voice as it is written in Kiddushin "let master send regards to Yalta" and he replied "Samuel said the voice of a woman is nakedness" and from this it seems that specifically the voice of sending or receiving regard for this arouses feelings of familiarity.	באשתו ובק״ש פירש הראב״ד ז״ל דאפשר דוקא ממקום צנוע שבה ועלה קאתי ר״ח למימר דשוק באשה מקום צנוע וערוה הוא ואפילו לגבי בעלה אף על פי שאינו מקום צנוע באיש, אבל פניה ידיה ורגליה וקול דבורה שאינו זמר ושערה מחוץ לצמתה שאינו מתכסה אין חוששין להם מפני שהוא רגיל בהן ולא טריד, ובאשה אחרת אסור להסתכל בשום מקום ואפי׳ באצבע קטנה ובשערה ואסור לשמוע אפי׳ קול דבורה כדאמרינן בקדושין [ע׳ א׳] לישדר מר שלמא לילתא אמר ליה הכי אמר שמואל קול באשה ערוה, ואלא מיהו נראה דדוקא קול של שאלת שלום או בהשבת שלום כי התם דאיכא קרוב הדעת,

Rashba quotes Raavad (Rabbi Abraham ben David 1125–1198) who writes that only parts of the body that are normally covered, including hair outside of her braid, or a woman's voice outside of her speaking voice, constitute a source of *ervah* during *Shema*. He brings the *shok* as an example, explaining that this is not a part of the body normally concealed by men, but since it is normally concealed by women, it has the power to stimulate. He also writes that a woman's *ervah* is not

Ervah

a problem for the woman herself since she can fulfill the *mitzvah* of *hallah* while naked. It is only a problem for a man when saying *Shema*.

In a similar vein, Ritva (Rabbi Yom Tov of Seville, 1260–1320) writes this explicitly in his commentary on Kiddushin:

Ritva on Kiddushin 82a	חידושי הריטב"א מסכת קידושין דף פב עמוד א
All is dependent on wisdom and the sake of heaven: This is the normative rule of Jewish law, that all is dependent on what a person sees in himself. If he needs to distance himself more, he must do so, even such that he not gaze upon women's undergarments when they are being washed. So too, if he sees in himself that his desires are subdued and under control and do not give rise to any impure thoughts, he may look at and speak to a woman with whom he is prohibited to engage in a sexual relationship and ask a married woman how she is doing. This explains the conduct of Rav Yohanan who looked at the women as they were immersing, without any erotic intent.	הכל לפי דעת שמים. וכן הלכתא דהכל כפי מה שאדם מכיר בעצמו, אם ראוי לו לעשות הרחקה ליצרו עושה ואפילו להסתכל בבגדי צבעונין של אשה אסור כדאיתא במסכת עבודה זרה (כ' ב'), ואם מכיר בעצמו שיצרו נכנע וכפוף לו ואין מעלה טינא כלל מותר לו להסתכל ולדבר עם הערוה ולשאול בשלום אשת איש, והיינו ההיא דרבי יוחנן (ב"מ פ"ד א') דיתיב אשערי טבילה ולא חייש איצר הרע.

According to Rashba's approach, the parts of a woman's body that must be covered while a man is reciting *Shema* are determined by the social standards of dress. Ritva, outside of the context of the recitation of *Shema*, places the onus on the man and emphasizes his responsibility for understanding what triggers his sexual arousal.

In the halakhic definitions of *ervah* found in the codes written by Rabbi Yaakov Ben Asher (1269–1343), author of Tur, and in Shulhan Arukh, written by Rabbi Joseph Karo (1488–1575), the halakhic opinion follows the Rashba that only parts of the body normally covered constitute halakhic *ervah* during *Shema*. However, in Even HaEzer 21:1, in the Laws of Prohibited Sexual Relations, they both strongly advocate against all interaction with women that could lead to sexual thoughts, beginning the relevant passage with a warning to men "to stay far, far away from women." While the language in Tur is identical, below is the text from Shulhan Arukh since it is a more widely studied text:

Shulhan Arukh *Even HaEzer* 21:1	שלחן ערוך אבן העזר כא:א
A person must stay very far from women. He is forbidden to signal with his hands or his feet, or to hint with his eyes, to one of the *arayos*. He is forbidden to be playful with her, to be frivolous in front of her, or to look upon her beauty. Even to smell the perfume upon her is forbidden. He is forbidden to gaze at women doing laundry. He is forbidden to gaze at the colorful garments of a woman whom he recognizes, even if she is not wearing them, lest he come to have [forbidden] thoughts about her. If one encounters a woman in the marketplace, he is forbidden to walk behind her, but rather [must] run so that she is beside or behind him. One may not pass by the door of a promiscuous woman [or: a prostitute], even four cubits [around 6–8 ft or 2–2.5 m] distant. If one gazes even at the little finger of a woman with the intent to have pleasure from it, it is as though he gazed at her shameful	צריך אדם להתרחק מהנשים מאד מאד ואסור לקרוץ בידיו או ברגליו ולרמוז בעיניו לאחד מה עריות ואסור לשחוק עמה להקל ראשו כנגדה או להביט ביופיה ואפילו להריח בבשמים שעליה אסור ואסור להסתכל בנשים שעומדות על הכביסה ואסור להסתכל בבגדי צבעונים של אשה שהוא מכירה אפי' אינם עליה שמא יבא להרהר בה. פגע אשה בשוק אסור להלך אחריה אלא רץ ומסלקה לצדדין או לאחריו ולא יעבור בפתח אשה זונה אפילו ברחוק ד' אמות והמסתכל אפילו באצבע קטנה של אשה

Ervah

place. It is forbidden to listen to the voice of an *ervah* or to look at her hair. If one intentionally does one of these things, we give him lashes of rebellion. These things are also forbidden in the case of ordinary biblical prohibitions.	ונתכוין ליהנות ממנה כאלו נסתכל בבית התורף (פי׳ ערוה) שלה ואסור לשמוע קול ערוה או לראות שערה והמתכוין לאחד מאלו הדברים מכין אותו מכת מרדות ואלו הדברים אסורים גם בחייבי לאוין:

The legal parameters for the recital of *Shema* are clear and defined in Shulhan Arukh. In contrast, the code of behavior cited above in Even HaEzer in the context of a mixed-gender society, is far from defined. The harsh rhetoric warning men away from women seems to represent an attempt to inspire fidelity to religious aspirations that nullify potential sexual misconduct beyond the strict boundaries of law.

Summary

From the Talmud on, the practical consequence of something being *ervah* is limited to the halakhic requirements for reciting *Shema*. Defining parts of women's bodies other than genitalia as *ervah* seems to be conceptual, a reflection of the concern that male sexual arousal can be a cause for distraction during the recitation of *Shema*. Beyond the laws of *Shema*, authorities such as Maimonides, Tur, and Shulhan Arukh stressed that men should avoid all possible engagement with women outside of family since women, covered or uncovered, can elicit sexual thoughts in men. However, there is no evidence of strict asceticism in the Talmud and subsequent rabbinic literature. Women are found in the marketplace. Women interact with men. Even married women interact with men outside of the home. Women are not invisible and they are not completely covered.

There are no actual laws of women's dress in the Talmud or post-Talmudic discussion, nor can any be found outside of the laws of *Shema* in any codes of law. Nonetheless, the *ervah* statements in

Berakhot become the foundation for defining women's standard of dress by directly addressing concern for male sexual arousal with a concrete and applied way to limit sexualization in religious society. It is noteworthy that the movement toward establishing defined laws of modest dress for women develops as men and women come into greater casual and social contact with one another at the same time that changing fashions expose more of a woman's body. Thus, the discourse around the *ervah* statements in Berakhot becomes a Talmudic anchor point for crafting a religious dress code. The formulation of halakhic guidelines on which body parts need to be covered including elbow, knee, and collar bone are subsequently derived from the idea that an uncovered handsbreadth is *ervah*, although there will be significant societal variations.

Nonetheless, in the most restrictive communities, the concept of habituation is employed so that a woman's face and hands may be always revealed. In Modern Orthodoxy there is more latitude, with a greater emphasis on habituation to permit the exposure of feet, calves, and forearms. In even more liberal communities, women will casually reveal more parts of their bodies, with habituation playing a far greater role in crafting dress code norms than halakhic analysis.

The concepts appearing in sources ranging from Rav Hai and Maimonides along with the concept of habituation introduced by Rashba and Ritva are essential when reviewing the topic of women and dress and allow for moderation when developing religious guidelines and boundaries for mixed gender interaction. Some of the questions that arise in Modern Orthodox environments ask how broadly habituation might be applied in a society where suggestive clothing and familiarity between sexes is widely accepted. It must be emphasized that while cultural norms allow for significant uncovering of women's bodies, it is ludicrous to suggest that no objective boundaries exist. We are surrounded by images designed to evoke sexual stimuli in both men and women. Familiarity is one parameter, while drawing sexual attention is another. The two coexist in a delicate dance that permits and limits simultaneously.

Chapter Four

WEARING PANTS IN THE COMMUNITY

MANY WOMEN WISH to make thoughtful decisions about clothing choices as a reflection of their religious commitment. When it comes specifically to the question of trousers, women might well question how they are compromising their modesty by wearing a garment that is worn for comfort and covers more of their bodies than skirts, especially when seated. If there is a halakhic basis for the prohibition of wearing pants, many women do not understand it, yet those who choose to wear pants are perceived as less committed to religious observance. This stereotype is unfortunately reinforced by the observed behavior of women in religious communities. Those who dress in longer sleeves and skirts are often more likely to attend synagogue services, wash their hands before eating bread, take care to say Grace after Meals, and fast the minor fasts, to give just a few pertinent examples. This "reality" is the backdrop to the many angst-filled conversations I have with students as they try to embark on the next stage of their religious journey, after seminary, usually on to secular college campuses. They seek to make choices that allow them to stay true to themselves as women who are critical thinkers with feminist tendencies while simultaneously wanting to grow spiritually and religiously through increased commitment to ritual and observance.

Uncovered

The Prohibition Against Women Wearing Men's Apparel

One of the main sources to address regarding women wearing pants is the prohibition against a woman wearing men's apparel set out in Deuteronomy:

Deuteronomy 22:5	דברים כב:ה
A woman must not put on man's apparel nor shall a man wear women's clothing, for whoever does these things is a *toevah* (translated as abhorrence or abomination) to the LORD your God.	ולא יהיה כלי גבר על אשה ולא ילבש גבר שמלת אשה כי תועבת ה' אלהך כל עשה אלה

The earliest rabbinic interpretation understands the verse to mean the following:

Sifrei Devarim Piska 226	ספרי דברים רכו
A woman must not put on man's apparel. Could this be teaching that a woman should not wear white garments nor should a man wear colored ones? Rather the verse concludes, "whoever does these things is *toevah* to the LORD your God." Only practices leading to *toevah* are forbidden. As a rule, a woman should not put on male garb and circulate among men, nor should a man adorn himself in a feminine way and circulate among women.	לא יהיה כלי גבר על אשה. וכי מה בא הכתוב ללמדנו? [אם] שלא תלבש אשה כלים לבנים, ואיש לא יתכסה בגדי צבעונים, [הרי כבר נאמר] "תועבה", דבר הבא לידי תועבה! [אלא] זה כללו של דבר - שלא תלבש אשה מה שהאיש לובש, ותלך לבין האנשים; והאיש לא יתקשט בתכשיטי נשים, וילך לבין הנשים.

Wearing Pants in the Community

R. Eliezer Ben Yaakov says: Whence do we know that a woman should not wear weaponry and go off to war? It says: "A woman must not put on man's apparel." A man shall not adorn himself in women's ornaments, as it says: "nor shall a man wear women's clothing."	ר"א בן יעקב אומר, [מנין] שלא תלבש אשה כלי זין, ותצא למלחמה? תלמוד לומר "לא יהיה כלי גבר על אשה." [ומנין] שאיש לא יתקשט בתכשיטי נשים? תלמוד לומר "ולא ילבש גבר שמלת אשה."

The Sifrei cites two interpretations of the verse in Deuteronomy that discusses cross-dressing. In the first, it explains that clothing is not the essence of the prohibition but rather, the resultant practices that lead to an act defined as *toevah*. The *midrash* then clarifies its approach: a woman who puts on men's clothing to circulate among men or a man who dresses like a woman to access exclusively female space both presumably do so to commit prohibited sexual acts.

The second voice, belonging to Rabbi Eliezer ben Yaakov, takes the clause to specifically refer to women wearing weaponry and going off to war and men adorning themselves in women's ornaments. This interpretation touches on questions of gender identity expressed through clothing or other accessories within the spaces in which they are worn. Until very recently, war was a profoundly and exclusively male experience and women had no place in such a setting. The *midrash* suggests that crossing over into such male space by a woman erodes the integrity of society and thus is a *toevah*. Rabbi Eliezer compares women's ornaments on men to men's battle garments or accessories on women. It is not about the intended practice in the apparel, as the first *tanna* in the *midrash* understood. The simple act of wearing the other gender's clothing is prohibited. For Rabbi Eliezer ben Yaakov, the prohibition presumably also concerns sexual indiscretion and promiscuity.[1]

---

1. This *midrash* has contemporary ramifications for women serving in the Israeli army. For an excellent analysis see Beit Hillel's responsum on the topic: *And Beit Hillel*

Uncovered

However, in the centuries following the *midrash*, the more prevalent understanding of the verse reflects the first *tanna*'s interpretation: what is prohibited is apparel that leads to acts defined as *toevah*.

If we look at Maimonides' understanding of this law, which he categorizes by a man's prohibition against adorning himself in women's ornaments, we find that he writes explicitly that these prohibited acts of cross-dressing by both men and women, are meant to arouse the senses to debauchery, or alternatively, for the purpose of idolatry.[2] In other words, this *mitzvah* intersects with possible transgression across two major categories of sin – sexual promiscuity and idolatry. He further alludes to religious cults that require cross-dressing as part of pagan worship, for instance, men wearing gold and pearls and women putting on armor and bearing swords:

Maimonides Sefer HaMitzvot, Lo Taaseh 40	ספר המצוות לרמב"ם מצות לא תעשה מ
That He prohibited also men to adorn themselves with women's ornaments. And that is His saying, *nor shall a man wear women's clothing.* And any man who adorns himself like this or wears what is well-known in that city to be an ornament specific to women – is lashed. And you should know that this procedure – meaning that the women adorn themselves with men's ornaments and the men adorn	והמצוה הארבעים היא שהזהיר האנשים גם כן מהתקשט בתכשיטי הנשים והוא אמרו יתעלה "ולא ילבש גבר שמלת אשה". וכל אדם שהתקשט גם כן או לבש מה שהוא מפורסם במקום ההוא שהוא תכשיט המיוחד לנשים לוקה. ודע שזאת הפעולה, כלומר היות הנשים מתקשטות בתכשיטי האנשים או

Says: Halakhic Rulings of the Rabbis and Rabbaniot of Beit Hillel (Hebrew), Yedioth Aharonoth Books, 2018, pp. 211–260.

2. Sefer Hamitzvot Negative Commandment 40.

themselves with women's ornaments – is done to arouse the drive for promiscuity, as is explained in the books written about this. And it is often placed in the stipulations for the making of some talismans and said, "If a man is occupied with it, he should wear women's garments and adorn himself with gold and pearls and that which is similar to them; but if it was a woman, she should wear armor and arm herself with swords." And this is very famous among those of this opinion.	האנשים בתכשיטי הנשים, פעמים תיעשה לעורר הטבע לזמה כמו שהוא מפורסם אצל הזונים ופעמים ייעשה למיני מעבודת עבודה זרה כמו שהוא מבואר בספרים המחוברים לזה. והרבה מה שיושם בתנאי בעשיית קצת הטלאסם ויאמר אם היה המתעסק בו אדם ילבש בגדי נשים ויתקשט בזהב ופנינים והדומים להם ואם היתה אשה תלבש השריין ותזדיין בחרבות. וזה מפורסם מאד אצל בעלי דעת זאת:

Like Maimonides and independent of him, the Sefer HaHinukh (published anonymously in thirteenth-century Spain) linked the biblical prohibition to two categories of sin:

Sefer HaHinukh Mitzvah 542	ספר החינוך מצוה תקמב
Among the roots of the commandment to distance our holy nation from matters of sexual immorality … And there is no doubt that if the clothes of men and women were the same, they would constantly mix – these with those – "and the world would be filled with promiscuity."	משרשי המצוה להרחיק מאומתנו הקדושה דבר ערוה... ואין ספק כי אם יהיו מלבושי האנשים והנשים שוים, יתערבו אלו עם אלו תמיד ומלאה הארץ זמה.

| And they also said in explaining this commandment that it is to distance all matters of idolatry, as the way of the worshipers of idolatry was with this. And I found these two reasons in the books of Rambam after I wrote them. | ועוד אמרו בטעם מצוה זו שהיא להרחיק כל עניין עבודה זרה שדרכן של עובדי עבודה זרה היה בכך. ואלה שני הטעמים מצאתים בספרי הרמב"ם ז"ל אחר כתבי אותם. |

The author writes that the root of the *mitzvah* is to remove both promiscuous behavior and all traces of idolatry from the holy nation. He concludes by noting that he found both reasons in Maimonides after he had already written them himself. Both men understand the dilution of gender boundaries as leading to untethered behavior associated with sexual promiscuity and/or idolatry.

Sefer HaHinukh further understands that the *purpose* of this *mitzvah* is to avoid the danger of men and women not being sufficiently distinguished one from the other, which could lead to licentiousness. In other words, he seems to advocate for a society that maintains clear gender separation through distinct external markers in dress that work to structure such separation.

This is also echoed in the commentary of Abraham Ibn Ezra:

Abraham Ibn Ezra Deuteronomy 22:5 (translation Raphael Blumberg[3])	אבן עזרא דברים כב:ה
A woman must not put on man's apparel. The purpose of a woman is to give birth, and if she goes out to war with the men, she will come to promiscuity and the same is the case for *nor shall the man wear women's clothing.* The purpose	לא יהיה כלי גבר. נסמכה בעבור צאת למלחמה כי האשה לא נבראת כי אם להקים הזרע ואם היא תצא עם אנשים למלחמה תבא בדרך לידי זנות

---

3. Found in Getsel Ellinson, *Women and the Mitzvot Vol. 2: The Modest Way*, The World Zionist Organization, 1992, p. 223.

is to prevent smooth faced men from mingling with women and then secretly committing adultery with them. And this shows that the custom in Israel, as in most kingdoms, is for the dress of men to not be like the dress of women but that there be a distinction between them.	וכן לא ילבש גבר והטעם זכר שלא נתמלא זקנו יתערב עם הנשים וינאף הוא והן ואינו יודע וזה יורה כי מנהג ישראל היה וכן ברובי המלכיות להיות מלבוש האנשים איננו כמלבוש הנשים רק הפרש ביניהם

While these sources are not halakhic in nature, they provide a window into an interpretive arc prevalent in both rabbinic and medieval commentaries around the basis for the prohibition in the Torah. To transgress, a man or woman needs intent. The overarching understanding is that what is *toevah* is the behavior that ensues when men and women exchange gendered clothing in a manner that is directly associated with promiscuity by concealing gender differences. When rabbinic authorities in the twentieth century return to the biblical verse in order to outlaw pants by anchoring it in the prohibition against women wearing men's apparel, they will deviate from this prevalent understanding of the *mitzvah* as will be presented later in this chapter.

It is possible to trace the halakhic positions taken by Maimonides, Tur, Shulhan Arukh, and rabbinic authorities after the sixteenth century, to the two positions outlined in the Sifrei.

The first position was concerned with masquerading as a member of the opposite sex for the purpose of engaging in prohibited behavior. Accordingly, wearing a single article of gendered clothing would most likely not achieve that goal. In contrast, Rabbi Eliezer's position was less focused on intention and more on the simple act of wearing the other gender's apparel or accessories. Even wearing a single-gendered item, regardless of behavior, might be considered a *toevah*:

Maimonides Mishneh Torah Laws of Idol Worship 12:10	רמב״ם משנה תורה הל׳ עבודת כוכבים פרק יב:י
A woman shall not adorn herself with the adornments of a man such as wearing a turban or a hat on her head or her wearing armor and the like, or her cutting her hair like a man. And a man shall not adorn himself with the adornment of a woman such as wearing colorful clothing and gold jewelry in a place where that [type of] clothing or jewelry are worn only by women. It all depends upon the custom of the land. A man who adorns himself with the adornments of a woman and a woman who adorns herself with the adornments of a man [are liable to] receive lashes.	י לא תעדה אשה עדי האיש כגון שתשים בראשה מצנפת או כובע או תלבש שריון וכיוצא בו או שתגלח ראשה כאיש. ולא יעדה איש עדי אשה כגון שילבש בגדי צבעונין וחלי זהב במקום שאין לובשין אותן הכלים ואין משימים אותו החלי אלא נשים, הכל כמנהג המדינה. איש שעדה עדי אשה ואשה שעדתה עדי איש לוקין.

When defining the prohibition in his halakhic code Mishneh Torah, Maimonides describes women who adorn themselves in a helmet, armor, or weaponry and men who put on women's jewelry or undertake the kind of grooming normally practiced by women. In other words, what is prohibited for each gender is wearing clothing definitively associated with the other gender. Interestingly, the resultant behavior which was important for understanding the reason for the *mitzvah* in his Sefer HaMitzvot, is deemed irrelevant when setting out halakhic guidelines. Furthermore, it is unclear whether a man or woman would need to be completely clothed in apparel/adornments of the opposite sex or if even one gendered garment would be sufficient to transgress. Nonetheless, Maimonides significantly inserts an important caveat – gendered clothing, accessories, and behavior are all according to local societal custom. In this statement, Maimonides recognizes that there is a significant socio-cultural component to the gendering of dress and behavior norms and that these can change, depending on time and place. This qualification will be particularly important in the twenty-first century when clothing and grooming habits become increasingly unisex.

Along those lines, Tur references local custom as determinative of gender norms around dress and apparel in the one brief law cited in Yoreh Deah around defining the biblical prohibition for women:

Tur Yoreh Deah 182	טור יורה דעה קפב
A woman may not wear clothing which local custom deems to be exclusively male nor may she cut her hair like a man.	לא תלבש אשה בגדים המיוחדין לאיש לפי מנהג המקום לא תגלח אשה כאיש

Rabbi Yoel Sirkis in his commentary Bayyit Hadash (known as Bakh) to the Tur added two elements for consideration when evaluating the prohibitive nature of wearing men's apparel. These will be echoed in two central commentaries on the Shulhan Arukh, known as Taz and Shakh:

Bayyit Hadash on Tur Yoreh Deah 182	בית חדש יורה דעה קפ"ב
The words of the Tur are unclear for it seems that in any situation it would be prohibited [for a woman to wear men's apparel] and this is not the case for the law is lenient in two respects. First of all, no prohibition applies, even against wearing something that makes one more attractive unless one does so to resemble the opposite sex. Clothing worn as protection against the summer sun or winter rain presents no prohibition...	דברי רבינו בדין זה סתומים דמשמע דבכל ענין אסור ואינו כן אלא יש היתר בשני דברים. האחד שאין איסור אפילו בדבר שהוא נוי וקישוט אלא אם כן באשה הלובשת בגדי איש להתדמות לאיש ואיש הלובש בגדי אשה להתדמות לאשה אבל אם לובשין כדי להגן מפני החמה בימות החמה

Second, there is no prohibition even to resemble the opposite sex unless they are items that are meant for beauty and adornment... Therefore, male garments that are known as a waistcoat, etc., and other male garments that women customarily wear when they go to market and sit in shops violate no prohibition. They are made only as clothing to cover the body, not for beautification or adornment. Moreover, women wear them only as a protection from exposure to the elements not to resemble men.	ובימות הגשמים מפני הגשמים אין שם איסור... והשני דאף להתדמות אין איסור אלא בדברים שהם עשויין לנוי ולקישוט ועל כן הני מלבושים של איש שקורין זופיצ״א וכיוצא בהם שאר מלבושים של איש שנוהגים הנשים ללבשן ולילך בהם לשוק ולישב בהן בחנות אין בהם איסור חדא שאינן עשויין כי אם ללבישה ולכסות בהן לא לנוי ולקישוט ועוד שאין האשה לובשתו אלא כדי שלא להצטער בצינה ובחמה ואין כוונתה להתדמות בהן לאיש אם כן אין בהם שום צד משני צדדי האיסור:

First and foremost, Bakh requires intent in both choosing to wear the clothing of the opposite sex in order to resemble them and beautifying oneself by doing so. If such clothing is worn even intentionally but without adornment or beautification, there is no prohibition.

Second (based on a Talmudic source in Nedarim), women or men who wear one another's clothing for protection against the summer sun or winter rain do not violate the prohibition in any way. In other words, if they are worn as clothing to cover the body rather than as accessories meant to blur gender distinction, they do not meet the criteria for prohibition.

Shulhan Arukh adds little beyond quoting Maimonides with regard to the relevant laws regarding men and women exchanging unquestionably gender apparel, although it is the Rema who adds the clause that gendered garments reflect local custom:

שולחן ערוך יורה דעה סימן קפב	Shulhan Arukh Yoreh Deah 182:5
ה לא תעדה אשה עדי האיש כגון שתשים בראשה מצנפת או כובע או תלבש שריון וכיוצא בו (ממלבושי האיש לפי מנהג המקום ההוא) (טור) או שתגלח ראשה כאיש. ולא יעדה איש עדי אשה כגון שילבש בגדי צבעונים וחלי זהב במקום שאין לובשין אותם הכלים ואין משימין אותו החלי אלא נשים. הגה ואפילו באחד מן הבגדים אסור אף על פי שניכרים בשאר בגדיהם שהוא איש או אשה.	A woman may not adorn herself in men's clothing, e.g., put on her head a turban or helmet, or wear armor, and so on (Rema: examples of male clothing in accordance with the local custom) (Tur) or shave her head like a man. A man may not clothe himself in the clothes of a women, e.g., wear colored clothing or golden ornaments in a place where only women wear those things. (Rema: Even wearing just one of the garments is forbidden, even if it is apparent by his other garments that this is a man or a woman.)

It is unclear from the language of Maimonides, Tur, and Shulhan Arukh whether wearing one unquestionably gendered garment violates the biblical prohibition. Bakh and others (Shakh and Taz) deflect this possibility, building on the interpretive exposition seen consistently from the first position in the Sifrei onward in which intent to commit promiscuous acts by blurring gender boundaries is essential to violating the biblical prohibition. It is interesting that Rema inserts the more stringent position of Rabbi Eliezer ben Yaakov cited in the Sifrei regarding the donning of only one gendered garment as prohibited.

As noted earlier, the majority opinion in halakhic literature follows the first position in the Sifrei which emphasized intentionality and subsequent behavior when gender is blurred. However, Rema includes the second minority opinion, disallowing the act of wearing one garment definitively belonging to the opposite sex as violating the biblical prohibition for men or women.

Summary

One of the main ideas that emerges from source analysis is that gender differentiation is a value in rabbinic sources of both a halakhic and non-halakhic nature. Dress is one of the ways in which gender separation is maintained and this ensures fidelity to holiness as reflected in sexual separation. If we remove the markers that police this separation, the possibility of sexual perversion is manifest. As expressed in Sefer HaHinukh, "And there is no doubt that if the clothes of men and women were the same, they would constantly mix – these with those – *and the world would be filled with promiscuity.*" The verse in Deuteronomy focuses on both men and women. They are equally held accountable for misleading the community of Israel by blurring the gender divide, and thus, opening doors to the betrayal of the covenant with God.

Trousers as Women's Apparel

The phenomenon of women wearing trousers began in the nineteenth century with women seeking both the literal and symbolic freedom that they provided. While it was initially against the law (well into the twentieth century in some Western countries), they nonetheless persisted.

Many religious leaders, Jewish and non-Jewish, protested. There was a universal concern that women would exhibit unladylike behavior, possibly veering toward promiscuity if allowed to wear pants. Such apparel was equated with the potential downfall of the family, the emasculation of men, and the concern that social and moral chaos would ensue if the gender differences represented by dress were to be obliterated.[4]

A look at the rabbinic responsa on pants reveals a very strong religious ideology against garments that are purported to blur gender differentiation or at the very least, represent blatant immodesty and promiscuity, threatening the very fabric of religious society.

The Rabbinic Reaction

One of the first rabbinic authorities to deal with the question of women wearing pants was Rabbi Yekutiel Teitelbaum, head of the rabbinic court in Sighet, Hungary, in the nineteenth century. In his responsa *Avnei Zedek*, he records a question about whether women are allowed to wear trousers under their clothing as protection against the cold. Rabbi Teitelbaum offers a learned halakhic discussion and concludes that such garments are permitted:

Avnei Tzedek Yoreh Deah 72 (translation Raphael Blumberg[5])	שו"ת אבני צדק חיו"ד סי' עב
During the winter, are women allowed to wear trousers under their clothing as protection against the cold? Answer: One may rely upon the view of Bah and Taz that even an outright male garment is permissible if worn as protection against the cold. Shakh forbade only a man's so dressing up that one cannot tell he is a man. His entire focus is on the person, not his garb, such that if a man wears only one female garment, and does not intend to resemble the opposite sex, he violates	אם מותר לנשים ללבוש מכנסים בחורף להגן מפני הצנה מתחת לבגדים. יש לסמוך ע"ד הב"ח והט"ז להתיר אפי' במלבוש איש ממש כשעושה להגן מפני הצנה, וגם הש"ך לא אסר אלא כשלובשת ממש בגדי איש בכל המלבושים עד שאינה ניכרת שהיא אשה, אבל מכנסים שהם רק בגד

---

4. http://the-toast.net/2014/08/07/wearing-pants-brief-history/; https://www.britannica.com/story/when-did-women-start-wearing-pants.

5. Found in Getsel Ellinson, *The Modest Way*, pp. 261–263.

no prohibition. Surely trousers beneath a woman's clothing, or even over them are permissible, since the woman will ultimately be recognized as such by her other clothing and since she is only wearing this garment as protection from the cold.

…Yet even without my answer, there is still no problem, for after investigation, I have become aware that women's trousers can be distinguished from men's being that the two are different. Thus there are two points in your favor: There is no intent to resemble men and they are different from a man's. Both here and in Poland, even pious modest women have long practiced this, without a complaint being heard (Note: Avnei Tzedek is talking about special loose-fitting work trousers).

A greater problem is the new phenomenon of women wearing men's hats and suits…these would seem to be forbidden and I have previously made an uproar about this, demanding that their forbidden status be publicized. Unfortunately, many trespass in this regard as well by wearing non-Jewish fashions. May God have mercy on us!

אחד אפי׳ ללובשו למעלה על המלבושים מותר, שהרי הב"ח התיר גם בבגד העליון שנקרא זיפוצא. ועוד שאפי׳ לד׳ האוסר יש להתיר המכנסים האלה, כי לאחר חקירה ודרישה נודע לי שהמכנסים של נשים ניכרים ומשונים ממכנסי אנשים, ונמצא דאיכא הכא תרתי לטיבותא שאינן להדמות לאנשים, וגם יש היכר בין מכנסים אלה של הנשים למכנסי האנשים. וכן נהגו להקל בזה כאן ובפולין אפי׳ נשים צנועות ואין פוצה פה.

אבל מה שנעשה חדשות בארץ, שהולכים איזה נשים, במלבוש הנקרא כובע (קאפעליש), או בגד הנקרא מענער ראק, שנראה לעינים, שאין זה, אלא להתדמות לאיש, והגם שמשונה קצת משל איש, מ"מ שמו עליו לכן זה וזה מכוער מאד, ונראה דאסור, וכבר הרעשתי ע"ז, וצווחתי בדרושים בקהל רב, וגם צויתי להכריז שאסור.

In his analysis, Avnei Zedek reflects the halakhic discourse that preceded him (and that was outlined above) on the topic of women wearing men's apparel. It is important to note two elements that appear in this responsum. The first is that the pants he is referring to are loose and formless. They are cut to fit women's bodies, but they seem suited for work rather than fashion. He acknowledges that pious women in Hungary and Poland are wearing these garments presumably because of the mobility it gave them to carry out certain jobs and to protect themselves in very cold climates from the winter chill. He writes specifically that they are not trying to imitate men and that the garments are somewhat modified for women. There is no attempt to disguise themselves, and there is no sexual allure to the garments.

The second is his attack on women who wear men's suits and hats, a trend occurring in the nineteenth century in Europe and the United States. This trend incensed the Avnei Zedek, who describes the look as "very ugly." Although he admits that there are some slight differences in the cut of the suits worn by women, to his mind, they are clearly menswear and women could be mistaken for men when wearing them. He maintains that such clothing violates a prohibition although he does not specify the source of the transgression. He could be referring to the prohibition against wearing men's apparel, but it is also possible that he is talking about a different prohibition found elsewhere in Shulhan Arukh (Yoreh Deah 171:1) forbidding an individual from dressing in the manner of the gentiles.

Overall, the Avnei Zedek presents a moderate position on the subject of women and pants, dismissing the prohibition of wearing men's apparel as being significant. However, it is clear that he is concerned about the breakdown of gender boundaries through cross-dressing in his attack on men's suits and hats being worn by women.

More reflective, however, of the general response to women wearing pants are the rabbinic authorities who show extreme antagonism to the garment. Two schools of thought emerge. One argues that pants are so gendered that there is no way to wear them without violating a biblical prohibition on women wearing male apparel. The other admits that there is no biblical prohibition, but that nonetheless, the garment is prohibited because it is immodest. In the rhetoric cited below, the sense of a religious war being waged is palpable, regardless of the interpretation behind the dissent.

Rabbi Yitzhak Yaakov Weiss in his responsa *Minchat Yitzhak* was asked about women wearing pants in the year 1958 while he was serving as the head of the rabbinic court in Manchester, England. The questioner asked about the source of the prohibition and added that women's pants are cut differently than men's and are also distinguishable by color so that gender boundaries are maintained in this form of dress:

Minchat Yitzhak Part II 108 (translation Raphael Blumberg[6])	מנחת יצחק חלק ב ק"ח
Answer: This question does not require elaborate investigation, for an outright prohibition is involved. Besides, ostentatious clothing such as this is produced, *a priori*, for sin and is associated with promiscuity. Even if they are not classed as "male apparel" wearing them still constitutes an "abominable act."	הנה אין דין זה צריך בושש דהוי איסור גמור, דחוץ מזה דבגדי שחץ כאלו, נעשים מתחילתם לעבירה, והם בגדי זימה, ומביאים לידי תועבה, ואף אם לא יהי' בכלל כלי גבר, המה בכלל תועבת ד' כל עושה אלה.

In the opening sentence, the *Minhat Yitzhak* maintains that there is an outright prohibition on women wearing pants, but in the second sentence, he reveals a bias, suffused with animosity toward these articles of clothing and those who wear them, above and beyond the nature of the prohibition. He states that such clothes are used for sin and promiscuity. Even if they would not be "male apparel," they would still be considered an abomination. He upholds his position that they are in fact "male apparel" and biblically prohibited, even though they do not fit into any of the categories for prohibited male

---

6. Ibid., p. 257.

apparel that we have seen in previous definitions of the prohibition from the Talmud until the twentieth century.

Rabbi Weiss argues that even if "the female version of these is a bit different from the male version, their labels will still apply, hence they should be forbidden." He even forbids a woman wearing pants at home while alone.

Below is another excerpt from the same responsum where he addresses women wearing pants to ski, considering that it is the appropriate garment for the sport:

| Is she allowed to wear trousers to go skiing, when skiing without them is difficult and when, if she falls, they actually provide an advantage? This seems to depend on a debate among the rabbinic authorities regarding whether a woman is allowed to wear male garb as protection against the elements. On close scrutiny however, it appears that even wearing such garments is forbidden according to all opinions....Even Shakh is lenient only where exposure to the elements is not a matter of choice. Yet who would allow her to wear male garb to go skiing? Better she should stay home and not dress this way…especially as a Torah prohibition is involved. | (ד) בדבר אם מותרת ללבוש מכנסים לצורך גלישה, דקשה לגלוש בלא מכנסים, וגם אם תפול, הוי לה למעליותא מבלא זה כמובן. אבל לאחר העיון נראה דבכעין נד"ד, אף שיהי' רק מלבוש א', אסור לכ"ע, דבודאי גם הש"ך מתיר רק כמו חמה וצינה, דאינו תלוי ברצונו למנוע מזה, משא"כ כה"ג דמי התיר לה לילך לגלוש, ולהלביש עצמה בבגדי אנשים, לא תגלוש ולא תלבוש... |

Rabbi Ovadia Hodaya (1889–1969, a member of the Beit Din Hagadol of the Israeli Rabbinate) offers an even more candid look at the "holy war" being waged against women wearing pants:

Yaskil Avdi Yoreh Deah Vol. 5 20: 6 (translation Raphael Blumberg and author)	שו"ת ישכיל עבדי ה יו"ד כ:
The prohibition of cross-dressing is not violated unless a man or woman wears trousers distinctly suited to the opposite sex. However, if they are equal in form there is no room for a prohibition…and especially if they are made specifically for each of them it is certainly permitted to wear them…only if the man wears women's pants that are different in form and are made for a woman and he wears it and similarly, a woman is prohibited to wear men's pants that are different in form from a woman's and are made for a man... For a different reason, however, they should be forbidden to women. Trousers are a wild, promiscuous and immodest garment for women since legs are separated from each other to the pudendum and it leads to sexual thoughts in those who see her and even to fornication…. Unfortunately, due to our sins there is no longer any separation between young men and women. All mingle together at work and school….a matter that will lead to fornication with such clothing for a young man, the fire burns in his loins and he cannot control himself and there is no guardian for sexual prohibition and for this reason trousers should be forbidden to women. Every man who truly fears the word of God must keep his daughters from	יוצא מכל זה האמור דעיקר האיסור אינו אלא בשצורתם משונה מהאיש לאשה וכן מאשה לאיש, אבל אם הם שוים בצורתם אין מקום איסור, אפילו מא' לשני, ורק ממדת חסידות כנ"ל, וכ"ש אם נעשה במיוחד להם דודאי דמותר ללובשו הם עצמם ובכן הוא הדבר בנ"ד, אין מקום נאסור אלא אם הדבר ילבש מכנסי גברת המשונים בצורתם ונעשה וזה מביא לידי הרהור מהמסתכל בה, ומביא גם לידי ניאוף....והוא הדבר בנ"ד שלדאבוננו, אין גדר בין בחורים לבחורות דכולם מעורבים יחד בין בעבודה בין בבתי הספר וכדומה...הדבר שיבואו לידי ניאוף במלבושם כאלה, שהבחור אש התאוה תבער בקרבו, ולא יכול להתאפק, ואין אפוטרופוס לעריות, וע"כ מטעם זה יש לאסור, וכל איש הירא וחרד לדבר ה', עניו להזהר ולשמור על בנותיו שלא

Wearing Pants in the Community

going out in such garb, lest it lead to real sexual offence...	יצאו במלבושים כאלה, דהוא מסרך סריך באיסור ערוה...

Pants are "wild and promiscuous" because they allow men to see the split in the legs of women. They draw attention to her *ervah* even if it is actually covered. Accordingly, habituation or local custom, both of which could be grounds for halakhic leniency in matters of women's dress, are irrelevant when something draws attention to *ervah*. He decries the mingling of the sexes that takes place in school and at work. The camp is being polluted. *Ervat davar* or conceptual *ervah* is driving away the presence of God.

The objection to pants thus remains even when the halakhic discourse regarding women wearing men's apparel could be resolved. It results in a far more insidious issue, for it involves a perceived breach of feminine modesty within society.

Rabbi Hodaya is one of the first to suggest that the split in the legs represents an insurmountable modesty violation. The halakhic source for his conclusion is unclear although perhaps this perception does not need further clarification in a community where the shape of women's bodies is meant to be hidden. Nonetheless, Rabbi Yehuda Henkin wonders about this halakhic claim in his responsum cited below. He explains that the phrase "spreading the legs" which Rabbi Hodaya uses in his rejection of pants actually refers in rabbinic literature to the movement a woman makes when spreading her legs during sexual intercourse. While this is an immodest position when exhibited outside of that particular act, it is certainly acceptable according to the Talmud when she rides on a horse or donkey:

Bnei Banim Part Four Paragraph 28	בני בנים חלק ד סימן כח
In the Torah it is referred to as...and its meaning is that a woman spreads her	במקרא הוא נקרא פישוק רגליים ופרושו שהאשה

legs in order to accept within her the male…and it is not modest to reference this movement unnecessarily, but it is permitted for a woman to spread her legs when necessary for instance, to ride on a donkey or horse. And I read that there is one who prohibits a woman from wearing pants because one thus sees the split in her legs and cited Pesachim 3a and this is incorrect and see the Meiri there. If the woman is not spreading her legs but walking normally, this is not the act described as spreading the legs even if she wears pants, and if she spreads her legs widely it is immodest even if she is wearing a long dress.	מרחיבה בין רגליה כדי לקבל עליה את הזכר.... ואינו מן הצניעות להזכיר תנועה זו ללא צורך, אבל מותר לאשה להרחיב בין רגליה לצורך וכגון לרכב על חמור או סוס. וראיתי מי שאסר לאשה ללבוש מכנסיים משום שאז רואים פסיקת רגליה וציין למסכת פסחים דף ג' עמוד א', ואינו נכון ועיי"ש במאירי. אם אין האשה מרחיבה בין רגליה אלא הולכת כרגיל אין זה פיסוק רגלים אפילו אם היא לובשת מכנסיים, ואם היא מרחיבה בין רגליה הרבה זה פיסוק רגלים ואינו צנוע אפילו אם היא לובשת שמלה ארוכה.

Rabbi Henkin concludes that a woman who walks and sits normally, even in pants, is not exhibiting immodest behavior. The garment is not the issue, explains Rabbi Henkin; the concern for an immodest pose is relevant either in pants or in a skirt. Pants do not intrinsically represent immodesty. Nonetheless, his analysis is overwhelmingly rejected in halakhic discourse in favor of Rabbi Hodaya and the claim that seeing the split between a woman's legs is fundamentally promiscuous.

We have thus presented two different rabbinic voices when addressing possible prohibitions with regard to women wearing pants. One presents the biblical prohibition of women wearing men's apparel as key to prohibiting the garment and the other, an insurmountable breach in modesty. While the purely halakhic issue of women wearing men's apparel can be avoided when trousers are worn for practical considerations or are clearly women's apparel that no man would wear, the view that trousers are *a priori* a breach of modesty is a deliberate impasse to revisiting the conversation through a purely halakhic analysis of earlier sources.

Those two positions – biblical prohibition and irrevocable breach in modesty – become fully integrated in a polemical exchange between Rabbi Ovadia Yosef and Rabbi Eliezer Waldenberg that includes a fair degree of hyperbole, notably in Rav Waldenberg's responsa, strongly suggesting that something larger is taking place within the halakhic conversation.

In the early 1970s, a school principal wrote to Rabbi Ovadia Yosef explaining that his female students were coming to school in miniskirts and there was little he could do to prevent this. He then asked whether trousers would be preferable. Rabbi Ovadia starts off his response by attacking the miniskirt, prohibiting it both because of sexual promiscuity and because it violates the injunction not to "imitate the non-Jews in their behavior…miniskirts are a sign of the promiscuous culture of the West."[7] He then analyzes the prohibition of "male apparel" and comes to the conclusion, after a lengthy analysis involving the Talmud and early and late rabbinic authorities, that pants which are made for women do not violate that prohibition. Even articles of clothing that are unisex do not violate the prohibition. However, he explains that pants are inadvisable:

---

7. Rabbi Ovadia is referring to the law codified in Shulhan Arukh Yoreh Deah 171:1 that prohibits going out in the way of idolators or wearing clothing specific to them. Rema adds that one must be separate from gentiles in dress and action. To Rav Ovadia, miniskirts represent sexual promiscuity and violate a clear prohibition of the law found in Shulhan Arukh.

Yabia Omer Part 6 Yoreh Deah 14 (translation Raphael Blumberg[8])	שו"ת יביע אומר חלק ו - יורה דעה סימן יד
Even so, I admit that *a priori* one should not allow young women to wear trousers since they are an arrogant form of dress that arouses the attention of onlookers more than a normal skirt or dress and provokes sinful thought. Fine Jewish girls should not wear them at all especially those that really cling to the body, for they cause men to stare and to entertain especially sinful thoughts..... If girls do not heed their parents' and teachers' wishes that they avoid especially short skirts and they go out in public with legs bared which constitutes excessively immodest behavior, we must choose the lesser of two evils and instruct them as a temporary provision to wear trousers…therefore where the girls will not listen to us to wear skirts that cover the knee, trousers are preferable until we influence them to wear the modest dress of all fine Jewish girls.	ומכל מקום מודה אני שאין להתיר כאן לכתחלה לבישת מכנסים אלה לבנות, כי בגדי שחץ הן, ומעוררות תשומת לב מיוחדת לרואיהן יותר מאשר שמלה או חצאית רגילה, ומביאות לידי הרהורים רעים. ואין לבנות ישראל הכשרות ללכת בהן כלל. ובפרט במכנסים המהודקות ממש על הגוף שגורמות הסתכלות והרהורים רעים ביתר שאת..... ומכל מקום אם אין הבנות שומעות לקול הורים ומורים להמנע מלבישת חצאיות קצרות ביותר, והולכות בשוק וירך מגולות, שהיא פריצות יתירה, יש לבחור הרע במיעוטו, ולהורות להן כהוראת שעה ללבוש מכנסים....

Rabbi Ovadia concludes that since there is no biblical prohibition, it comes down to questions of decorum in dress. Pants, he writes, are preferable since they at least cover the entire leg. Miniskirts are

---

8. Getsel Ellinson, *A Modest Way*, pp. 265–267.

a graver violation of modesty norms than pants because they expose the *shok*, which he defines as thigh and which is a form of *ervah*. This kind of garment comes close to exposing the actual *ervah* and must be vehemently discouraged.

Although he does not prohibit them outright, Rav Ovadia is not comfortable with women wearing pants. He calls them an arrogant form of dress that attracts the attention of onlookers. He is also aware that the young women who are resisting parental and school authority may very well leave the schools and slip farther away from a life of religious observance. The difficult decision to allow pants shows his full awareness of the complex reality of the situation.

Nonetheless, it is hardly surprising, given all that we saw above, that Rabbi Eliezer Waldenberg attacked Rabbi Ovadia Yosef for his perceived soft position on pants:

Tzitz Eliezer Vol. XI, 62 (translation Raphael Blumberg[9])	שו"ת ציץ אליעזר חלק יא סימן סב
Regarding the prohibition of "a woman must not put on men's apparel" I was astonished to hear of any possibility of permitting this arrogant clothing called pants which has spread due to our many sins among many of the girls in our generation... Our greatest legal authorities have raised their voices against those who by seeing a pretext for leniency regarding women's trousers have made themselves "scoundrels with Torah approval." They have ruled that the Torah simply forbids such trousers with these words "A woman shall not wear male articles" (Deuteronomy 22:5).	באיסור לא יהיה כלי גבר על אשה במלבושים. (א) נדהמתי לשמוע על מקום צידוד היתר לבגדי השחץ מכנסים שנפרץ הדבר בעוה"ר אצל הרבה מבנות דורינו, וכעוכלא לדנא דמי זה להכתוב מזה בשו"ת אבני צדק חיו"ד סי' ע"ב.... וא"כ מה דמות נערוך להקיש מזה למכנסי - השחץ שפשתה המספחת ללבוש כיום, הרי אך

---

9. Ibid., pp. 259–260.

Clearly, none of the halakhic differentiations presented by the *poskim* apply to shameful garments such as these. By their very nature, their abominable arrogance is evident for all to see, as are the lustful thoughts of those who wear them. By exposing the shape of the leg and by accentuating the figure, they are the living fulfillment of "They make a tinkling with their feet" (Isaiah 3:16). It goes without saying that they are forbidden in terms of *kli gever*. Such trousers lay a wicked trap to ensnare young Jewish males in the net of promiscuity. They are almost certainly to be considered accessories of fornication. Hidden in their very shape and form is a poisonous incitement to sexually forbidden acts.	סמויות עינים הוא לבוא לדמות זה להיא דהאבני צדק, הרי בכאן כוונת ההתדמות והקישוט לשם פריצות בולט לעין, וכאילו חרוט עליהן כרזה - גדולה שחלק אין להם בתורת תלבושת הצניעות שמלמדת תוה"ק לבנות ישראל. וכמוני היום כיושב זה למעלה משלשים שנה על כס ההוראה והדיינות יודע ועד על התוצאות המרות ממרור של הרס משפחות רבות בעטיין של פריקת עול והתערטלות מהתלבושת הצניעותית, והיא אם - כל - חטאת.

Rabbi Waldenberg condemns the few rabbinic authorities who hold that pants are not male articles. They are not only men's apparel, writes Rabbi Waldenberg, but also serve as conduits to lust and sexual thoughts. To his mind, they are *ervah* personified. Though there may not be even a *tefah* uncovered on the woman's body when she wears them, this kind of clothing is so sexually perverse that he calls them accessories of fornication. In contrast to Rabbi Ovadia Yosef, he feels the miniskirt is preferable to pants because it fits into the accepted category of women's apparel:

Tzitz Eliezer continued	ציץ אליעזר המשך
And in truth, wearing pants causes drawing close to abomination, even	ולמעשה יש בלבישת מכנסיים גם גרמת

| worse than the wearing of a mini-skirt for according to what is told, the promiscuous males stand in the middle of the street or at the side with the promiscuous females, the type who wear pants and they draw near to one another and rub against one another through the pants, something that can be avoided when wearing a dress. | התקרבות לתועבה, ומבחינת מה עוד יותר מהלבוש הקצר של השמלה, דכפי הנשמע עומדים הפרוצים באמצע הרחוב או בפנה ממנו עם פרוצות כאלה לובשות המכנסיים ומתקרבים זל"ז ומתחככים דרך המכנסיים, דבר שהוא מן הנמנע אם לובשת שמלה וד"ל. |

These two rabbinic approaches reflect the different worldviews of each authority. Rabbi Ovadia Yosef was willing to acknowledge the present reality of women's dress even though he protested its inevitability. Pants were a given and preferable to more immodest forms of dress that revealed more of a woman's body. Rabbi Waldenberg, in contrast, felt that any acknowledgment was to be seen as a concession that would cause greater damage in the future. To his mind, it was better to totally and absolutely reject pants as an option rather than accept the reality as a given.[10]

Besides Rav Ovadia, other rabbinic voices emerged reflecting the moderate position already set out by Avnei Zedek over 100 years ago.

Rabbi Yehuda Henkin describes a conversation about women wearing pants that he had with his grandfather, Rabbi Yosef Henkin, who was a major halakhic authority in the twentieth century:[11]

---

10. Ariel Picar, *Rabbi Ovadia Yosef's Response to Contemporary Reality in his Halakhic Writings* (Doctoral Thesis, Hebrew), Tevet 5763, pp. 86–89.

11. Bnei Banim 2, p. 211 Article 38.

Uncovered

בני בנים א מאמר א:לח	Benei Banim I Article 1:38 (translation Deracheha[12])
שאלתי אותו זצלה"ה אם מותר לאשה ללבוש מכנסים והשיב לי שאם המכנסים רפויים ואינם מהודקים להגוף אינו רואה בזה שום איסור ואדרבה יש בו משום צניעות, אבל אם הם מהודקים ודבוקים להגוף אין ללבוש אותם. [אם חשב זה האופן השני לאיסור גמור או רק לדבר שאינו ראוי לעשות לדאבוני הרב לא ידדתי לסוף דעתו בזה.	I asked him [my grandfather Rav Yosef Eliyahu Henkin] if it is permitted for a woman to wear pants. He answered me that if the pants are loose and do not cling to the body, he does not see any prohibition in that. On the contrary, such clothing can have a quality of modesty. But if they are tight and cling to the body, one should not wear them. [And to my sorrow, I did not ask him specifically whether he thought that it was outright prohibited to wear such pants or whether it was something that should not be done.]

It is interesting that Rabbi Yosef Henkin recognized the potential of greater modesty for women when they are wearing loose pants along with the parallel "danger" in tight, clinging ones. Rabbi Yehuda Henkin seems to have adopted his grandfather's ruling for he did not further comment beyond this paragraph and the one cited above where he refuted the idea that seeing the split in a woman's legs stems from a clear prohibition.

Rabbi Nachum Rabinowitz issued a similar ruling, specifying loose pants and reliance on local customs and social mores as reasons to permit:

---

12. Deracheha.org is a Har Etzion initiative in partnership with the Virtual Beit Midrash and Beit Midrash Migdal Oz. It provides halakhic resources on topics having to do with women and *mitzvot*.

Wearing Pants in the Community

Si'ach Nachum 109 (translation Deracheha)	שו"ת שיח נחום קט, לבוש מכנסי חצאית
Therefore, women's pants that are modest, if the matter is accepted in the community in which you live, are permissible. Regarding a tunic over pants, if it covers most of the thigh (the area between the pelvis and the knee), then the legs are covered, and the upper part of the leg is also covered as with a skirt, and this is modest dress… However, if you go to a place where this is not accepted, as when you travel to visit a community where women do not go about thus, it is fitting to respect the manner of dress in that place…In matters of clothing, there are matters that are *halachot*, and there are matters that are customs that are set by social mores of that time and place… In all matters of modesty of clothing, a person should not have his path depend only on the technicalities of the law, but rather it is fitting to respect local customs of the society of those who observe Torah and *mitzvot* with which one wishes to affiliate.	לפיכך, מכנסיים שהם מיוחדים לנשים והם צנועים, אם הדבר מקובל ביישוב שאת גרה בו הדבר מותר. באשר לטוניקה על המכנסיים, אם הכיסוי מכסה את רוב הירך (החלק שבין האגן לברך), הרי גם הרגליים מכוסות ואף החלק העליון של הרגל מכוסה כדמות חצאית, והרי זה לבוש צנוע….אמנם אם את הולכת למקום בו הדבר אינו מקובל, וכגון שאת נוסעת להתארח ביישוב ששם אין נוהגות להלך כך, מן הראוי לכבד את דרכי הלבוש באותו מקום….בעניינים של לבוש יש דברים שהם הלכות, ויש דברים שהם מנהגים שנקבעים על ידי דפוסים חברתיים של זמן ומקום… בכלל בעניני צניעות במלבושים אל לו לאדם להעמיד את דרכו רק על שורת הדין, אלא מן הראוי לכבד את מנהגי המקום של חברת שומרי תורה ומצוות אליה הוא רוצה להשתייך

Rabbi Rabinowitz reinforces much of the analysis brought earlier in the chapter. He does not relate to the prohibition on wearing men's apparel nor does he define pants as an essentially promiscuous garment. He considers the possibility that pants can be modest on their own and additionally includes the option of wearing a tunic or long shirt over a pair of pants, covering the split in the legs which came up in previous responsa. Finally, he speaks to the importance of matters of dress – "matters that are customs that are set by social mores of that time and place" –reflecting to a large degree the idea of habituation neutralizing the immodesty of exposure or in this case, a garment, that was presented in the previous chapter.

Female Respectability

The pants topic touches not only on questions of *shok*, *ervah*, and women wearing men's apparel but also on matters of communal identity and gender affiliation. In a brief analysis that appeared in the journal *Tradition*,[13] Rabbi J. David Bleich goes beyond the strictly halakhic questions of male apparel and male sexual desire to a broader issue involving rabbinic authority and community:[14]

> A number of years ago, the question of the propriety of slacks was presented to a number of prominent scholars by Rabbi Yom Tov Lippa Deutsch… All of the Rabbis whose views on this matter are published in *Taharat Yom Tov* replied in the negative…
> …While there is little doubt that in many instances the type of slacks currently in vogue do not conform with halakhic norms of modest dress, it is difficult to agree that this must necessarily always be the case. For example, an ensemble including slacks designed to be worn under a long modestly cut tunic does not appear to be inherently immodest… The governing concern is that those viewed as exemplars

---

13. *Tradition*, Volume 16:1, 1976, pp. 155–158.

14. Rabbi Aryeh Leibowitz in a recent YU podcast (2017) expressed a similar distinction. https://www.yutorah.org/lectures/lecture.cfm/845396/rabbi-aryeh-lebowitz/ten-minute-halacha-women-wearing-pants/

Wearing Pants in the Community

> of Torah study, whether male or female, comport themselves in a way which enhances rather than detracts from the honor and esteem in which Torah is held. Hence, it would seem that as long as slacks are viewed as improper attire by significant segments of the Jewish community, the wearing of such garb by those charged with bearing the banner of Torah should not be sanctioned.

After reviewing the halakhic source material presented in this chapter, Rabbi Bleich considers a third possibility – the socioreligious aspect. He brings an innovative suggestion when he refers the reader to a section of Mishneh Torah[15] in which Maimonides describes garb appropriate for a Torah scholar and concludes that both men and women who study Torah and reflect the values of a life committed to Torah should also wear clothing that remind them to comport themselves accordingly and identify them with such a lifestyle. This represents a sharp turn away from the discourse around sexuality, promiscuity, and *ervah*. It is noteworthy that in the 1970s, at the beginning of the shift toward increased Torah and Talmud study for women, Rabbi Bleich acknowledged the changing reality in which women can be heralded as exemplars of Torah study. For this reason, he suggests, women who are "charged with bearing the banner of Torah" should not wear pants.

Finally, Rabbi Getsel Ellinson presents a nuanced approach in his in-depth analysis of women and pants that focuses more on the religious community's standards of identity and belonging:[16]

> Another factor that must be taken into account, however, is the existence of a community of modest Jewish girls with their own standard. The fact that they are careful to wear only skirts affords significant weight to this structure. By wearing a skirt, a Jewish girl

---

15. Maimonides, Laws of Knowledge 5:9.
16. Getsel Ellinson, *A Modest Way*, pp. 192–193, footnote 138 (translation Raphael Blumberg).

> identifies with this group and separates herself from other permissive circles.
>
> To a certain extent, in the last few decades the skirt has become a sort of "yarmulka" for the scrupulously observant girl who strives to follow our Sages' ethical guidelines as reflected in their halakhic rulings. By her refusal to wear trousers, she demonstrably declares that she is unwilling to resign herself to the dictates of modern style and that she takes exception to the immorality so rampant these days in society at large.
>
> For the modest young woman who comes into contact with that society in the context of her daily work or study, this last factor has special import. Such girls need a constant reminder that they do not identify with the values and lifestyle of their surroundings. My daughter once scored this point saying, "Even if it could be proven beyond the shadow of a doubt that there is nothing wrong with wearing trousers, I would still continue to avoid them."

Ellinson was the first to place the choice ultimately made by women at the center of his assessment. He regarded it as an empowering statement on the part of young women to choose a dress code that distinguishes them from society at large. By calling the skirt the equivalent of the "yarmulka,"[17] Ellinson moved away from questions of modesty and male sexual arousal and focused instead on identity, values, and lifestyle. In quoting his daughter at the end of the footnote, he consciously included a woman's voice in his writing, something that was not present in any of the other rabbinic sources quoted.

Although there is room to permit women wearing pants while nonetheless asserting certain modesty guidelines for this choice, it is extremely rare for Rabbi Henkin or Rabinowitz's responsa to be taught in Modern Orthodox schools and seminaries. A colleague of mine was censured for bringing this source material to her students in a seminary that sees many of its alumna going to secular college

---

17. *Yarmulke* is a head covering also known as a *kippah*, worn to signify Jewish religious affiliation.

campuses. On this topic, there is usually one halakhic position presented which unequivocally rejects pants.

Concluding Thoughts

To sum up all that was presented in this chapter, there are three halakhic/educational approaches that emerge from within the halakhic discourse.

The first approach prohibits women from wearing pants because it violates the prohibition on wearing men's apparel, striving to anchor its protest against such arrogant and sexualized articles of clothing in a biblical prohibition. It is clear that the widespread shift toward women's pants in society required a strong counter-argument toward absolute indisputable prohibition. On one hand, this anchors the discourse in a biblical text, giving clarity to the prohibitive nature of the practice. On the other hand, doing so feels contrived, since it contradicts the actual nature of the prohibition as interpreted for 2,000 years. It is hard to equate pants with the prohibition on wearing men's apparel based on the halakhic analysis above since wearing pants does not innately involve a desire to disguise gender or exemplify sexual promiscuity. Today, pants are simply a garment, without relation to gender, worn to cover the body in the same way that shirts, sweaters, and socks describe garments that clothe different parts of the body and have no gender association. What differentiates men's garments from women's garments are cut, color, and sometimes fabric. There is some overlap today regarding some of these categories. For example, men might wear pink shirts, a color once exclusive to women, and women will wear men's sweaters, and halakhic literature does not protest such crossing over. Much of this overlap is dictated by fashion norms and has little to do with the biblical prohibition.[18] Furthermore, there is a substantive difference between the cut of men's

---

18. For example, men and women may shop for the same items of clothing in different departments within the same store. Even boyfriend jeans or boyfriend sweaters, while suggestive of men's clothing, are actually cut for women's bodies and sold in the women's department.

and women's pants, including jeans, and women are certainly not trying to resemble men when they wear these garments. Pants today are so ubiquitous that, in fact, women may draw more male attention by wearing a skirt! Should we go out to the marketplace to see people who are dressed respectfully and respectably, we would encounter women wearing pants – both loose and tight – to work, school, and for elegant dress. In the words of Rabbi Ellinson, "It is difficult to sustain this idea [prohibition of wearing men's apparel]…and it seems that the ruling of the authorities stems not so much from formal halakhic considerations as from an aversion to the phenomenon itself and to the tendencies it reflects."[19]

The second approach veers away from the biblical prohibition and focuses instead on concepts of *ervah*, gender separation, and modesty norms. Recent responsa, instead of acknowledging a changing reality and the existence of societal standards wherein women wear pants, voice a clear protest by decrying the desecration inherent in the wearing of such garments, leading to abomination, perversion, and absolute moral anarchy. Such virulent rhetoric – using words like libertine, wanton, loose, and licentious – suggest a certain inability in formulating a carefully constructed halakhic argument to prohibit such apparel. The language deters any rational conversation. From the opening sentences of any of the responsa in this school of thought it is non-negotiable. Modest skirts are the only option that a religious society can countenance.

It is my sense that this masks an underlying concern that in wearing a garment that had previously been limited to men, women will be emboldened toward other feminist attitudes. This obliteration, seen through the eyes of a traditional society based on gender distinction, reflects a sense of social and moral chaos and upheaval within the fabric of the family. This fear is particularly exacerbated at a time when the separation of men from women in greater society, as well as in some religious spaces, has begun to dissolve.

The third and most moderate approach is less source-based and

---

19. Ellinson, *A Modest Way*, p. 220.

more focused on the skirt as a sign of religious commitment and identity. This has been in many ways the most successful argument presented in modern religious communities and schools, since it avoids focusing on male *yetzer* and wearing men's apparel. If we look at dress as reflecting religious affiliation and identity, a religious man has *tallit* and *tefillin* to mark him in sacred spaces and *kippah* and *tzitzit* in public spaces, while women have no parallel ritual garments. It has been suggested that the skirt, although not a ritual garment per se, serves as a sign of religious identity in the manner of *kippah* for men.[20] In this way, the skirt is presented as an empowering choice on the part of women to identify with the objectives of a God-fearing religious society. Along these lines, but in a separate vein, young women are educated to believe that skirts of a certain length along with longer sleeves represent a greater form of self-respect by desexualizing the way they dress, in line with the norms of religious societal expectation. In other words, choosing to dress more modestly, in contrast to secular standards which uncover women, is a form of religious empowerment that will lead to more respectful and respectable interaction between the genders. Women could thus see themselves as partners in this initiative.

I have found, however, that this third approach fails to convince some of the women searching for clarity when making personal decisions around pants, despite its deliberate move to steer away from the language of promiscuity and male sexual desire. It nonetheless further widens the chasm between men and women in Modern Orthodox settings where boys and girls learn side by side and men and women work together as equals. They understand how skirts or long clothing that demonstrate a woman's *Avodat Hashem* (commitment to

---

20. The *kippah* is the head covering initially worn by married men at times of prayer and Torah study that gradually evolved into a sign of Jewish identity to be worn at all times in many, but not all, communities. Today it is worn at all times, in many different shapes and sizes, by most men and boys affiliated with Orthodox observance as a sign of identity. In non-Orthodox communities, it is worn by men and, most recently, by women, at times of prayer or religious ceremonies taking place in synagogues.

God) work well in ultra-Orthodox communities where men also have a clear dress code that identifies them as belonging to strict religious commitment. In contrast, in Modern Orthodoxy, men's clothing is not very restricted beyond the basic requirements of respectability. Religious men can wear shorts and t-shirts in the summer without restriction. It is true that men wear *kippah* and *tzitzit*, but it is acceptable for an Orthodox man to remove his *kippah* at work if he feels uncomfortable (or he can wear a baseball cap in a more casual setting) and *tzitzit* are almost always tucked out of sight. In such communities, the skirts and sleeves required of women can feel jarringly out of keeping with their "religious lifestyle."

I often urge my students to avoid defining their religious commitment solely around the decision to wear or not wear pants. We talk about the Jewish concept of modesty, which, as a central value, should inspire thoughtfulness in dress, language, and comportment, equally affecting men and women. When the prophet Micah preached, *Walk modestly with God*, he was exhorting the people of Israel to strive for a quality that should infuse the very essence of our lives, bringing them (and us) closer to the Divine image within.

When women choose to wear only skirts, then that choice should inspire greater attention paid to how external deportment can serve to fuel true religious growth rather than relying on a stock uniform to replace internal development. In the same manner, when women choose to wear pants (preferably, modestly cut and not skin tight), then they should feel even more motivated to visibly increase their participation in Orthodox prayer quorums and Torah classes, to reinforce their own commitment to *halakhah*, and change social perceptions of what committed Orthodox women look like. Their clear adherence to *halakhah* could challenge religious communities to rethink the paradigms around standards of dress. Instead of constantly fighting and/or resenting modesty norms imposed upon them, women should strive to make thoughtful decisions regarding their choices of dress and how it reflects their inner commitment to Torah and *mitzvot*.

Chapter Five

The Voice of a Woman

> *Sweet is your voice and your countenance is alluring*
> (Song of Songs 2:14).

As has been discussed in previous chapters, there is ongoing universal concern in rabbinic and, specifically, halakhic discourse over sexual distraction of men when interacting with women. Much of the focus has been on the potential visual stimulus presented by women's bodies. However, there is rabbinic awareness that sight is not the only sense that requires a man's vigilance in order to distance himself from sexual arousal. In this chapter, the sensory stimulus of sound, specifically when men hear women's voices, becomes another channel for apprehension with regard to mixed gender interaction and male sexuality.

The halakhic perspective on this issue is yet another component of the meta-halakhic conversation regarding female identity in Orthodox Judaism and how religious society seeks to desexualize both sacred and non-sacred spaces by cautioning men and restricting women.

Samuel's Statement: Three Citations

The Talmudic text in Tractate Berakhot serves as the main source for the introduction of women and *ervah* into rabbinic discourse on this topic.[1] The context is a man's ability to recite *Shema* in a situation where he may be distracted due to the sensuality of a woman:

B. Talmud Berakhot 24a	תלמוד בבלי מסכת ברכות דף כד עמ' א
Samuel stated: A woman's voice is considered *ervah*, as it is stated: *Sweet is your voice and your countenance is alluring* (Song of Songs 2:14).	אמר שמואל: קול באשה ערוה, שנאמר: "כִּי קוֹלֵךְ עָרֵב וּמַרְאֵיךְ נָאוֶה".

The Talmud quotes Samuel stating that the voice of a woman is nakedness and citing a poetic expression of love from a verse in Song of Songs to support his claim. The text does not seem to have any obvious practical application other than a warning against the sensuality of a woman's voice which may lead to sexual thoughts.

The second reference appears in the Jerusalem Talmud:

J. Talmud, Hallah, 2:1	תלמוד ירושלמי מסכת חלה, פרק ב הל' א
Samuel said: A woman's voice is considered *ervah*. What is the reason? "It shall be that from the voice of her whoring, the land will be polluted" (Jeremiah 3:9).	שמואל אמר: קול באשה ערוה. מה טעם? "וְהָיָה מִקּוֹל זְנוּתָהּ וַתֶּחֱנַף הָאָרֶץ וְגוֹ'".

The Jerusalem Talmud cites a verse from Jeremiah which provides more insight into Samuel's statement than the verse in Song of Songs, since it refers to a "voice of whoring." The Talmud brings Samuel's statement immediately after a Tannaitic text that shockingly declares when a man gazes at the body of an *ervah*, it is as if he engaged in intercourse with her. In other words, visual stimuli can inflame a man's

---

1. See Chapters One and Two for a detailed analysis of the Talmudic text.

The Voice of a Woman

desire and create a framework that will lead to prohibited intercourse. This juxtaposition to Samuel's statement suggests that not only is visual stimulation dangerous for a man trying to avoid promiscuity, audible stimulation can be as well.

Samuel's statement appears in one more place in the Talmud:

B. Talmud Kiddushin 70a	תלמוד בבלי מסכת קידושין דף ע עמ' א
[Rav Naḥman] He said to him: Let my daughter Donag come pour us drinks. [Rav Yehuda] He said to him: This is what Samuel says: One may not make use of a woman. [Rav Naḥman]: She is a minor. [Rav Yehuda retorted]: Samuel explicitly says: One may not make use of a woman at all, whether she is an adult or a minor. [Rav Naḥman suggested]: Let the Master send greetings to my wife Yalta. [Rav Yehuda] He said to him: This is what Samuel says: A woman's voice is *ervah*. [Rav Naḥman responded]: It is possible [to do so] through an agent. [Rav Yehuda said to him]: This is what Samuel says: One may not send greetings to a woman (even with a messenger). [Rav Naḥman countered]: Through her husband! [Rav Yehuda] He said to him: This is what Samuel says: One may not send greetings to a woman at all.	אמר ליה: תיתי דונג תשקינן. אמר ליה, הכי אמר שמואל: אין משתמשים באשה. קטנה היא! בפירוש אמר שמואל: אין משתמשים באשה כלל, בין גדולה בין קטנה. נשדר ליה מר שלמא לילתא. א"ל, הכי אמר שמואל: קול באשה ערוה. אפשר ע"י שליח! א"ל, הכי אמר שמואל: אין שואלין בשלום אשה. על ידי בעלה! אמר ליה: הכי אמר שמואל: אין שואלין בשלום אשה כלל.

The discussion brought in Kiddushin raises the broader issue of social interaction between men and women. Rav Yehuda repeatedly rejects

Uncovered

Rav Nahman's attempts to involve his daughter Donag and his wife Yalta in the hospitality extended toward him, quoting Samuel each time.

Rav Nahman and Rav Yehuda were contemporaries living in Babylon in the third century. Both headed influential yeshivas; Rav Nahman was the head of the Nehardeah yeshiva while Rav Yehuda headed the Pumpedita yeshiva. It is noteworthy that Rav Nahman does not agree with Rav Yehuda and encourages him to include the women in his family in their social encounter. In fact, he finds it insulting that Rav Yehuda will not speak or even send greetings to his wife.

The "voice of a woman is *ervah*" is only one of a number of Samuel's sayings restricting interaction between men and women. Clearly, Rav Yehuda understands Samuel's statement as restrictive of all conversation with women, even to the extent of sending greetings through her husband.[2] However, hearing a woman's voice is the only restriction where the severity of *ervah* is invoked.[3]

---

2. There is a similar statement in Mishnah Avot (1:5): "Engage not in too much conversation with women. They said this with regard to one's own wife, how much more [does the rule apply] with regard to another man's wife. From here the Sages said: as long as a man engages in too much conversation with women, he causes evil to himself, he neglects the study of the Torah, and in the end he will inherit *gehinnom*." The Mishnah in Avot warns that interaction between the sexes can lead a man to *gehinnom* and one should limit but not eliminate conversation with women. It neither prohibits such interaction nor singles out the woman's voice as specifically problematic. The Talmudic passage in Kiddushin is more extreme, forbidding not just casual conversation but even words of greeting.

3. Dr. Aharon Amit suggests that Samuel's statement which is native to the unit in Berakhot is brought into Kiddushin by later redactors since some of the manuscripts and early print editions are missing the text of "Samuel said the voice of a woman is *ervah*." To Amit, this explains the absence of Samuel's statement with all of its implications in the vast majority of post-Talmudic commentary when commenting on Kiddushin. The halakhic implications that emerge from Kiddushin would essentially force us to understand Samuel's statement as including the speaking voice of the woman, which matches the text in the Jerusalem Talmud (citing Jeremiah, "the voice of her whoring"). This, however, is not the conclusion of halakhic authorities.

The Voice of a Woman

To summarize, Samuel's statement associating a woman's voice with *ervah* appears in three places in rabbinic literature, with none of them directly referring to singing. Post-Talmudic interpretation of the sources will be paramount in extracting practical applications, since the Talmudic statements themselves give no such clarity.

A Ban on Song

A second selection of Talmudic sources is also relevant to this discussion. These sources present an attitude of suspicion about song in general and have less to do with women singing, but they are important nonetheless for our analysis:

Mishnah Sotah 9:11	משנה סוטה פרק ט משנה יא
When the Sanhedrin ceased, song ceased from the places of feasting, as it is said, "They drink their wine without song" (Isaiah 24:9).	משבטלה סנהדרין, בטלה השיר מבית המשתאות, שנאמר: בַּשִּׁיר לֹא יִשְׁתּוּ־יָיִן וגו׳.
Sotah 48a	מס׳ סוטה דף מח עמ׳ א
Rav Huna said: The song of those who pull ships and lead the herd is permitted, of weavers is forbidden. Rav Yosef said: If men sing and women respond, this is licentiousness. If women sing and men respond, it causes the evil inclination to burn as if setting fire to sawdust. The abolishment of the [latter] should precede the [former]. Rabbi Yohanan said: Anyone who drinks accompanied by four musical	אמר רב הונא: זמרא דנגדי ודבקרי שרי דגרדאי אסיר... אמר רב יוסף: זמרי גברי וענו נשי פריצותא. זמרי נשי וענו גברי כאש בנעורת. למאי נפקא מינה? לבטולי הא מקמי הא. אמר ר׳ יוחנן כל השותה בארבעה מיני זמר מביא חמש פורעניות לעולם

> instruments – brings upon the world five punishments, as it is written (Isaiah 5:11): "Woe to those who rise early in the morning, pursuers of strong drinks, who stay up late into the night; wine will inflame them, and it will be that the fiddle and the harp, the drum and the pipe, and wine at their parties, and they will not behold the actions of God…"
>
> שנאמר: "הוֹי מַשְׁכִּימֵי בַבֹּקֶר שֵׁכָר יִרְדֹּפוּ מְאַחֲרֵי בַנֶּשֶׁף יַיִן יַדְלִיקֵם: וְהָיָה כִנּוֹר וָנֶבֶל תֹּף וְחָלִיל וָיַיִן מִשְׁתֵּיהֶם וְאֵת פֹּעַל יְהֹוָה לֹא יַבִּיטוּ.."

The Mishnah records how song was banned from celebrations in the wake of the loss of Judean autonomy to the Romans ("when the Sanhedrin ceased"). Later Talmudic sources appear to express reservations about song in general although it is not clear how those reservations relate to the Mishnah. Rav Huna says that boat haulers and those who lead the herd are permitted to sing but weavers are prohibited.[4] Rav Yosef cautions harshly against men singing with women answering (in song) and women singing with men answering. He calls the former immodest and the latter he compares to setting fire to sawdust, presumably because of the potential conflagration when the women and men interact in such a way. The Talmud does not pause to define the type or content of the songs being sung, nor does it quote Samuel saying the voice of a woman is *ervah*. In the next passage it quotes Rabbi Yohanan who warns against drinking and listening to musical instruments, for that will bring calamity to the world. The Talmud then moves to the next part of the Mishnah which has nothing to do with song or with women.

The text from Tractate Sotah about men singing with women and women singing with men is sometimes cited as another source that prohibits *kol isha*. However, no connection is made to Samuel's statement or to *ervah*, nor are any proof texts from Scripture cited.

---

4. Rashi in his commentary explains that boat haulers and herders need song in order to inspire them to do their physically strenuous work. In contrast, weavers sing frivolously.

The Voice of a Woman

In the parallel passage in the Jerusalem Talmud, there is no direct reference to herders, weavers, or men and women, but the passage explains why song was banned in the absence of the Sanhedrin:

J. Talmud Sotah 9:12	תלמוד ירושלמי מסכת סוטה פרק ט' הל' יב
Rav Hisda said, in earlier times the fear of the Sanhedrin was on them and they did not include lewd language in song. But now when the fear of the court is no longer on them they include lewd language in song.	אמר רב חסדא בראשונה היתה אימת סנהדרין עליהן ולא היו אומרים דברי נבלה בשיר. אבל עכשיו שאין אימת סנהדרין עליהן הן אומרים דברי נבלה בשיר.

The problem, according to the Jerusalem Talmud, is the content of the songs rather than the identity of the singers. This ultimately has the potential to lead to promiscuity, a thematic concern in rabbinic literature.

Read together with the Babylonian Talmud's teaching, the overarching concern is about song leading to immodest interaction between men and women. In the source from Sotah, the text is sending a warning about songs containing giddiness and immodesty, inasmuch as Rav Yosef's statement is situated between Rav Huna who denounces the weavers' songs and Rabbi Yohanan who warns against drinking accompanied by music. Women and men singing together increases the frivolity and potential licentiousness. The conversation seems to have little bearing on any practical halakhic conversation around the parameters of *kol isha* except to caution against immodest lyrics or behavior while singing. It is noteworthy that Samuel's statement that a woman's voice is *ervah* is absent.

The Talmudic sources cited above refer to post-Temple restrictions and concerns for debauchery stemming from songs with inappropriate and crude content particularly when men and women sing together.

Uncovered

The Talmud takes a strict position against song and music at all gatherings, particularly those involving wine and women. It appears that in Tannaitic times, Jews were expected to completely abstain from music as a sign of mourning. In Amoraic times, the rabbis tried to dissuade people from engaging in song and music, with a few exceptions.

It is worth noting several responsa presented by *ge'onim* condemning the practice of women entertainers performing at men's gatherings that do not rely on the trope "the voice of a woman is *ervah*." As will be brought below, Samuel's statement about *kol isha* seems to have been regarded by Rav Hai and Rabbeinu Hananel and other *ge'onim* as relevant only to the recitation of *Shema*. The responsa object to these women entertainers because their performance is immodest and not because they are singing in the presence of men.[5] This halakhic approach fits well with the Talmudic sources in Sotah, Gittin, and the Jerusalem Talmud where lyrics with obscenity or frivolity in mixed company are condemned out of concern that they will lead to promiscuity.

Similarly, in a responsum regarding Jewish men listening to Arab

---

5. See Otzar HaGe'onim Sotah, pp. 272–272, section 143. Mixed entertainment is condemned in this source as promiscuous, and the *ge'onim* argue that both the men and the women should be excommunicated for partaking in such entertainment. A few lines later, the Ga'on also condemns men who play instruments even in settings where there are only men, and he also commends those who avoid playing drums during the bridal ceremony. In Otzar HaGe'onim Sukkah, pp. 69–70, section 189, the Ga'on condemns men and women sitting together at festive meals outside of family, extended to include aunts and sisters. In Otzar HaGe'onim Gittin, pp. 8–9, section 18, the Ga'on is asked about a custom in the house of bride and groom for women to play drums and tambourines and bring gentiles who gladden with harp and string instruments. He answers that song, blessings, and music are permitted and encouraged in the home of the bride and groom. He then condemns a type of love song sung at these gatherings under the influence of the Ishmaelites. He explains that after the Sanhedrin was disbanded, the songs of the Ishmaelites were prohibited but not the songs of Israel, with the exception of certain work songs which did not have ugly lyrics. He reiterates the teaching in Sotah that men and women singing one to the other is prohibited particularly at festive occasions because of the possible licentiousness.

The Voice of a Woman

women singing, Maimonides protests the practice because of the content of the songs and the wine being consumed. He cites Samuel's statement as follows: *the voice of a woman is nakedness...even more so if the woman is singing.*[6] Although Maimonides' premise is that Samuel's statement refers to the speaking voice of a woman (and certainly to her singing voice) as codified in his Laws of Sexual Prohibitions (see below), he emphasizes both in this responsa and in his Laws that it is the focus on sexual pleasure that constitutes a prohibition. In a licentious environment of wine and song (and gentile women!), his concern for impropriety is clear. It does not automatically indicate a blanket prohibition on women speaking or singing.

From both Talmudic and post-Talmudic sources, it seems that the Sages were never completely successful in eradicating music and song – even frivolous song – from Jewish celebrations.[7] Notably, most of these sources do not mention any halakhic issue of women singing per se. It is unequivocal that songs of a sexual, licentious nature are prohibited both in single-sex and mixed company. However, this does not imply any prohibition of women singing songs of a non-sexual nature such as folk songs, religious songs, or lullabies.

Post-Talmudic Interpretation

The practical status of a woman's voice was a matter of discussion among the *rishonim*, the post-Talmudic authorities who continued to interpret and institute *halakhah* in the years 1000–1500 CE. Roughly speaking, three schools of thought emerged. The first rejected the entire premise of *kol isha* as being halakhically irrelevant. This is most prominently seen in the writings of the eleventh-century Talmudist and halakhic authority Rabbi Isaac Alfasi, known as the Rif, who omits the entire *ervah* unit in Berakhot as well as most of the section in Kiddushin quoted in the name of Samuel from recounting of the

---

6. Yehoshua Blau, *Responsa of Moses B. Maimon, Mekizei Nirdamim* (Jerusalem: 1969) vol. 2, Responsum no. 224, pp. 398–400.
7. See Boaz Cohen, *Law and Tradition in Judaism*, pp. 167–181.

halakhic sections of the Talmud. This suggests that he viewed the statements as rhetorical rather than halakhic.

It is noteworthy that the only dictum he allows to stand intact is the statement of Rav Yehuda in the name of Samuel that a man must not inquire after the welfare of a married woman via a messenger (not her husband). The implication by the Rif is less about the voice of the woman and more about a married woman potentially entering into a type of surreptitious relationship with another man, lest it lead to adultery. In a similar vein, Rashi in Kiddushin writes, "lest through inquiry after her welfare (not through her husband) they will become familiar with each other through their messenger and come to love one another." It is the character of the relationship and the form of communication that is of concern rather than the voice of the woman.

The second approach explores the parameters of *kol isha* only within the context of the laws of *Shema*. Accordingly, some reason that familiarity and habituation can neutralize the *ervah* component of a woman's voice, including her singing voice even though it can theoretically be a distraction for a man when saying *Shema*.

The third approach is broader than the second although it uses a similar methodology in the end toward leniency. Here the argument is that in general a women's voice serves as a sexual trigger for a man, but only when he listens with the intention of deriving pleasure from it. Here too, familiarity and habituation can neutralize the *ervah* component of *kol isha*. In some of these sources there is a lack of clarity whether only the singing voice of a woman is of concern or also the speaking voice.

The second approach is most common among both *ga'onim* and early *rishonim* where the focus is on a man hearing a woman's voice when reciting *Shema*. Rav Hai Ga'on (tenth century), for instance, wrote that a man should not say *Shema* when a woman is singing, but if she is talking normally or if he can concentrate while she is singing, it is permitted.[8] Rabbeinu Hananel (tenth century) writes that even though a woman's voice is not seen, it can nonetheless

---

8. Otzar HaGe'onim, Berakhot, Peirushim, pp. 30, section 102.

The Voice of a Woman

stimulate. However, he argues, if the man is accustomed to the voice of a woman, there is no halakhic issue.[9]

A third example of this approach with reference to a woman singing is found in the commentary of Mordekhai[10] (thirteenth century), where he claims, at first, that both *Shema* and other holy pursuits like learning Torah should be prohibited for men when in the presence of a woman's singing voice but then quotes the Sefer HaYireim who writes "that because of our sins we sit among the gentiles and therefore we are not careful not to learn Torah in the presence of non-Jewish women singing, and so ruled the author of Halakhot Gedolot and so ruled Rabbeinu Hananel."

Mordekhai focuses on a man hearing a woman's singing voice rather than her speaking voice not only when saying *Shema* but also when learning Torah. Hearing non-Jewish women singing should have prevented men from praying or learning because of direct exposure to *kol isha* which is *ervah*. However, familiarity neutralizes this as a sexual distraction even when focusing on a holy ritual.

All three of these commentators would certainly permit a man's wife to be present and vocal, along with any woman with whom he is familiar, while he is saying *Shema* (and according to Mordekhai when he is learning Torah, without concern for distraction). Furthermore, these early commentaries are directing attention entirely to the subjective perspective of the man. If he is distracted, he may not recite *Shema*. There are no limitations or warnings aimed at women.

We can presume that according to these early authorities familiarity can neutralize the concern for male *yetzer* or sexual drive while saying *Shema* and certainly, although not specified, outside of the sanctified space of prayer and Torah study. This approach opens greater possibilities for casual interaction between the sexes and, more specifically, the opportunity for women to sing in front of men. It is further reinforced in the commentary of three additional *rishonim*

---

9. Otzar HaGe'onim, Berakhot, Commentary of Rabbeinu Hananel, p. 25, section 84.
10. Mordekhai, Berakhot, Chapter Mi SheMeito, 247:80.

who go beyond the parameters of *Shema* to a more general analysis of *kol isha*:

Commentary of Rashba on Berakhot 24a	חידושי הרשב"א מסכת ברכות דף כד עמוד א
(Quoting the Raavad)….However, her face, hands, feet, and her speaking voice that is not a singing voice and her hair outside of her veil which is not covered causes no concern (for sexual thoughts) because he is accustomed to them and is not distracted, and in another woman it is prohibited to look at any area of her, including her little finger and her hair and it is prohibited to hear her speaking voice as it is written in Kiddushin "let master send regards to Yalta" and he replied "Samuel said the voice of a woman is nakedness" and from this it seems that specifically the voice of sending or receiving regard for this arouses feelings of familiarity.	... אבל פניה ידיה ורגליה וקול דבורה שאינו זמר ושערה מחוץ לצמתה שאינו מתכסה אין חוששין להם מפני שהוא רגיל בהן ולא טריד, ובאשה אחרת אסור להסתכל בשום מקום ואפי' באצבע קטנה ובשערה ואסור לשמוע אפי' קול דבורה כדאמרינן בקדושין [ע' א'] לישדר מר שלמא לילתא אמר ליה הכי אמר שמואל קול באשה ערוה, ואלא מיהו נראה דדוקא קול של שאלת שלום או בהשבת שלום כי התם דאיכא קרוב הדעת...

Rashba, quoting Raavad, presents the possibility for greater leniency and greater stringency regarding *kol isha*. Citing Raavad he acknowledges that familiarity as exemplified by a man's wife can neutralize *ervah*. This fits well with the approach of other commentaries we have seen above. However, he then states unequivocally that based on Samuel's statement in Kiddushin, it seems that a man cannot hear another woman's speaking voice! Nonetheless, he steps back from such stringency and concludes that only hearing a woman's voice in a way that breeds feelings of closeness such as sending or receiving regards would be prohibited and not general social discourse. This concern for a growing closeness between a man and woman (he does not specify a married woman) is similar to Rif's concern for possible adultery when men and women correspond via a messenger.

Ritva (Rabbi Yom Tov of Seville, 1260–1320), presents a more flexible and subjective criterion, placing the burden completely on the man and his awareness of his sexual desire. He writes this explicitly in his commentary on Kiddushin:

Ritva Kiddushin 82a	חידושי הריטב"א מסכת קידושין דף פב עמוד א
All is dependent on wisdom and the sake of heaven: This is the normative rule of Jewish law, that all is dependent on what a person sees in himself. If he needs to distance himself more, he must do so, even such that he not gaze upon women's undergarments when they are being washed. So too, if he sees in himself that his desires are subdued and under control and do not give rise to any impure thoughts, he may look at and speak to a woman with whom he is prohibited to engage in a sexual relationship and ask a married woman how she is doing. This explains the conduct of Rav Yohanan who looked at the women as they were immersing, without any erotic intent.	הכל לפי דעת שמים. וכן הלכתא דהכל כפי מה שאדם מכיר בעצמו, אם ראוי לו לעשות הרחקה ליצרו עושה ואפילו להסתכל בבגדי צבעונין של אשה אסור כדאיתא במסכת עבודה זרה (כ' ב'), ואם מכיר בעצמו שיצרו נכנע וכפוף לו ואין מעלה טינא כלל מותר לו להסתכל ולדבר עם הערוה ולשאול בשלום אשת איש, והיינו ההיא דרבי יוחנן (ב"מ פ"ד א') דיתיב אשערי טבילה ולא חייש איצר הרע.

The onus here is placed upon men to be sensitive to sexual arousal triggers, even as it normalizes mixed-gender association with the assumption that some (many?) men can interact with women in a non-sexual manner.

One final source is noteworthy. Rabbeinu Asher (thirteenth century), known as Rosh, does not mention the caveat of familiarity or intention to derive sexual pleasure, nor does he distinguish between a woman's speaking and singing voice. However, his commentary on Berakhot is vague and it is difficult to extrapolate what he is referring to when he mentions *kol isha*.

Rosh Berakhot 3:37	רא"ש ברכות ג:לז
Samuel said: A woman's voice is *ervah*, as it is said, "For your voice is sweet," explanation: to hear [in general] and not [specifically] for the matter of *Keri'at Shema*.	אמר שמואל קול באשה ערוה שנאמר כי קולך ערב פירוש לשמוע ולא לעניין ק"ש [=קריאת שמע].

To summarize, many of the approaches expressed in the post-Talmudic era establish that there is no broad prohibition against a man hearing a woman's voice. These *rishonim* distinguish between different voices – voices associated with or leading to sexual pleasure or intimacy on one hand, and voices that do not invite sexual thoughts on the other. Even in the seemingly more restrictive approach which supports Samuel's statement that the voice of a woman is *ervah*, content and context matter.

Maimonides[11] specifies intent to derive sexual pleasure as determinative of transgression when listening to a woman's voice:

Maimonides Mishneh Torah Laws of Sexual Prohibitions 21:2	רמב"ם משנה תורה הלכות איסורי ביאה כא:ב
One who engages in these behaviors is	הָעוֹשֶׂה דָּבָר מֵחֲקוֹת אֵלּוּ

---

11. Maimonides, Laws of Sexual Prohibitions, 21:2.

The Voice of a Woman

suspected of committing *arayot* (sexually prohibited acts). And it's forbidden for a person to intimate with his hands or feet or to hint with his eyes to any of the *arayot* (a woman sexually prohibited to him) or to laugh with her or to engage in light-headedness. And even to smell her perfume or to gaze at her beauty is forbidden. And one who engages in this deliberately receives lashes of rebelliousness. And one who gazes even at the little finger of a woman intending to derive sexual pleasure is comparable to one who looks at her genitalia. And even to hear the voice of an *ervah* or to look at her hair is forbidden.	הֲרֵי הוּא חָשׁוּד עַל הָעֲרָיוֹת. וְאָסוּר לְאָדָם לִקְרֹץ בְּיָדָיו וּבְרַגְלָיו אוֹ לִרְמֹז בְּעֵינָיו לְאַחַת מִן הָעֲרָיוֹת אוֹ לִשְׂחֹק עִמָּהּ אוֹ לְהָקֵל רֹאשׁ. וַאֲפִלּוּ לְהָרִיחַ בְּשָׂמִים שֶׁעָלֶיהָ אוֹ לְהַבִּיט בְּיָפְיָהּ אָסוּר. וּמַכִּין לַמִּתְכַּוֵּן לְדָבָר זֶה מַכַּת מַרְדּוּת. וְהַמִּסְתַּכֵּל אֲפִלּוּ בְּאֶצְבַּע קְטַנָּה שֶׁל אִשָּׁה וְנִתְכַּוֵּן לֵהָנוֹת כְּמִי שֶׁנִּסְתַּכֵּל בִּמְקוֹם הַתֹּרֶף. וַאֲפִלּוּ לִשְׁמֹעַ קוֹל הָעֶרְוָה אוֹ לִרְאוֹת שְׂעָרָהּ אָסוּר:

While strong concern is expressed for subjective factors regarding female-male interactions that can turn an innocent interaction into one charged with sexual possibility (for instance, sending regards to a married woman via a messenger who is not her husband), there does not seem to be a outright prohibition on women singing in front of men. Maimonides ignores *kol isha* in his Laws of *Shema*, citing the prohibition on a man hearing a woman's voice only in Laws of Sexual Prohibitions (above) which relates to the general conduct between men and women. He does not distinguish between a woman's speaking and singing voice. If there is intent to derive sexual pleasure, hearing the voice of a woman is prohibited in any circumstance. This suggests that even Maimonides *could* agree that familiarity, as noted in the writings of major halakhic authorities from the early Middle Ages onward, or lack of intent to derive sexual pleasure using his own language, could be applied to permit women's speaking and singing voices in the company of men.

This halakhic opinion was expressed by Rabbi Yehuda Herzl Henkin in recent years:

"We have seen, then, that there exists a trend – not a dominant trend, but a trend – within halakhic thought that in interactions between the sexes that might ordinarily lead to *hirhur* (sexual thoughts), frequency and familiarity of contact can be a mitigating factor, and that a community can legitimately rely on this in using the services of and speaking to and looking at women."[12]

While he does not specifically reference women singing, certainly his emphasis on familiarity as a significant halakhic factor could be extended in that direction, particularly in light of the trend seen in *ge'onim* and *rishonim* above. However, Rabbi Henkin, recognizing that the familiarity approach could be taken to an extreme in the modern secular world in which the boundaries around speech, dress, and comportment are minimal, added an important caveat:

"No degree of frequency and familiarity can legitimize what is intrinsically or intentionally sexually stimulating. Examples are immodest or provocative dress, erotic performances and entertainment and other pitfalls too numerous to be listed. A sin indulged in a thousand times remains a sin."[13]

This last point is a fitting response to those who might apply the halakhic concept of familiarity to remove most boundaries in a world in which a normative dress code is almost non-existent, ubiquitous sexualization of language is prevalent in daily conversation (particularly in the lyrics of many songs), and "nakedness" is virtually everywhere. Nothing is further from the halakhic truth. Certain behaviors, including types of dress and language, remain sexualized regardless of familiarity and can never be permitted.

If the laws of *kol isha* in contemporary *halakhic* practice would rest on Samuel's statement in the Talmud as interpreted by the *ge'onim* and *rishonim*, there should not be a prohibition on women singing in the presence of men *a priori*; content and context would be the only considerations.

---

12. Yehuda Henkin, *Equality Lost*, p. 81.

13. Ibid., p. 82.

The Voice of a Woman

From the Shulhan Arukh Until Today

We will begin the final section of this chapter with a discussion of the Shulhan Arukh's treatment of these questions given its centrality in all contemporary halakhic analysis. In Even HaEzer, the section of the Shulhan Arukh that deals with matters of women and *halakhah*, Rabbi Yosef Karo paraphrases Maimonides in laying out his concerns related to interaction between the sexes:

Shulhan Arukh Even HaEzer 21:1	שלחן ערוך אבן העזר סי' כא
A person must stay very very far from women. He is forbidden to signal with his hands or his feet, or to hint with his eyes, to one of the women who is prohibited to him. He is forbidden to be playful with her, to be frivolous in front of her, or to look upon her beauty. Even to smell the perfume upon her is forbidden. He is forbidden to gaze at women doing laundry. He is forbidden to gaze at the colorful garments of a woman whom he knows, even if she is not wearing them, lest he come to have [forbidden] thoughts about her. If one encounters a woman in the marketplace, he is forbidden to walk behind her, but rather [must] run so that she is beside or behind him. One may not pass by the door of a promiscuous woman [or: a prostitute], even four cubits [around 6–8 ft or 2–2.5 m] distant. If one gazes even at the little finger of a woman with the intent to have pleasure from it, it is as though he gazed at her shameful place. It is forbidden to listen	א צריך אדם להתרחק מהנשים מאד מאד ואסור לקרוץ בידיו או ברגליו ולרמוז בעיניו לאחד מהעריות. ואסור לשחוק עמה להקל ראשו כנגדה או להביט ביופיה ואפילו להריח בבשמים שעליה אסור ואסור להסתכל בנשים שעומדות על הכביסה ואסור להסתכל בבגדי צבעונים של אשה שהוא מכירה אפי' אינם עליה שמא יבא להרהר בה. פגע אשה בשוק אסור להלך אחריה אלא רץ ומסלקה לצדדין או לאחריו. ולא יעבור בפתח אשה זונה אפילו ברחוק ד' אמות. והמסתכל אפילו באצבע קטנה של אשה ונתכוין ליהנות ממנה כאלו נסתכל

to the voice of an *ervah* or to look at her hair. If one intentionally does one of these things, we give him lashes of rebellion…..	בבית התורף שלה. ואסור לשמוע קול ערוה או לראות שערה. והמתכוין לאחד מאלו הדברים מכין אותו מכת מרדות....

Shulhan Arukh, building on Talmudic texts and passages in Rif, Rosh, and Maimonides, advocates strict gender separation in order to prevent men from having sexual thoughts. While he writes that it is forbidden to hear the voice of a woman prohibited to him, he does not focus on the singing voice as being uniquely erotic. As with Maimonides, intent to derive sexual pleasure is what turns any male-female interaction into one that is prohibited for men.

Elsewhere, in Orah Hayyim, a section that deals with prayer, Shabbat, and Festivals, Shulhan Arukh specifically references a woman's singing voice:

Shulhan Arukh, Orah Hayyim 75:4	שלחן ערוך אורח חיים סי׳ עה
One should be careful [i.e., refrain] from hearing a woman's singing voice at the time of the recitation of the *Shema*. Gloss [by Rabbi Moshe Isserles]: And even of his wife. But a voice that one is familiar with is not [considered] *ervah*.	ד יש ליזהר משמיעת קול זמר אשה בשעת קריאת שמע. הגה: ואפילו באשתו. אבל קול הרגיל בו אינו ערוה.

There are a few things to note in the text cited above. *One should be careful [i.e., refrain] from hearing a woman's singing voice* suggests that a woman's speaking voice is not a concern even during *Shema*, which is a familiar conclusion from some of the earlier commentaries such as Rabbeinu Hananel. In his gloss to Shulhan Arukh, Rabbi Moshe Isserles adds that *"a voice that one is familiar with is not [considered] ervah."*

The Voice of a Woman

In summary, Shulhan Arukh in the laws of *Shema* warns a man to refrain from hearing a woman's singing voice while saying *Shema*. In Even HaEzer he warns men to stay far away from women and when he speaks of a man refraining from hearing a prohibited woman's voice he speaks generically without specifying her singing voice, building perhaps on his understanding that Samuel is concerned that familiarity will ensue. However, he adds the important caveat that only if there is intent to derive sexual pleasure is such interaction prohibited for a man." By integrating the texts from Even HaEzer and Orah Hayyim, it seems that the singing voice of a woman is not inherently prohibited unless it causes sexual thoughts.

Modernity and Kol Isha

Despite all that we have seen until now, the premise that a woman's singing voice has the requisite potential to trigger male sexual response or foster promiscuity regardless of context and content remains a factor in halakhic literature, particularly in modernity. How did this come to be?

The shift toward defining *kol isha* as a prohibition relating specifically to a man hearing a woman's singing voice in all contexts is well reflected in the seventeenth-century commentary of Rabbi Abraham Gombiner, known as Magen Avraham, on the Shulhan Arukh, and later in the early twentieth-century commentary of Mishnah Berurah written by Rabbi Israel Meir Kagan, known as Hafetz Haim:

Magen Abraham Laws of *Shema* 75:3	מגן אברהם על שולחן ערוך אורח חיים הל' קריאת שמע סי' עה סעיף ג
6. Singing voice of a woman. Even a single woman. And see the laws of Even HaEzer [in Shulhan Arukh] chapter 21 that the singing voice of a married	ו זמר אשה. אפילו פנויה. וע' בא"ע סימן כ"א דקול זמר אשת איש לעולם

woman is always prohibited but her speaking voice is permitted.	אסור לשמוע אבל קול דבורה שרי:

Magen Avraham adds an important caveat not mentioned in Shulhan Arukh: the prohibition in Even Haezer (i.e., not during *Shema*) involves a married woman's (forbidden under the *arayot* laws) singing voice at all times, regardless of the man's intent or the content and context of lyrics and environment in which the singing takes place. While some *rishonim* apply a blanket restriction to a man hearing a woman's singing voice when saying *Shema*, this move toward a uniform, all-encompassing prohibition (upon men) seems to be an innovation that has no precedent.

In the late nineteenth century, Rabbi Israel Meir Kagan, author of the Mishnah Berurah, took the idea of prohibiting men from hearing women singing one step further:

Mishnah Berurah Laws of *Shema* 75:3	משנה ברורה הלכות קריאת שמע סי' עה סעיף ג
17. "Singing of a woman." Even a single woman. However, if it is not during *Shema*, hearing the singing voice of a woman is permitted but he must not have intent to derive pleasure from it so that he not come to have sexual thoughts. The singing voice of a married woman and of all other sexually prohibited women is always prohibited and the single woman who is a *niddah* (menstruant) is also in the category of a sexually prohibited woman. And our single women (literally virgins) are all presumed *niddot* from the time of their	(יז) זמר אשה - אפילו פנויה. אבל שלא בשעת קריאת שמע שרי, אך שלא יכוין להנות מזה כדי שלא יבוא לידי הרהור. וזמר אשת איש וכן כל העריות לעולם אסור לשמוע, וכן פנויה שהיא נדה מכלל עריות היא. ובתולות דידן כולם בחזקת נדות הן משיגיע להן זמן וסת. וקול זמר פנויה נכרית היא גם כן בכלל ערוה ואסור לשמוע בין כהן ובין ישראל.

The Voice of a Woman

first menstrual cycle.[14] 18. "That he is familiar with." What [Rabbi Isserles] means to say is that since it is a voice he is accustomed to, he will not be aroused to sexual thoughts.[15] And even that of a married woman. But even so, it is prohibited to have intent to derive pleasure from her speaking for it is prohibited even to look at her clothing in order to derive (sexual) pleasure.	(יח) הרגיל בו - רצונו לומר, כיון שרגיל בו לא יבוא לידי הרהור ואפילו מאשת איש. ואפילו הכי אסור לכוין להנות מדיבורה שהרי אפילו בבגדיה אסור להסתכל להנות:

Mishnah Berurah initially acknowledged that an unmarried woman could, potentially, be permitted to sing in front of men in contexts outside of a man reciting *Shema*. He then concluded that since all unmarried women past childhood are presumably *niddah* and thus are sexually prohibited to all men, there is no way to permit them to sing at all in front of men. This ruling led many Orthodox communities to restrict girls from singing in any public or communal setting beyond the age of 11, and sometimes even 9, when a girl could potentially begin to menstruate.

In essence, Samuel's statement *kol b'isha ervah* became a blanket prohibition on women singing in front of men, and the methodology outlined earlier – that the prohibition actually applies to women speaking and singing and only when content or context is sexualized – almost completely disappears. Familiarity and intent (which could be mitigated by context and circumstance) are rendered irrelevant,

---

14. A female, regardless of age, becomes halakhically *niddah* when she menstruates for the first time and until she immerses in the *mikvah* even after bleeding stops. Since women are prohibited from immersing in the *mikvah* until the eve of marriage, all single women from their first period onward are defined halakhically as *niddah* and sexually prohibited to all men. This will be further addressed in a later chapter of the book about *niddah* and sexual intimacy.
15. The Mishnah Berurah understands this to mean a woman's speaking voice. He has already issued a blanket prohibition on the singing voice of all women from puberty onward.

replaced by objective sexualization of women's singing voices in *halakhah*.

Nonetheless, there are isolated rabbinic voices that reject this determination, three of which will be examined below. The scope of the prohibition is discussed in the *Sedei Hemed* by Rabbi Haim Hezekiah Medini, a nineteenth-century rabbinic scholar from Jerusalem. He affirms that most rabbinic authorities of his time indeed prohibited men from listening to women sing. However, he cites Rabbi Aharon de Toledo, the author of *Divrei Hefetz* (published in Salonika in 1798), who permitted it "so long as it is not a voice of lust-provoked songs and the listener does not intend to derive pleasure from her voice." *Divrei Hefetz* expresses concern about music that might contain illicit content and thus lead to inappropriate sexualized thoughts and/or behavior, but not about the sexualization of a woman's singing voice.

While I only brought the Magen Avraham and Mishnah Berurah above to illustrate the shift toward uniform stringency, it is a shift that is broadly represented in halakhic sources across the religious world. By the nineteenth century, Rabbi Toledo, who most accurately reflects the halakhic discourse presented in the Talmudic and post-Talmudic sources outlined in the chapter, had become a minority opinion. Despite the strong majority opinion, Rabbi Medini acknowledges that Rabbi Toledo's halakhic position is a legitimate one.[16] Nonetheless, most contemporary responsa ignore the analysis brought in *Divrei Hefetz*, but they do so without any proof text to undermine his thesis. Given that it is dated post-Shulhan Arukh and is based on earlier rabbinic texts dating back to the Talmud, Rabbi Toledo's ruling could remain relevant for rabbinic authorities seeking support for a more lenient opinion on the matter of *kol isha*.

Around the same time that Rabbi Medini was writing his encyclopedia in Jerusalem, Rabbi Azriel Hildesheimer and Rabbi

---

16. "One who sees *Divrei Hefetz*'s words will rightfully deem them cogent. And even though it is surely correct to act stringently, not in accordance with the aforementioned words of the *Divrei Hefetz*, in any case they are not, Heaven forbid classified as inscrutable words." *Sedei Hemed*, section 20, principle 42 (vol. 5, p. 282).

The Voice of a Woman

Samson Raphael Hirsch, two leading rabbinic authorities from the more modern Jewish communities in Germany, permitted men and women to sing Shabbat songs (*zemirot*) together in a family setting. They avoided an outright rejection of the prevalent ruling which unilaterally prohibited men from hearing women sing, instead basing their leniency on an unprecedented but innovative argument. They used the Talmudic assertion that תרי קלי לא משתמעי - *two voices cannot be heard simultaneously*. This idea appears in Tractate Rosh HaShanah to explain why two people cannot read Torah together because it is difficult to hear the words read in a discerning manner.[17] Rabbis Hildesheimer and Hirsch innovatively suggest that if women sing with men or at least two women sing together, it nullifies the concern for sexual promiscuity since *halakhah* recognizes that two simultaneous voices are difficult to distinguish. Based on Talmudic and post-Talmudic discourse brought above, this approach should not have even been necessary. Songs sung around a table at home and focused on the sanctity of Shabbat involve neither promiscuous behavior nor obscene lyrics, and men hearing women singing such songs would not violate *kol isha* by any of the earlier criteria (unless there was specific intent to derive sexual pleasure!) It illustrates the necessity of constructing a halakhic argument to override what had become the majority halakhic opinion. While the "two voices" construct did not become the mainstream Orthodox approach, some observant communities rely on it to permit women to sing at the Shabbat table, in a mixed choir with men, or even to allow a group of women to perform together in a modest setting with appropriate lyrics.

The final rabbinic authority who played a significant role in reintroducing a moderate approach to men hearing women sing was Rabbi Yechiel Yaakov Weinberg, author of the *Seridei Eish*. Rabbi Weinberg wrote a responsum in which he permitted boys and girls to sing together during youth group activities in France after World

---

17. Rosh HaShanah 27a.

War II. He advocated adopting this permissive approach in deference to the urgent religious crisis unfolding in France at the time:

Responsa Seridei Eish 1:77 (translation Deracheha)	שו"ת שרידי אש א:עז
…When I came to Berlin, I saw that in Orthodox homes men and women sang sacred *zemirot* together on Shabbat, and I was amazed at this custom, which violates an explicit *halachah*… However, after research and investigation, it was told to me that Rav Azriel Hildesheimer and also Rav Samson Raphael Hirsch in Frankfurt am Main permitted singing together for sacred *zemirot*. The reason is that "two voices are not heard," and since they sing together there is no concern of a prohibition, but I was not comfortable with this… I searched and found in *Sedei Chemed, s.v. Kol*, that he brought in the name of a Sephardi Rav to permit sacred *zemirot* of men and women together …Afterwards, I saw it brought in the name of Chida in his book *Devash Le-fi, s.v. Kuf*, that when there is dwelling of the *Shechina* it is permitted for a woman to sing and there is no problem of inappropriate thoughts. One can at least rely on what he brought from Sedei Chemed, that with sacred songs we are not concerned with inappropriate thoughts … The opinion of those who are stringent is to prohibit during *keri'at Shema* in any manner. But at times not during *keri'at Shema* there is certainly no prohibition	כי בבואי לברלין ראיתי בבתי החרדים מזמרים אנשים ונשים…יחד זמירות קודש בשבת, והשתוממתי למנהג זה שהוא נגד דין מפורש…ואולם אחרי חקירה ודרישה נאמר לי כי הגאון הצדיק ר"ע [=רב עזריאל] הילדסהיימר ז"ל וכן הגרש"ר [=הגאון רב שמשון רפאל] הירש ז"ל בפרנקפורט על נהר מיין התירו בזמירות קודש לזמר יחד והטעם משום דתרי קלא לא משתמעי וכיון שמזמרים יחד אין חשש איסור, אבל לא נחה דעתי בזה….וחפשתי ומצאתי בשדי חמד מערכת קול, שהביא בשם רב ספרדי להתיר זמירות קודש של אנשים ונשים יחד…ואח"כ [=ואחר כך] ראיתי מובא בשם החיד"א בספרו דבש לפי מערכת ק', שבשעת השראת שכינה שריא לאשה לשורר וליכא משום הרהור,

222

unless he has intention to enjoy, as according to the Rambam's opinion. If so, one can say that with sacred *zemirot* we are not concerned that they would intend to enjoy a woman's voice… If so, one can say that with sacred *zemirot* we are not concerned that they would intend to enjoy a woman's voice…There is room to say, that with sacred *zemirot* the *zemer* awakens holy feelings and not thoughts of sin…. One can say that since those who sing sacred *zemirot* also intend for the sake of Heaven, in order to awaken religious feelings among the girls and to plant in their hearts affection for the sacred things of Israel, one can rely on those who are lenient. See *Yoma* 69a regarding Shimon Ha-tzadik: "A time to do for God, [they have abrogated Your Torah] etc., and Rashi there.…

ועכ"פ [=ועל כל פנים] יש סמך למה שהביא בשד"ח הנ"ל [=בשדי חמד הנזכר לעיל], שבשירי קודש לא חיישינן להרהור. ..ודעת המחמירים לאסור בשעת ק"ש [=קריאת שמע] בכל אופן, אבל שלא בשעת ק"ש [=קריאת שמע] בודאי שאינו אסור אלא כשמתכוין להנות וכדעת הרמב"ם הנ"ל [=הנזכר לעיל], וא"כ [=ואם כן] יש לומר שבזמירות קודש אין לחוש שיתכוונו להנות מקול אשה...יש מקום לומר, שבזמירות קודש הזמר מעורר רגש קודש ולא הרהור עבירה. ... יש לומר כיון שהמזמרים זמירות קודש ג"כ [=גם כן] מתכוונים לש"ש [=לשם שמים], כדי לעורר רגשות דתיים אצל הבנות ולטעת בלבם חיבה לקדשי ישראל, יש לסמוך על המקילים. ועי[ין] במס[כ]ת יומא ס"ט, א גבי שמעון הצדיק: עת לעשות לה' [הפרו תורתך] וכו' ובפירש"י [=ובפירוש רש"י] שם....

Fueled by the awareness that halakhic stringency would only lead to greater assimilation and rejection of religious practice, Rabbi Weinberg felt that it was a time of crisis which mandated leniency in order to protect Torah observance. To this end, he wrote that the prohibition regarding men hearing women sing was based on custom and practices of modesty, and not explicit *halakhah*. He recognized that the mixed youth group activities that included singing together, were succeeding in creating a warm, inviting framework that brought estranged boys and girls closer to Judaism. For this reason, he suggested that despite the prohibition of *kol isha* based on the halakhic rulings of *aharonim* (later rabbinic authorities), the ban should be overridden based on the principle *et la'asot la'hashem* which translates as *there is a time to act on behalf of the Lord, [even at the cost of] breaking laws of the Torah*. He suggested that the relative lightness of the *kol isha* prohibition and the seriousness of the possible consequences of maintaining the prohibition commended this course to him.

Thus, Rabbi Weinberg advocated for a return to the earlier halakhic approaches that we have seen above, in which context, intent, and familiarity can guide the halakhic discourse rather than the immutable fear that all mixed gender interaction is inherently sexual. More importantly, he recognized that women would feel alienated and take great offense at the suggestion that their voices might be objectified and sexualized by men, requiring them to be silenced.

In a like manner many years later, Rabbi Ovadia Yosef permitted women to sing *zemirot* in the company of men on Shabbat, relying on Rabbi Weinberg. In a beautifully descriptive responsa, he acknowledged the close spiritual and religious relationship between the male rabbinic educators and their female students and the importance of maintaining that level of inspiration through the singing of *zemirot* together around the Shabbat table.[18] Rabbi Saul Berman, a Modern Orthodox halakhic thinker, in a comprehensive analysis of the halakhic sources about women singing, summarized the increased stringency in the approach of *aharonim* in a very long halakhic analysis he published in 1980:[19]

---

18. https://www.machonso.org/hamaayan/?gilayon=35&id=1104

19. Saul Berman, *Kol Isha*, Rabbi Joseph H. Lookstein Memorial Volume, edited by

The Voice of a Woman

> Rabbi Saul Berman, *Kol Isha*
>
> ....For the Aharonim [later rabbinic authorities]... "the voice of a woman is nakedness" is a declaration that a woman's singing voice, under all circumstances, is to be considered a form of nudity to be exposed exclusively to one's husband. In light of this proposition, it is understandable that the Aharonim virtually totally discard the limiting principle of accustomedness which the Rishonim [early rabbinic authorities] used so extensively. One might suggest that being accustomed to a woman's voice limits its distracting quality, or limits the likelihood of its arousing someone to perform an illicit act of intercourse. But the Aharonim, in effect, suggest, that being accustomed to seeing a woman's nudity in no way makes the act itself permissible...
> *Regarding the position of Rabbi Weinberg he concludes as follows:*
> ....The importance of this position [of Rabbi Weinberg] lies in the fact that it constitutes a major departure from the treatment of a woman's singing voice as a form of nudity. It reinstates the tradition of the Rishonim [early rabbinic authorities], that the ban on a woman's voice is functionally motivated and is related to the likelihood of its resulting in illicit sexual activity.

In general, Rabbi Berman's article was written as an attempt to reinstate the earlier halakhic approaches toward allowing women to sing in front of men. Ultimately, it had little impact on the behavior within most Orthodox communities. However, in recent years, *kol isha* was revisited in Israel by some rabbinic authorities. The incident that led to this was an event in which religious soldiers and officers abruptly walked out of an Israeli army ceremony because women were singing, thereby breaking protocol and offending their fellow soldiers and commanders. In the wake of that incident, Rabbi Moshe Lichtenstein of Yeshivat Har Etzion and Rabbi David Bigman of Yeshivat Ma'ale Gilboa wrote responsa that permitted women to sing – even alone – in religious or national settings.

Reflecting the halakhic positions of the Talmud and post-Talmud

---

Leon Landman, Ktav Publishing, 1980, pp. 45–66.

interpreters, Rabbi Bigman writes that women could be permitted to sing if the context and atmosphere of the gathering are appropriate and the lyrics of the song, dress of the singer, body language, and musical style are not provocative:[20]

> Rabbi David Bigman, *A New Analysis of "Kol B'Isha Erva"* (translation Yedidya Schwartz)
>
> According to this approach, there is no problem with those among our daughters who are modest and upstanding to develop a career in singing, even within the general culture, as long as they do not make concessions of the refined foundations of Torah culture, and do not cooperate with the vulgar, commercialized aspects of the culture surrounding us.

In an article published in two mainstream Orthodox journals of *halakhah*, Rabbi Moshe Lichtenstein,[21] after an extensive analysis of the topic, concurs with Rabbi Weinberg's position, recognizing that the needs of the generation are great and for many Orthodox men, women's singing voices are familiar and cause no possible sexual thoughts or distraction. Furthermore, he writes that he does not need to upend the halakhic structure, as he can rely comfortably on the earlier halakhic discourse from the Talmud onward.

Nonetheless, despite a clear outline of halakhic thought that opens the possibility for being more lenient, the majority of halakhic opinions are extremely reluctant to follow the Lichtenstein/Bigman examples. For instance, in his essay "The Parameters of *Kol Isha*," Rabbi Chaim Jachter opens by stating unequivocally that "the Gemara (Berakhot 24a) records the prohibition of *kol isha*" as a starting point for an analysis that limits and rejects possible moderation for men

---

20. Bigman, David, *A New Analysis of "Kol B'Isha Erva,"* https://www.jewishideas.org/article/new-analysis-kol-bisha-erva, translated from Hebrew by Yedidya Schwartz.

21. Techumim Volume 32 (Hebrew) and Moshe Lichtenstein, "Kol Isha: A Women's Voice," *Tradition*, Spring 2013 Issue 46, 1, pp. 9–25.

The Voice of a Woman

hearing women sing.[22] Much of mainstream Orthodoxy has favored a non-negotiable and very stringent perspective about women singing in front of men. This perspective has been invoked beyond actual singing to prevent women from saying *kaddish*, as if even hearing a woman's voice praying in a synagogue violates a sacred taboo that will distract men who are meant to be focused on matters of sanctity.

In essence, *kol isha* has become a sort of battleground in which religious communities are tested regarding their fidelity to perceived halakhic observance. This not only affects the discourse regarding women singing but also has implications for women reciting *kaddish* in synagogue, and I have heard it used to restrict women from giving lectures or Torah classes to men.

A popular Jewish website aimed at explaining Judaism to those less affiliated presents this perceived ideology behind the restriction:[23]

> **Excerpted from Aish.com**
>
> Men and women have different criteria for sexual arousal. Hearing a woman sing is sexually arousing for a man….While it might be hard for a woman to imagine such a thing, the Sages are very in tune with human nature – and this rule has been observed by Jews for thousands of years. So with this in mind, when the Torah sets up barriers to protect society's moral fabric, the emphasis was placed to counter the reality of man's weaker character in these areas. Hearing the pleasant melody of a woman singing is just one way a man could become aroused, therefore he should avoid this medium, given that we are obligated to refrain from exposing ourselves to erotic situations.

Interestingly, a woman's voice weighing in on the topic sounds different and yet, contains some of the same concerns expressed above:

---

22. https://www.koltorah.org/halachah/the-parameters-of-kol-isha-by-rabbi-chaim-jachter
23. https://www.aish.com/atr/Kol_Isha.html

> Avital Macales, interviewed by Varda Epstein, "Count the Stars," Jerusalem Post, November 11, 2014
>
> In recent years, I began to better understand the complexity of [kol isha], and I challenged myself more about whether or not I wanted to get out there and perform in front of mixed audiences... After much thought I came to the decision that I'm still going to sing only in front of women and my personal reason is... There's a certain intimacy that I want to bring to the stage. I want to be completely intimate with my audience, and I don't want anything to block that. I just want to be completely open, and I feel completely open in front of an all-women's audience.

While I appreciate Macales' honesty, I cannot help but wonder if her argument could not easily be calibrated with those *rishonim* who talk about context, content, and intent so that a performer seeking that sort of intimacy with her audience should indeed restrict herself to women only. Just as a man, in the words of Ritva, needs to know his sexual triggers when around women, so too women. Furthermore, her argument could also be used to prevent men from performing for women on the grounds that it creates intimacy that can lead to sexual thoughts. Why is it that women's sexual thoughts are innocuous and only men's are dangerous if the fear of adultery or promiscuous sex lurks behind the *kol isha* restriction?

It is my hope that this chapter has helped explain the halakhic process that has unfolded over the course of the last several hundred years, leading toward an unyielding halakhic attitude of stringency. This restrictive "innovation" prohibiting women from singing in front of men or even being heard at all in the synagogue when saying *kaddish* has been adopted by many as the only legitimate halakhic approach to *kol isha*,[24] but it does not need to serve as the final note.

---

24. In the year I said *kaddish* for my mother, I was fortunate that in most places, I was not asked to say it inaudibly although I have heard women tell me that they were explicitly told not to say *kaddish* out loud because of *kol isha*. This is probably due to ignorance. A thorough look at *kaddish* sources collated by Rahel Berkovits in

The Voice of a Woman

The source analysis presented here is meant to give shape to the possibility of reclaiming the "traditional" approach, dating back to the Talmud, one that permits women to raise their voices in joyful song and prayer without fear of sexualizing society.

"A Daughter's Recitation of Mourner's Kaddish," JOFA, 2011, reveals no relevant source material citing *kol isha* as a factor in preventing women from saying *kaddish*. Rav Ovadia Yosef's son, Rav Yitzhak Yosef, writes explicitly that *kol isha* is not a concern when a woman says *kaddish* from the women's section and cites the source in Megilla 23a (brought above) that prevents women from reading from Torah because of congregational honor and not because of *kol isha*. See *She'elot Utshuvot Yehavveh Da'at*, Vol. 4 #15.

Chapter Six

Women and Hair Covering – *Dat Yehudit*

Among observant Jews, it is standard practice for a woman to begin to cover her hair once she marries.[1] It is impossible to ignore the enormous and varied range of hair covering apparel that one sees when walking through different Orthodox communities. These can include colorful headbands, a baseball cap or fedora, various sized scarves and large patterned wraps, broad brimmed hats, or human hair wigs that cover some or all of the hair. There are communities where women wear wigs and a second head covering, and in some Hassidic communities, women shave their hair and wear a kerchief or wig over their bald heads. At the same time, a sizable minority of observant women do not cover their hair at all outside of religious settings such as synagogues or when lighting Shabbat candles. This topic, touching as it does on identity, femininity, sexuality, and modesty, is a matter of no small import, and many women seek to make this practice "their own" through textual study and independent decision-making.

Before we explore some of the contemporary aspects of hair covering, we may ask: where does the obligation of hair covering begin? People often wonder if the practice is biblically based or

---

1. For an excellent review of the *halakhot* here, see https://www.etzion.org.il/en/talmud/seder-nashim/massekhet-ketubot/head-covering

rabbinically mandated. Furthermore, if there is a clear obligation with an attendant prohibition, why do a substantial number of women choose not to cover their hair even as they are committed to the rigorous observance of Shabbat, *kashrut*, and many other *halakhot* that define their lives as observant Jews?

I have divided the topic of hair covering into two chapters. In this chapter, I offer a textual analysis of the sources from the Mishnah and Talmud specifically around the idea of *dat yehudit* (literally, Jewish practice) that is a significant factor in understanding the rabbinic perspective on head covering. In the next chapter, I will discuss Rav Sheshet's statement in Berakhot that "hair of a woman is *ervah*."

Mishnah Ketubot: *Dat Moshe* and *Dat Yehudit*

Mishnah Ketubot 7:6	משנה מסכת כתובות פרק ז
The following are to be divorced without receiving their *ketubah*: A wife who violates *dat moshe* or *dat yehudit*. What is [regarded as a violation of] *dat moshe*? Feeding [her husband] untithed food, having intercourse with him while she is *nidda*,[2] not separating *hallah*,[3] or making vows and not fulfilling them. What is [considered to be a violation of] *dat yehudit*? Going out with her head uncovered, spinning in the marketplace, or conversing with every man.	ו אלו יוצאות שלא בכתובה: העוברת על דת משה ויהודית. ואיזו היא דת משה? מאכילתו שאינו מעושר, ומשמשתו נדה, ולא קוצה לה חלה, ונודרת ואינה מקיימת. ואיזוהי דת יהודית? יוצאה וראשה פרוע, וטווה בשוק, ומדברת עם כל אדם.

---

2. When a woman experiences significant uterine bleeding (e.g., menstruation, miscarriage, birth), she becomes sexually prohibited to her permitted sexual partner (e.g., her husband) until the bleeding stops and she immerses in a ritual bath known as a *mikvah*. Throughout this period of time she is known as a nidda. See Chapter Eight for a more detailed discussion on the topic.

3. During the Temple period, people would separate a portion of their dough in order

Women and Hair Covering – Dat Yehudit

In this Mishnaic passage, the text introduces examples of offensive behavior on the part of the wife that gives legitimate cause to her husband to divorce her without paying her *ketubah*. They are separated into two categories. The first is termed *dat moshe* and the second *dat yehudit* (or *dat yehudim* in some manuscripts of the Mishnah). These unusual terms appear infrequently in the Talmud and their translation is not straightforward.[4]

The consequences for the violation of *dat moshe* or *dat yehudit* are specific to a married woman, leading to divorce and forfeit of her *ketubah*.[5] The Mishnah presents the list of violations of *dat moshe*: feeding her husband untithed food, having relations with her husband when she is a *niddah*, neglecting to separate the *hallah* portion of the household dough, and taking vows without fulfilling them. These four examples have direct implications for the husband and are grounds for divorce. Conspicuously absent are violations of severe biblical prohibitions, such as desecrating Shabbat, eating non-kosher food, or thievery. In other words, her transgression of biblical law, if it only affects her, does not cause her to forfeit her *ketubah*. The forfeiture is

---

to give it to the priest. This was known as the hallah offering. After the destruction of the Temple, rabbinic law mandated that the portion be separated and burned to commemorate the hallah offering. This was often perceived as a woman's *mitzvah* because of her role in the home, although male bakers had the same obligation.

4. The Koren Talmud which uses the Steinsaltz translation, translates as follows: a woman who violates the precepts of Moses, i.e., *halakhah*, or the precepts of Jewish women, i.e., custom. This translation of *dat yehudit* is based on the interpretation of many *rishonim* including Rashi and Maimonides. Soncino translates: a wife who transgresses the law of Moshe or [one who transgresses] Jewish practice.

5. The *ketubah* is the Jewish marriage document of ancient origin in which a man promises to support his wife during marriage and, in the case of death or divorce, commits to repaying her dowry together with a fixed sum of money to ensure her of financial support when she loses the protection of a husband. The *ketubah* continues to be part of the marriage ceremony to this day and is signed and given to the wife under the *huppah*, the Jewish bridal canopy, although it does not play as central a financial role today as it did in previous times.

Uncovered

only exercised when she violates these examples of *dat moshe,* and, in doing so, causes her husband to sin.[6]

The Mishnah then presents the list of violations of *dat yehudit*. Included in the list are a woman going out with a bared head, spinning in the marketplace, and talking to men. The parallel Tosefta in Tractate Ketubot adds several other violations: going out with clothing open on both sides, baring arms, coarse familiarity with servants, and bathing with all [men and women] in the bathhouse.[7] Loss of *ketubah* serves as a severe penalty and clearly was meant to be a significant deterrent to all of the behaviors cited in the Mishnah.

Given the severity with which adultery is treated both in the biblical text and in all ancient societies, the practice of *dat yehudit* may reflect Jewish society's desire to prevent promiscuous behavior on the part of married women. Not only women but also men are called upon to uphold these standards. The Tosefta in Sotah 5:9 reinforces this:

Tosefta Sotah 5:9	תוספתא מסכת סוטה פרק ה הל' ט
Rabbi Meir would say: Just as there are different attitudes in consumption of food, so are there different attitudes with regard to women. Some men, if a fly [merely] passes over his cup, he sets it aside and does not taste it. That [fly in the cup refers to]	היה ר' מאיר אומר: כשם שדיעות במאכל כך דיעות בנשים. יש לך אדם שהזבוב עובר על גבי כוסו מניחו ואין

---

6. *Responsa* of the Rosh 32:8 quoted in Getsel Ellinson, *A Modest Way*, p. 130.

7. Tosefta Ketubot 7:6. The Tosefta does not distinguish between the first category of *dat moshe* as presented in the Mishnah in which the woman deceives the man into transgression and the second category of *dat yehudit* in which she behaves in an unseemly manner. They are simply described as *dat moshe* and Israel, suggesting that neither are purely biblical or rabbinic law. The Babylonian Talmud retains the *dat moshe/dat yehudit* terminology in line with the Mishnah and ignores the Tosefta's usage of *dat moshe* and Israel, as do all subsequent post-rabbinic discussions on this topic.

Women and Hair Covering – Dat Yehudit

corrupted women, when he wishes to divorce his wife [but has not done it yet].	טוֹעֲמוֹ. זה חלק רע בנשים שנתן עיניו באשתו לגרשה.
Some men, if a fly falls into his cup, he throws it out and does not drink it. And this is the trait of Papus ben Yehuda, who would lock [the door of the house] before his wife, and would leave.	יש לך אדם שהזבוב שוכן בתוך כוסו זורקו ואין שותהו, כגון פפוס בן יהודה שנעל דלת בפני אשתו ויצא.
And there is a man where, if a fly falls in his cup, he throws [the fly] out and then drinks it. This is the trait of any man who sees her speak to her neighbors and relatives, and leaves her be.	ויש לך אדם שהזבוב נופל בתוך כוסו זורקו ושותהו. זו מדת כל אדם שראה את אשתו שמדברת עם שכיניה ועם קרובותיה ומניחה.
And there is a man where, if a fly falls into the plate, he crushes it and eats it. And this is the trait of a corrupted man who sees his wife go out with her head uncovered, her heart is familiar towards her manservants, her heart is familiar towards her maidservants, and spins thread in the marketplace, and [whose garment is] open on both sides, and bathes and plays with all. This is the command from the Torah to divorce her, for it is stated [Deuteronomy 24:1-2] "[When a man takes a wife and marries her, then it comes to pass, if she finds no favor in his eyes,] because he hath found some unseemly thing in her, [that he writes her a bill of divorce, and gives it in her hand,] and sends her out of his house... [and she departs out of his house, and goes and becomes another man's wife.]"	יש לך אדם שהזבוב נופל בתוך תמחוי שלו נטלו מוצצו וזורקו ואוכל את מה שבתוכה. זו מדת אדם רשע שראה את אשתו יוצאת וראשה פרוע, יצאת וצדדיה פרומים, לבה גס בעבדיה, לבה גס בשפחותיה, יוצא וטווה בשוק, רוחצת ומשחקת עם כל אדם, מצוה לגרשה שנ' כי יקח איש אשה ובעלה וגו' ויצאה מעמו וגו'.

According to this text, a man is held accountable for the way he responds to the immodest behavior of his wife. It is reflective of the patriarchal nature of society that a man has authority over his wife and is expected to take responsibility for her breaking the norms of acceptable conduct in society. The types of behavior that a man is criticized for tolerating in his wife are similar to those found in the Mishnah and Tosefta in Ketubot cited above. While not directly a matter for the courts, since there are no witnesses that adultery has taken place, men are strongly urged, if not required, to divorce such women as a sanction to deter such behavior in Jewish society.

Going Out With a Bared Head

The Mishnah states that a married woman who goes out with her head uncovered violates *dat yehudit*. In other words, an uncovered head is a violation of Jewish norms, not a biblical violation. Nonetheless, the Mishnah is unequivocal that such behavior is grounds for divorce without *ketubah*,

The Babylonian Talmud challenges the categorization of head covering as merely a matter of *dat yehudit*. In the ensuing discussion, the Talmud asserts unequivocally that going out bareheaded violates biblical law:

Ketubot 72a	כתובות דף עב עמ' א
"And who is considered a woman who violates *dat yehudit*? One who goes out with her head uncovered." [The Talmud challenges] The prohibition against a woman going out with her head uncovered is biblical law! as it is written: "And he shall uncover the head of the woman" (Numbers 5:18).	ואיזוהי דת יהודית? יוצאה וראשה פרוע. ראשה פרוע, דאורייתא היא! דכתיב: וּפָרַע אֶת רֹאשׁ הָאִשָּׁה.

The biblical verse cited as textual support for hair covering in the Talmud is found in the context of a portion dealing with a woman accused by her husband of adultery, and there are no witnesses to the act. In rabbinic texts, this woman is referred to as a *sotah*, literally,

Women and Hair Covering – Dat Yehudit

"one who goes astray." There is no way to determine in court whether this woman has sinned or whether her husband has been overcome by jealousy.[8] Given the severity of the accusation and the lack of evidence, the woman is brought before the High Priest to undergo a ritual that will establish her guilt or her innocence. One of the steps involves a ritual that involves an act of *p'ra* to her head:

Numbers 5:18	במדבר פרק ה
After he has made the woman stand before the LORD, the priest shall uncover/dishevel the woman's head and place upon her hands the meal offering of remembrance, which is a meal offering of jealousy. And in the priest's hands shall be the water of bitterness that induces the spell.	יח וְהֶעֱמִיד הַכֹּהֵן אֶת־הָאִשָּׁה, לִפְנֵי ה', וּפָרַע אֶת־רֹאשׁ הָאִשָּׁה, וְנָתַן עַל־כַּפֶּיהָ אֵת מִנְחַת הַזִּכָּרוֹן מִנְחַת קְנָאֹת הִוא; וּבְיַד הַכֹּהֵן יִהְיוּ, מֵי הַמָּרִים הַמְאָרֲרִים.

I have often been asked to explain, even justify, the meaning of the proof text as the source for head covering. It must be noted that the halakhic interpretation does not necessarily adhere to the literal meaning of the Torah.

However, it is interesting to trace the literal meaning of the biblical verse in order to tease out, to some degree, the evolution of interpretation within the halakhic discussion. Based on recent scholarship,[9] it seems the Hebrew word *p'ra*, in biblical times, most likely meant to dishevel or scatter. Similarly, in the ancient language

---

8. Numbers 5:11–31.
9. Amnon Shapira, "*Peri'at Rosh HaIsha MaHe?*" Beit Mikra 45b (5760), pp. 177–184. Shapira studied the two-letter roots of *p'ra* in the Bible and concluded that all of them mean to confuse/let loose/scatter/dishevel. The verb *p'ra* appears six times in the context of head/hair. Out of the six verses, three are associated with the hair of the priests, one refers to the leper, one to the nazarite, and only the verse cited above refers to a woman's head. The other verses are: Leviticus 10:6, 21:10, 13:45, Numbers 6:5, and Ezekiel 44:20.

of Akkadian which was spoken around the time that the Torah was given, *pe-ra wasarat* means hair that is loosened. It is likely that the original ceremony involved a ritual in which the priest loosened the woman's bound hair in order to humiliate her. Thus, the accused woman stands before the priest holding a poor offering of barley sheaves, her hair disheveled, and forced to drink water with some dirt and ink that held God's name dissolved in it. According to this interpretation, the ritual does not describe the removal of a head covering, nor is there any indication from any other biblical text that such a head covering was mandated by the Bible.

In the [pre-Rabbinic] Second Temple period, biblical commentaries such as the Greek translation of the Bible known as Septuagint interpret the ritual as the removal of a head covering, as do Philo and Josephus.[10] They insert a word into their transmission of the text that indicates the removal of a veil or head covering worn by a woman accused of adultery. The purpose of the *sotah* ritual, as understood by these early interpreters, was clearly to expose and humiliate the woman by baring her head. The intent is no different from the way dishevelment of hair would have humiliated her in the previously suggested biblical reading.

These two different, but somewhat overlapping, interpretations of the word *p'ra* can be found in rabbinic texts as well. The dominant approach follows the tradition of removal or uncovering.[11] However, in the secondary approach, reflected in a number of Tannaitic sources, *p'ra* is interpreted as being similar to the Hebrew root *s'tr*, meaning to loosen.[12] These will be examined below. It is largely acknowledged, even

---

10. Septuagint Numbers 5:18; Philo, *The Special Laws* iii, 57; Josephus, *Antiquities* Book 3, Chapter 11:6.

11. For instance, in a totally unrelated ceremony, during male circumcision, the second stage of the ritual is known as *p'ria*, or the uncovering of the corona after the foreskin is removed. The clear meaning of this word in the circumcision ritual helps elucidate the normative rabbinic translation in interpreting the *sotah* ritual as described in the biblical passage. See Mishnah Shabbat 19:2.

12. Menahem Izhak Kahane, *Sifre on Numbers: An Annotated Edition*, Part I, Magnes Press, 2011, pp 129–131.

Women and Hair Covering – Dat Yehudit

in those texts, that while dishevelment might have been the original meaning of *p'ra* in the Bible, in the Rabbinic period uncovering is the more prevalent interpretation.

The *Sotah* Ritual

Before returning to the Talmudic passage in Ketubot which links the act of a woman going out with a bared head to the *sotah* passage, we will examine several Tannaitic sources that describe the *sotah* ritual, specifically the act of uncovering her head and disheveling her hair. In *Sifrei Bamidbar*, there is a passage that describes what happens when the priest approaches the *sotah* to do *p'ria*:

Sifrei Bamidbar 11	ספרי במדבר פרשת נשא פיסקא יא
"And he shall uncover/dishevel the head of the woman." The priest moved behind her and uncovered/disheveled her head in order to fulfill the *mitzvah* of *p'ria*, according to Rabbi Yishmael. Another opinion. Learn from this that the daughters of Israel should cover their heads. And even though there is no proof of this, there is an allusion to it, "And Tamar took ashes and put them on her head" (II Samuel 13:19).	וּפָרַע אֶת רֹאשׁ הָאִשָּׁה. כהן נפנה לאחוריה ופורעה כדי לקיים בה מצות פריעה. דברי ר' ישמעאל. דבר אחר, לימד על בנות ישראל שיהו מכסות ראשיהן. ואף על פי שאין ראייה לדבר זכר לדבר: וַתִּקַּח תָּמָר אֵפֶר עַל רֹאשָׁהּ.

The first opinion, attributed to Rabbi Yishmael, explains that the priest stands behind the woman when performing the *p'ria*, but does not supply any further details as to what the *p'ria* looks like.

The second opinion, which is anonymous, extrapolates from the biblical passage that the daughters of Israel should cover their heads. This is most likely the source for the Babylonian Talmud's assertion that women's head covering is biblical in nature.

Uncovered

Mishnah Sotah 1:5	משנה מסכת סוטה פרק א
...And a priest grasps her garment – if it tears, it tears; if it unravels, it unravels – until he has bared her bosom, and he loosens her hair. Rabbi Judah says: if her bosom is beautiful, he does not bare it; if her hair is beautiful, he does not loosen it.	ה... וכהן אוחז בבגדיה. אם נקרעו נקרעו אם נפרמו נפרמו עד שהוא מגלה את לבה וסותר את שערה. ר' יהודה אומר אם היה לבה נאה לא היה מגלהו ואם היה שערה נאה לא היה סותרו:

The Mishnah in Sotah does not describe the act of baring her head. It describes the act as being one of loosening or unbinding, from the Hebrew root *s'tr*. Interestingly, Rabbi Judah then comments that her hair should not be loosened if her hair is especially attractive, for fear that it will encourage sexual thoughts among the onlookers rather than serve as a deterrent since the hair was seen as an act of sexual intimacy potentially overshadowing the intended humiliation:[13]

Tosefta Sotah 3:2–3	תוספתא מס' סוטה פרק ג
2. And so you find with the accused wife, by the same measure which she behaved, retribution is metered out to her. She stood before the man so as to be attractive to him, therefore the priest stands her before all to show her disgrace as it is written: And the priest stood the women before God.	ב וכן אתה מוצא בסוטה שבמדה שמדדה בה מדדו לה. היא עמדה לפניו כדי שתהא נאה לפניו לפיכך כהן מעמידה לפני הכל להראות קלונה, שנ' וְהֶעֱמִיד הַכֹּהֵן אֶת הָאִשָּׁה לִפְנֵי ה'.

---

13. There are other rabbinic sources that help further our understanding of the word *p'ra* as it evolves from the possibly earlier meaning "loosening" to the more accepted rabbinic definition of "uncovering." See Mishnah Ketubot 2:1, Mishnah Bava Kamma 8:6.

3. She spread beautiful shawls for him, therefore the priest removes the *kippah* (cover) from her head and places it at his feet. She braided her hair for him, therefore the priest loosens her hair. She adorned her face, therefore her face turns yellow. She colored her eyes blue for him. Therefore, her eyes bulge out.	ג היא פירסה לו סדין, לכך כהן נוטל כפה מעל ראשה ומניחה תחת רגליו. היא קולעה לו שערה לפיכך כהן סותרו. היא קישטה לו פניה לפיכך פניה מוריקות. היא כחלה לו עיניה לפיכך עיניה בולטות.

The Mishnah and Tosefta each describe a graphic and fairly violent ritual meant to expose and condemn female promiscuity.[14] The process described of uncovering the woman's hair and body is clearly intended to humiliate and disgrace the accused for disrobing for her lover.

The interpretation of the ritual in the Tosefta involves two stages that incorporate the two meanings of the word *p'ra*: the priest first bares her head by removing her *kippah* (head covering). He then loosens her braided hair. Loosening her braids was seen as an act of sexual intimacy, far beyond the simple removal of the *kippah*. For this reason, Rabbi Judah, in the Mishnah, insists that the second stage of loosening be carried out judiciously.

Summary

While the biblical word *p'ra* most likely meant to dishevel or scatter, by the Rabbinic era the priest is described, in some Tannaitic texts, as uncovering the woman's head. For some women, the lack of a clear biblical proscription, or even description, is alienating and fails to convince them of the *d'orayta* (Torah mandated) nature of the practice. However, as we will see in the next source, from the Talmud onward it is indisputably accepted that there is some form of obligation for married women to cover their heads regardless of

---

14. The rabbis of the Talmud debate whether the ritual was actually ever carried out. For an academic analysis, see Ishay Rosen-Zvi, *The Mishnaic Sotah Ritual*, Brill, 2012.

the halakhic "leap" from the literal understanding of the Sotah ritual to the Sifrei to the Babylonian Talmud's assertion that head covering is biblically mandated.

The Babylonian Talmud

B. Talmud Ketubot 72a	תלמוד בבלי מסכת כתובות דף עב עמ' א
And what is *dat yehudit*? One who goes out with her head uncovered. Going out with her head uncovered is forbidden by biblical law! as it is written: "And he shall uncover the head of the woman" (Numbers 5:18). And the school of Rabbi Yishmael taught: It is a warning to the daughters of Israel not to go out with their heads uncovered.	ואיזוהי דת יהודית? יוצאה וראשה פרוע: ראשה פרוע דאורייתא היא! דכתיב: "ופרע את ראש האשה." ותנא דבי רבי ישמעאל: אזהרה לבנות ישראל שלא יצאו בפרוע ראש.

As mentioned previously, in this passage the Babylonian Talmud reacts to this example of *dat yehudit* in the Mishnah by stating that having an uncovered head is forbidden by biblical law, based on the passage in Numbers regarding the *sotah*. It quotes a midrashic interpretation that sounds very similar to that found in the Sifrei brought above.

In his commentary, Rashi offers two explanations for the Talmud's position that head covering is based on a biblical verse and is defined as a *d'orayta*, Torah mandated:

Rashi B. Talmud Ketubot 72a	רש"י מסכת כתובות דף עב עמ' א
....A warning [to the daughters of Israel] – From the fact that we disgrace her measure for measure, commensurate to her act of making herself attractive to	...אזהרה - מדעבדינן לה הכי לנוולה מדה כנגד מדה כמו שעשתה להתנאות על

| her lover [by uncovering/loosening her hair] we can infer that it is forbidden. Alternatively, since Scripture states, "And he shall uncover/loosen," we can infer from this that at that time her head was not uncovered/loosened. We thus deduce that it is not the practice of the daughters of Israel to go out with their heads uncovered/loosened. That is the main explanation. | בועלה, מכלל דאסור. א"נ מדכתיב "ופרע" מכלל דההוא שעתא לאו פרועה הות. שמע מינה אין דרך בנות ישראל לצאת פרועות ראש. וכן עיקר. |

In the first explanation, Rashi echoes the Tosefta brought above,[15] inferring the prohibition from the punishment. Since her punishment involves the disgrace of having her hair exposed or disheveled in public it can be inferred that her sin was of a similar nature, i.e., the act of exposing and/or letting down her hair for her lover. Since the sin is inferred in the Torah, it can be considered *d'orayta* as per the Talmud's declaration that a woman going out with bared head violates a *d'orayta*.

In Rashi's second explanation, the practice of head covering, classified as *dat yehudit* in the Mishnah, is anchored in a biblical verse and therefore upgraded to a biblical obligation. In this reading, there is a synergy between the practice described in Sifrei in which daughters of Israel did not go out with bared heads and the act of uncovering that serves to humiliate the accused *sotah*. The biblical text is descriptive rather than proscriptive yet the *midrash halakhah* understands it to reflect the practice of the daughters of Israel; therefore, it ultimately can be defined as *d'orayta*. However, it does not have a clear textual anchor in the text.

The Talmud continues:

---

15. Tosefta Sotah 3:2.

According to biblical law, a basket [*kalata*], is sufficient. However, according to *dat yehudit*, covering her head with just a basket – is also prohibited. Rabbi Asi said that Rabbi Yohanan said: With a basket, there is no uncovered head!	דאורייתא קלתה שפיר דמי, דת יהודית - אפילו קלתה נמי אסור. אמר רבי אסי אמר ר' יוחנן, קלתה אין בה משום פרוע ראש.
Rabbi Zeira discussed it: Where? If we say in the marketplace, this is a violation of *dat yehudit*. And if you say rather that he means she appears this way in her own courtyard, if so, you have not allowed any daughter of our father Abraham to remain with her husband. Abaye said, and some say that Rav Kahana said: From one courtyard to another courtyard or via an alleyway.	הוי בה רבי זירא, היכא? אילימא בשוק, דת יהודית היא! ואלא בחצר. אם כן, לא הנחת בת לאברהם אבינו שיושבת תחת בעלה! אמר אביי, ואיתימא רב כהנא: מחצר לחצר ודרך מבוי.

The Talmudic statement that a married woman's uncovered head violates a biblical prohibition and the Mishnah's classification of the practice as *dat yehudit* seem to be in contradiction. The Talmud resolves this conflict by proposing that the Mishnah assumed that women who went out were at least wearing a *kalata*, meaning a basket, on their heads, thereby fulfilling the mandatory minimum requirement for head covering according to biblical law.[16]

Thus, according to Talmudic reasoning, the Mishnah had no need to raise the issue of the biblical requirement, because it was obvious that all women would be wearing at least a basket. Following this

---

16. In his commentary to the Talmud, Rashi explains that the *kalata* was literally a basket with a receptacle on the bottom that was attached to her head and a receptacle on top to hold small accessories such as needles.

Women and Hair Covering – Dat Yehudit

logic, the Mishnah refers only to the practice expected of Jewish women, defined as *dat yehudit*, to wear a secondary head covering.

The parallel discussion in the Jerusalem Talmud brings an almost identical statement in the name of Rabbi Yohanan, who rules that going out with a single head covering is not in violation of a prohibition against going out with a bared head. Interestingly, the Jerusalem Talmud does not cite the verse from Numbers as proof text. Rather, it seems to define the *dat yehudit* requirement as the only reason for the practice as per the straightforward reading of the Mishnah. Similar to the Babylonian Talmud's conclusion, the Jerusalem Talmud rejects the possibility of such a minimal single head covering and restricts a woman wearing only a head covering called *kapaltin* (as well as R. Yohanan's position that one head covering is sufficient (to sparsely populated courtyards and alleyways.

The different approaches found in the Babylonian and Jerusalem Talmuds are reflected in the writings of major rabbinic authorities in the Middle Ages:

Maimonides Mishneh Torah Laws of Ishut, 24:11	רמב"ם משנה תורה הלכות אישות פרק כד:יא
If a woman has done one of the following, she is considered to have violated *dat moshe*: going out in the marketplace with the hair of her head uncovered, making vows or taking oaths and not fulfilling them, having intercourse with her husband during the period of her menstruation, not setting apart the dough offering, or feeding her husband forbidden foods – insects, reptiles, and the carcasses of unslaughtered beasts go without saying, but even foods that are untithed.	ואלו הן הדברים שאם עשת אחד מהן עברה על דת משה: יוצאה בשוק ושער ראשה גלוי, או שנודרת או נשבעת ואינה מקיימת, או ששמשה מטתה והיא נדה, או שאינה קוצה לה חלה, או שהאכילה את בעלה דברים אסורים ואין צריך לומר שקצים ורמשים ונבלות אלא דברים שאינן מעושרין.

Uncovered

Maimonides enumerates the ways in which a woman can be divorced without a *ketubah* based on violations of *dat moshe*. These are exactly the same infractions listed in the Mishnah as *dat moshe*, with one exception, "going out in the marketplace with the hair of her head uncovered." The Mishnah classified this infraction explicitly as *dat yehudit*. However, Maimonides formulated the law in accordance with the Babylonian Talmud's determination that there is a biblical obligation for married women to cover their heads.[17]

These two parallel positions around the obligation of a woman's head covering (is it of biblical origin or *dat yehudit*) are outlined in the earlier work of two Talmudists from the thirteenth century: Rabbi Moshe of Coucy who wrote *Sefer Mitzvot Gadol* in the first half of the century, followed by Rabbi Yitzhak of Corbeil who wrote *Sefer Mitzvot Katan* in the second half of the century. Rabbi Coucy echoes Maimonides and classifies a woman's obligation to cover her hair as *dat moshe*; only the secondary head covering is *dat yehudit*. Rabbi Corbeil does not consider head covering to fall into the category of *dat moshe* at all. Head coverings are classified as *dat yehudit*. Within this category, distinctions are made between different spaces and the type of head coverings that must be worn in each space:

---

17. One example in Maimonides' list is clearly rabbinic and thus, begs the question of how he is defining *dat moshe*. Notably, he quotes the Mishnah's statement that she has sexual relations while she is menstruant but explains that she was not actually biblically *niddah*. Rather, she was in danger of being prohibited because of a uterine blood stain in violation of a rabbinic prohibition. He uses the distinct rabbinic language of *ketem* – a blood stain – explaining in detail that she tells her husband that her *ketem* has been permitted by a sage and he finds out that she has lied. He then brings the example of a woman who is considered *niddah* by her neighbors (because she was seen wearing the clothes women wear when *niddah*) and, nonetheless, sleeps with her husband. This, too, is rabbinically prohibited since there is a suggestion of menstruation but not actual proof. Such behavior is certainly considered a serious deviation from religious norms of behavior but does not violate a biblical prohibition. It has been suggested that for Maimonides, *dat moshe* is not a category strictly based on biblical law but includes severe rabbinic prohibitions that border on biblical violations.

Women and Hair Covering – Dat Yehudit

Sefer Mitzvot Gadol, Positive Commandment 48	Amudei Golah (Sefer Mitzvot Katan), *Mitzvah* 184
If a woman has done one of the following, she is considered to have violated *dat moshe* as presented in the seventh chapter of Ketubot: Going out in the marketplace with the hair of her head uncovered, as the school of R. Yishmael taught, "And he shall uncover her head" (Numbers 5:18), this is a warning to the daughters of Israel that they should not go out with uncovered head; making vows or taking oaths and not fulfilling them; having intercourse with her husband during the period of her menstruation; not setting apart the dough offering; or feeding her husband forbidden foods – insects, reptiles, and the carcasses of unslaughtered beasts go without saying, but even foods that are untithed… What is considered to be *dat yehudit*? Those are the modest practices which the daughters of Israel practice. If a woman has done one of the following, she is considered to have violated *dat yehudit*: Going from one courtyard to another by way of an alley with her head uncovered and without the headscarf that all other women wear, even though her hair is covered by a kerchief and not uncovered entirely…	To divorce one's wife, as it is written, "If a man finds evidence of sexual misconduct on her part, he shall write her a bill of divorce and place it in her hand" (Deuteromy 24:1). Evidence of sexual misconduct, such as violating *dat moshe*: Feeding him untithed food, having intercourse with him during the period of her menstruation, not setting apart the dough offering, or making vows and not fulfilling them; or such as violating *dat yehudit*: Going out to the marketplace with her head uncovered, even with a workbasket on her head if she goes out into the public domain – in our society, the hair net called *kupia* is equivalent to the workbasket; but it is permissible to go from one courtyard to another by way of an alley – or spinning in the marketplace with rouge on her face – R. Hananel explained that she spins red wool near her face so that it casts a red glow on her cheeks – or acting flirtatiously with the young men.

Uncovered

Reflected in the two sources above is a kind of ambiguity that remains ongoing regarding the binding obligation for women to cover their hair. While the majority opinion of post-Talmudic discourse reflects the B. Talmud's position of *d'orayta*, there remains a strong indication nonetheless that head covering is a *dat yehudit* obligation (rather than *d'orayta*) as per the Mishnah.

Interestingly, Shulhan Arukh categorized the obligation of head covering as *dat yehudit* although his language is almost verbatim taken from Maimonides:

Shulhan Arukh, Even HaEzer 115:4	שולחן ערוך אבן העזר הל' כתובות סי' קטו
What is *dat yehudit*? The modesty customs practiced by the daughters of Israel. And these are the things that if she violated one of them has transgressed *dat yehudit*: Going out to the marketplace or populated alleyway or courtyard in which many pass through and her head is bare and she does not have on it the headscarf like all of the women even though her hair is covered with a kerchief.	ד איזו היא דת יהודית? הוא מנהג הצניעות שנהגו בנות ישראל. ואלו הם הדברים שאם עשתה אחת מהם עברה על דת יהודית: יוצאת לשוק או למבוי מפולש או בחצר שהרבים בוקעים בו וראשה פרוע ואין עליה רדיד ככל הנשים, אף על פי ששערה מכוסה במטפחות.

Rabbi Yosef Karo uses the language of the Mishneh Torah in describing the types of hair covering *redid* (headscarf) and *mitpahat* (kerchief) as opposed to the *kalata* of the Talmud (retained by Tur in his code). We do not exactly know what types of head covering these might be, although presumably they covered much of the head and hair. However, he stops short of using Maimonides' classification of uncovered hair as a violation of *dat moshe*.

Regardless of the provenance of the obligation, there is an

Women and Hair Covering – Dat Yehudit

undisputed expectation in both of the Talmuds as well as in the *rishonim* and *aharonim* that married women cover their heads.

And in a Woman's Courtyard?

B. Talmud Ketubot 72b	תלמוד בבלי מסכת כתובות עב
Rabbi Zeira discussed it: Where? If we say in the marketplace, this is a violation of *dat yehudit*. And if you say rather that he means she appears this way in her own courtyard, if so, you have not allowed any daughter of our father Abraham to remain with her husband. Abaye said, and some say that Rav Kahana said: From one courtyard to another courtyard or via an alleyway.	הוי בה רבי זירא, היכא? אילימא בשוק, דת יהודית היא! אלא בחצר. אם כן, לא הנחת בת לאברהם אבינו שיושבת תחת בעלה! אמר אביי, ואיתימא רב כהנא: מחצר לחצר ודרך מבוי.

At the end of the *sugya*, the Talmud addresses a woman's obligation to wear a head covering in her own courtyard or private outdoor space. The Talmud then ends with the following, *If so, you have not allowed any daughter of our father Abraham to remain with her husband!*[18] The Talmud concludes that based on the common practice of women,

---

18. This expression, *If so, you have not allowed any daughter of our father Abraham to remain with her husband*, appears in one other source, in B. Talmud Gittin 89a. The Talmud discusses a woman's behavior in the marketplace, although it does not define it as *dat yehudit*. A series of behaviors in the marketplace are just cause for divorce according to Rabbi Meir because they are considered licentious. Examples include eating, walking with an extended neck (arrogantly), or nursing one's child. Rabbi Akiva cites the instance of a woman being talked about by women spinning in the moonlight, regarding her promiscuity with men. Rabbi Yohanan ben Nuri replies that if so (if you force divorce in such a case), you will not allow any daughter of our father Abraham to remain with her husband, for all women will end up under suspicion if such gossip is to be believed.

Uncovered

there is no requirement for married women to cover their heads in their own courtyards even in the presence of others. [19] Certainly, such behavior could not be one which was grounds for divorce without a *ketubah*.[20]

Maimonides, cited above, does not define or refer to what a woman is expected to cover in her own courtyard. Future authorities will disagree on this specific matter when discussing his position. Rabbi Joseph Karo interprets Maimonides as being lenient with regard to a bared head in a courtyard while Rabbi Joel Sirkis rules that Maimonides prohibited women in their private courtyards from going out with bared heads.[21]

Is the Basket Enough?

In later halakhic discourse, the question of how much hair a woman is required to cover becomes a focal point among rabbinic authorities. The earlier Talmudic texts are far from conclusive with regard to defining a specific amount of the head or hair that must be concealed. This is particularly apparent in the Talmudic discussion above where an argument about *kalata* ensues. The Talmud initially states that a *kalata* alone is perceived as bared head according to the standards of *dat yehudit*, even though it fulfills the biblical requirement. In contrast, Rabbi Yohanan states that a woman who goes out with a *kalata* does not have a bared head. Presumably, Rabbi Yohanan's position is that the *kalata* is sufficient to fulfill the requirements of *dat yehudit*.

Since the Talmud's methodology is to prefer finding a resolution to two seemingly conflicting statements rather than present them as opposing positions, it reframes Rabbi Yohanan's statement to be applicable in semi-private space only. According to this reading, in a

---

19. Ritva on Ketubot 72b, based on Rashi, suggests that a woman could go with a bared head, if only a small number of people are in the vicinity.
20. According to Rashi and Tosafot's understanding of this passage. See their commentary to Ketubot 72b.
21. Beit Yosef and Bah on Tur Even HaEzer 115.

public space like the marketplace, Rabbi Yohanan would agree that another head covering is required. The resolution of the two positions in this manner results in the following conclusion: the biblical requirement can be fulfilled with a single head covering like a *kalata*. It also fulfills the *dat yehudit* requirement in less populated areas like alleyways and between courtyards. However, in the marketplace, *dat yehudit* requires an additional head covering beyond the basket.

Types of Head Covering

An inquiry into the types of head coverings and hair ornaments mentioned in rabbinic texts will be helpful in trying to ascertain what women were wearing and how this might concretize some of the theoretical discussion presented above. As mentioned earlier, there is a curious lack of definition. The specifics of how much hair must be covered and what type of covering is acceptable will emerge much later in halakhic discourse.

The *kippah*, which is a head covering worn by men and women, appears among a list of articles of clothing a married woman is entitled to receive upon getting married.[22] A *kippah* for her head was an essential garment, along with a belt and shoes.

Neither Mishnah nor Talmud discuss the requisite size of this *kippah*,[23] nor are any other head coverings mentioned on the list. As

---

22. Mishnah Ketubot 5:8 …And he must provide her with a bed, a mattress, and a reed mat. He must also give her a *kippah* for her head, a girdle for her loins, and shoes every festival, and clothing [valued] at fifty *zuz* [a specific unit of money] every year…

23. The *kippah* is mentioned in passing in Ketubot 75a. The Mishnah states that if a man vows not to marry a woman with blemishes and she is found to have blemishes, the *kiddushin* is annulled. The Talmud discusses the blemishes in question and one of the examples is a mole on her forehead. A question is raised: if the mole is on her forehead, surely he saw it and was reconciled to it! The Talmud answers that it was hidden under the *kippah* on her head so that it is sometimes visible and sometimes not. In this source, it is suggested that the *kippah* was something worn by a woman even before marriage and sometimes covered the forehead and sometimes did not. Neither here nor in the source above, is any size or definition given to the *kippah*. As with many Talmudic sources, it is hard to draw final conclusions regarding the

cited above in Tosefta Sotah 7:3, the priest removes the *kippah* from her head before disheveling her hair, suggesting that at minimum, a married woman would be wearing this head covering when out in public.

Going Out on Shabbat

Mishnah Shabbat Chapter 6:1, 5	משנה מסכת שבת פרק ו
1 - With what may a woman go out and with what may she not go out? A woman may not go out with wool ribbons, nor with flax ribbons, nor with straps on her head…Nor [may she go out] with a frontlet [on her forehead], nor with bangles if they are not fastened to her cap; nor with a cap [under the headdress] into the public domain… 5 - A woman may go out with braids of hair whether of her own [hair], or of another woman, or of an animal. [She may go out] with a frontlet [on her forehead], or with bangles if they are sewn [to the cap]; with a kabul [under the headdress] or with a wig into the courtyard….	א - במה אישה יוצאה, ובמה אינה יוצאה? לא תצא אישה לא בחוטי צמר, ולא בחוטי פשתן, ולא ברצועות, שבראשה…ולא בטוטפת, ולא בסנבוטין, בזמן שאינן תפורין, ולא בכבול ברשות הרבים… ה - יוצאה אישה בחוטי שיער, בין משלה ובין משל חברתה ובין משל בהמה, בטוטפת ובסנבוטין בזמן שהן תפורין; ובכבול ובפיאה נוכרית בחצר…

In Tractate Shabbat, the Mishnah in chapter 6 brings descriptions of hair ornaments that cannot be worn in the public domain on Shabbat (Mishnah 1), and ornaments that can be worn in the public domain (Mishnah 5). The discussion is focused on concern for objects that can be easily removed since a woman may remove her jewelry and

---

kippah and the obligation of women to cover their heads. Pictures from Pompei contemporaneous with the Mishnaic period show women wearing caps that sit on top of their heads but do not cover their hair. It seems to be a net contained within the strictures of a cap. This fits the general implied meaning of *kippah* in the text.

Women and Hair Covering – Dat Yehudit

carry it more than four cubits in a public space (*reshut harabim*), which would violate a biblical prohibition. For this reason, women are not allowed to wear such ornaments, even into their courtyards lest they leave their courtyards and come to carry in public space. In contrast, Mishnah 5 brings examples of hair ornaments that are tied tightly and cannot be easily removed. These, in comparison to loosely tied ornaments, can be worn into a public space.[24] The importance of these *mishnayot* for our topic is that it gives detailed descriptions of what sort of hair ornaments and head coverings women were wearing at the time. The scholar Ze'ev Safrai, in his commentary to the *mishnayot* in Shabbat and Ketubot, integrates different rabbinic sources to summarize the practice of women's head and hair covering. In his opinion, Jewish women covered their heads with a cap or net onto which were woven or attached ornaments. The hair was not fully covered, but the net or cap was obligatory, presumably to fulfill the requirements of *dat yehudit* according to the Mishnah in Ketubot.[25] While there is no reference to *dat yehudit* or biblical requirement to cover hair (and certainly not to *ervah*) in the Talmudic discussion

---

24. In parallel, the Mishnah mentions that the looser hair ornaments such as ribbons or ornaments not tightly attached, could be worn into the *mikvah* while the woman immersed because their looseness did not preclude water from saturating the women's hair completely. The more tightly tied ornaments could not be worn during immersion.

25. See Ze'ev Safrai, Mishnat Eretz Israel, Tractate Ketubot – B (Nashim 3), Lipshitz Publishing House College, Jerusalem, 2013, pp. 437–447, and Ze'ev Safrai, Mishnat Eretz Israel, Tractate Shabbat – A (Moed 1) Lipshitz Publishing House College, Jerusalem, 2020, pp. 210–211, pp. 236–238. Paintings from the Mishnaic period have been found that show non-Jewish women wearing hair ornaments that match those described in Tractate Shabbat. A golden hair net is seen holding back the hair of a woman in Pompeii. Bangles and frontlets appear in another fresco attached to a band or ribbon held in place at the top of her head. In all of the frescoes the woman's hair is neatly combed and parted. In some frescoes the woman wears a cap. Whether Jewish women in the time of the Mishnah wore a unique head covering is impossible to prove. Some rabbinic sources suggest that non-Jewish women, because of their immodesty, went out with completely uncovered hair. Others suggest that they wore a partial head covering while Jewish women wore an additional head covering.

around hair ornaments worn on Shabbat, these descriptive Mishnaic sources seem to reinforce the overall rabbinic attitude toward hair covering in line with modesty customs and the accepted norms of women's hair accessories of the time.

Head Covering Practices in the Rabbinic Era

Outside of the central discussion of head covering found in Ketubot, there are scattered references throughout the Talmudic corpus in both halakhic and *aggadic* texts referencing married women covering their heads and some of their hair. While they do not pertain to the halakhic discussions brought above, the casual manner in which women's head covering is assumed reflects the expectation in Jewish society that women go out in head coverings:

Genesis Rabbah Parasha 17	בראשית רבה (וילנא) פרשה יז
Why does a man go out bareheaded while a woman goes out with her head covered? He said to them: She is like one who has done wrong and is ashamed before people, therefore she goes out with her head covered.	... ומפני מה האיש יוצא ראשו מגולה והאשה ראשה מכוסה? אמר להן לאחד שעבר עבירה והוא מתבייש מבני אדם, לפיכך יוצאת וראשה מכוסה.

For instance, women covering their heads appears in a long midrashic discourse on gender differences between men and women found in Genesis Rabbah. The first part of the *midrash* (not cited) describes biological and social differences between men and women. It then brings a different type of interpretation based on character, cited above: women cover their heads out of shame because they brought sin into the world, a central theme in the passage. This source which is descriptive rather than proscriptive reflects the societal expectations of Jewish women at the time. An almost identical sentiment is found in Avot of Rabbi Natan.[26]

Head Covering for Unmarried Women

Dat moshe and *dat yehudit* appear in the Mishnah and Talmud in the context of a married woman and the possible loss of *ketubah*. Maimonides likewise quotes these in his chapter on the Laws of Matrimony (הלכות אישות), as cited above. However, in the Laws of Prohibited Sexual Relations (הלכות איסורי ביאה), Maimonides prohibits both married and unmarried women from going to the marketplace with their hair uncovered:

Maimonides, Laws of Sexual Prohibitions, 21:17	רמב״ם משנה תורה הלכות איסורי ביאה פרק כא
Daughters of Israel should not walk in the marketplace with uncovered heads, whether unmarried or married.	יז לא יהלכו בנות ישראל פרועי ראש בשוק אחת פנויה ואחת אשת איש

This seems to echo the plain language of the Tannaitic text, Sifrei, cited earlier in the chapter:

Sifrei Bamidbar 11	ספרי במדבר פרשת נשא פיסקא יא
Another opinion. Learn from this that the daughters of Israel should cover their heads. And even though there is	דבר אחר, לימד על בנות ישראל שיהו מכסות ראשיהן. ואף על פי שאין

---

26. Avot of Rabbi Natan Version B, Chapter 9 Clause One: Why does woman cover her head and man not cover his head? A parable. To what may this be compared? To a woman who disgraced herself and because she disgraced herself, she is ashamed in the presence of people. In the same way, Eve disgraced herself and caused her daughters to cover their heads.

no proof of this, there is an allusion to it, "And Tamar took ashes and put them on her head" (II Samuel 13:19).	רְאָיָיה לְדָבָר זֵכֶר לְדָבָר: וַתִּקַּח תָּמָר אֵפֶר עַל רֹאשָׁהּ.

Whereas Sifrei used the ambiguous term "daughters of Israel," Maimonides stated unequivocally that all women, married and unmarried, should cover their heads in the marketplace. Nonetheless, as can be seen in the language and context of where this law appears in Mishneh Torah, this passage is about proper conduct and does not involve an outright halakhic obligation.[27] Indeed, this requirement for single women to cover their heads in the marketplace is not found in earlier halakhic sources[28] and is not codified into later *halakhah*. It is most likely reflective of modesty norms that were prevalent in the Muslim world at the time and place in which Maimonides lived.

Conclusions

Two central positions on the topic emerge from these rabbinic texts. The earlier Tannaitic sources, particularly the Mishnah, Tosefta, and one opinion in the Sifrei, regard hair covering as a binding practice on the daughters of Israel, classified in the Mishnah as *dat yehudit*. Uncovering one's head in the marketplace was associated with promiscuous behavior, which is why a married woman who went about with an uncovered head could be divorced without receiving her *ketubah*.

The second position emerges from the Babylonian Talmud in Ketubot, which is the only Talmudic-era source in which it is stated

---

27. Many commentaries on Maimonides try to interpret this *halakhah* as referring to previously married women such as widows or divorcees. This is both because in practice single women did not cover their hair and because a Mishnah in Ketubot Chapter 2:1 states clearly that a virgin bride goes to her wedding canopy with a bared head or loosened hair. However, Maimonides uses the language of פנויה in *halakhah* 3 and clarifies that it means both a virgin and a non-virgin.

28. It appears both in Tur Even HaEzer 22 and Shulhan Arukh Even HaEzer 21:2, taken verbatim from Maimonides.

clearly that women's head covering involves a biblical obligation. Given the centrality of the Babylonian Talmud in post-Talmudic halakhic discussion, its conclusion that head covering is of *d'orayta* origin had an enormous impact on all post-Talmudic halakhic discourse and is seen by many as authoritative in a way that the earlier rabbinic sources were not.

I have often been asked to "justify" the meaning of the biblical proof text in Sotah as the source for head covering since the Talmud quotes it as the basis of the practice. This type of anachronistic critique questioning the authenticity of *halakhah* has become popular among modern scholars. According to this approach, if the conventional halakhic discourse deviates from the original meaning of the biblical verse, it erodes the authenticity of the practice.[29] While it is interesting to trace the literal meaning of the biblical text in order to tease out the evolution of the halakhic discussion, it must be noted that the Talmud is based on Oral Law (*torah she'baal peh*), which is not bound to the literal meaning of the written Torah and never has been. Head covering for women is an excellent example of the manner in which the Talmud extrapolates a halakhic decision from a biblical verse, even when it is not necessarily the literal meaning of that verse.

Notably, there are no references to a woman's hair being *ervah* in all of the sources brought in this chapter nor is there indication of how much of the head or hair was covered. This reinforces the ambiguity around the legal implications of the "*ervah* statements" in Berakhot, specifically Rav Sheshet who says that the hair of a woman is *ervah*. The interplay between *dat yehudit* and *ervah* will be the focus of the next chapter.

---

29. Even if this verse is interpreted literally as loosening or disheveling the hair, it is clear that women did not appear in public with their hair down as women do today.

Chapter Seven

Women and Hair Covering – *Ervah*

One of the most prevalent informal explanations given for the halakhic mandate of head covering is that, after the wedding ceremony, a woman's hair becomes *ervah*, meaning a type of nakedness, to be seen only by her husband and associated with their sexual intimacy. In the previous chapter, rabbinic texts were cited and analyzed regarding the earliest documented practice of women's head covering, yet nowhere in those discussions was hair referenced as *ervah*. It bears asking, how did the idea that a married woman's hair is *ervah* become part of the halakhic discourse?

In previous Chapters Three, Four, and Five, an extensive analysis of the concept and context of *ervah* and its applications in the Talmudic text was undertaken. Now I will return to the relevant statement regarding hair covering and trace the impact it has had on applied *halakhah*:

B. Talmud Berakhot 24a	תלמוד בבלי מסכת ברכות דף כד עמ' א
Rav Sheshet said: Hair in a woman is *ervah*, as it is written (Song of Songs 4:1), "Your hair is like a flock of goats."	אמר רב ששת: שער באשה ערוה, שנאמר שַׂעְרֵךְ כְּעֵדֶר הָעִזִּים.

Uncovered

The statement by Rav Sheshet that hair is *ervah* appears only once in the Babylonian Talmud. It is not repeated or referenced anywhere in Tannaitic sources or in the Jerusalem Talmud, and it does not lead to any further discussion. Although many sources indicate that married women covered their heads and wore hair ornaments and accessories, it is significant that none of those sources reference Rav Sheshet's statement. This dovetails with the amorphous nature of the entire *ervah* passage in Berakhot, in which a woman's voice, leg [*shok*], hair, and even uncovered pinky is considered *ervah*, and its relevance to applied practice. See Chapter Three for a longer, more in-depth analysis of the topic.

Introducing Kimhit and the Zohar

Head covering based on *dat yehudit* does not specify that all hair must be covered. It also differentiates between the marketplace in which head covering is obligatory and private space where it is not. However, in the post-Talmudic period, the halakhic discussion around hair covering comes to be dominated by the concept of *ervah* rather than *dat yehudit*, perhaps to some extent due to the influence of the Zohar. Zohar, the foundational work in the literature of Jewish mystical thought, introduces an unprecedented and uniquely stringent position in requiring that no hair ever be uncovered on the head of a married woman, even in the privacy of her own home. This position did not become normative immediately, but over the course of time, its impact on *halakhah* is impossible to ignore and it gradually became presented as an ideal in many observant communities.

The inspiration for the Zohar's approach seems to come from a Talmudic passage about a woman named Kimhit:

B. Talmud Yoma 47a	תלמוד בבלי מסכת יומא דף מז עמ' א
It was taught in a Beraita: Kimhit had seven sons and all served as high priests.	תנו רבנן: שבעה בנים היו לה לקמחית וכולן שמשו

260

Women and Hair Covering – Ervah

The Sages asked her how she merited this and she answered: "The walls of my house have never seen the hairs of my head." They said to her, "Many have done so without benefiting."	בכהונה גדולה. אמרו לה חכמים: מה עשית שזכית לכך? - אמרה להם: מימי לא ראו קורות ביתי קלעי שערי. אמרו לה: הרבה עשו כן, ולא הועילו.

The response of the Sages to Kimḥit is startling. They are not impressed with her excessive piety, nor do they validate it by suggesting that all women behave in a similar way.[1] Nonetheless, the Zohar references this passage when it requires that "a woman must not allow even the walls of her house to see a single hair of her head."

Zohar Parashat Naso, 3:125b–126a (translation Daniel C. Matt)[2]	זוהר (במדבר) פרשת נשא [המתחיל בדף קכא עמוד א]
R. Ḥizkiyah said: May a stupor come upon the man who allows his wife to expose the hair of her head! This is one of the rules of household modesty. A woman who exposes her hair for adornment brings poverty upon the household, causes her children to be mediocre in their generation, and causes an alien element to abide in the home. Who causes this? That hair exposed on her head. Now if this is so within the house, how much more so on the street – and how much more so with any other impudence! Therefore, *Your wife*	אתתא דאפיקת משערא דרישה לבר לאתתקנא ביה גרים מסכנותא לביתא וגרים לבנהא דלא יתחשבון בדרא וגרים מלה אחרא דשריא בביתא מאן גרים דא ההוא שערא דאתחזי מרישה לבר, ומה בביתא האי כ״ש בשוקא וכ״ש חציפותא אחרא ובגין כך אשתך כגפן פוריה בירכתי ביתך,

---

1. The Talmud even asks, sardonically, how it came about that her seven sons all served as high priests, since the commission of high priest was supposed to be for life!
2. *The Zohar*, Pritzker Edition, Stanford University Press, 2014, pp. 302–303.

shall be like a fruitful vine in the recesses of your house (Psalms 128:3).
R. Yehudah stated: The hair of the head of a woman being exposed causes other hair [i.e., harsh forces above (Daniel C. Matt)] to be exposed, tainting her. Therefore, a woman must not allow even the walls of her house to see one hair of her head, let alone outside.
"Come and see: Just as in the male, hair is harshest of all, so too for the female. Go and see how much damage is caused by a woman's hair! It has effect above, it has effect below. It causes her husband to be cursed; it causes poverty; it brings an alien element into the home; it deprives her children of repute. May the Compassionate One save us from their impudence.
So, a woman must be concealed in the corners of the house. And if she does so, what is written? *Your children are like olive shoots around your table* (Psalms 128:3). What is meant by like olive shoots? Just as an olive tree does not shed its leaves in either winter or summer, and always retains more value than other trees, so her children excel all other inhabitants of the world. Furthermore, her husband is blessed in all: with blessings from above and blessings from below, with wealth, with children and with grandchildren. ...

אמר ר' יהודה שערא דרישא [דף קכו עמוד א] דאתתא דאתגלייא גרים שערא אחרא לאתגלייא ולאפגמא לה בגין כך בעיא אתתא דאפילו טסירי דביתא לא יחמון שערא חד מרישא כ"ש לבר, ת"ח כמה בדכורא שערא הוא חומרא דכלא הכי נמי לנוקבא, פוק חמי כמה פגימו גרים ההוא שערא דאתתא, גרים לעילא גרים לתתא גרים לבעלה דאתלטייא גרים מסכנותא גרים מלה אחרא בביתא גרים דיסתלק חשיבותא מבנהא, רחמנא לישזבון מחציפו דלהון, ועל דא בעיא אתתא לאתכסייא בזיוותי דביתא ואי עבדת כן מה כתיב (תהלים קכח) בניך כשתילי זיתים, מהו כשתילי זיתים, מה זית דא בין בסתווא בין בקייטא לא אתאבידו טרפוי ותדיר אשתכח ביה חשיבות יתיר על שאר אילנין, כך בהא יסתלקון בחשיבו על שאר בני עלמא ולא עוד, אלא דבעלה מתברך בכלא ברכאן דלעילא ברכאן דלתתא בעותרא בבנין בבני בנין....

Women and Hair Covering – Ervah

The Zohar mandates that a woman cover all of the hair on her head, even in the innermost part of her home, in order to protect her husband and family. Her exposed hair could unleash terrible misfortune into the world, connecting to powerful external forces in the spheres above that could cause harm in the world below. One may speculate that the terrifying language of the Zohar had repercussions for the practices of many Jewish communities that wanted to ensure divine protection from tragedy and ill will, inspiring women to be vigilant about covering their hair. It is known from responsa that the Zohar was influential in some communities in Ashkenaz, even as it was clear that it went far beyond all halakhic requirements. In some Hassidic communities, it remains the source for the custom to completely shave off a woman's hair after her wedding, to ensure that there is never a possibility of exposed hair.[3]

The Responsa of Maharam Alshakar

Rabbi Moses son of Isaac Alshakar (known as Maharam Alshakar), who lived in the fifteenth and sixteenth centuries and served communities in Tunisia, Greece, and Cairo, wrote a responsum about women whose practice it was to uncover some of their hair, in which he rejected the stringent approach of the Zohar as standard practice. The questioner wished to know if the community had cause to protest such a liberal practice. Maharam Alshakar explains (and as we have seen in the earlier discussions of *ervah*) that the definition of *ervah* depends largely on the behavioral norms of a given community.[4]

Since this *responsum* has exerted enormous influence over later halakhic authorities, including those of today, a large selection will be quoted below:

---

3. This is coupled with a fear that even a single hair protruding from the waters of the ritual bath (*mikvah*) will invalidate the immersion of women. See Ellinson, *A Modest Way*, pp. 161–162.

4. It is interesting that Maharam completely ignores the concept of *dat yehudit*, despite its prominence in the Talmudic discussions. This is rather unusual with regard to post-Talmudic discourse, and its absence is hard to explain unless one could argue its presence is assumed.

Uncovered

Maharam Alshakar 35 (translation by Nechama Goldman Barash)	שו"ת מהר"ם אלשקר סימן לה
I was asked a question by a friend about women who expose some of their hair outside of the veil for beauty and whether we should be concerned for the teachings of a person who said this is a break from tradition and an absolute prohibition for it is explicitly said that a woman's hair is *ervah*, and therefore it is appropriate to rebuke them and warn them not to expose their hair. Answer: It is clear that there is no reason to be concerned for this [partially exposed] hair at all since the custom is to expose it and even for *Kriat Shema*. And the hair that is *ervah* is only with regard to hair that a woman is accustomed to cover – and it is thus written in the Talmud that Rabbi Isaac said a handbreadth of a woman is *ervah*, meaning a handbreadth that is normally covered… Furthermore, it is expressly permitted [to uncover this hair] and even for *Shema* and women were accustomed to uncovering and certainly the daughters of Israel were accustomed to such in the days of the Mishnah and Talmud. And it is possible that this was the practice even during the time of the Temple. "A woman must adorn herself but leave her lower temple untouched" (Bava Batra 60b). And the Arukh wrote that when a	תלמסאן שאלה שאלת ממני הידיד אם יש לחוש לאלו הנשים שנהגו לגלות שערן מחוץ לצמתן להתנאות בו לפי מה ששמעונו מי שהורה ואמר כי שקר נחלו אמותינו הנוהגות לגלותו כי הוא איסור גמור ובפי' אמרו ז"ל שער באשה ערוה ולכן ראוי להוכיחן ולהזהירן שלא לגלותו. תשובה. איברא דאין בית מיחוש לאותו שער כלל כיון שנהגו לגלותו ואפילו לק"ש. וההיא דשער באשה ערוה לא מיירי אלא בשער שדרך האשה לכסותו דומיא דטפח והכי איתה בגמרא אמ"ר יצחק טפח באשה ערוה פי' טפח שדרכה לכסות... אדרבה שהתירוהו בפירוש ואפילו לק"ש והעידו שנהגו לגלותו ובודאי כי כן היו נוהגות בנות ישראל בימי חכמי המשנה והתלמוד ז"ל ואיפש' דאפילו בעודן על אדמתן בזמן שבית המקדש קיים כדאיתא בהדיא בפרק חזקת הבתים

Women and Hair Covering – Ervah

woman wrapped up her hair she would leave some out between her ears and forehead opposite the sides of her face and she brings lime and applies it to the hair that she does not braid and lets it fall and creates a bang with it. But a rich woman combs it with perfumes and good oils until the hairs stick together.

And this is the custom today, that the women wrap their hair and leave out hair on the temples that falls onto their face and the Sages called this "temples" as we will explain and it is customary to comb this hair with perfumes and oils like the rich women in days gone by even though it seems that it is not appropriate to do this because of the destruction [over which women would refrain from removing the hair at their temples in mourning] as is written there…

And all that you will find in the Zohar, who was stringent regarding uncovering of hair of the woman, it is possible this was when the custom was to cover but in the Talmud it is clear that it was only talking about hair normally covered and during the recital of *Shema*.

דאמרינן התם "עושה אשה כל תכשיטיה ומשיירת דבר מועט". מאי היא רב אמר בת צדעא שנ' אם אשכחך ירושלם וגומ' ופירש בעל הערוך ז"ל דכתיב בתשובות כשהאשה קולעת שערה משיירת ממנו דבר מועט בין אזניה לפדחתה כנגד צדעתה ומביאה סיד טרוף כשהוא חבוט וטחה אותו שער ואינה קולעת אותו אלא מטילה כנגד פניה זה עושה בת עניים. אבל עשירה שורקתו בבשמים ובשמן טוב כדי שיתחברו שערות זו בזו ולא תהיה כאבלות ויתיפו ע"כ.

וזה המנהג בעצמו הוא מנהג הנשים היום שהאשה קולעת כל שערה ומשיירת שער הצדעים יורד על פניה והוא הוקרא בלשון חכמים "בת צידעא" כמו שנתבאר ונהוגות גם כן לשרוק אותו בבשמים ושמן הטוב כעשירות של אותו הזמן אף על גב דלא חזי למיעבד הכי זכר לחרבן הבית כדאיתא התם...

וכל מה שתמצא בספר הזוהר מקפיד על גלוי שער האשה איפשר דבשער

And there is nothing else to say, we rely on the Talmud and the custom. And let us stand and cry out at those who prohibit this hair for a woman in her household because *hair of a woman is ervah* without knowing about which hair we are talking about and what the *halakhah* is as stated in the Talmud and if this is the case then according to their approach, the eyebrow hair should also be prohibited for it says "hair" and it is also written that all of the hair [of the nazir] shall be shaved, his head and his beard and his eyebrows, etc. "and certainly her face, hands and feet" Should these too be prohibited" And what difference does this [eyebrow] hair make? And if it is because it is the custom for it to be uncovered, here too it is the custom for this hair to be uncovered…

And were I less fearful, I would even say for those women who have been exiled from the land of the uncircumcised (Christendom), whose practice was to cover all of their hair when they were there, they should not be warned about uncovering since they have established their dwelling place here and they are not planning to return. …

שדרכה לכסותו משתעי דבגמר' סתמא נמי קאמר ואמרינן דלא איתמר אלא במה שדרכה לכסות ולק"ש. ואם יש דבר אחר אנן אתלמוא ואמנהגא סמכינן. ובואו ונצווח על אלו האוסרים אותו שער לאשה בתוך ביתה מהייא דשער באשה ערוה בבלי דעת באי זה שער אמרו ולמאי הילכתא איתמ' בגמ' ואלא מעתה לפי דרכם שער גבות עיניה נמי היה להם לאסור דשער קרייה רחמנא נמי דכתיב יגלח את כל שערו את ראשו ואת זקנו ואת גבות עיניו וגומ' וכל שכן פניה ידיה ורגליה דהוה להו נמי למיסרן ומאי שנא אותו שער ואי משום דדרכן להיות מגולין האי נמי דרכו להיות מגולה. ואלמלא דמסתפינא הוה אמינא דאפילו אותן הנשים שבאו מגורשות מארצות הערלים שהיו נוהגות לכסותו כשהיו שם אין להזהירן שלא לגלותו כיון שקבעו דירתן בכאן ואין לומר בהן דעתן לשוב לארצם. ....

Women and Hair Covering – Ervah

...And even more so, with these women who have no intent to return to their original lands, for they did not cover all of their hair because of a prohibition but rather because that was the custom of the women, even the non-Jewish women, to cover all hair. Therefore, even those who would cover all of their hair in their former dwelling place should be allowed to follow the custom of their current dwelling place. And in many situations, the rabbis were lenient in order to avoid a wife becoming repulsive to her husband. And there is no need to continue to explain at length.

Moshe Alshakar

וכל שכן באלו הנשים דליכא למימ' בהו דעתן לשוב לארצם כמו שכתבנו וכל שכן דאפי' בארץ לא היו מכסות אותו משום איסור אלא שלא היה מנהג ארץ לגלותו דאפילו רוב הגויות לא היו נוהגות לגלותו. הילכך אפי' לאותן שהיו נוהגות לכסותו בארצן ראוי להניחן לנהוג כמנהג הארץ אשר גרו בה. ומעשה אמותן הקדושות בידיהן כמו שהוכחנו מהיא דפרק חזקת הבתים דלעיל ובכמה וכמה דברים הקילו רבותינו ז"ל כדי שלא תתגנה האשה על בעלה. ואין צורך באורך. נאם המעוטף באהבתך ולפרידתך קירות לבו מקרקר. משה ן' אל אשקר. נ"ר.

In his responsum, Maharam Alshakar addresses the practice of women in the questioner's community to leave some of their hair uncovered and in doing so, offers a definition for when hair is considered *ervah*. Citing Rashba and many other authorities (not cited in the excerpt above but found in the full responsum), Maharam Alshakar argues that hair that is normally uncovered does not fall under the category of *ervah* even for *Shema* and that this is true not only with regard to one's wife but also with regard to other women. He quotes Rav Natan the son of Yehiel, known as Arukh, who lived in the eleventh century and studied with the last of the *ge'onim*. Rav Natan described how it was acceptable that when a woman wrapped up her hair she would leave some exposed between her ears and forehead on opposite sides of her face using perfumes and fine oils to comb the hair extending past the veil. Four hundred years later, the Maharam notes that the women still do the same, wrapping their hair and leaving hair exposed on the sides, descending over the face.

He concludes by ruling that if a woman goes from a place in which the custom was to cover all her hair to a place where the custom is to allow hair to extend from the veil and frame the face, then women should be allowed to act in accordance with local custom. In other words, he is not concerned that this hair might be considered *ervah* since it reflects the accepted practice of women regarding hair covering, and men will not be sexually aroused by seeing it.

Maharam states an important principle that had already been stated previously by some *rishonim*: hair that is normally uncovered is not considered *ervah* even for the purposes of reciting *Shema*. The type of hair covering required for married women depends on the accepted practice of women in a community. Jewish women's" customs "with regard to hair covering will be the benchmark in defining which hair is considered *ervah*. Furthermore, he suggests that women have been uncovering some hair dating all the way back to the Temple. While it is my opinion that the spirit of *dat yehudit* hovers between the lines of the responsa particularly when focusing on the behavioral norms of women covering their heads, the Maharam Alshakar's *responsa* is representative of the halakhic focus shifting to greater concern for *ervah*. While Maharam Alshakar refuted the Zohar and ruled that some hair could be exposed, there is a move in the following centuries toward greater stringency around *ervah*. For example, Rabbi Moshe Sofer, known as the *Hatam Sofer*, who lived in the eighteenth century, wrote that while the Zohar is not *halakhah*, it has supplanted *halakhah* in firmly defining that women should cover all of their hair all of the time.

Women and Hair Covering – Ervah

Responsa Hatam Sofer Part 1 (Orach Chayim) No. 36 (adapted from the translation of Raphael Blumberg[5])	שו"ת חתם סופר חלק א (אורח חיים) סי' לו
In our region, non-Jewish women do not cover their hair, but Jewish women, scrupulously heeding the words of the Zohar, are quite cautious on this point. Were contemporary authorities to gather for a vote, they might declare, in accordance with the line explained in the Talmud that there is room to be permissive according to the interpretation of Arukh, rather than the Rashbam, [i.e., that the hair outside the tresses need not be covered] and that the *halakhah* is not like the Zohar. Nonetheless, since the custom of the Zohar has caught on….the custom supplants the law, becoming established in its stead… And the general principle is any hair on the head and forehead of a married woman, even in her room, is *ervah* if she does not wear a kerchief on her head, and a hat as well in the market and courtyard where many pass through.	והאמנם בארצותינו שהאומות יוצאות פרועי ראש ואמותינו לא יצאו ונזהרו מאד וחשו לדברי הזוהר והקפידו על זה מאד, אף על גב דאילו היינו עומדים למנין לקבוע הלכה היינו אומרים דאותה שורה מבוארת בש"ס להיתר היינו עפ"י פי' הערוך דלא כרשב"ם ואין הלכה כהזוהר, מ"מ כיון שתפסו המנהג כהזוהר על זה כ' מהר"א שטיין מנהג עוקר הלכה ונעשה הלכה קבוע… הכלל היוצא כל שום שער בשום מקום בראש ופדחת בנשואה אפילו בחדרה ערוה היא אם לא שיש לה מטפחת בראשה ובשוק וחצר של רבים גם כובע…

In his responsum, Hatam Sofer writes that he adopted the Zohar's position since it had become the prevalent custom "in our lands," thereby overturning and supplanting the law. He concedes that this is not the halakhic consensus based on the Talmudic discussion or the *rishonim*, and he agrees with the ideas presented by Maharam Alshaker in principle (although he does not explicitly cite him). He concludes,

---

5. Getsel Ellinson, *The Modest Way*, pp. 158–159.

however, that although according to *halakhah* the practice of women and how much they cover determines what hair is *ervah*, in fact, the custom based on the Zohar supplants the straightforward *halakhah*. This is consistent with Hatam Sofer's attitude in general that custom ultimately determines *halakhah*, even if it replaces or uproots a more straightforward or earlier understanding of the *halakhah*.

Styles began to change at the end of the nineteenth century, and in addition to the pants revolution discussed in Chapter Four, it became the norm in general society for women to be seen in public with their heads uncovered and their hair loose. As a result, women in Jewish communities also began to follow the local fashions and stopped covering their hair. This posed a challenge to rabbinic authorities. Were these women flouting *halakhah*, or could *halakhah* reflect the changed reality? As was analyzed in the previous chapter, a man could divorce his wife if she did not conform to *dat yehudit* practices, but what if she uncovered her hair in conformity with what had become acceptable Jewish practice? Could this be reconciled with the Babylonian Talmud concluding that the obligation for head covering has a biblical origin? In parallel, Rav Sheshet in Berakhot said that women's hair is *ervah*. However, the majority of *rishonim* agreed that *ervah* does not apply to areas of the body that are normally exposed, and this included hair for unmarried women and hair for married women that was typically exposed (e.g., fell outside of their head covering). Could this be extended to all hair if the trend was to completely uncover, thus removing the status of *ervah* from women's hair completely?

Nineteenth-century halakhic compendiums in both Ashkenazic and Sepharadic communities began to acknowledge the actuality of observant women uncovering their heads. Rabbi Yehiel Mikhel Epstein, author of the Arukh HaShulkhan, who lived in Belarus in the nineteenth and early twentieth century, a century after the Hatam Sofer, was one of the first to address this issue:

Women and Hair Covering – Ervah

Arukh HaShulkhan Even HaEzer 21:4	ערוך השלחן אבן העזר כא:ד
Daughters of Israel should not go with bared heads in the marketplace, single women such as widows and divorcees and married women alike. And to go with a bared head in the public thoroughfare is prohibited from the Torah as it is written regarding the *sotah*: "And he bared the head," meaning she does not normally go out like this…	לא תלכנה בנות ישראל פרועות ראש בשוק, אחת פנויה כגון אלמנה וגרושה ואחת אשת איש. ולילך פרועת ראש ברשות הרבים אסור מן התורה, דכתיב בסוטה: וּפָרַע אֶת רֹאשׁ הָאִשָּׁה – מכלל דאינה הולכת כה.

Like virtually all post-Talmud discussion on head covering, Arukh HaShulkhan rules that uncovering the head (for a married woman) is prohibited, as inferred from the *sotah* passage in the Torah. Nonetheless, in practice, married women in his community were flouting rabbinic authority in this regard, a reality that he protests in the laws of *Shema* in Orakh Chaim:

Arukh HaShulkhan *Orakh Hayyim* 75:7 (translation Rafael Blumberg[6])	ערוך השולחן אורח חיים סי' עה
Let us decry the tragic circumstances that have befallen our generation due to our many sins. Jewish women become lax and appear in public bareheaded, and our cries have been to no avail. The incidence of married women exposing their hair like the virgins is a spreading blight! Woe to us that such is our lot!	ז ועתה בואו ונצווח על פרצות דורינו בעוונותינו הרבים שזה שנים רבות שנפרצו בנות ישראל בעון זה והולכות בגילוי הראש וכל מה שצעקנו על זה הוא לא לעזר ולא להועיל ועתה פשתה המספחת שהנשואות הולכות

---

6. Getsel Ellinson, *A Modest Way*, p. 204.

> Even so, it should be legally permitted, at least, for us to pray or recite blessings in the presence of the bare head. Since most women go that way now, it has become like an exposed part of the body.
> As was written in the *Mordekhai* in the name of *Raaviah*, "All we have said about erotic stimulant refers specifically to parts normally unexposed. A virgin's customarily exposing her hair poses no problem, because it causes no erotic thought." Since our married women go out this way there as well, no erotic thought results.

> בשערותן כמו הבתולות, אוי לנו שעלתה בימינו כך! מיהו עכ"פ לדינא נראה שמותר לנו להתפלל ולברך נגד ראשיהן המגולות כיון שעתה רובן הולכות כך והוה כמקומות המגולים בגופה וכמ"ש המרדכי בשם ראבי"ה בספ"ג וז"ל: כל הדברים שהזכרנו לערוה דוקא בדבר שאין רגילות להגלות אבל בתולה הרגילה בגילוי שיער לא חיישינן דליכא הרהור עכ"ל. וכיון שאצלינו גם הנשואות כן, ממילא דליכא הרהור.

While bemoaning this behavior, which he regards as violating a *d'orayta* practice, he rules that habituation of seeing women's hair causes it to cease being *ervah* even when reciting the *Shema*! As a result of eliminating *ervah* as a concern, the amount of head and hair to cover could become solely a matter of *dat yehudit* (rather than *ervah*) as will be presented below.

Similarly, in another part of the world, Ben Ish Hai (Yosef Hayyim 1835–1909) in Baghdad, writes about pious, modest women who uncover their heads:

Women and Hair Covering – Ervah

Ben Ish Hai, Sefer Hukei Nashim, Chapter 17 (adapted from the translation by Moshe Schapiro)	בן איש חי, ספר חקי הנשים, פרק י"ז
First and foremost, a woman must dress in a modest manner and her appearance must be arranged according to accepted customs (of dress). This means that no part of her body other than her face, hands and neck may be exposed. The rest of her body must remain carefully concealed. Women have observed [the manners of] the women of Europe where it is acceptable for women to speak to strangers, yet the Jewish women [of Europe] nevertheless dress in accordance with the above-mentioned guidelines, do not reveal their bodies, only their faces and necks, the palms of their hands and their heads. And although it is true that many of their women do not cover their hair, which is strictly prohibited according to our Law, they have a justification, for they say in their defense that this practice was not accepted among all of their women, [and] both Jewish and non-Jewish women uncover their hair, just like they uncover their hands and their faces and looking at them does not cause immodest thoughts among the men.	תחילה – אופן מלבושיה והופעתה צריכה להיות מסודרת על המנהגים הנחוצים. אסור לה לעשות שום דגמת וצורת לבוש אשר יגלה משהוא מבשרה. כי האשה אסור לה שיתגלה דבר מגופה, רק פניה, צוארה וכפות ידיה. ושאר אבריה כלם עטופים. והיבטו הנשים על אנשי אירופה, מנהג לא להסתר מפני זרים, ובכל זאת מלבושיהם מסדרים, לא מתגלה מגופם, רק פניהם וצוארם, כפות ידיהם וראשם. ונכון ששערם מגלה, ולפי הדין שלנו אסור הדבר, אבל יש להם איזה התנצלות, כי אומרים לא נתישב המנהג הזה אצל כל נשותיהם, מבנות אמתם חוץ לאמתם, נעשה גלוי השער כמו גלוי פניהם וכפות ידיהם ואינו גורם הרהור אצל האנשים במבט עיניהם.

Ben Ish Hai, like Arukh Hashulkhan, writes that *halakhah* obligates women to cover their hair. However, he puts forth a justification for

273

Uncovered

the defense of those women who are going around with uncovered hair by equating it to uncovered hands and faces which do not cause any sort of sexual stimulation. He also concedes that Jewish women in Europe dressed modestly in general, albeit with bared heads, and does not issue an absolute ruling in this regard. It is interesting that across the Jewish world, from Baghdad to Belarus and Lithuania, women began uncovering their hair following contemporary styles and the acceptance to uncover among non-Jewish women.

In his twentieth-century *responsa*, Rabbi Moshe Feinstein largely follows the position set out by Arukh HaShulkhan, arguing that women's hair can no longer be considered *ervah* since it is commonly left uncovered, even in Jewish society.[7] Nonetheless, the elimination of ervah does not negate the uncontested biblical prohibition for a married woman to go out with an uncovered head. Rav Moshe makes innovative use of the ervah passage in Berakhot to define the parameters of *dat yehudit*; the amount of hair that a woman may leave uncovered in a public venue. The statement in Tractate Berakhot, *the tefah of a woman is ervah*, was understood by the *rishonim* onward to mean that up to a tefah of what is normally covered can be seen by a man when reciting the *Shema*. Rav Moshe allows women to uncover up to a *tefah* (approximately 8 cm) of their hair, as is permitted with other places on a woman's body that are considered *ervah*:

Igrot Moshe Even HaEzer 1:58 (adapted from the translation by Raphael Blumberg[8])	שו"ת אגרות משה אבן העזר חלק א סימן נח
The actual prohibition is stated in Tractate Ketubot 72b, in the name of Rabbi Yishmael who read *p'ra* the	הנה עצם האיסור נאמר בכתובות דף ע"ב תנא דב"ר ישמעאל מקרא

---

7. *Igrot Moshe, Orah Hayyim* I:42 "Even the married women became accustomed to go with heads uncovered. Even though it is prohibited, it is not *ervah* regarding *Keri'at Shema* and words of Torah".

8. Getsel Ellinson, *A Modest Way*, pp. 159–160.

Women and Hair Covering – Ervah

head of the woman as a warning to the daughters of Israel not to go out with unkempt heads and it is not stated that Jewish women should not go out with their hair uncovered. In other words, it depends on the degree of dishevelment – at issue is the hair of the head being unkempt – not merely uncovered. As a few exposed strands cannot render all her hair "unkempt" their exposure poses no problem. For if the prohibition was referring to all hair, it would have been appropriate to write that any small amount of hair is significant but when it specifies head, it is clear that it is talking about the entire head...

...and even those who cite the Remah who writes that for a woman other than his wife, even less than a *tefah* is *ervah*, one should not make this distinction with hair, for the actual flesh is different since...unmarried women do not need to cover their hair, nor does a married woman not need to cover in her house...

Coming from so great a scholar as Hatam Sofer both the first law [to cover all of her hair] and the second law [the strict practice of covering the hair at home] are worthy ones to follow, especially as it achieves the modesty of Kimhit, mentioned by Darkei Moshe. Even so, it is clear that those who wish to be lenient ...should not be considered to violate *dat yehudit* God Forbid. Even a pious Torah scholar should not avoid marrying such a woman, if she is herself God-fearing scrupulously observant and of good

דופרע את ראש האשה אזהרה לבנות ישראל שלא יצאו בפרוע ראש, ולא נאמר אזהרה שלא יצאו בשערותיהן מגולות, משמע שתלוי בחשיבות פריעה על הראש בכולל שבשביל גילוי מעט שערות אין להחשיב שהראש הוא פרוע. שאם היה נאמר האיסור על השערות היה שייך לומר שנידון כל מעט שערות בפני עצמן אבל כשנאמר על הראש הרי יש לידון על הראש בכולל.

...גם בשערות יש חלוק זה דאין מקום להחמיר בשערות יותר מגופה כיון דכל האיסור הוא משום שנחשבו מקום מכוסה, וממילא נראה דאף להי"א שברמ"א דבאשה אחרת אפילו רפחות מטפח הוא ערוה נמי לא יפלוג בשער, דשאני בשר דבכל הנשים הוא מקום מכוסה .... דהא בתולות אין מכסות וכן בביתה אינה צריכה לכסות...

ולכן שיטת החת"ס בזה הוא דבר תמוה. ....ולכן לדינא אף שמן הראוי שיחמירו הנשים לכסות

| character. But [the amount to leave out] is about 2 fingerbreadths in height, since the face is approximately two *tefahim*, and it will be in total, less than *tefah* of exposed hair and more than that is prohibited. | כדסובר החת"ס הואיל ויצא מפומיה דגאון גדול כמותו ... ובדין השני הא איכא גם מעלה דצניעיות דקמחית שכתב הד"מ, אבל פשוט שאלו הרוצות להקל בשני הדינים אין להחשיבן לעוברות על דת יהודית ח"ו, ואין להמנע אפילו לת"ח ויר"ש מלישא אשה כזו אם היא יראת שמים ומדקדקת במצות ובעלת מדות. אבל הוא רק ערך ב' אצבעות בגובה שהפנים הוא ערך ב' טפחים ויהיה בצרוף פחות מטפח ויותר אסורה. |

This blending of the boundaries of *ervah* into *dat yehudit* gave women a degree of latitude in permitting some of their hair to be uncovered, in contrast to the Zohar and the subsequent approaches based on it. Accordingly, some women uncover their hair in the front or in the back or even at the top of their heads as long as it does not exceed the *tefah* limit.

Although the idea that a source of *ervah* can lose its status due to familiarity is well established in the *rishonim*, not all halakhic authorities agree with Arukh HaShulhan's analysis. Mishnah Berurah, written in the early twentieth century by Rav Yisrael Meir Kagan, known as Hafetz Hayim, remains steadfast in his position that a married woman's hair remains eternally *ervah*:

Women and Hair Covering – Ervah

Mishnah Berurah 75:10 (adapted from the translation of Raphael Blumberg[9])	משנה ברורה סימן עה
Hair that is accustomed to be covered – even if it is her practice only to cover in the market and not in the house or courtyard – in any event, it is *ervah* according to all opinions, even in the house and it is prohibited to recite [the *Shema*] opposite if even a little is uncovered. And know, that even if the way of a woman and her friends is to go in the market with an uncovered head in the matter of the promiscuous women, it is prohibited, similar to the manner of uncovering the *shok*, which is prohibited according to all, since the hair must be covered by law..... [and there is a Torah prohibition for it is written "and he bared the head of the woman," which means her head was covered]. Furthermore, all daughters of Israel who hold by *dat moshe* are careful about covering this from ancestral times until now, as it is in the category of *ervah* and it is prohibited to recite *Shema* in its presence. It [Shulkhan Arukh] only comes to exclude unmarried women for whom it is permitted to go with an uncovered head, or, in the case of married women, it singled out hair that falls out of the veil (or hair net), for this is dependent on local custom. [However] if the	(י) שדרכה לכסותו - ואפילו אם אין דרכה לכסותו רק בשוק ולא בבית ובחצר מכל מקום בכלל ערוה היא לכו"ע אפילו בבית ואסור שם לקרות נגדה אם נתגלה קצת מהן. ודע עוד דאפילו אם דרך אשה זו וחברותיה באותו מקום לילך בגילוי הראש בשוק כדרך הפרוצות אסור וכמו לענין גילוי שוקה דאסור בכל גווני וכנ"ל בסק"ב כיון שצריכות לכסות השערות מצד הדין [ויש בזה איסור תורה מדכתיב ופרע את ראש האשה מכלל שהיא מכוסה]. וגם כל בנות ישראל המחזיקות בדת משה נזהרות מזה מימות אבותינו מעולם ועד עתה בכלל ערוה היא ואסור לקרות כנגדן. ולא בא למעט רק בתולות שמותרות לילך בראש פרוע או כגון שער היוצא מחוץ לצמתן שזה תלוי במנהג

---

9. Ellinson, pp. 202.

| daughters of Israel do not allow any hair to be revealed, even the smallest amount, then it is (all) in the category of *ervah* and it is prohibited to recite [*Shema*] in its presence. Otherwise, it does not, since men are used to seeing it. | המקומות שאם מנהג בנות ישראל בזה המקום ליזהר שלא לצאת אפילו מעט מן המעט חוץ לקישוריה ממילא בכלל ערוה היא ואסור לקרות כנגדן וא"ל מותר דכיון שרגילין בהן ליכא הרהורא וכדלקמיה: |

According to Mishnah Berurah, hair remains *ervah*, even if the normal practice in the marketplace is for women to uncover their hair. Since, according to his analysis, the [married] daughters of Israel covered their hair from the giving of the Torah onward, to do otherwise is to display *ervah*, akin to an exposed thigh, regardless of what is considered acceptable in general society. As most people would agree that hair today is no more sexual than an exposed face, the idea of a married woman's hair reflecting nakedness seems, to some people, to be a form of religious extremism. The Mishnah Berurah recognizes the discrepancy in comparing exposed flesh to exposed hair, acknowledging that unmarried women's hair is not *ervah*, because the custom is that unmarried women do not cover their hair. However, and this is the important part of his interpretation, he addresses this point by arguing that since it is prohibited by *halakhah* for married women to go out with bared heads independent of its *ervah* status, their hair becomes *ervah* after marriage by definition, regardless of local custom. Nonetheless, he is not as extreme as Zohar or Hatam Sofer, and he does allow for some hair to be exposed where it is the accepted custom as seen in the Maharam et al.

In contrast, at around the same time that Rabbi Kagan wrote Mishneh Berurah, Rabbi Yosef Messas, a halakhic authority in Morocco in the twentieth century, defends the practice of married women in North Africa who started to go out with uncovered hair after they were influenced by contemporary French fashion.

Rabbi Messas concluded that the obligation for married women to cover their heads in public, and its biblical basis derived from uncovering the *sotah*'s head in the Torah, was relevant only when head covering was the dominant custom within the Jewish community:

Rav Yosef Messas, Collected Writings Volume 3, p. 211	הרב יוסף משאש אוצר המכתבים כרך 3, עמ' ריא
There was a strict prohibition for married women to uncover their head, here, following the traditional practice, and so it was in all cities of the Maghreb before the arrival of the French, but within a short time of their arrival, the daughters of Israel broke this boundary…no reproof was of use…and now all of the women go out with bare heads, hair uncovered…and therefore I endeavor to find merit in their ways [*le-lamed aleihen zechut*], for it is impossible to conceive of returning the matter as it was…and when I looked into the writings of halakhic authorities that preceded me, I found only stringency upon stringency and prohibition upon prohibition…	איסור גלוי הראש לנשואות היה חמור אצלנו פה מחזק[ה], וכן בכל ערי המערב טרם בוא הצרפתים, אך אחרי בואם במעט זמן, פרצו בנות ישראל גדר בזה.... לא הועילה שום תוכחת... ועתה כל הנשים יוצאות בריש גלי פרועי שער...ובכן נתתי לבי ללמד עליהם זכות, כי אי אפשר להעלות על לב להחזיר הדבר כמאז... ובגשתי לחפש בדברי הפוסקי[ם] אשר לפני, מצאתי רק חומרא על חומרא ואסור על אסור...
Ibid., p. 213	הרב יוסף משאש אוצר המכתבים עמ' ריג
The prohibition is not about uncovered hair per se, but rather about the daughters of Israel who were accustomed to cover their heads, because at the time that it was considered modest for a woman to do so, and a woman who uncovered her	אין האסור מצד עצם הדבר של גילוי שער, רק מצד מנהג בנות ישראל שנהגו לכסות ראשן, משום שחשבו בזמנם שיש בזה צניעות לאשה, והמגלה

hair was considered to be breaking the barriers of modesty, and for this reason the Torah warned all daughters of Israel not to behave contrary to the custom of the daughters of Israel. Accordingly, now that all the daughters of Israel have concurred that there is no issue of modesty in covering the head…the prohibition has been fundamentally uprooted and has become permissible.	שערה נחשבת פורצת גדר הצניעות, ולזה הזהירה תורה לכל בת ישראל שלא תעשה הפך מנהג בנות ישראל בזה. וא״כ]=ואם כן[עתה שכל בנות ישראל הסכימה דעתן שאין להן בכסוי הראש שום צניעות... נעקר האסור מעיקרו ונעשה היתר.

In a radical departure from the entire halakhic discourse in the wake of the B. Talmud's declaration that head covering for married women is a biblical obligation, Rav Messas contextualizes the biblical passage in Sotah based on his understanding of Rashi's commentary. Based on Rashi (and the Tosefta), he explains that the purpose of uncovering the *sotah*'s hair was disgrace and humiliation. This was pertinent, he writes, because at the time it was considered immodest or coarse for a woman's head to be uncovered. He concludes that since *dat yehudit* is based on societal norms and communal practice, if women stop covering their hair without societal consequence, the practice is no longer halakhically binding.[10] While Rabbi Messas was boldly innovative in finding justification for the increasing practice of observant women to uncover their hair, in truth, his approach, while interesting and even convincing, has largely been rejected. Most tellingly, Rav Ovadia Yosef, one of the foremost halakhic authorities

---

10. Whether or not one agrees with Rav Messas's conclusions, it reflected the increased practice of women in his time, and it is the responsibility of a halakhic authority to reinterpret and redirect halakhic conversation in keeping with the needs of his community. It is not fundamentally different from the great halakhic leap taken by the Hatam Sofer in mandating that women cover all of their hair even in the privacy of their own homes. The two voices, those of Rav Messas and the Hatam Sofer, reflect the two ends of the spectrum of halakhic discourse. To this day, there are Orthodox women whose practices reflect each of these positions.

in Israel in the twentieth century, accepted Rav Messas's approach in principle, but rejected the possibility that the biblical obligation is linked in any way to contemporary practice. He prefered to follow the guidelines of Maharam Alshakar, cited earlier in the chapter:

Yabia Omer, Even HaEzer 4:3 (translation Michael Broyde)	יביע אומר אבן העזר ד, סימן ג
Today, it has become widespread practice for God-fearing women to go out with a kerchief or hat, but without an additional headscarf or veil, and no one makes a fuss. We must conclude that only the basic covering of one's hair, which is biblical in nature, is obligatory irrespective of changes in practice, and is unchanging for all time. However, with respect to the modest practices of Jewish women, whatever the contemporary practice is although it is lenient, can be accepted. This accords with the ruling of Maharam Alshakar who permits women, in places where the practice is for all to do so, to go about with hair protruding from outside their tresses.	והנה היום פשט המנהג שהנשים יראות ה' יוצאות במטפחת או בכובע בלבד בלי צעיף או רביד, ואין פוצה פה ומצפצף. וע"כ דדוקא עצם כיסוי הראש שהוא דאורייתא הוא מחייב המציאות לעולם ולא ישתנה בשום זמן, אבל מנהג בנות ישראל שנהגו לצניעות כל שהמנהג בכל העיר להקל אזלינן בתר מנהגא. ודמי למ"ש מהר"ם אלשקר (סי' לה) להתיר במקום שנהגו הנשים לצאת בשערות שחוץ לצמתן. ע"ש.

Rav Ovadia affirms that the immutable obligation of head covering, based on the biblical text, cannot be overturned by a change in common practice. However, in the source cited above he was willing to be lenient as to the form of head covering, based on the accepted practice in a given community.[11]

---

11. It should be noted that in other sources he is more stringent about the amount of hair that must be covered.

Conclusion

In the late nineteenth and early twentieth centuries, in parts of Europe and its colonies, it had become common practice for women to go out with bared heads. In keeping with the times, religious married women, among them the wives of prominent rabbis, began to go out with bared heads, despite formidable rabbinic opposition. This influenced the rabbinic discourse, with authorities such as Rabbi Messas and Ben Ish Hai willing to recognize that *dat yehudit* no longer included head covering for married women. Had more major halakhic voices agreed with their positions, it is possible that women would not be covering their hair today outside of the most restrictive communities.

Nonetheless, the majority of rabbinic opinion stood firm, both among Sephardi and Ashkenazi authorities, that head covering remained obligatory. While a small percentage of Orthodox women wear the double hair coverings required by the Talmud, Maimonides, and Shulkhan Arukh, in many communities, women cover all or most of their hair, even in the privacy of their home.

Modern Practice and Interpretation

Several developments over the last half century should be noted when discussing women's hair covering today.. First, many women who identify as Torah observant – keeping Shabbat, *kashrut*, and *mikvah*, praying in an Orthodox synagogue, sending their children to Orthodox schools – nonetheless continue the trend that began in the nineteenth century and do not cover their hair at all. It is my experience that usually this is not based on strict adherence to *halakhah* in the manner of Rav Messas or Ben Ish Hai. Rather it is usually due to reasons of comfort, fashion, the custom of the woman's mother (who did not cover her hair), or because it does not speak to a woman as a meaningful *mitzvah*. Furthermore, it is no longer considered grounds for divorce without receiving *ketubah*[12] nor are these women prevented in any way from participating in communal

---

12. *Igrot Moshe, Even HaEzer*, Vol 1: 114; *Yabia Omer* Vol. III, *Even HaEzer* 21.

events or being fully part of a religious community. In fact, a man without a *kippah* stands out far more than a woman without a head covering at any religious gathering since single women are expected to bare their heads in public.

Second, there has been an increase of female voices actively engaged in studying the sources and searching for significance behind the practice of hair covering. Following are a sampling of different learned women who have expressed opinions about their decision to cover their hair:

Rabbanit Oriya Mevorach, "Why Do I Love my Head-Covering?" (Translation from Deracheha)

I'm aware that my full head-covering labels me as a *frum* woman, even though my attitudes might surprise people who have stereotypes about religious people…I am happy for people to see me first of all as a *frum* (observant) woman and only afterwards to get to know me deeply and be as surprised as they wish.

Rabbanit Chana Henkin, "Mo'adon Ovedot Hashem" (translation from Deracheha):

When a man and woman marry, the barriers of modesty between them fall. This is an expression of the bonding of the couple together as "they became one flesh." From now on, the members of the couple will stand together on the same side of the barrier of modesty that separates them and other people. At the same time that Halakha sanctifies the physical connection between the couple, it creates a special barrier around the couple. The same halakha that allows the woman to reveal a handbreadth [to her husband], obligates her to cover a handbreadth [with regard to everyone else]. Halakha says to the woman: things that were forbidden are now permitted.
But revealing the head in public – which was permitted – becomes forbidden. Thus a balance is created and holiness is preserved in this new and sensitive situation.

> Rabbanit Dr. Meirav (Tubul) Kahana, from Olam Katan, May 2019 (translation from Deracheha)
>
> At the end of the day, after all the discussion and clarification of the matter of head-covering, its value and significance, we also need to say simply and with submission that thus the Oral Torah taught us, that the basis of head-covering is a Torah-level obligation. It is so difficult to exercise the muscle of submission regarding matters that are not understood and clear to us. To simply fulfill them because so commanded the Creator of the world. Especially in our generation, thinking and enlightened on the one hand, connecting and feeling on the other – what isn't understood or what we don't "feel" remains out of bounds. Indeed, we must look deeply, clarify, investigate and understand; there is great importance in connecting with mitzvot and to fulfilling them in joy. But the beginning and end of all mitzva fulfillment is the aspect of doing the will of one's Creator…

Some of these voices express a sense of the dignity inherent in the *mitzvah*, symbolic identification of a married woman in public, the expression of humility before God in the manner of a *kippah*, the need for greater modesty once married, and connecting to a female ritual. Women's voices weighing in on this topic is in and of itself an innovation. For the first time in Jewish history women are being heard as they embrace and/or grapple with the gender differences in halakhic Judaism. While attempts to find meaning are always welcome, it is also important to recognize that none of the reasons mentioned above (dignity, symbolic identification, humility) are explicitly stated in the rabbinic and halakhic sources. The source in Tractate Ketubot states that a married woman has to cover her head when going out in public along with a series of other behaviors that mandate her modesty. In Tractate Berakhot, the concern is solely for a man's sexual arousal. In other words, interpretive meaning has the potential to infuse a given ritual with greater significance, but to my mind it does not fully uproot any of the earlier original discussions that gave shape and definition to the practice.

Third, many young women, particularly in Israel, who cover

Women and Hair Covering – Ervah

only a fraction of their hair, have come to regard hair covering as a women's *mitzvah*, seeking to observe it on their own terms outside of the parameters set out by rabbinic authorities. As often happens, particularly for women learning about gendered *mitzvot*, there can be a simultaneous movement toward and away from the practice. Many are not interested in protecting men from *ervah* or in measuring how much of their head must be covered by estimating the area of a *tefah*. At the same time, they are attracted to a Jewish female ritual dating back thousands of years. They choose to cover their head symbolically, as a sign of their status as married women and in connection to an established women's practice.

One of the styles most reflective of this trend is a wide headband which covers the top of the head but very little hair. According to Rav Ovadia's definition above that any practice of head covering practiced by the daughters of Israel is legitimate, such a hair covering should be validated by rabbinic authorities, but often it is not. Below is a *responsum* of Rabbi Nachum Rabinovitch who echoes the sentiment cited above in the name of Rav Ovadia:

Si'ach Nachum 105 (translation adapted from Deracheha)	שו"ת שיח נחום סימן קה
However, even when a covering is required, if a small amount of the hair emerges from under the covering, that's also fine…and Beit Yosef cites the Rashba in the name of Ra'avad: "Her face and hands and feet…and her hair outside of her hair-binding, which isn't covered – we aren't concerned about them"…In summary, according to basic *halakhah* one must cover most of the hair of the head, but it is permissible to leave out a bit of hair, and not specifically a certain amount of hair,	... אולם גם כשצריך כיסוי, אם מקצת מן השיער יוצא מחוץ לכיסוי גם זה בסדר, ... ובבית יוסף שם מביא את הרשב"א בשם הראב"ד: "פניה וידיה ורגליה.... ושערה מחוץ לצמתה שאינה מתכסה אין חוששין להן."... לסיכום: מעיקר הדין צריך לכסות את רוב שיער הראש, אבל מותר להוציא קצת שיער,

but as is customary in the community of those who keep Torah and *mitzvot* to which she belongs.	ולאו דווקא שיעור מסוים אלא כפי הנהוג בחברה של שומרי תורה ומצוות אליה היא משתייכת.

Rabbi Rabinovitch does not define what part of the head can be left uncovered. He emphasizes that the determining factor is the practice in a community committed to Torah and *mitzvot*. In addition, Rabbi Rabinovitch was known to agree publicly that a headband, if accepted by the community as a head covering, would be an acceptable halakhic application of *dat yehudit*. He did not, however, write this in a formal *responsum* and, as noted, women who cover their hair in this way do not usually ask for rabbinic permission.

Similar to the headband, the wig as a head covering is a fascinating issue in which rabbinic authority interacts and, to some degree, clashes with women's desire to be fashionable and look attractive. It seems that as far back as the Mishnah in Shabbat,[13] women wore wigs made out of human or animal hair. It is not clear whether the Mishnaic wig is similar to the human hair wigs worn by religious women today or was used only as a hair extension, to thicken a woman's own hair. What is clear from the Mishnah and subsequent Talmudic discussion is that she is considered to be more attractive with it than without it which is why she is allowed to wear it into the courtyard on Shabbat.

More than one thousand years after the Mishnah, as *ervah* dominated the discourse, with rabbis calling on women to cover all of their hair, wigs seemed to be an ideal solution. They cover all of a woman's hair and yet, she remains attractive to her husband, an ongoing concern addressed by the Sages and the post-Talmudic authorities with regard to hair and head coverings. Four hundred years ago, Rabbi Yehoshua Boaz in his book *Shiltei Giborim*, anticipated

---

13. Mishnah Shabbat Chapter 6 Mishna 5: A woman may go out with strands of hair, whether from her own, or whether from another, or whether they are from an animal.... with a woolen cap or with a wig to the courtyard....

Women and Hair Covering – Ervah

the trend of human hair wigs in different shades of color and varying styles and even wigs that are not discernable from natural hair and are often more attractive than a woman's own hair. In his gloss to the *Rif* he asserted that a woman's hair constitutes *ervah* only when it is attached to her scalp.[14] Whether the wig is made of her own hair or that of another woman's, even if it is an "adornment creating the impression of uncovered hair, it poses no problem."

Thus, a permissive halakhic framework was established, particularly within communities most insistent that a married woman's hair is *ervah* and must be completely covered. Nonetheless, wigs remained and continue to remain a subject of controversy given the increased attraction and attention they can bring to a married woman. There are rabbinic voices that forbid women from wearing attractive wigs due to concerns for immodesty and latent promiscuity, for example, the nineteenth-century Rabbi Hayyim Hazekiah Medini in his book *Sdei Hemed*:

Sdei Hemed, Asefat Dinim 4:3 (translation Raphael Blumberg[15])	שדי חמד אסיפת דינים אות ד סימן ג:
It has been clearly proven that the wig should not be permitted to married women…and this is in accordance with the law. For us in the Diaspora, all the exiles we have experienced until today in France, Spain, Portugal etc. have been due to the envy aroused against us by the lack of a discernable difference between Jew and nobleman. Even if there is no outright prohibition, it is still improper for married Jewish women to wear wigs in our region.	הוכיחו בראיות ברורות שאין להתיר פאה נכרית לנשואות...זה מצד הדין, אנו בגולה, כל הגירושים עד היום הזה מצרפת, ספרד פורטוגל וכדומה, כולן היו מחמת הקנאה שמעוררת עלינו, שלא ניכר בחוצות וברחובות הבדל בין איש יהודי לאחד השרים. אף אם אין

---

14. Shiltei Giborim, gloss to Rif Shabbat 29a (chapter 6), aleph.
15. Ellinson, pp. 150–151.

It is immodest and not for such women were we redeemed from Egypt. Here, where the custom has not spread and the strict view has taken hold, it is obviously forbidden to breach it. Our women do not wear wigs and those women from cities in which the custom is breached are an inconsequential minority. Heaven forbid that we should learn from their corruption.	איסור גמור, מכל מקום לא נאות לנשים נשואות מבני אמהות לעשות כן במקומינו, כי אין זה מדרכי הצניאות ולא בשביל נשים כאלו נגאלו ממצרים. פיטא שמבומותינ שלא נתפשט המנהג, כבר קבלנו דעות האוסרים, ואסור לפרוץ גדר, במבומותינו לא נמצ מנהג זה, וא המצא ימצא אחת מעיר פורצת גדר, בטלה במיעוטה, וחלילה לנו ללמוד.

In contrast, Rav Moshe Feinstein ruled that wigs are permissible and rejected any concern for immodesty even when a wig strongly resembled or exceeded the attractive quality of a woman's hair. Common Ashkenazi practice is to permit wigs in even the most stringent of communities, although some require a hat on top of the wig:

Igrot Moshe Even HaEzer Vol. II, 12 (translation Raphael Blumberg[16])	אגרות משה אבן העזר ב סימן יב
Although some sages forbid the use of wigs, most allow it, including our chief halakhic authorities. Since we find no prohibition in the Talmud, we cannotlearn from other sources that forbid it because of *mar'it ayin*, possible suspicion on the part of others.	אף שיש מי שחושש לאזור פאה נכרית, מכל מקום רוב רבותינו מתירים גם אלו שאנו סומכים עליהם לעיקרי ההוראה. כיוון שלא מצאנו איסור בגמרא, אין

---

16. Ibid., pp. 152–153.

Women and Hair Covering – Ervah

One can usually discern that a woman is wearing a wig, and even if a man cannot tell, in the vast majority of cases a woman can. Those few instances in which a woman cannot tell, provide the rabbis with insufficient reasons to forbid it. Another reason not to apply *mar'it ayin*: Everyone knows that a woman may be wearing a wig, and will assume her to be reputable.

You cannot halakhically prevent your esteemed Rebbetzin from wearing a wig. Even if you wish to be strict, you may not force your own strictures upon her for this is exclusively her realm. She is behaving lawfully following the majority view, the one that seems right and you cannot be strict with her even if she does not cover her wig at all.

ללמוד ממקומות אחרים שאסרו משום מראית עין. זאת ועוד, רוב הפעמים ניכר שהשערות הם מפאת נכרית, ואף אם אינו ניכר לאנשים, לנשים ודאי ניכר ברובא דרובא. בשביל מה שנזדמן לעתים רחוקות שאינו ניכר, לא אסרו. ויש עוד טעם גדול לא לאסור משום מראית העין, כיוון שיודע לכל שיש ללבוש פאה נכרית, והיא מוחזקת לאשה כשרה.

להלכה, אין כובדו יכול מנוע מאשתו הרבנית החשובה מללבוש פאה נכרית, שאף אם הוא רוצה להחמיר אינו יכול להטיל חומרותין עליה, שזהו רק דין שלה. כיוון שהיא עושה כדין, שהוא דעת רוב הפוסקים, וגם נראה כדעתם, אינו יכול להחמיר עליה, אף אם לא תכסה כלל את הפאה.

I particularly appreciate Rav Moshe's strong rebuke to the husband who is trying to restrict his wife from wearing a wig because of his own personal wish to be stringent. As Rav Moshe writes, "this is exclusively her realm" and since she is behaving according to the majority opinion, he has no right to interfere with her practice!

Notably, the last Lubavitcher Rebbe, Rav Menachem Mendel Schneerson, strongly endorsed the wearing of wigs:

> **Likutei Sichot 13, p. 189**
>
> Wearing a *shaitel* (wig) has a beneficial impact on children and grandchildren, livelihood and health, as the Zohar states…when a Jewish woman walks in the street without a hair covering, there is not a discernable difference between her and others. However, when she wears a *shaitel*, one can tell that she is a Jewish religious woman… A woman who wears a scarf on her head will tend to take it off in certain cases because of discomfort. This in contrast to a woman who wears a wig. Even if President Eisenhower were to walk in, she will not remove it.

The Rebbe felt so strongly about wigs being an ideal form of hair covering that a special fund was established in Chabad for needy brides to assist them in buying beautiful wigs that would assure their complete compliance with the full *mitzvah* of hair covering. Today the technology of wigs has evolved (and along with it the price) so that the top of the wig is engineered with materials that completely mimic the appearance of a woman's scalp seen through the part in the wig and make it even harder to tell when a woman is wearing a wig.

It is interesting that in Modern Orthodox communities, the full wig quickly evolved into the fall, a hair piece which starts further back on the women's head, allowing her natural hair to blend seamlessly into the added hair. The adaptation of the wig into the fall with better quality engineering and higher quality hair shows how women have extended the boundaries of the permissible by adapting the specific medium (in this case, the constantly improving wig making techniques) in a way that empowers and beautifies them.

Even in Sephardi communities, it has proven impossible to ban the wearing of wigs despite Rav Ovadia strongly condemning their use and criticizing Sephardi women who reject their own traditions and rabbinic rulings in favor of the customs and rulings of Ashkenazi rabbis:

Women and Hair Covering – Ervah

Yabia Omer, Vol. V. Even HaEzer 5 (author's translation)	יביע אומר חלק ה - אבן העזר סימן ה
We need not be so impressed by the wives of rabbis and Hassidic leaders wearing wigs, for it runs counter to our Sages consent. And I know from several rabbis that they are not strong enough to protest their wives on this matter, even though they are not comfortable with this practice....and we must not learn from women's practice for they have no wisdom except for handicrafts, for we must rely on our Sages who have ruled on this manner.....and I was surprised with what I saw written in Igrot Moshe on the matter of a wig... and what he says is not coherent at all. And the essence is like the majority of the *aharonim* mentioned above who prohibited (the wig), and it is a great *mitzvah* to publicize this prohibition to the many and specifically to the Sephardi women who from time immemorial have treated it as forbidden and only now have begun to learn from those women contrary to the attitude of our Sages… And any woman who undertakes to preserve and practice our Sages' ruling, prohibiting a woman from leaving her home without a hat or scarf that covers the entire head, will reap all the Torah's blessings and will merit holy offspring, children who wax great in Torah and the pristine fear of God.	ואין להתפעל כל כך ממה שעינינו הרואות כמה נשי רבנים ואדמורי"ם שמקילות בזה, כי שלא ברצון חכמים עושים, וידעתי מכמה רבנים שאין ידם תקיפה למחות בנשותיהם על פתגם דנא, אף על פי שאין דעתם נוחה ממנהג זה... ואין לנו ללמוד ממנהג נשים שאין להן חכמה אלא בפלך, שאנו אין לנו אלא דברי רבותינו הפוסקים ... וגם הלום ראיתי מ"ש בשו"ת אגרות משה (מה"ת אה"ע פי' יב), בהיתר פאה נכרית. ע"ש. ואין דבריו מחוורים כלל. והעיקר כדברי רוב ככל האחרונים הנ"ל לאסור בזה, ומצוה רבה לפרסם האיסור ברבים, ובפרט לספרדיות שנהגו לאסור מימות עולם ומשנים קדמוניות, ורק כעת התחילו ללמוד מאלו המורות היתר לעצמן שלא ברצון חכמים... וכל אשה המקבלת עליה לשמור לעשות ככל דברי רבותינו הפוסקים שאסרו

> הדבר בכל תוקף, ולצאת
> אך ורק בכובע או מטפחת
> המכסה את כל ראשה,
> תתברך בכל הברכות
> שבתורה, ובמזוני רויחי
> ובבני סמיכי, ותזכה לראות
> זרע קודש בנים גדולים
> בתורה ויראת ה׳ טהורה,
> מורי הוראות בישראל

While there are Sephardi rabbis who allow wigs, the majority opinion in that community continues to reject them, based on the requirement for an obvious head covering. Nonetheless, women in those communities are increasingly choosing wigs, influenced and inspired by their *haredi* Ashkenazi counterparts.

As the world has become smaller and women from communities with different customs and practices live alongside and interact socially with one another, women are taking ownership of a practice they have come to define as a *mitzvah* by deciding how to cover their hair, influenced more by other women than by straightforward rabbinic instructions, and in this way, perhaps, reasserting the truest ideal of *dat yehudit* practice.

Chapter Eight – Part One

Sexual Intimacy

The Laws of Family Purity

IN THE COURSE of this chapter, many of the concepts regarding the Jewish laws that govern sexual intimacy will be presented and explained. However, a very short description of the basic structure of the *halakhot* governing sexual intimacy is necessary at the outset.

When a woman menstruates (or experiences any significant uterine bleeding), she becomes prohibited from engaging in sexual relations. Once the bleeding ceases, she must count seven days during which she is clean of blood, followed by immersion in a ritual bath known as a *mikvah*. Until the menstruating woman counts clean days and immerses, she is referred to as a *niddah*.

Throughout the seven days of counting, a woman is expected to perform daily vaginal inspections to be certain that the uterine bleeding has stopped. At the end of the seventh day, around nightfall, she begins to prepare for immersion in the *mikvah*. This requires a detailed inspection of her body from head to toe to ensure that the immersion will be free of any impediments between any part of her body and the water.

Religious couples are well aware that having sexual relations while *niddah* is punishable by *karet* – being "cut off" from the people.[1]

---

1. *Karet*, or "severance" is the punishment for transgressing one of 36 prohibitions,

This heightens their sense of religious responsibility when considering whether to keep these laws scrupulously or not.

Intercourse is not the only restriction during this period. In order to discourage proximity which may lead to sexual arousal, a series of laws known as *harkhakot* (literally, "laws of distancing measures") evolved to protect the couple from behaving in a sexual way while nonetheless living together, reminding them throughout this time that they are sexually prohibited. These include an absolute restriction on all forms of touch, separate beds, increased modesty in dress and language, limitations while eating together, and refraining from handing things to one another.

Niddah laws are often grouped with Shabbat and *kashrut* as the central tenets of a halakhically observant way of life.

At the same time, they are fundamentally different in several ways. First, for men and women who have grown up keeping *halakhah*, praxis from a young age brings familiarity with key traditions and practices and instills meaning into rituals that are performed most often within families and communities. *Niddah*, in contrast, has long been shrouded in an opaque silence with a sense of the taboo surrounding it. It is largely left undiscussed until marriage since sharing relevant information necessitates conversations about menstruation, female anatomy, and sexuality. These are all topics that are avoided out of a sense of modesty. Furthermore, there is a sense that such

---

including, for example, eating on Yom Kippur, eating leavened bread on Passover, eating the blood of an animal, or a man dying without being circumcised. These transgressions are synonymous with a betrayal of God's covenant, extending conceptually above and beyond the actual transgression; hence the punishment is severance from the nation commanded to adhere to holiness in order to mimic God who is holy. While transgressions that incur *karet* are often presented as irreparable, in truth, the model of repentance works here as it does for all sin. Unfortunately, in an attempt to ensure compliance, women have told me about bride instructors who have frightened them with stark warnings about the grave and permanent spiritual destruction they will bring to their husbands and children if they do not keep these laws scrupulously. Educationally, this does more harm than good, in my opinion. Reinforcing an empowering outlook which reminds the couple that they are in an ongoing aspirational relationship with God that at times challenges all of us is often a more effective approach in inspiring compliance.

Sexual Intimacy

discussions are irrelevant in a society that espouses strict celibacy before marriage. For this reason *niddah* laws are most frequently referred to as laws of *Taharat Ha-Mishpacha* or Family Purity Laws. This euphemism, which began to appear in the nineteenth century, removed the uncomfortable concepts of uterine blood, purity/impurity, and sexuality, even implicitly, from the terminology. Compared to other *mitzvot* which are publicly performed, children often have no awareness that their mothers immerse in a *mikvah*. At most, toward the end of high school, girls are given some minimal education about the *halakhot* involving *mikvah*, which may include a trip to the *mikvah* to introduce some of the concepts and familiarize them with a ritual that will be theirs to practice in the future. While such a trip could potentially provide an opportunity to engage in the issue of Judaism and sexuality, I have been told by students from many different schools both in Israel and abroad, that these classes do not usually foster a safe environment for students to ask personal questions. In addition, the subject matter is nearly always presented in a romantic and positive way, without any nuance that could potentially imply that couples, and specifically women, struggle with keeping these laws. No framework prepares young women for what lies ahead in their not-so-distant future. For young men there is even less information given about *niddah* laws before marriage. Introduction to *Taharat Ha-Mishpacha* in any sort of comprehensive, educationally coherent way is effectively non-existent, despite its importance in the halakhic corpus, the fairly regular references to *niddah* and *zavah* throughout the Talmud, and the expectation that the laws will be observed immediately upon marriage.

In contrast, I have seen in my decades of teaching that presenting the *halakhot* from high school onward, with a framework for authentic question and answer sessions on the topic of *halakhah* and sexuality, creates a far more personally meaningful opportunity for students to consider the application of these laws to them long before they become "practically relevant." This is the case for women and men. I have taken unmarried men to the women's *mikvah* during daytime hours when it is not in use. It allows them to see firsthand the space in which women are meant to immerse and ask their own questions about the experience. During one visit, a young man, recently observant, said he would be more willing to consider incorporating *mikvah* into his future marriage because he now understood the physical framework along with the *mitzvah's* potential meaning. Since these laws equally affect men and women, it is my opinion that husbands would be better able to appreciate and support their wives if they come into marriage with a better understanding of what is being taught to women.

The Biblical Laws of *Niddah*

The laws that define the status of uterine blood are complex and are derived from two different sections in Leviticus. One is in the context of the code of sexual prohibitions, and the other is in the context of regulations of purity/impurity prescribed for those wishing to enter the Tabernacle and later the Temple. This duality is the primary challenge in understanding the laws of *niddah*. The two aspects are intertwined in Talmudic discussion, despite the seeming irrelevance of purity/impurity once the Temple has been destroyed.

Sexually Prohibited Relationships

Leviticus Chapter 18 opens with the prohibition of incest and sexual relations between family members. Adultery, bestiality, and sexual relations between two men are included in the list as well.

The ensuing chapter, Chapter 19, opens with a call to holiness: *Speak to the whole Israelite community and say to them: You shall be holy, for I the Lord your God, am holy.* The medieval Bible commentator Rashi writes, at the opening of Chapter 19, that the laws of sexual prohibition which appear in Chapter 18 are so significant that they comprise the essence of holiness:

Sexual Intimacy

Rashi, Leviticus 19:2	רש"י ויקרא יט:ב
You shall be holy. Separate from sexual prohibition and from [sexual] transgression for everywhere you find a fence against sexual prohibition, you find holiness.	קדשים תהיו. הוו פרושים מן העריות ומן העבירה, שכל מקום שאתה מוצא גדר ערוה אתה מוצא קדושה.

The paradigm of "holiness" is not only for a select few, but for the entire nation. In imitating God's holiness, we make holiness our objective. Unlike impurity which can be incurred involuntarily, holiness is achieved by voluntarily choosing to follow in God's way. It is an ongoing process, an act of partnership between the Israelite nation and God. Holiness is realized by engaging only in permitted behaviors and refraining from the prohibited in our daily activities, including restrictions on the food we eat and, central to our discussion, sexual behavior. These boundaries are essentially what distinguish us from the other nations: a fundamental aspect of our relationship with God, who has chosen to distinguish us.

In Chapter 20, the topic of sexual boundaries is revisited with punishments presented for each transgression; the punishment of *karet* is assigned to the man and woman who deliberately engage in sexual relations while the woman is a *niddah*.

Leviticus 20:18	ויקרא כ:יח
If a man lies with a woman in her infirmity and uncovers her nakedness, he has laid bare her flow and she has exposed the source of her blood; both of them shall be cut off from among their people.	וְאִישׁ אֲשֶׁר יִשְׁכַּב אֶת אִשָּׁה דָּוָה, וְגִלָּה אֶת־עֶרְוָתָהּ אֶת מְקֹרָהּ הֶעֱרָה, וְהִוא, גִּלְּתָה אֶת־מְקוֹר דָּמֶיהָ וְנִכְרְתוּ שְׁנֵיהֶם, מִקֶּרֶב עַמָּם.

Sanctified sexuality is an intrinsic part of the covenantal relationship and symbolic of what is demanded of us as we aspire to integrate the Divine spirit into our lives. It affects not only prohibited relationships but also permitted ones, for the *niddah* is in a fundamentally permitted sexual relationship, except during times of uterine bleeding. This sets her apart from other sexual prohibitions mentioned.

Niddah and the Laws of Impurity (*Tumah*)

In order to fully comprehend the concept of *niddah*, one needs to refer back to Leviticus Chapters 12–15. It is here that the Bible introduces the boundaries of *ritual* purity and impurity.

Ritual impurity is not forbidden in the Torah. In fact, God does not warn the nation to avoid impurity with *Thou shall not* language in contrast to most of the Torah's prohibitions. It is not about bodily cleanliness in the classic sense. A person can be hygienically clean but impure, while another person can be filthy and pure. Maimonides writes this distinction clearly at the end of his laws of *mikvah*:

Maimonides Mishneh Torah Laws of *Mikvaot*, Chapter 11, Halakhah 12	רמב״ם משנה תורה הלכות מקוואות פרק יא, הלכה יב
It is obviously clear that the laws concerning defilements and purities are biblical decrees, and not things which the human mind can determine; they are classified as divine statutes. So too, immersion as a means of ridding oneself from defilement is included among the divine statutes. Defilement is not mud or filth to be removed with water, but is a matter of biblical decree; it depends on the heart's intent....	דָּבָר בָּרוּר וְגָלוּי שֶׁהַטֻּמְאוֹת וְהַטָּהֳרוֹת גְּזֵרוֹת הַכָּתוּב הֵן. וְאֵינָן מִדְּבָרִים שֶׁדַּעְתּוֹ שֶׁל אָדָם מַכְרַעְתּוֹ. וַהֲרֵי הֵן מִכְּלַל הַחֻקִּים. וְכֵן הַטְּבִילָה מִן הַטֻּמְאוֹת מִכְּלַל הַחֻקִּים הוּא שֶׁאֵין הַטֻּמְאָה טִיט אוֹ צוֹאָה שֶׁתַּעֲבֹר בְּמַיִם אֶלָּא גְּזֵרַת הַכָּתוּב הִיא וְהַדָּבָר תָּלוּי בְּכַוָּנַת הַלֵּב.

At the end of Chapter 15, God tells Moses and Aaron to warn the nation to stay away from the Tabernacle when in a state of *ritual* impurity, upon pain of death.

Sexual Intimacy

Leviticus 15:31	ויקרא פרק טו:כא
You shall warn the Israelites from their impurity, lest they die as a result of their impurity by defiling My Tabernacle which is among them.	וְהִזַּרְתֶּם אֶת-בְּנֵי-יִשְׂרָאֵל, מִטֻּמְאָתָם; וְלֹא יָמֻתוּ בְּטֻמְאָתָם, בְּטַמְּאָם אֶת-מִשְׁכָּנִי אֲשֶׁר בְּתוֹכָם.

Ritual impurity is a consequence of being human. It is not, in its essence, about moral culpability or transgression, nor is it about spiritual distance from God. Men and women who are in a state of *ritual* impurity are still fully obligated to keep the Torah's commandments. *Ritual* impurity only precludes them from partaking in rituals and sacrifices within the Temple precinct. Proximity to God's direct presence, in the Tabernacle/Temple, requires utmost vigilance. Additionally, these biblically mandated sources of *ritual* impurity are highly "contagious," demanding caution and awareness of one's bodily state, particularly for the priestly community. In the next section, five bodily states of *ritual* impurity that occur as a result of discharge from sexual organs will be presented. Uterine blood is just one example.

Birth

The first mention of *ritual* impurity due to bodily emissions is a mother after birth:

Leviticus 12:1–8	ויקרא פרק יב
1 The LORD spoke to Moses, saying: 2 Speak to the Israelite people thus: When a woman conceives and gives birth to a male, she shall be impure seven days; she shall be impure as at the time of her *niddut*.	א וַיְדַבֵּר ה' אֶל-מֹשֶׁה לֵּאמֹר. ב דַּבֵּר אֶל-בְּנֵי יִשְׂרָאֵל, לֵאמֹר, אִשָּׁה כִּי תַזְרִיעַ, וְיָלְדָה זָכָר--וְטָמְאָה שִׁבְעַת יָמִים, כִּימֵי נִדַּת דְּוֹתָהּ תִּטְמָא.

> 3 On the eighth day, the flesh of his foreskin shall be circumcised.—
> 4 She shall remain in a state of blood purification for thirty-three days: she shall not touch any consecrated thing, nor enter the sanctuary until her period of purification is completed.
> 5 If she gives birth to a female, she shall be impure two weeks as during her menstruation, and she shall remain in a state of blood purification for sixty-six days.

> ג וּבַיּוֹם, הַשְּׁמִינִי, יִמּוֹל, בְּשַׂר עָרְלָתוֹ.
> ד וּשְׁלֹשִׁים יוֹם וּשְׁלֹשֶׁת יָמִים, תֵּשֵׁב בִּדְמֵי טָהֳרָה; בְּכָל-קֹדֶשׁ לֹא-תִגָּע, וְאֶל-הַמִּקְדָּשׁ לֹא תָבֹא, עַד-מְלֹאת, יְמֵי טָהֳרָהּ.
> ה וְאִם-נְקֵבָה תֵלֵד, וְטָמְאָה שְׁבֻעַיִם כְּנִדָּתָהּ; וְשִׁשִּׁים יוֹם וְשֵׁשֶׁת יָמִים, תֵּשֵׁב עַל-דְּמֵי טָהֳרָה.

The birthing woman is described as a *niddah*: "She shall be *impure* as at the time of her *niddut*" (Leviticus 12:2), even though the laws of *niddah* are only to be found later in Chapter 15. In addition, the birthing woman, uniquely, has 2 periods of purification: the first is like the *niddah* which lasts for 7 days (double for birthing a girl); the second period lasts for 33 days (or 66 days, again double for a girl) in which she experiences what is defined as blood of "purity." Only at the end of the second phase is she allowed to return to God's sanctuary and bring sacrifices that include a sin offering and a burnt offering.[2]

---

2. The Torah prescribes a sin offering as part of the process of purification for impurities that involve a life-threatening situation (childbirth), pathological bodily emissions from sexual organs (*zav* and *zavah*), or disease (i.e., leprosy). For all of these, the purification process is at least seven days. These laws seem to underscore the fact that a sin offering serves a different purpose in the context of purity/impurity from the classic sin offering which is brought as penance for a transgressive act. Normally, sin is a manifestation of our ability to make choices freely, for right or for wrong. In the world of purity/impurity, the physical manifestations of the body are involuntary and are not subject to the exercise of free will, and yet they still mandate a sin offering.

Sexual Intimacy

Seminal Emissions and Uterine Bleeding

Leviticus 15	ויקרא פרק טו
1 The LORD spoke to Moses and Aaron, saying: Speak to the Israelite people and say to them: 2 When any man has a penile discharge, he is impure. 3 The impurity from his discharge shall mean the following – whether there is flow from his penis or it is stopped up so that there is no discharge, his impurity means this... 4 Any bedding on which the one with the discharge lies shall be impure, and every object on which he sits shall be impure. 13 ...When one with a discharge becomes clean of his discharge, he shall count off seven clean days, wash his clothes, and bathe his body in living water; and then he shall be pure. 16 When a man has an emission of semen, he shall bathe his whole body in water and remain impure until evening. 17 All cloth or leather on which semen falls shall be washed in water and remain impure until evening. 18 And a woman who lays with a man who ejaculates, they shall bathe in water and remain impure until evening.	א וַיְדַבֵּר ה' אֶל-מֹשֶׁה וְאֶל-אַהֲרֹן לֵאמֹר. ב דַּבְּרוּ אֶל-בְּנֵי יִשְׂרָאֵל, וַאֲמַרְתֶּם אֲלֵהֶם: אִישׁ אִישׁ, כִּי יִהְיֶה זָב מִבְּשָׂרוֹ--זוֹבוֹ, טָמֵא הוּא. ג וְזֹאת תִּהְיֶה טֻמְאָתוֹ, בְּזוֹבוֹ: רָר בְּשָׂרוֹ אֶת-זוֹבוֹ, אוֹ-הֶחְתִּים בְּשָׂרוֹ מִזּוֹבוֹ--טֻמְאָתוֹ, הִוא. ד כָּל-הַמִּשְׁכָּב, אֲשֶׁר יִשְׁכַּב עָלָיו הַזָּב--יִטְמָא; וְכָל-הַכְּלִי אֲשֶׁר-יֵשֵׁב עָלָיו, יִטְמָא. יג וְכִי-יִטְהַר הַזָּב, מִזּוֹבוֹ--וְסָפַר לוֹ שִׁבְעַת יָמִים לְטָהֳרָתוֹ, וְכִבֶּס בְּגָדָיו; וְרָחַץ בְּשָׂרוֹ בְּמַיִם חַיִּים, וְטָהֵר. טו וְאִישׁ, כִּי-תֵצֵא מִמֶּנּוּ שִׁכְבַת-זָרַע--וְרָחַץ בַּמַּיִם אֶת-כָּל-בְּשָׂרוֹ, וְטָמֵא עַד-הָעָרֶב. יז וְכָל-בֶּגֶד וְכָל-עוֹר, אֲשֶׁר-יִהְיֶה עָלָיו שִׁכְבַת-זָרַע--וְכֻבַּס בַּמַּיִם, וְטָמֵא עַד-הָעָרֶב. יח וְאִשָּׁה, אֲשֶׁר יִשְׁכַּב אִישׁ אֹתָהּ שִׁכְבַת-זָרַע--וְרָחֲצוּ בַמַּיִם, וְטָמְאוּ עַד-הָעָרֶב.

19 When a woman has a discharge, her discharge being blood from her body, she shall remain in her impurity seven days; whoever touches her shall be impure until evening.
24 …And if a man lies with her, her impurity is communicated to him; he shall be impure seven days, and any bedding on which he lies shall become impure.
25 When a woman has had a discharge of blood for many days, not at the time of her menstruation, or when she has a discharge beyond her menstrual period, she shall be impure, as she would be at the time of her menstruation, for as long as her discharge lasts.
28 …When she becomes clean of her discharge, she shall count off seven days, and after that, she shall be pure.
31 You shall put the Israelites on guard against their impurity, lest they die through their impurity by defiling My Tabernacle which is among them.

יט וְאִשָּׁה כִּי-תִהְיֶה זָבָה, דָּם יִהְיֶה זֹבָהּ בִּבְשָׂרָהּ--שִׁבְעַת יָמִים תִּהְיֶה בְנִדָּתָהּ, וְכָל-הַנֹּגֵעַ בָּהּ יִטְמָא עַד-הָעָרֶב.
כד וְאִם שָׁכֹב יִשְׁכַּב אִישׁ אֹתָהּ, וּתְהִי נִדָּתָהּ עָלָיו--וְטָמֵא, שִׁבְעַת יָמִים; וְכָל-הַמִּשְׁכָּב אֲשֶׁר-יִשְׁכַּב עָלָיו, יִטְמָא.
כה וְאִשָּׁה כִּי-יָזוּב זוֹב דָּמָהּ יָמִים רַבִּים, בְּלֹא עֶת-נִדָּתָהּ, אוֹ כִי-תָזוּב, עַל-נִדָּתָהּ: כָּל-יְמֵי זוֹב טֻמְאָתָהּ, כִּימֵי נִדָּתָהּ תִּהְיֶה--טְמֵאָה הִוא.
כח וְאִם-טָהֲרָה, מִזּוֹבָהּ--וְסָפְרָה לָּהּ שִׁבְעַת יָמִים, וְאַחַר תִּטְהָר.
לא וְהִזַּרְתֶּם אֶת-בְּנֵי יִשְׂרָאֵל, מִטֻּמְאָתָם; וְלֹא יָמֻתוּ בְּטֻמְאָתָם, בְּטַמְּאָם אֶת-מִשְׁכָּנִי אֲשֶׁר בְּתוֹכָם.

Seminal emission and menstruation are normal, healthy physical states. Both are necessary to create life, and yet they cause impurity. These *ritual* impurities are bracketed by the more extreme types of emissions, *zav* and *zavah*, which are abnormal resulting in a more stringent level of impurity.

Some women recoil from the idea that a natural occurrence in their body causes them to be impure. For this reason, it is important to study these chapters in context, understand that there are myriad causes for impurity, and note that men's and women's bodies are equally subject to impurity. *Ritual* impurity does not bar anyone from the normal daily and weekly rituals that make up their covenantal relationship with God. The practical implication of this status at the

Sexual Intimacy

time of the Temple was to be barred from the Temple precinct and sacrificial worship.

To summarize, the categories of *ritual* impurity for men and women are:

- **Zav** - A man who has a pathological emission is called a *zav*; he becomes *ritually* pure only after seven clean days without discharge, followed by immersion in a *mikvah* and the sacrifice of sin and burnt offerings.

- **Seminal Emission** - A man who has a seminal emission becomes *ritually* impure. To become *ritually* pure, he must immerse in a *mikvah* and wait until nightfall.

- **Niddah** - A menstruating woman is obligated to wait seven days from the onset of bleeding and then immerse in the *mikvah* and wait until nightfall to become *ritually* pure.[3]

- **Zavah** - A woman who experiences uterine bleeding not at the time of her menses or beyond the seven days allotted for normal menstruation is known as a *zavah*. *Zavah* is the feminine noun form of the word *zav* in Hebrew, and like the *zav*, her purification requires 7 clean days without discharge, immersion, and sacrifices.

Based on tradition, the Sages determined that a woman is a *zavah* only if she experiences uterine bleeding during the 11 days following the 7 days of *niddah* (the shortest possible menstrual cycle, in their opinion), i.e., from day 8 through day 18 of the menstrual cycle. From day 19 onward it is considered the onset of *niddah* blood.[4]

---

3. Water is not specifically referenced regarding the *niddah* or the *zavah*. Given that water appears in all purification rituals in some capacity, it is reasonable to conclude from the biblical text that the references to water in purifying the *zav* and *zera* (semen) are relevant for the *niddah* and *zavah* as well.

4. It bears mentioning that this explanation follows the majority opinion among commentaries of Talmud. Maimonides, however, ruled that from the moment a woman first menstruated, the first 7 days are *niddah* days to be followed by 11 *zavah*

Uncovered

Additionally, they determined that there are two categories of *zavah*:

a. If a woman bleeds for one or two days, she is required to wait one more day before she can immerse. After nightfall of that "clean" day, she immerses in a *mikvah* and becomes pure. Her status is one of *zavah ketanah* ("minor *zavah*"). [5]

b. If a woman bleeds for three days or more, she has bled for "many days" as described in the Torah. She is required to count seven days clean of blood as described in Torah and only then may she immerse. Her status is one of *zavah gedolah* ("major *zavah*").

In this way, a woman was expected to track the seven days of menstrual bleeding followed by careful awareness of the next eleven days in case she would see blood and become a minor or major *zavah*. The two categories of *zavah* and one of *niddah*, together with the rules for impure and pure blood following the birth of a boy or girl, created a convoluted arrangement of laws requiring vigilance, regular monitoring, and awareness of discharge within women's bodies. This complexity is important to understanding the move toward a uniform system of *halakhah* applicable to all types of uterine bleeding.

---

days followed by 7 *niddah* days, etc., making the cycles dependent only on that first menses, regardless of a woman's personal biological cycle, stopped only by periods of childbirth. Her status was to be calculated on a calendar in which *niddah* and *zavah* were eternally predetermined by her first period. It should be noted that in all of these calculations, there is a lack of real understanding of why the bleeding is occurring along with a sense that there is no way to differentiate between the quality of the different bleeds, even though a Talmudic tradition suggests otherwise. In line with rabbinic thinking, there is an attempt to create order and definition without reflection of the reality of the situation. In other words, the system of law will determine the woman's status rather than her own perception or experience of what is happening from within her body. Women's voices are completely absent from all of these deliberations.

5. This category became superfluous following R. Yehuda HaNasi's ruling presented below.

Sexual Intimacy

The Unification of *Niddah* and *Zavah*

Although the system of *ritual* purity laws ceased to be practiced in the generations after the destruction of the Temple, the prohibition of sexual relations with a woman experiencing uterine blood, based on the verse in Leviticus 18:19, was still very much mandated.[6] Moreover, according to Leviticus 20:18 the punishment for both men and women who engage in sexual relations while *niddah* is *karet*.

At the end of the Tannaitic period (circa 200 CE), Rabbi Yehuda HaNasi (Judah the Prince) began the process of conflating the status of *niddah* with that of *zavah* into a uniform halakhic system. As shown in the textual analysis above, *niddah* was expected to last for no more than seven days. Any bleeding after that period defined her as either a major or minor *zavah* (see chart above).

B. Talmud Niddah 66a	תלמוד בבלי מסכת נידה סו עמ' א
Rav Yosef said that Rav Yehuda said that Rav said: Rabbi Yehuda HaNasi decreed that in the fields (rural areas), if she saw blood for one day, she must sit six days. If she experiences bleeding for two days, she must sit six days. If she experiences bleeding for three days she must sit seven clean days.	אמר רב יוסף אמר רב יהודה אמר רב התקין רבי בשדות ראתה יום אחד תשב ששה והוא שנים תשב ששה והן שלשה תשב שבעה נקיים.

Rabbi Yehuda HaNasi presented three rulings for women living far from rabbinic courts ("the fields"). These rulings were intended to eliminate the uncertainty around *niddah* for unlearned women and simplify the required behavior whenever there was an emission of uterine blood. This was achieved by taking the stringent approach in all cases. His rulings:

---

6. The birthing women is called a *niddah* and so is the *zavah* which means all women with significant uterine bleeding are sexually prohibited except for the interim days after birth when the blood, at least by Torah law, was deemed *tahor* (pure).

1. A woman who experienced one day of bleeding should wait six additional days before immersing (although women's periods are on average four to six days). Rabbi Yehuda HaNasi ruled stringently, to avoid any doubt; lest even uterine bleeding that lasts one day could be considered menstrual blood rendering the woman a *niddah*.

2. If a woman experienced two days of bleeding, Rabbi Yehuda HaNasi reasoned that since the first day of bleeding could theoretically be non-menstrual, it should not be included in the *niddah*'s seven days of counting. The second day could be either *niddah* blood or not. Thus, according to his ruling, the seven days **could** only be counted from the second day of bleeding (in case the first day was not *niddah* blood and the second day was *niddah* blood) to complete the seven *niddah* days.

3. If a woman experienced three days of bleeding, Rabbi Yehuda HaNasi ruled that she should always regard herself as a *zavah* and required seven "clean" days, i.e., without blood, before immersing.

Looking at this last ruling, it is clear that Rabbi Yehuda HaNasi took an enormous step toward conflating *niddah* with *zavah*. Unlike the system sketched out above where *niddah* days flowed into (no pun intended) *zavah* days for a maximum of 18 days total before the system "reset" itself, Rabbi Yehuda HaNasi instituted a system dependent only on the duration of the flow and not the time of month.

In practice, Rabbi Yehuda HaNasi's ordinance specified six clean days after one or two days of blood and seven clean days after three or more days of blood. This still had the potential to be confusing. It is hardly surprising that in the next line of Talmud, we have the famous statement of Rabbi Zeira who lived circa 300 CE, which completely eliminated the separation between *niddah* and *zavah* for women everywhere:

Sexual Intimacy

B. Talmud Niddah 66a	תלמוד בבלי מסכת נדה דף סו עמ' א
R. Zeira said: The daughters of Israel took it upon themselves to be stringent. Even if they saw a drop of blood the size of a mustard seed they would abstain for seven clean days.	אמר ר' זירא: בנות ישראל החמירו על עצמן שאפילו רואות טפת דם כחרדל יושבות עליה שבעה נקיים.

It is worth noting that R. Zeira's statement, which credits the daughters of Israel for taking upon themselves a new stringency, actually added only one more day to what Rabbi Yehuda HaNasi had enacted for women in the fields, as explained above. More significantly, his statement expanded the ruling to all women. The statement *a drop of blood the size of a mustard seed* is more of a rhetorical exaggeration than a halakhically accurate statement. A mustard-seed size of a drop of blood does not render a woman prohibited unless other significant halakhic criteria are met.[7] Nonetheless, for thousands of years there has been a valorization of the pious daughters of Israel who are credited with influencing the shift to a uniform system of counting seven clean days before immersing.[8] On one hand, this narrative gives halakhic agency to women, crediting them for having a hand

---

7. Specifically, *hargashah*, which is a specifically defined sensation that a woman experiences where she feels her uterus or cervix open to release blood. Barring that sensation, according to the Talmud, a woman is not considered a *niddah* on a biblical level. This criterion remains relevant in contemporary halakhic rulings towards leniency; if a woman has not experienced *hargashah*, although she sees a small amount of uterine blood, it may be possible to permit her.

8. There are many other elements that went into the uniform way in which *niddah* is practiced. For practical *halakhah*, see Rabbi Eliashiv Knohl's excellent book, *The Marriage Covenant, A Guide to Jewish Marriage*, 2008, and Dr. Deena Zimmerman's book, *Lifetime Companion to the Laws of Jewish Family Life*, Urim Publications, 2011. For academic feminist readings of *niddah*, see Charlotte Fonrobert, *Menstrual Purity*, Stanford, 2000; Rachel Biale, *Women and Jewish Law*, Schocken, 1984, pp. 147–174; and Judith Hauptman, *Rereading the Rabbis*, Westview, 1998, pp. 147–175.

in halakhic practice by choosing stringency so as to clarify their own practice. On the other hand, it is also a source of frustration for some women in the modern era who feel they would be better served by the original models of *niddah* and *zavah* which distinguished between menstruation and other forms of uterine bleeding based on individual internal timing of uterine bleeding. For this reason, it is important to understand that Rabbi Yehuda HaNasi was far more influential in setting up a single halakhic framework for the purposes of clarity in transmission of these halakhot than R. Zeira's later claim about the "daughters of Israel."[9]

The famous fourteenth-century Talmudist, Menachem ben Solomon HaMeiri elucidates this in his commentary:

Meiri Berakhot 31a	המאירי על מסכת ברכות דף לא עמ' א
The daughters of Israel later adopted an additional stringency…Moreover, they felt it would be more convenient if the counting were the same for all women, so one woman would not be counting six days, and another woman seven.	בנות ישראל החמירו עוד אח"כ וחששו שמא בראיה אחת שתקנו חכמים ו' נקיים אפשר לענין שיגיע לידי טעות הגע עצמך שהיתה זבה וסופרת ז' נקיים ושמא מתוך שכבר עמדה לה ה' ו' ימים בטהרה היא סבורה שהוא תחלת נדה ולא תמנה אלא ו' נקיים ואף על פי שחששא

---

[9]. While *dam tohar* – postpartum bleeding defined as "pure blood" in Torah– was maintained for some centuries in a number of communities, ultimately birth was treated in the same way as all uterine bleeding and required seven clean days following cessation of bleeding.

Sexual Intimacy

| The committed women said to each other, "There's not such a big difference between six and seven," so they established for themselves that each time they saw blood, they would treat it like definitive *zavah*, and even if it were only the size of a mustard seed, which is clearly from a closed womb, not an open one. | זו רחוקה היא שהרי ספירת ז' דבר הניכר הוא מ"מ יש לחוש בקצת נשים שאינן בקיאות. וכן, שהדבר נוח להם להיות המנין שוה בכלן ולא תהיה זו מונה ו' וזו ז' דנו בעצמן בנות זריזות מה לנו בעיכוב יום אחד ואין בין ו' לז' אלא יום אחד בלבד לפיכך תקנו בעצמן שכל ראייה שתראה אף שלא במנין הנקיות יהו חוששות עליו לזיבה גמורה ואפי' דם טפה כחרדל שהדברים מוכיחים בה שהיא יוצאת ממעין סתום ולא ממעין. |

This shift towards uniformity is cited in the Talmud as a seminal example of "conclusive *halakhah*"[10] and for 1,700 years has remained unchallenged as the foundation for how *niddah* laws are practiced in the post-Temple era.

Shifting Attitudes Toward *Niddah* Laws

The last 50 years has brought increased interest in women proactively tracking their fertility, gaining increased understanding of their sexuality, and seeking greater autonomy over their bodies. This trend reflects the overall increase in accessible information and resources on female sexuality, fueled by the feminist movement and the sexual revolution. The awareness of sexual abuse and trauma most recently exposed by the #MeToo revolution has also contributed greatly to wariness regarding any sense of coercion over what women are asked to do with their bodies.

---

10. B. Talmud Niddah 31a.

Uncovered

Based on decades of teaching, lecturing, and informally speaking to women on this topic, I have heard many stories reflecting a wide variety of responses to the impact *niddah* has on women's sense of self, feelings toward their bodies, sexuality, fertility, autonomy, and, of course, marriage. The following is a brief synopsis of some of those voices.

Starting with the positive, many women feel that these laws foster respect for women, their bodies, menstrual cycles, and sexual needs by indicating that sexual relations are not the only medium for intimacy, thus mandating regular breaks from sexual interaction. There is a sense that immersion in the *mikvah* connects them to their female ancestry dating back thousands of years, from the period of the Bible and Talmud onward. Heroic stories have been passed on about women who immersed under adverse conditions and endured hardships – at times under terrible persecution – with a sense of responsibility towards ensuring the purity of the Jewish family. The *mikvah*, it should be noted, is traditionally one of the first buildings built in a Jewish community as a sign of its commitment to the sanctity of sexuality within marriage and continuity through childbearing. Many women feel empowered by a *mitzvah* that is exclusively a "woman's *mitzvah*" being directly tied, as it is, to the female cycle and life-bearing potential of their bodies.

While this positivity has been the almost exclusive narrative in mainstream Orthodox literature about *niddah*, for some women, including those who have an affirmative relationship with their sexuality and their bodies, this kind of halakhic intervention about a natural biological process can feel primitive, coercive, or misogynistic. I have heard women express an uncomfortable sense that the rabbis are "in their bodies," given the detailed attention paid to this most intimate part of their bodies in texts authored almost exclusively by men. This type of reflexive response by some women has led to a cacophony of voices, especially on social media, demanding a reevaluation of halakhic sources that speak about women's bodies.[11]

---

11. There are women who are making the (non-halakhic) decision to keep *niddah* on

Sexual Intimacy

Finally, there are women who have complicated relationships with their bodies and sexuality due to religious education, body shaming, lifelong avoidance of their vulva (because of religious instruction or cultural taboos), or, sadly but increasingly prevalent, women who are survivors of sexual trauma. More recently, awareness of women suffering from OCD and the painful reality in which they engage with these extremely detailed laws has come to the forefront of halakhic discourse. The added stress of laws forcing these women to directly interact with the source of their anxiety – often without any therapeutic process– can complicate the transition towards halakhic compliance and sexual intimacy.[12] Thankfully, greater awareness due to the articulation of women's voices in this area, along with ongoing rabbinic attention focused on alleviating distress, has led to compassionate halakhic solutions in many of these situations.

---

their own terms, choosing which aspects are meaningful and reasonable for them personally to uphold. Following are two examples, each with different halakhic weight. The first is a refusal to do *bedikot*, internal vaginal exams women are instructed to perform to prove cessation of uterine blood, for the duration of the seven clean days before immersion in the *mikvah*. Some of this rejection has to do with sexual trauma or vaginismus, in which case there is room for halakhic leniency. However, for some women this decision is based on a more straightforward rejection of the halakhic requirement of intrusive vaginal inspections that they deem unnecessary. Women have said to me they know when their periods end and even if it means waiting an extra day or two to make sure all bleeding has stopped before counting seven clean days, they prefer this to performing *bedikot*. The second, which will be addressed below, is the shift to keep seven days of *niddah*, as was the practice prior to the ruling of R. Yehudah HaNasi, rather than the seven clean days of *zavah*.

12. Some women in the religious world have been told never to touch or insert anything, including tampons, into their vaginas to protect their virginity, an instruction that exhibits gross ignorance of female anatomy. The hymen is a thin fleshy tissue found just inside the vaginal opening. It stretches when anything is inserted vaginally, like a tampon or a finger. Sexual intercourse causes it to stretch even more and in some women with a thicker tissue, there will be tearing. However, the myth of hymenal bleeding proving virginity must be debunked. Some women never bleed, even with no prior sexual experience, and some women bleed from vaginal tearing after sexual relations even after many years of experience. The hymen does not necessarily tear or disappear and in many cases it is impossible for a doctor to "know" whether a woman is a virgin or not based on hymenal tissue.

Modern Challenges to *Niddah*

Within the observant community, the increased awareness of women about their bodies led to the shocking realization that some women were not becoming pregnant because of *niddah* laws. As explained above, women are sexually prohibited for approximately 11–13 days per cycle. For a woman trying to get pregnant, the timing of sexual intercourse to coincide with ovulation is crucial. Contemporary books on the laws of *niddah* often emphasize how the timing of *mikvah* immersion coincides with the most fertile days of the month. This is generally true for women who have cycles of at least 26 days and bleed for no more than 5. However, some women ovulate a day or two prior to their immersion because they bleed for more than 5 days and/or their cycles are shorter than 26 days. Simply put, it has been proven that abiding by *halakhah* actually prevents a small minority of women from having intercourse during their most fertile time of the month. As a result, they are unable to conceive! Looking back at *responsa* literature over the last 2,000 years, one cannot help but wonder if some of the women who were divorced by their husbands due to infertility[13] were unable to have children solely because of the extended rabbinic stringency of 7 clean days.

Once this phenomenon was discovered, the initial halakhic response was to work with doctors who would administer a short course of hormones in order to push off ovulation. This maintained fidelity to the halakhic requirement of the seven clean days and enabled women to time their ovulation to correspond to the days after immersing in the *mikvah*. However, when the negative impact of hormones was considered, doctors and observant women began to ask why they were being administered potentially harmful medical treatment to resolve an issue that was halakhic in nature.

Senior ob/gyn Dr. Daniel Rosenak, himself an Orthodox Jew with a thriving practice in an ultra-Orthodox neighborhood, was one of the driving forces in upsetting the status quo. He published a paper

---

13. A man can divorce his wife if she is barren for 10 years. B. Talmud Yevamot 64a, Shulhan Arukh Even HaEzer 154:10.

Sexual Intimacy

with four other doctors,[14] which he subsequently expanded to a book,[15] arguing that precoital ovulation (ovulation taking place at a time when sexual intercourse was forbidden because of Jewish law) accounted for infertility in a significant number of religious couples.[16] In addition, he championed a return to biblical *niddah* (colloquially referred to as *niddah d'orayta*) due to its beneficial impact on female sexuality and fertility. Women's libidos, for instance, increase incrementally during the seven days after menstruation as they move toward ovulation, and begin to decrease in the days that follow. The rabbinic *niddah* system prohibits sexual relations on some of these most sexually charged days.

Rosenak's publicly endorsed attitude unleashed a firestorm of debate around strict compliance with Rabbi Yehuda HaNasi's stringency in the face of possible "halakhic infertility," given the centrality Judaism places on the *mitzvah* of procreation. In addition, religious couples began to question the impact of the rabbinic system overall on their sexuality and intimacy.[17]

Outside of very carefully controlled leniencies given in cases of true halakhic infertility, rabbis were quick to condemn any suggestion that we return to *niddah d'orayta*. Two *yoatzot halakhah*, Dr. Deena Zimmerman[18] and Dr. Tova Ganzel, carried out a serious assessment of

---

14. Ronit Haimov-Kochman, et al. "Infertility Associated with Precoital Ovulation in Observant Jewish Couples; Prevalence, Treatment, Efficacy and Side Effects." *IMAJ*, vol. 14, February 2012, pp 100–103.

15. Daniel Rosenak, *To Restore the Splendour: The Real Meaning of Severity in Applying Jewish Marital Traditions* [Hebrew] Tel Aviv, 2011.

16. Rosenak also ethically questioned the need to inject hormones for non-medical reasons.

17. Dr. Rosenak spoke to many audiences as both a medical professional and Orthodox Jew advocating for a return to biblical *niddah*. I attended and subsequently moderated one of these sessions. Both times the sessions were packed with couples eager to hear Dr. Rosenak's views. It was clear from the questions that the majority of the attendees were not suffering from halakhic infertility. Rather, there was an eagerness to hear a position that championed shortening the rabbinic structure of *niddah* and the significant impact it has on their sexuality.

18. Dr. Zimmerman is a family physician, and Dr. Ganzel is a professor of Bible Studies.

Rosenak's claim and concluded that his numbers were greatly inflated. While some women were indeed suffering from ovulation prior to *mikvah* immersion, a larger number who were claiming halakhic infertility were in fact being overly stringent with their practice of *niddah* laws. Better education on how to accurately count clean days became a major focus of the *yoetzet halakhah* community and helped many women immerse a day or two earlier without resorting to a restructuring of rabbinic law.[19]

Another factor, abutting the halakhic infertility conversation, has been increased interest by women in the fertility awareness method (FAM).[20] To become proficient, a woman must spend several months with a trained professional learning how to assess the signs of ovulation accurately in her body. In the process, she learns to identify the signs of fertility through the hormonal imprint that changes as she moves toward and away from ovulation. In this way, using natural methods, a woman can gain control over her fertility and sexuality.[21] Similar to Rosenak's findings, some women who are attracted to this method feel alienated by the *halakhah*'s inflexible and uniform structure which has little to do with their internal biological consciousness and their experience of fertility and sexuality.

Both were among the first graduates of the Yoatzot Halacha program at Nishmat. For a detailed explanation of Yoatzot Halacha, see Chapter Two where the history and character of the program is described.

19. For example, some women were waiting an extra day or two because they thought, incorrectly, that clean days required an absence of any color at all on the internal examination cloths. This unnecessary stringency was what was causing them to miss ovulation, rather than rabbinic law.

20. The FAM campaign in Israel was spearheaded by Michal Schonbrun, who learned the technique in the United States and brought it back to Israel 30 years ago. In 2006, she began training women to teach this method. Since then, the number of women interested in FAM has risen steadily into the thousands.

21. For couples who are trying to become pregnant, it allows them to pinpoint the fertile days and increase the statistical probability of pregnancy by having sexual relations at the most potentially fertile time. For couples who want to prevent pregnancy, this method allows the woman to limit the use of contraception to fertile days only, which are five to six days a cycle.

Additionally, the internet has made information more accessible. Today there are public forums where mini communities of observant couples have decided to keep *niddah d'orayta*. I have personally taught couples before marriage who let me know that they are choosing to keep *niddah d'orayta* rather than the required seven clean days following cessation of bleeding. We agree that I will teach them the core curriculum that I teach all couples but there is a tacit understanding of what they will keep "for real". Additionally, a number of women confided to me that they reverted to *niddah d'orayta* (without rabbinic approval) because they were simply unable to completely refrain from sexual activity for the longer duration required by rabbinic law. There is a feeling in some circles that Rabbi Yehuda HaNassi's stringencies, originally designed to protect "women of the fields" from accidentally transgressing the laws of *niddah*, have paradoxically become a stumbling block that leads to transgression. Attitudes toward *niddah* laws are additionally exacerbated by the difficulty some people have in refraining from all touch for the entire prohibited period (this topic is addressed in Part Two of the chapter). Some feel it is preferable to immerse after seven days rather than refrain from touching for longer.

While this conversation has to some degree grabbed the attention of the rabbinic community, though many are either ignorant of the trend or ignore it, there has been unanimous rejection at least publicly of any sort of endorsement. Due to the privacy inherent to the topic, it is very difficult to gather accurate information beyond couples who are public about their decisions in this regard.

In general, women are gaining confidence in their ability to ask questions as they seek greater agency in this area of *halakhah*, along with deeper religious meaning and empowerment through their *mikvah* practice. Additionally, many husbands want to better understand what is involved so that they can better support their wives. Hundreds of thousands of *niddah*-related questions have come to the Nishmat hotline,[22] which is only a fraction of the myriad questions that both

---

22. See Chapter Two for a discussion about Yoatzot Halacha and Nishmat. Graduates of a rigorous two-year training program in *halakhah* supplemented by courses in

male and female halakhic authorities are asked regularly on the topic. It is clear that there is heightened awareness and acute relief in finding an outlet for asking personal questions. As someone who answers halakhic questions in this area daily, I am regularly moved by women who urgently want to be sexually permitted but are committed to keeping *halakhah* even when it is difficult, whether they are newlyweds or approaching menopause. They call with the fervent hope they will be permitted to their husbands despite the uterine bleeding that they fear will make them prohibited. Often, I am able to help them find a halakhic solution, and their subsequent gratitude, which, at times, is fervent and quite emotional, is testimony to how these laws impact people's lives on the most profoundly intimate levels.

---

sexuality, gynecology, infertility, and psychology, answer questions every night on a hotline.

Chapter Eight – Part Two

Behavior When the Couple is Prohibited by Laws of *Niddah*

The Perpetual Honeymoon?

IN THE TWENTIETH century, a romantic reframing of the *niddah* laws promoted family purity laws as the key to eternal sustainability of the Jewish marriage, distinguishing it from the hedonistic world of free, meaningless, self-indulgent sexual relationships promoted by secular liberal culture as the individual's right. At the height of the sexual revolution, Rabbi Dr. Norman Lamm, president of Yeshiva University, wrote his famous pamphlet, *A Hedge of Roses*, in which he explained that these laws inculcate a positive yet modest attitude towards sexuality.[1] He saw the laws of *niddah*, with their monthly repetitions of permitted and prohibited times for sexual relations, as creating a "perpetual honeymoon" for the couple by creating a genuine "I-Thou" relationship between partners. It was his opinion (which reflected the prevailing sentiment in Orthodoxy) that because of these laws, Orthodox Jewish marriages enjoy a high degree of sexual intensity and that Jewish law is the key to erotic fulfillment.

---

1. Norman Lamm, *A Hedge of Roses*, Feldheim, New York, 1966.

> **Excerpted from *A Hedge of Roses*:**
>
> Unrestricted approachability leads to over-indulgence. And this over-familiarity with its consequent satiety and boredom and ennui, is a direct and powerful cause of martial disharmony. When, however, the couple follows the Torah's sexual discipline and observes this period of separation, the ugly spectre of over-fulfillment and habituation is banished and the refreshing zest of early love is ever-present.... The separation is a prelude to reunion. This separation, too, which Judaism commands as part of the observance of Family Purity, is that which puts the poetry back into marriage...it is the pause that refreshes all of married life.[2]

Many subsequent works continued (and continue) to endorse the "perpetual honeymoon" theory with the intent to make *niddah* laws more directly relevant and meaningful to the modern observant couple. The biblical text, however, promises no such rewards. As was seen in the previous chapter, the laws of *niddah* first appear in the Bible as part of the section of laws on states of *ritual* purity/impurity. The prohibition of sexual relations with a woman who is a *niddah* appears separately, among the laws of sexual prohibitions. Neither passage promises rewards for keeping these laws, although severe punishment is incurred with transgression.

Rabbi Meir, circa second century CE, seems to be the first Rabbinic Sage to suggest a greater meaning to the practice:

B. Talmud Niddah 31b	תלמוד בבלי מסכת נדה דף לא עמ' ב
Rabbi Meir used to say: Why does the Torah state that a woman retains her *niddah* status for seven days? Because he becomes accustomed to being with	תניא, היה ר"מ אומר: מפני מה אמרה תורה נדה לשבעה - מפני שרגיל בה,

---

2. Ibid., pp. 58–60.

Behavior When the Couple is Prohibited by Laws of Niddah

| her and becomes repulsed by her. The Torah said: Let her be forbidden to him for seven days so that she will be as dear to her husband as when she entered the *huppah*. | וקץ בה, אמרה תורה: תהא טמאה שבעה ימים, כדי שתהא חביבה על בעלה כשעת כניסתה לחופה. |

Rabbi Meir proposed that the prohibited days serve as a sort of aphrodisiac for the husband, preventing overfamiliarity that could turn into contempt. It is noteworthy that he referred to a total of seven days of separation; in other words, his statement predated the shift to the more stringent requirement for seven clean days after the menstrual bleeding has ceased. Forbidden fruit is always sweeter, says the author of Proverbs, and Rabbi Meir suggested that the Torah's approach encouraged sexual fidelity and satisfaction on the part of the husband.

Despite his focus on male desire, Rabbi Meir (and later, Rabbi Lamm) was insightful in recognizing that sexual desire can erode due to familiarity and boredom, and that the sexual relationship is an important, even central piece in fostering intimacy and love. In a similar way, well-known psycho-therapist Esther Perel's bestselling book *Mating in Captivity*[3] explores the paradoxical union of domesticity and sexual desire, giving various insights on how to maintain passion in a long-term monogamous relationship.

> Excerpted from *Mating in Captivity*:
>
> Love enjoys knowing everything about you; desire needs mystery. Love likes to shrink the distance that exists between me and you, while desire is energized by it. If intimacy grows through repetition and familiarity, eroticism is numbed by repetition…love is about having; desire is about wanting…too often, as couples settle into the comforts of love, they cease to fan the flame of desire.[4]

---

3. Esther Perel, *Mating in Captivity*, First Harper, 2007.

4. Ibid., p. 37.

The structure of *niddah* laws, with clearly defined boundaries of sexual and non-sexual space, has the potential to foster greater sexual desire and passion through the distancing it requires throughout a couple's married life. The non-sexual days might infuse the sexual days with more intensity and the laws add value to the overall relationship, particularly when there is a disparity between the sexual needs in the relationship.[5] While this "benefit" may not be automatic, particularly in the beginning when couples are trying to establish a positive sexual rhythm, eventually it can become an appreciated part of their intimacy.[6]

However, the laws of *niddah* are far from a magical panacea that ensures sexual pleasure or saves troubled relationships.[7] For some couples, the laws of *niddah* never result in the promised benefit of greater intimacy and a perpetual honeymoon. Not infrequently, *niddah* laws can create tension, highlighting either the disparity in

---

5. To illustrate, structured sexual and non-sexual spaces, as regimented by *niddah* laws, can be helpful in developing a healthy balance using different "love languages" to express intimacy and connection. For a spouse who prefers non-physical and/or non-sexual communication, *niddah* can create a natural "break" from sexual expectation and allow for alternative expressions of love without rejecting the overtures of their more physical/sexual partner. In addition, the less sexual partner can find that they are more available during the sexually permitted days given the defined nature of the sexual space.

6. It is my experience that *niddah* laws are most successful when the couple honestly acknowledges the impact these laws will have on their particular relationship. Thinking sensitively about one another's needs as they enter and exit the sexual and non-sexual spaces determined by *niddah* laws will help a couple set realistic expectations of what they can anticipate from and give to one another. Ultimately, couples who can articulate healthy goal setting for both sexual and non-sexual spaces can help foster the closeness they are working to build and maintain in their marriage with *niddah* as part of that process.

7. The increase in religious sex therapists trained to work with rabbis and advise couples even in the most sexually restricted communities attest to the reluctant acknowledgment that men and women are seeking sexual satisfaction more than ever before. The internet has provided an anonymous platform in which religious men and women – from Modern Orthodox to the most restrictive Hassidic communities – are opening up their bedroom doors to expose a frightening lack of information, resources, and satisfaction.

Behavior When the Couple is Prohibited by Laws of Niddah

sexual needs between the couple or leaving one or both feeling lonely and alienated from one another. I have heard many women express gratitude for the childbearing years when *mikvah* does not factor into their lives at all.

In that vein, the following story exemplifies a reality that is very rarely mentioned when teaching *niddah* and illustrates some of what was described above. A woman called me with the following question. She had switched to a hormonal IUD and had gone for seven years without menstruating. Confronted with the possibility of becoming *niddah* due to some breakthrough (uterine) bleeding, I jokingly suggested that maybe it was time for a break. She earnestly responded that she would be happy if she never needed the *mikvah* since *niddah* had never been beneficial for her marital intimacy. She had, luckily, found a solution that removed *niddah* and *mikvah* completely from the equation.

Women are increasingly challenging the narrative which asserts that all couples need to replenish libidinal reserves in order to enjoy sexuality in a monogamous relationship. Couples for whom sexual and physical intimacy is central to their interaction, find removing it akin to lack of oxygen, leaving them straining to infuse emotional intimacy into their marriage during the non-sexual days. Others express issues with time management in overprogrammed lives leaving them little time to focus on sexuality when there is too short a window available with 12–13 days of non-sexual space in every cycle.

Rabbinic authorities are becoming more aware of the stress that restricted sexuality can place on observant couples. It has resulted in a halakhic solution that extends permitted days by encouraging women to double and triple pack their prescribed contraceptive pills to avoid becoming prohibited.[8] This strategy exposes how tenuous,

---

8. If the woman has been prescribed hormonal contraception by a doctor, she can usually extend the number of permitted days by continuously taking active pills. This does not work for every woman, but it can provide relief when a cycle is extended from 4 weeks to 6, 8, 10, and even 12 weeks. There are preparations on the market that are manufactured with 12 consecutive weeks of active pills. Some women who have finished with their childbearing opt for an intrauterine device

and, in extreme cases, fraudulent, the romanticizing of *niddah* laws can feel to couples who struggle to find meaning in or benefit from their practice of *halakhah*.

Forbidden Touch – Biblical or Rabbinic?

While restrictions on sexual relations can be challenging, the halakhic requirement that bans all intimate physical contact from the onset of uterine bleeding until immersion in the *mikvah* is far more difficult for many couples.

Rabbinic authorities are in agreement that sexual touch is prohibited between people who are sexually prohibited to one another. However, there is disagreement in the early rabbinic sources as to whether sexual touch is prohibited on a *d'orayta* (biblical) or a rabbinic level, based on their interpretation of the relevant verses in Torah. I will be focusing on touch between a man and his wife when she is *niddah*, and the relevant proof texts will be cited. However, as will be clear from Maimonides below, the same logical interpretation is applied in all forbidden relationships (e.g., between a man and another man's wife or a single man and woman):

Leviticus 18:19	ויקרא פרק יח
Do not come near a woman during her period of uncleanness to uncover her nakedness.	יט וְאֶל אִשָּׁה בְּנִדַּת טֻמְאָתָהּ לֹא תִקְרַב לְגַלּוֹת עֶרְוָתָהּ.

The *midrash halakhah* on Leviticus, Sifra, analyzes the words *do not come near* to indicate a prohibition above and beyond the prohibition of intercourse:

---

with hormones which can be left in for up to 5 years. Once the body adjusts to the IUD (in some cases immediately and in others after a few months of frequent breakthrough bleeding), women can spend years without any uterine bleeding.

Behavior When the Couple is Prohibited by Laws of Niddah

Sifra Aharei Mot Chapter 13	ספרא אחרי מות פרק יג
"Do not come near a woman during her period of uncleanness to uncover her nakedness" (Leviticus 18:19). I only know that intercourse is forbidden. From where do we derive that any intimacy is forbidden? It is written: "Do not come near." I only know this regarding a *niddah* (menstruating woman). How do I know it applies to all forbidden liaisons? It is written: "None of you shall come near anyone of his own flesh to uncover nakedness: I am the LORD."	וְאֶל אִשָּׁה בְּנִדַּת טֻמְאָתָהּ לֹא תִקְרַב לְגַלּוֹת עֶרְוָתָהּ. אין לי אלא שלא יגלה, מנין שלא יקרב? תלמוד לומר לא תִקְרַב. אין לי אלא נידה בל תקרב בל תגלה, מנין לכל העריות בל תקרבו ובל תגלו? תלמוד לומר: לֹא תִקְרְבוּ לְגַלּוֹת...אֲנִי ה׳.

It is noteworthy that Sifra does not explicitly define what the prohibition entails. However, Avot D'Rabbi Natan, using the same literary structure as Sifra, goes into specific detail about what is prohibited. These details will later be reflected in the laws codified by Maimonides:

Avot D'Rabbi Natan A Chapter 2	מסכתות קטנות מסכת אבות דרבי נתן נוסחא א פרק ב
What "safeguard" has the Torah made to its words? It says "Do not come near a woman during her period of uncleanness." (Leviticus 18:19). May the man hug her, kiss her, or have idle chat with her [short of intercourse]? The verse says: "Do not come near!" May the woman sleep with him on one bed while clothed? The verse says: "Do not come near!"	איזהו סייג שעשתה תורה לדבריה? הרי הוא אומר: וְאֶל־אִשָּׁה בְּנִדַּת טֻמְאָתָהּ־־לֹא תִקְרַב, יכול יחבקנה וינשקנה וידבר עמה דברים בטלים? ת״ל לֹא תִקְרַב. יכול תישן עמו בבגדיה על המטה ת״ל לֹא תִקְרַב.

323

Uncovered

Avot D'Rabbi Natan specifies hugging, kissing, and sleeping in one bed while wearing clothing as being in violation of the biblical command *do not come near*. This and the Sifra text seems to be the source that Maimonides relies on to prohibit sexual touch as *d'orayta* (biblical) law in both Sefer Hamitzvot and Mishneh Torah. Subsequently, this became the dominant halakhic position, and the one that is almost exclusively cited:[9]

Maimonides Sefer Hamitzvot, Negative Precept 353	ספר המצוות מצוות לא תעשה שנ"ג
He prohibited approaching one of these forbidden sexual relations – even without intercourse – such as [with] hugging and kissing, and similar such licentious acts. And that is His saying about its prohibition, "Each and every man – to any of his close kin – you shall not come near to uncover nakedness" (Leviticus 18:6) – as if to say, do not make any approach that leads to uncovering nakedness (sexual intercourse). And the language of the Sifra (Sifra, Acharei Mot, Chapter 13:15) is, "'You shall not come near to uncover nakedness' - I only know of nakedness. From where [do we know] not to come near? [Hence] we learn to say, 'To a woman, while in her menstrual impurity, you shall not come near to uncover her nakedness' (Leviticus 18:19). I only know about a menstruant, that she is [forbidden] with, do not come near and with,	הזהיר מהקרב אל אחת מהעריות האלו ואפילו בלא ביאה כגון חבוק ונשיקה והדומה להם מן הפעולות הזרות, והוא אמרו באזהרה מזה איש איש אל כל שאר בשרו לא תקרבו לגלות ערוה, כאילו יאמר לא תקרבו שום קירוב שיביא לגלות ערוה. ולשון ספרא לא תקרבו לגלות ערוה אין לי אלא שלא יגלה מנין שלא יקרב תלמוד לומר ואל אשה בנדת טומאתה לא תקרב, אין לי אלא נדה שהיא בבל תקרב ובל תגלה מנין

---

9. Maimonides, however, does not include the restriction on sleeping in a bed while clothed as a biblical prohibition.

324

Behavior When the Couple is Prohibited by Laws of Niddah

do not reveal. From where [do we know] about all of the sexual prohibitions, that they are [forbidden] with, do not come near and with, do not reveal? [Hence] we learn to say, 'you shall not come near to uncover.'" And there (Sifra, Acharei Mot, Chapter 13:21), they said, "'Their souls shall be cut off, those who do' (Leviticus 18:29) – what do we learn to say [from this]? Because it is stated, 'You shall not come near,' perhaps they would be liable for excision for [even] for coming near? [Hence] we learn from the scripture, 'who do' – and not those who come near."	לכל העריות שהן בבל תקרבו ובל תגלו תלמוד לומר לא תקרבו לגלות, ושם אמרו ונכרתו הנפשות העושות מה תלמוד לומר לפי שנאמר לא תקרבו יכול יהיו חייבים כרת על הקריבה תלמוד לומר העושות ולא הקרבות.

It is clear that Maimonides considers sexual touch, like hugging and kissing, to be in violation of a negative commandment. He acknowledges, nonetheless, that they are not equivalent to the act of "doing," meaning sexual relations, so someone who transgresses the commandment of "do not come near" would not be subject to *karet* or being cut off.

In Mishneh Torah, he codifies the law more concisely and clearly:

Maimonides Mishnah Torah Laws of Prohibited Sexual Relations 21:1	רמב"ם משנה תורה הלכות איסורי ביאה, פרק כא
Anyone who performs non-vaginal intercourse with one of the forbidden relationships, or who hugs and kisses in a sexual way and takes pleasure in physical intimacy, receives lashes for a biblical transgression, as it says (Leviticus 18:30), "Do not do any of these abominable customs etc.," and	א כל הבא על ערווה מן העריות דרך אברים, או שחיבק ונישק דרך תאווה ונהנה בקירוב בשר--הרי זה לוקה מן התורה. שנאמר: לְבִלְתִּי עֲשׂוֹת מֵחֻקּוֹת הַתּוֹעֵבֹת, ונאמר:

325

it says (Leviticus 18:6), "Do not come near to uncover nakedness," which is to say do not come near to acts which might bring you to transgressing sexual prohibitions.	לֹא תִקְרְבוּ לְגַלּוֹת עֶרְוָה. כלומר, לא תקרבו לדברים המביאין לידי גילוי ערווה.

Maimonides writes that in order to violate a negative prohibition in all prohibited sexual relations there must be two conditions: there must be intent (*hugs and kisses in a sexual way*) and/or sexual pleasure (*takes sexual pleasure*) derived from the act. In fact, the examples he brings are explicitly sexualized, particularly his use of the term for non-penetrative sexual relations (דרך אברים). Based on his interpretation that sexual touch violates a biblical prohibition, it is understandable that the rabbinic attitude toward any form of touch, even if it is non-sexual, is to be halakhically wary.

Other early post-Talmudic authorities took issue with Maimonides' determination that sexual touch in prohibited relationships is a violation of a biblical prohibition, the most well-known being Nahmanides:

Nahmanides Comments to Maimonides' Sefer Hamitzvot, Negative Precept 353	השגות הרמב"ן לספר המצוות להרמב"ם מצות לא תעשה שנ"ג
Maimonides cited an explicit *baraita* text, a respected authority upon which to base his opinion, but upon scrutiny of the Talmud it is not so. Acts such as hugging and kissing do not violate a negative precept of the Torah, but rather a rabbinic prohibition…an *asmakhta*. Although the Sages linked their precautionary measure to a Torah verse, they did not intend to interpret	והנה הרב מצא הברייתא הזו המפורשת ותלה דבריו באילן גדול. אבל כפי העיון בתלמוד אין הדבר כן שיהיה בקריבה שאין בה גלוי ערוה כגון חבוק ונשוק לאו ומלקות. ...נבין מהם כי אצלם זה האיסור מדרבנן... אבל אין זה עיקר

Behavior When the Couple is Prohibited by Laws of Niddah

the biblical verse as literally referring to intimate acts.	מדרש בלאו הזה אלא קרא אסמכתא בעלמא.

In contrast to Maimonides, Nahmanides understands that sexually touching a prohibited woman is a rabbinic prohibition and only the actual "uncovering of nakedness" (the biblical euphemism for penetrative intercourse) violates a biblical commandment. He brings evidence for this from the Talmud, in which Rabbi Pedat is cited as limiting the biblical prohibition to sexual relations only:

B. Talmud Shabbat 13a	תלמוד בבלי מסכת שבת דף יג עמ' א
They asked: Regarding a niddah, may she sleep with her husband in one bed while she is in her clothes and he is in his clothes?... Come and hear: "And he has not eaten upon the mountains, neither has he lifted up his eyes to the idols of the house of Israel, neither has he defiled his neighbor's wife, neither has he come near to a woman in her impurity" (Ezekiel 18:6). This verse juxtaposes a menstruating woman to his neighbor's wife. Just as lying together with his neighbor's wife, even when he is in his clothes and she is in her clothes, is prohibited, so too, lying with his wife when she is menstruating, even when he is in his clothes and she is in her clothes, is prohibited. And this conclusion disagrees with the opinion of Rabbi Pedat, as Rabbi Pedat said: The Torah only prohibited intimacy that involves engaging in	איבעיא להו: נדה, מהו שתישן עם בעלה היא בבגדה והוא בבגדו?... תא שמע: אֶל־הֶהָרִים, לֹא אָכָל, וְעֵינָיו לֹא נָשָׂא, אֶל־גִּלּוּלֵי בֵּית יִשְׂרָאֵל; וְאֶת־אֵשֶׁת רֵעֵהוּ לֹא טִמֵּא, וְאֶל־אִשָּׁה נִדָּה לֹא יִקְרָב. מקיש אשה נדה לאשת רעהו. מה אשת רעהו - הוא בבגדו והיא בבגדה אסור, אף אשתו נדה - הוא בבגדו והיא בבגדה אסור. שמע מינה. ופליגא דרבי פדת, דאמר רבי פדת: לא אסרה תורה אלא קורבה של גלוי עריות

| prohibited sexual relations, as it is stated: *A person shall not come near anyone of his own flesh to uncover their nakedness* (Leviticus 18:6). | בלבד, שנאמר: אִישׁ אִישׁ אֶל־כָּל־שְׁאֵר בְּשָׂרוֹ, לֹא תִקְרְבוּ לְגַלּוֹת עֶרְוָה. |

Since the Talmud does not categorically refute Rabbi Pedat – for example, by quoting the Sifra which unequivocally prohibited sexual touch on a biblical level – it was clear to Nahmanides that the prohibition of sexual touch with a *niddah* does not violate a biblical precept (perhaps because the source for the prohibition in this text is from the Book of Ezekiel). He concludes that sexual touching is rabbinically prohibited, serving as a "safeguard" or a protective expansion of the biblical law in order to prevent a situation that might ultimately lead to sexual relations. This does not imply that Nahmanides would be casually permissive about sexual touch. However, had his approach become the dominant one, it could certainly have led to more nuance in some of the questions that arise around emotional and service-based (e.g., non-emotional, clinical or professional) touch that will be presented below. In other words, once sexual touch violates a rabbinic rather than biblical prohibition, all other touch that is non-sexual become safeguards to the rabbinic rather than biblical law.

Ordinary Interaction and Touch

A mythical story about Elijah the prophet, brought in Tractate Shabbat, expresses great suspicion over casual touch between husband and wife when she is a *niddah*, regardless of their intent. It was widely quoted in the post-Talmudic era as a proof text that even the most casual of touch between husband and wife is forbidden. This story becomes one of the well-known sources for the ruling that all touch, even non-sexual touch, is prohibited, perhaps even a blanket violation of biblical law:[10]

---

10. Ibid.

Behavior When the Couple is Prohibited by Laws of Niddah

B. Talmud Shabbat 13a–b	תלמוד בבלי מסכת שבת דף יג עמוד א–ב
The school of Eliyahu taught: There was an incident involving one student who studied much Mishnah and read much Torah, and served Torah scholars extensively, and, nevertheless, died at half his days. His wife would take his phylacteries and go around with them to synagogues and study halls, and ask: It is written in the Torah: "For it is your life and the length of your days" (Deuteronomy 30:20). If so, my husband who studied much Mishnah, and read much Torah, and served Torah scholars extensively, why did he die at half his days? No one would respond to her at all. Elijah said: One time I was a guest in her house, and she was relating that entire event to me. And I said to her: My daughter, during the period of your menstruation, how did he act toward you? She said to me: Heaven forbid, he did not touch me even with his little finger. And I asked her: During your white days (seven clean of blood days before immersion), how did he act toward you? She said to me: He ate with me, and drank with me, and slept with me with bodily contact and, it did not enter his mind about something else (meaning sexual relations). And I said to her: Blessed is the Omnipresent who killed him, as he did not show	תני דבי אליהו: מעשה בתלמיד אחד ששנה הרבה וקרא הרבה, ושימש תלמידי חכמים הרבה, ומת בחצי ימיו. והיתה אשתו נוטלת תפיליו ומחזרתם בבתי כנסיות ובבתי מדרשות, ואמרה להם: כתיב בתורה כי הוא חייך ואורך ימיך, בעלי ששנה הרבה וקרא הרבה, ושימש תלמידי חכמים הרבה - מפני מה מת בחצי ימיו? ולא היה אדם מחזירה דבר. פעם אחת נתארחתי אצלה והיתה מסיחה כל אותו מאורע. ואמרתי לה: בתי, בימי נדותך מה הוא אצלך? אמרה לי: חס ושלום, אפילו באצבע קטנה לא נגע בי. - בימי לבוניך מהו אצלך? - אכל עמי, ושתה עמי, וישן עמי בקירוב בשר, ולא עלתה דעתו על דבר אחר. ואמרתי לה:

329

respect to the Torah. The Torah said: "And to a woman in the separation of her impurity you should not come near" (Leviticus 18:19) (even mere affectionate or casual contact is prohibited).	ברוך המקום שהרגו, שלא נשא פנים לתורה, שהרי אמרה תורה ואל אשה בנדת טומאתה לא תקרב.

In the story, we are told of the untimely death of a young scholar who spent much time in the Beit Midrash learning Torah and serving Torah scholars. His inconsolable widow tries to find answers to the eternal question of theodicy, most particularly because the Torah has promised life to one who follows in the way of a Torah scholarship. In the course of the narrative, she reveals an interesting bifurcation in behavior between days of bleeding and the clean days before immersion. While she was actively menstruating, the couple maintained a strict separation. He did not even touch her little finger![11] The husband, intensely aware of her impure state, took great pains to maintain distance. However, once the bleeding stopped, although still prohibited from sexual relations, the couple resumed modified intimacy during the seven "clean" days, including sleeping in close proximity to one another (although each in their own coverlet), eating together, and allowing their "flesh" to touch, albeit without any sexual intention.[12]

Elijah's response to her story is to unsympathetically explain

---

11. The little finger of a woman was analyzed earlier in Chapter Three since it appears in the Berakhot *sugya* on sources of *ervah*. While seemingly a most innocuous part of the body, it is cited as a possible trigger for male sexual arousal if a man has intent to derive pleasure from gazing at it. Touch would be even more potentially arousing. It will appear again in the halakhic sources prohibiting passing items one from the other when the couple is prohibited lest their little fingers come to touch.

12. During the Middle Ages, as documented in halakhic responsa, women treated the days of bleeding and the seven clean days differently. At some point, women in Ashkenaz even immersed twice – after seven days like a biblical *niddah* and after seven clean days like the *zavah*. Sexual relations would only be resumed after the second immersion, but certain intimate interaction was permitted already after the first immersion. Many *rishonim* were opposed to this behavior.

that God did well to kill her husband. The deceased's transgression, explains Elijah, was intimate interaction while she was still prohibited, even though they had no sexual intent. This story unequivocally views direct touch as transgressive with Elijah citing the Biblical verse *do not come near a woman who is a niddah* as a proof text that justifies the husband's untimely death.[13]

This story is prominently cited in the halakhic discourse. It serves to reinforce the need for complete physical separation throughout the period of prohibition, with no distinction between days of bleeding and clean days. The question of whether non-sexual touch is prohibited biblically or rabbinically continues to be evaluated in light of the story, which reflects an overall negative and forbidding attitude towards any touch between husband and wife for the duration of the *niddah* period.

Touch or Die?

In his commentary to Tur, Rabbi Yosef Karo, author of the Shulhan Arukh, takes the discussion regarding touching a *niddah* to an unprecedented level which has tremendous impact on the later halakhic discourse. He claims that since Maimonides classified sexual touch as an accessory to *arayot*, laws of sexual prohibition, and this category of law makes up one of the three types of sin that one must forfeit one's life for rather than transgress[14], sexually touching a forbidden relation, including a man's *niddah* wife, might very well carry the same weight[15]. While almost no one goes that far, this stringency in approach will permeate the halakhic discussion

---

13. It is reminiscent of the text in Leviticus Chapter 15, warning both men and women from approaching God's presence in the Tabernacle while in a state of impurity on pain of death. Elijah echoes the spirit of that warning in reinforcing the death sentence for those who choose to "approach" the *niddah*.

14. These categories include idolatory, sexual prohibition, and murder. While Judaism normally takes all precautions to safeguard life including the transgression of all commandments, these three categories are inviolate and are known as laws for which one lays down one's life rather than transgress.

15. Beit Yosef, Yoreh Deah, 195:17.

around touch between a husband and his *niddah* wife, even though the premise (that touching a *niddah* is so severe as to require giving up one's life) is largely rejected.

Notably, there are some major rabbinic authorities like Noda b'Yehudah,[16] Pnei Yehoshua,[17] and Avnei Nezer[18] who rule that full sexual relations with a *niddah*, although resulting in the severe punishment of *karet*, does not fall into the category of *arayot* like incest and adultery. One of the supporting arguments given for this distinction is that the child born to a *niddah* is not categorized as *mamzer*, a child born out of halakhic adulterous[19] or incestuous relations. Thus, it cannot be considered a prohibition for which one lays down one's life. Nonetheless, there is consistent, ongoing reluctance to permit any form of touch between a husband and his *niddah* wife regardless of the category of law it falls into. Nowhere is this more apparent than when dealing with questions of illness while a woman is *niddah*:

---

16. Noda b'Yehudah, Even HaEzer 55.
    And in truth, a *niddah* is not considered a matter of *ervah* even though it results in *karet*, as is proven from the language of Tosafot… since in any event *kiddushin* takes hold [when the woman is *niddah*], and the unborn child is "kosher" [meaning there is no halakhic stigma to being born to a *niddah*] and there is a "permissibility" to this prohibition through *mikvah* immersion [in other words it is not a permanent prohibition like incest but can be rectified], but the rest of the sexual prohibitions in their entirety, in this regard, are a matter of *ervah*…

17. Responsa Pnei Yehoshua 2:44.

18. Avnei Nezer, Yoreh Deah 461:10.
    And therefore, since the niddah does not create a *mamzer* nor does the woman become a *zonah* following sexual intercourse, we do not kill the pursuer in order to save his soul (in other words, this is not an act for which one lays down one's life – to avoid sex with a *niddah* - in comparison to incest or adultery in which case we kill the pursuer to save his soul) and there no connection to murder (this refers to Talmudic methodology known as *hekesh*) and he will transgress and not be killed, and there is no accessory to sexual prohibitions known as *gilui arayot* since this is a different type of prohibition entirely. And it requires great investigation.

19. Halakhic adultery is defined as sexual relations between a married woman and Jewish man who is not her husband.

Behavior When the Couple is Prohibited by Laws of Niddah

Caring for an Ill Husband

Shulhan Arukh Yoreh Deah 195:15	שולחן ערוך יורה דעה הל' נדה סי' קצה
If the husband falls ill, and there is no one to care for him besides his *niddah* wife, she is permitted to care for him. She must take the utmost caution to avoid washing his face, hands and feet and making the bed in front of him.	טו אם הוא חולה ואין לו מי שישמשנו זולתה, מותרת לשמשו רק שתזהר ביותר שתוכל להזהר מהרחצת פניו ידיו ורגליו והצעת המטה בפניו.

The Shulhan Arukh permits a woman to care for her husband when he is ill if there is no one to care for him. While he cautions the *niddah* wife to avoid washing her husband's hands or face or making the bed in his presence, he does not actually prohibit her from carrying out these activities when her husband is ill. It appears that if there is no one else to serve him, she can do what is necessary to alleviate his suffering. He bases his ruling on Rabbi Israel Isserlein, known as Terumat Hadeshen, who lived 100 years prior and ruled that when the husband is ill the wife can care for him although she should assiduously avoid touching him. Should she be forced to do so, he permits it, writing that it lacks sexual overtones since her husband is ill and weakened and will thus be able to control his sexual response.[20]

Caring for a Wife When She Is Ill

In contrast to the law above regarding the husband, there is no hint of leniency in the language of the Shulhan Arukh when it is the wife who is ill:

---

20. Terumat HaDeshen 252.

Shulhan Arukh, Yoreh Deah 195:16	שולחן ערוך יורה דעה הל' נדה סי' קצה
If a *niddah* becomes ill, her husband cannot attend to her in a way that involves touch, e.g., to help her into or out of bed. Rema: And if there is no one to help her, he is permitted to do everything and this is common practice if she greatly needs assistance.	טז אשה חולה והיא נדה, אסור לבעלה ליגע בה כדי לשמשה, כגון להקימה ולהשכיבה ולסמכה. [הגה] וי"א דאם אין לה מי שישמשנה, מותר בכל, וכן נוהגין אם צריכה הרבה לכך.

Shulhan Arukh, Yoreh Deah 195:17	שולחן ערוך יורה דעה הל' נדה סי' קצה
If her husband is a doctor, it is prohibited for him to feel for her pulse. Rema: And based on what I wrote above, that we rule leniently if she needs him to care for her, it is certainly permitted for him to feel for her pulse if there is no other doctor, she needs him, and her illness puts her in danger.	יז אם בעלה רופא, אסור למשש לה הדפק. הגה: ולפי מה שכתבתי דנוהגין היתר אם צריכה אליו דמשמש לה, כ"ש דמותר למשש לה הדפק אם אין רופא אחר וצריכה אליו ויש סכנה בחליה.

The Shulhan Arukh does not seem to allow for any moderation, even if there is no one else to care for the wife, as was the case for the sick husband. This is due to the concern that a healthy man cannot be expected to control his sexual urges when his wife is ill. He cites the Terumat Hadeshen who wrote in his commentary that when the wife is ill and her husband is well, there is no room for leniency since "his sexual urge may overcome him and he will convince her to submit and there is no deterrent to his having relations with her when she is ill."[21]

Rabbi Moses Isserles, in his gloss to Shulhan Arukh, inserts his

---

21. Terumat Hadeshen 252.

opinion on both passages cited above to allow a husband to care for his sick *niddah* wife. Furthermore, he states that this is common practice. In the first passage, he rules outright that if there is no one else to care for her, her husband may do so, including helping her in and out of bed. In the second passage, Rema assumes that the physician husband is checking her pulse to establish the degree of danger she is in and thus permits it even though the Shulhan Arukh explicitly prohibits it.

It is worth noting that the degree of illness or whether the wife is in danger are not taken into consideration as circumstances that might allow for leniency in Shulkhan Arukh. For this reason, the nineteenth-century halakhic authority Rabbi Yechiel Michel Epstein takes pains to make it clear in his halakhic code, Arukh Hashulhan, that in case of danger the Shulhan Arukh would unequivocally allow a husband to care for his wife and explains that the argument between him and Rema is only when the wife is not in physical danger.[22]

To summarize, if a woman's life is in danger, it is agreed by the overwhelming majority of authorities that her husband may do all that is necessary to assist her. However, if she is not in danger and touch is necessary to alleviate physical suffering, there are conflicting opinions. Even Rav Elyashiv Knohl, considered a moderate in matters of *niddah*, writes: "One should also try to minimize direct physical contact where possible, using a thick garment or blanket as a barrier when holding or supporting an ill spouse. If these issues arise one should consult a rabbi about how to deal with the situation."[23]

---

22. Arukh Hashulhan Yoreh Deah 195:26–27.
"The explanation of the matters above is that the Rema and the author of the Shulhan Arukh both reason that in a case of danger it is permitted and even though the Beit Yosef seems doubtful for perhaps he agreed with the opinion of the Rambam who reasoned that all physical touch in matters of sexual prohibitions in the Torah are biblically prohibited and thus may not be permitted even in case of danger. In any event it is clear here that he would permit in case of danger…and certainly a professional doctor can check her 'hidden organs' if such is necessary since he is doing his job."

23. Elyashiv Knohl, *The Marriage Covenant*, 2008, p. 146.

Support During the Birthing Process

Birthing women become prohibited like a *niddah* once there is significant uterine blood flow or once the woman becomes fully dilated.[24] Therefore, the question of physically assisting one's wife during childbirth is somewhat comparable to the previous topic of assisting a *niddah* when she is ill. It is worth noting that the halakhic question of a husband assisting during birth is a very contemporary one, reflecting the modern trend of encouraging men to enter the birthing room. Until the late twentieth century, husbands were essentially banned from witnessing their wives' labor, and it was unthinkable that a man would hold his wife's hand or massage her back as she pushed the baby out into the world. This reality has changed significantly. Husbands are now encouraged to physically support their wives throughout labor and birth. Many actively seek and desire a partnering role during their child's birth. Rabbinic authorities have responded to this new reality with a plethora of opinions, running the gamut from lenient to stringent, as is commonly found in halakhic decision-making.

One of the first questions that was addressed by rabbinic authorities was whether the husband could be in the birthing room given the prohibition of directly looking at the vulva.[25] While many rabbis permit husbands to be present at birth, the instruction is for them

---

24. There are differences of opinion regarding the point in labor at which the couple becomes prohibited. Until the woman is in active labor, as long as there is no flow of blood resembling the flow of menstruation, she can wear panty liners or colored underwear and ignore bleeding. Once she is 10 centimeters dilated, according to all opinions, she becomes a *niddah*. This is the stage at which she is ready to push. For clear halakhic guidance, see books by Dr. Deena Zimmerman or Rabbi Knohl on the topic.

25. There are differences of opinion as to whether a man can ever look at his wife's vulva even when permitted. Such opinions continue to be reflective of a conservative attitude towards sexual exploration based on halakhic discourse. It is not the topic of this chapter but remains something that deserves great attention and awareness of enormous changes in hygiene, attitudes toward female genitalia, and interest in more direct interaction and exploration of women's bodies by men and women as part of their sexual intimacy.

Behavior When the Couple is Prohibited by Laws of Niddah

to remain by the woman's head to avoid seeing the baby emerge.[26] Another question that engenders tremendous debate is whether the husband can continue to touch his wife while she is giving birth, even after she becomes prohibited. Until the mid-1990s, there were no moderate rabbinic positions to be found, at least publicly. However, over the last three decades, as attitudes towards men in the birthing room have significantly changed, there has been a shift and some authorities permit it based on the school of Rema brought above about assisting the wife when she is ill.

This serves as an important illustration of the halakhic reluctance to permit emotional or support touch to the woman toward the end of childbirth or afterward during her recovery. On one hand, it is indisputable that the birthing woman is defined in *halakhah* as one whose life is in danger. Shabbat may be violated in any way necessary to assist her. *Kashrut* laws may be suspended if she has an unnatural craving for unkosher food, and she may eat and drink as necessary on Yom Kippur. Maimonides codifies the Talmudic law that a candle may be lit for a blind woman in labor on Shabbat if she requests it in order to give her "peace of mind," even though the light has no practical purpose. It thus seems counterintuitive that there is very little leniency with respect to the possibility of a husband providing his wife with emotionally supportive touch (in contrast to more clinical service touch) during and after birth. Given the seeming impossibility of having sexual relations with a birthing woman and her status as a person in physical danger during and sometimes after birth, there would seem to be room for leniency. However, in halakhic discourse, the nature of the touch, whether sexual or non-sexual, is hardly raised. All touch is potentially sexual especially if the man is healthy, even if the couple has no intention or possibility of having sexual relations.

To quote Rabbi Knohl who as mentioned above was one of the most moderate public voices on *niddah* law: "Most prenatal courses encourage the husband to massage his wife during labor, but Jewish law prohibits this [once the couple becomes prohibited]. If

---

26. For example, *Responsa Bnei Banim* 1:33.

a woman is terribly anxious before the birth and feels that she will need her husband's touch to calm her, the couple should consult a rabbi. Obviously, if there is any threat to the woman's health, then whatever is required to soothe her is permitted. But such situations are extremely rare; normally there is no reason to fear for the woman's health."[27]

This statement contains an internal contradiction. On one hand, we treat the woman in labor as if her life is in danger regarding Shabbat (most relevant) and *kashrut* (less relevant today). When it comes to emotionally supportive touch, however, Rabbi Knohl discourages it because her life is not *really* in danger. This sentiment is reflective of the deep discomfort of rabbis with the topic of permitting touch, particularly emotionally supportive touch, even when there is perceived need to support the woman's health. Perhaps this is because there is no concern that violating Shabbat for a birthing woman will lead to a more casual attitude to the laws of Shabbat. In contrast, there is a constant concern that allowing the couple to touch when prohibited will lead to a complete dissolution of sexual boundaries. From a halakhic perspective, it is best to ask a female relative or hire a doula to provide emotionally supportive touch throughout labor and during the birth.

Mental Illness

In comparison to physical illness, where the man or woman can halakhically be permitted to physically assist their spouse when no one else is around to do so, the touch provided to someone suffering from mental anguish is not adressed in the halakhic literature. As a result, it has been very difficult for rabbinic authorities to consider this as a necessary circumstance for which allowances could be made.

Unfortunately, this halakhic wariness might be perceived by men and women afflicted with mental health conditions as a lack of empathy or true understanding of the degree of suffering. I recently sat with a bride who suffers from terrible anxiety. She told me that

---

27. Elyashiv Knohl, *The Marriage Covenant*, 2008, p. 187.

Behavior When the Couple is Prohibited by Laws of Niddah

if the rabbis understood the degree of her suffering and the acute necessity for touch to alleviate her distress, they would absolutely regard it as threatening to life!

For men and women suffering from depression, anxiety, OCD, and other mental disorders, studies show that touch is essential in facilitating calm and emotional healing in times of mental anguish. The removal of touch from the marital relationship for 11–13 days can cause mental anguish for the spouse expressly needing physical closeness during this prohibited time.

In fact, mental illness has had little serious consideration in halakhic sources outside of very primitive boundaries presented in the Talmud with no incorporation of modern medical resources or findings reflecting changes made to the field. For this reason, Rabbi Yonatan Rosensweig extensively researched mental illness and *halakhah*, consulting with a wide range of Orthodox and ultra-Orthodox rabbis along with psychiatrists. In his book *Nafshi Bishe'elati: The Halakhot of Mental Health*, he examines the mental health crisis happening at every level of the greater religious community and halakhic responses to a wide variety of questions having to do with Shabbat, fasting on Yom Kippur, *kashrut*, prayer, honoring parents, laws of mourning, and much more. With regard to a couple who are prohibited to touch, he brings a spectrum of opinions along with comprehensive halakhic analysis ranging from those who prohibit all touch to those who are willing to permit a range of touch (hand-holding to a full embrace, preferably with a garment in between the bodies rather than skin to skin contact) in situations of mental distress.[28] In a similar vein, Rabbi Yitzhak Ronis published an article in the journal *Assia* in which he used an innovative multilayered halakhic argument to suggest that in cases of great emotional need there is room to permit couples to "support one another even though the woman is *niddah* at the time."[29]

---

28. Yonatan Rosensweig and Shmuel Harris, *Nafshi Bishe'elati: The Halakot of Mental Health* (Hebrew), pp. 156–163.

29. Yitzhak Roniss, "With Regard to Rabbinic Laws of Separation at Times of Acute Mental Trauma," Assia 106–107, 5777 (Hebrew), pp. 136–139.

To illustrate (and this is only one of many similar stories), a woman struggling with infertility contacted me. She was trying to get pregnant although chances were slim. She had suffered several miscarriages and after the most recent one, found herself suffused with sadness and depression. She was crying regularly. Since she was a *niddah* after the miscarriage (as are all women), her husband could not touch her, and they would not touch without rabbinic permission, despite her mental and emotional desperation.

I called two different rabbis whom I trusted, both renowned halakhic authorities in *niddah* as well as in other areas of Jewish law, to consult about the case. One allowed touching but without full-body contact. This leniency was based on the principle of *shinui* which means that there is enough of a change to the prohibited act to remove it from the category of biblical prohibition so that although rabbinically prohibited, in light of the circumstances, it could be permitted. The other rabbi was less restrictive, allowing touch without gloves and without defined boundaries, as long as the couple could be trusted to avoid sexual touch. He relied on the ruling of the nineteenth-century Rabbi Avraham David Wahrman in his *Ezer Mikodesh* who considers affectionate non-sexual touch to be rabbinically rather than biblically prohibited.[30] He concluded that in extenuating circumstances such as this one, rabbinic law could be waived. Both of their approaches relied on sources that prohibit sexual touch but leave open the possibility of a lenient ruling in extreme circumstances for non-sexual emotional touch.

Overall, these are welcome halakhic voices that bring nuance and moderation to complex situations that an increasing number of observant couples are finding themselves forced to navigate.

---

30. The *Ezer Mikodesh* Even HaEzer 20:1, is one of the only sources I have come across who distinguishes between sexual affection (*hibat biah*) and physical affection (*hibat ahavah*). Only touch that is meant for intercourse is prohibited from the Torah, he explains in his commentary to Even HaEzer. Affectionate touch, akin to touch between a father and daughter, is rabbinically prohibited between a husband and his *niddah* wife. This acknowledgment of emotional touch as rabbinically prohibited should allow for some latitude in cases of mental anguish.

Behavior When the Couple is Prohibited by Laws of Niddah

Emotional Touch

Having looked at halakhic sources that govern behavior throughout the *niddah* period between husband and wife, I want to circle back to the questions that arise around emotional touch. The rabbinic consensus is that non-sexual touch between two people who are in a sexual relationship can easily lead to sexual touch and therefore must be avoided during the *niddah* period. Although the need for emotional touch is not addressed in the halakhic sources, we must recognize that it is quite commonplace (and normal) for non-sexual emotional touch to release feelings of arousal unexpectedly. What may start out as purely asexual can very easily cross over into the sexual. Since *halakhah* often demands clarity and clear boundaries, it is easier to eliminate all touch than to navigate the subjective experience of individual men and women who may or may not become sexually aroused through non-sexual touch. For this reason, the halakhic discourse reflects a deep resistance to permitting any sort of direct contact between husband and wife when the woman is *niddah*, even when it is clearly non-sexual touch.

As we saw above, the only exceptions regard direct threats to life or serious illness, and most sources show little concern for emotional well-being. This can create tremendous dissonance for couples, particularly when touch is a central expression of the emotional intimacy between them. For many men and women, touch is the dominant way that they feel connected, nurtured, and contained. Studies have shown that humans have brain pathways that are specifically dedicated to detecting affectionate touch in order to communicate that we are safe, loved, and not alone.[31] Removing it can create a bewildering sense of loneliness that extends for almost two weeks within the marital relationship. Furthermore, there are a significant number of couples who experience weeks and sometimes months of separation. I have counseled women after miscarriage, childbirth, and most notably,

---

31. Tara Parker-Pope, "*How to Hug During a Pandemic*," *The New York Times*, June 4, 2020, www.nytimes.com/2020/06/04/well/family/coronavirus-pandemic-hug-mask.html

during perimenopause who spend extended periods of time unable to immerse in the *mikvah*. Too often, none of the many leniencies in the halakhic toolbox are able to help for long and the couple has to grapple with the anguish of physical separation in addition to the difficult hormonal challenges experienced by the woman in her body. One woman in perimenopause told me that she felt that despite all of their best efforts and their commitment to *halakhah*, she and her husband were living like brother and sister and their marital intimacy was deeply eroding due to the weeks of *niddah* separation they were enduring.

Rabbi Shaul David Bozcko of Israel published a post on Facebook that was intended to give couples a degree of freedom when considering when and how to incorporate touch into their relationship during prohibited days.

In a few sentences, he summarized the core of prohibited touch as being that which is foreplay to sexual relations. For Maimonides and his school of *halakhah*, such touch is biblically prohibited; for Nahmanides such touch is rabbinically prohibited. He wrote that couples should take four principles into consideration when making a decision when and how to touch:

1. The halakhic principle of human dignity which allows for the violation of rabbinic law when someone's honor or dignity is being compromised.

2. Anguish as halakhic grounds for violating rabbinic law.

3. A patient whose life is not in danger for whom rabbinic law can be violated.

4. Concern that keeping rabbinic law could lead to the violation of biblical law.

In his post he wrote that by publicizing these principles, his intent was to allow couples to make their own decisions without living in fear that there is no way to be lenient when there is necessity. While these principles would not allow for ongoing casual affection, it would

Behavior When the Couple is Prohibited by Laws of Niddah

allow couples to have some degree of emotional and physical support as deemed necessary by their individual circumstances particularly when there are extended periods of prohibition.

Further Halakhic Safeguards – *Harkhakot*

As described in the previous chapter, the mandated non-sexual space lasts, on average, 11–13 days a cycle. However, intercourse and sexual touch are not the only restrictions during this time. In order to govern the desexualization of the relationship, a series of restrictions known as *harkhakot* (distancing measures) evolved in order to remind the couple regularly, throughout this time, that they are prohibited. These include separate beds, limitations while eating together, and refraining from handing things to one another:

Arukh Hashulhan Yoreh Deah 195:1	ערוך השולחן יורה דעה סימן קצה
It is known that the prohibition of the *niddah* is like all of the sexual prohibitions in the Torah that result in *karet*; however, with regard to distancing oneself from her, restrictions are different. There are things that are more stringent in comparison to the other prohibitions such as passing things into her hand or taking from her hand and so on as will be explained below and there are many more leniencies in her regard such as permitting him to [sexually] enjoy looking at her in a way that is prohibited for those relatives that are prohibited to him. Likewise, seclusion with his wife during *niddah* is permitted	א ידוע שנדה היא ככל העריות שכל העריות הן בכרת וכן נדה היא בכרת ובעניין ההרחקה ממנה איננה שוה לכל העריות יש בדברים שהחמירו בה יותר מבכל העריות כמו ליתן בידה או ליטול מידה וכיוצא בזה כמו שיתבאר לפנינו ויש שהקילו בה יותר כמו שמותר ליהנות בראייתה ובכל העריות פשיטא שאסור אפילו ההסתכלות וכן יחוד דבכל העריות אסור להתייחד ועם אשתו נדה היחוד

| but not with women [such as relatives] who are prohibited to him. As the rabbis said (Sanhedrin 37a), the Torah creates a hedge of roses. It testifies that we, with only a mild warning and a minimal separation, separate ourselves from sin and when she says: I have seen red like a rose, he immediately separates. | מותר וכן אמרו חז"ל [סנהדרין ל"ז א] סוגה בשושנים התורה העידה עלינו שאפילו כסוגה בשושנים לא יפרצו בה פרצות כלומר באזהרה קלה ובהבדלה מועטת נפרשים מן העבירה [רש"י ד"ה סוגה] וכשאומרת כשושנה אדומה ראיתי מיד פורש ממנה [תוס' ד"ה התורה]: |

As the Arukh Hashulkhan aptly notes, a married man is allowed to have sexual thoughts about his wife, even when she is prohibited to him and he is allowed to be alone with her, even in the bedroom. However, he is not allowed to touch her in any way for the duration of the *niddah* period. The challenge of how to desexualize the relationship within the framework of shared living space is what guides the next series of laws.

There is a great deal of trepidation regarding male sexual desire often referred to in the Talmud as the *yetzer hara* – the evil inclination. This *yetzer* is a potential source of distraction that can turn a man away from his religious obligations, including prayer, Torah study, and a meaningful connection with the Divine. Even within a permitted, sanctified marital relationship, there is concern that men will be unable to control their sexual desire at times when their wives are prohibited. The early rabbinic text Avot D'Rabbi Natan goes as far as to propose that women should deliberately make themselves unattractive in order to protect their husbands:

Behavior When the Couple is Prohibited by Laws of Niddah

Avot D'Rabbi Natan A, Chapter 2	מסכתות קטנות מסכת אבות דרבי נתן נוסחא א פרק ב
What "safeguard" has the Torah made to its words? It says "Do not come near a woman during her period of uncleanness." (Leviticus 18:19). Then, may the man hug her, kiss her, or have idle chat with her [short of intercourse]? The verse says: "Do not come near!" Then, may the woman sleep with him on one bed with her clothes on [short of being naked]? The verse says: "Do not come near!" Can it be that she may wash her face and put on eye shadow? The Torah says: "in her menstrual infirmity[32]" (Leviticus 15:33). All of the days of her *niddah*, she should be shunned. From here they said, all women who intentionally make themselves repulsive while in their period of *niddah* will be blessed and all who adorn themselves during their *niddah*, the Sages are displeased with them.	איזהו סייג שעשתה תורה לדבריה? הרי הוא אומר: וְאֶל-אִשָּׁה בְּנִדַּת טֻמְאָתָהּ- לֹא תִקְרַב, יכול יחבקנה וינשקנה וידבר עמה דברים בטלים? ת"ל לֹא תִקְרָב. יכול תישן עמו בבגדיה על המטה ת"ל לֹא תִקְרָב. יכול תרחץ פניה ותכחול [את] עיניה ת"ל וְהַדָּוָה בְּנִדָּתָהּ. כל ימים שבנדתה תהיה בנדוי. מכאן אמרו כל המנולת עצמה בימי נדתה רוח חכמים נוחה הימנה וכל המקשטת עצמה בימי נדתה אין רוח חכמים נוחה הימנה:

We have already seen an analysis of the forbidden touch framework. However, that is not considered a strong enough framework according

---

32. There is wordplay here that is hard to catch in the English. The word *niddah* identifies a woman who is menstruating. As has been explained, in her menstruant state a woman is impure and sexually prohibited. Although she must have distance from her husband, she is not isolated from her home or the other members of her family. In this midrashic text, the author exaggerates the root *n'da* which can mean isolation to suggest the woman must be isolated, even shunned during this period to protect the husband from sexual deviancy for the duration of the prohibited period until she immerses in a *mikvah*.

to the majority Talmudic opinion to keep the man from "coming near" the woman. There must be other restrictions incorporated into their relationship to prevent the man from actualizing his sexual desire. This culminates in an extreme suggestion in the source above: women should make themselves unattractive in order to neutralize their husbands' sexual desire! Fortunately this idea is rejected by Rabbi Akiva below:

B. Talmud Shabbat 64b	תלמוד בבלי מסכת שבת דף סד עמ' ב
As we learned in a Tannaitic source: "in her menstrual infirmity." The early authorities said that she may not apply makeup nor put on colorful clothes. [That was] until Rabbi Akiva came and taught: If you hold this view you will soon make her unattractive to her husband and eventually he will divorce her. So how shall we understand "in her menstrual infirmity" [according to R. Akiva]? In her state of separation – until she immerses in water.	כדתניא: וְהַדָּוָה בְּנִדָּתָהּ, זקנים הראשונים אמרו: שלא תכחול ולא תפקוס ולא תתקשט בבגדי צבעונין. עד שבא רבי עקיבא ולימד: אם כן אתה מגנה על בעלה, ונמצא בעלה מגרשה. אלא מה תלמוד לומר וְהַדָּוָה בְּנִדָּתָהּ - בנדתה תהא עד שתבא במים.

The "early authorities" cited here seem to be reflective of the source in Avot D'Rabbi Natan. Rabbi Akiva astutely notes that if a woman makes no effort to groom herself for an extended period of time, she may indeed end up becoming repulsive to her husband, resulting in divorce. Rabbi Akiva understands that the marital relationship is fundamentally a sexual one and that desire cannot be denied so totally that a man cannot stand to look at his wife. Sexual attraction must exist on a continuum, even when prohibited, or it will lead to an untenable situation within the marriage in which the man will come to revile his wife as a sexual partner. The discipline to desexualize the

Behavior When the Couple is Prohibited by Laws of Niddah

interaction will have to come from elsewhere and not at the expense of a woman's attractiveness.

A woman (or man) is even permitted to perform loving acts for her (his) spouse with some modification, even when *niddah*. In Tractate Ketubot, the Talmud relates a series of stories in which wives poured their husbands wine while *niddah*:

B. Talmud Ketubot 61a	תלמוד בבלי מסכת כתובות דף סא עמ' א
Rav Yitzḥak bar Hananya said that Rav Huna said: All tasks that a wife performs for her husband, a menstruating woman may similarly perform for her husband, except for: Pouring his cup, making his bed, and washing his face, hands, and feet…. *And pouring a cup of wine.* Shmuel's wife would switch hands and pour with her left hand. Abaye's would place it on top of a barrel. Rava's on his pillow. Rav Pappa's wife would place it on the bench.	אמר רב יצחק בר חנניא אמר רב הונא: כל מלאכות שהאשה עושה לבעלה - נדה עושה לבעלה, חוץ ממזיגת הכוס, והצעת המטה, והרחצת פניו ידיו ורגליו. ... ומזיגת הכוס. שמואל, מחלפא ליה דביתהו בידא דשמאלא. אביי, מנחא ליה אפומא דכובא. רבא, אבי סדיא. רב פפא, אשרשיפא.

This first paragraph limits a wife from pouring her husband wine, making his bed, and washing her husband's hands, feet, and face when she is a *niddah*. All three have an element of intimacy and are not merely routine household tasks. For this reason, all three are prohibited while she is a *niddah*, according to Rav Yitzḥak bar Hananya.

In four vignettes that follow in the second paragraph (above), the Amoraim in Babylonia relate how their wives continued to pour their wine albeit with slight changes. The wives of these Amoraim continued to perform an intimate act for their spouses (mixing and serving them wine which was highly personal), but with mindful awareness of the non-sexual space they are sharing by means of slight changes in behavior. This principle, maintaining intimacy and yet reminding the husband and wife that she is *niddah*, is codified into *halakhah* in both Mishneh Torah[33] and Shulkhan Arukh.[34] In presenting these four vignettes, the Talmud teaches us that each couple can be creative in finding the right balance that works for them; maintaining intimacy, yet reminding themselves not to cross the line into sexual activity.

Desexualizing the Most Sexual Space: The Bedroom

Shulhan Arukh Yoreh Deah Laws of *Niddah* 195:6	שולחן ערוך יורה דעה הל׳ נדה סי׳ קצה
He should not sleep with her in one bed, even if each is in their own clothing and they are not touching one another. Rema: And even if each one has their own blanket and even if they are lying in two beds and the beds are touching, this is prohibited.	ו לא יישן עמה במטה, אפילו כל אחד בבגדו ואין נוגעין זה בזה. הגה: ואפילו יש לכל אחד מצע בפני עצמו, ואפילו אם שוכבים בשתי מטות והמטות נוגעות זו בזו, אסור.

Despite overarching concern for male *yetzer* and prohibited sexual behavior, *halakhah* does not require the couple to sleep in separate rooms. However, one bed with two blankets as per Rav Pedat's suggestion (cited above in Tractate Shabbat 13a) was rejected by Talmudic law. Although a bed wide enough so that two people could sleep on it without touching remained a viable halakhic option into the Middle Ages, the determinative *halakhah* from the Shulhan Arukh onward is to require two beds with a minimum separation preventing

---

33. Maimonides Mishneh Torah, Laws of Marriage, 21:8.
34. Shulkhan Arukh Yoreh Deah 195:10.

Behavior When the Couple is Prohibited by Laws of Niddah

the beds from touching.[35] This separation serves to remind the couple that they are in a non-sexual space while simultaneously preserving intimacy by allowing them to lie side by side throughout the night, interacting, sharing, and simply being next to one another.

Eating Together

Shulhan Arukh Yoreh Deah Laws of *Niddah* 195:3	שולחן ערוך יורה דעה הל׳ נדה סי׳ קצה
He should not eat with her at the same table unless there is some sort of object distinguishing between his plate and her plate such as bread or a pitcher, or each one should eat on their own placemat/tablecloth. Rema: And some say that a separation between his plate and hers is necessary specifically when they do not share a plate when she is permitted, but if they eat from one plate when she is permitted, then it is enough that each	ג לא יאכל עמה על השלחן אא״כ יש שום שינוי שיהיה שום דבר מפסיק בין קערה שלו לקערה שלה, לחם או קנקן, או שיאכל כל אחד במפה שלו. הגה: וי״א דצריכין הפסק בין קערה שלו לקערה שלה היינו דוקא כשאינן אוכלין בקערה אחת כשהיא

---

35. Some couples separate their beds with a small gap while others place a piece of furniture between them. The bed design can be reflective of different approaches to *niddah* and the way in which the couple wants to desexualize their relationship in accordance with their halakhic practice. In Israel, a "Jewish bed" was developed for the religious market, which has a shared headboard and one bed frame but separate mattresses. The frames move to separate the beds to whatever distance is chosen. When the couple is permitted, the bed frames are pushed together so that one sheet can be snugly placed over both mattresses.
Some couples prefer a double bed with one of them sleeping on a trundle bed or mattress on the floor during the prohibited time. Other couples resist having two beds and want to know if there are any halakhic alternatives. If they make the non-halakhic decision to buy one large bed, I suggest they act in the manner of couples who find themselves as guests in a hotel or guest bedroom with only one bed while prohibited: Create two spaces in the manner of Rabbi Pedat. Minimally, separate blankets and pillows should be used; if possible, a barrier of sorts should be placed in the middle of the bed.

one eats from their own plate and they do not need any other object to separate them. And this is the practice. And there are some who say it is prohibited for him to eat from her leftovers just as it is prohibited for him to drink from what is left in her cup, as will be explained. 4 He should not drink from what is left in a cup that she drinks from. Rema: Only if no person drank from her cup in between or, if the contents of the cup were emptied into another cup, even if it is returned to the original cup [he can drink]; and if she drank and he does not know that she drank from this cup and he wishes to drink from her cup, she does not need to tell him not to drink. And she is permitted to drink from a cup he drank from. And if she drank from this cup, there are some who say that he can drink what is left, since she has already left, there is no intimacy in the act.	טהורה, אבל אם אוכלין בקערה אחת כשהיא טהורה סגי אם אוכלת בקערה בפני עצמה, וא״צ היכר אחר, וכן נוהגין. י״א שאסור לו לאכול משיורי מאכל שלה, כמו שאסור לשתות משיורי כוס שלה, וכמו שיתבאר. ד לא ישתה משיורי כוס ששתתה היא. הגה: אם לא שמפסיק אדם אחר ביניהם או שהורק מכוס זה אל כוס אחר אפילו הוחזר לכוס ראשון. ואם שתתה והוא אינו יודע ורוצה לשתות מכוס שלה, אינה צריכה להגיד לו שלא ישתה. והיא מותרת לשתות מכוס ששתה הוא. ואם שתתה מכוס י״א שמותר לו לשתות המותר, דמאחר שכבר הלכה אין כאן חבה.

In the same vein as the attention directed towards the bedroom, there is both wariness and nuanced permissiveness at meals. Dining together is often a shared experience for friends and family, creating connection and fostering intimacy and familiarity. Like the bedroom, minimal boundaries are put in place to avoid sexual intimacy. They can prepare food for one another and sit down and enjoy the meal together. Slight changes in behavior are enough to allow for normalcy. The *halakhah* creates a framework in which the couple can eat together, with minor reminders that they are prohibited. For example, the requirement that

Behavior When the Couple is Prohibited by Laws of Niddah

they mark their status on the table in some minimal way. Any item that stands out as unusual can be used for this purpose. There is a similar halakhic requirement when two friends eat milk and meat at the same table. By placing an unusual object on the table, the diners are reminded that they are not to eat from one another's plate. In the case of the couple, it is there to remind them they are to be aware of their current staus and maintain a non-sexual relationship.

Passing from Hand to Hand

Tosafot Shabbat 13b	תוספות מסכת שבת דף יג עמ' ב ד"ה בימי
And Rashi forbade himself from passing a key from his hand to hers (his wife's) during the days of her *niddut*.	ורש"י היה נוהג איסור להושיט מפתח מידו לידה בימי נדות.
Mahzor Vitri 499	מחזור ויטרי סימן תצט
It is the law that it is prohibited [for a man] to touch his wife during all the days of her *niddah*, even her little finger… There are some who are careful even not to pass her any object. And at the very least it is good to be careful not to pass her any kind of food or drink. It is good and proper to be careful not to pass [anything] from his hand to her hand. And the same holds for her clean days, until she immerses.	דין שאסור ליגע לאשתו כל ימי נידתה אפי' באצבע קטנה. ויש נזהרין אפילו להושיט לה שום דבר. ולכל הפחות דבר של מאכל ומשתה טוב ונכון מליזהר שלא יושיט מידו לידה. וכן בימי ליבונה וספירתה עד שתטבול:

שולחן ערוך יורה דעה סי׳ קצה	Shulhan Arukh Yoreh Deah 195:2
ב לא יגע בה אפילו באצבע קטנה, ולא יושיט מידו לידה שום דבר ולא יקבלנו מידה, שמא יגע בבשרה. (וכן על ידי זריקה מידו לידה או להיפך, אסור).	And he should not touch her even on her little finger and he should not pass anything from his hand to hers and not accept anything from her hand lest he come to touch her flesh (also, throwing from his hand to hers or the opposite is prohibited).

People often wonder whether the restriction on directly passing to one another when the woman is *niddah* is a stringency or actual *halakhah*. It is a practice that seems to have originated with the famous biblical and Talmudic commentary Rashi (eleventh century), who did not pass keys to his wife, which began to be quoted in many halakhic sources afterwards. Eventually it became codified in the Shulhan Arukh where it is written that a man must not pass an object to his wife lest he brush against her little finger. The reference to the little finger, which appeared in Berakhot as a possible source of *ervah* if a man looks with intent, intimates that even inadvertently brushing against the little finger of his *niddah* wife could unleash sexual feelings and must be avoided.

For some couples, this restriction borders on the offensive by suggesting that a man's sexual desire is so uncontrollable that the couple must avoid passing things to one another in order to avoid triggering it. Men do not normally become uncontrollably excited by inadvertently touching their wife's hand! However, the *harkhakot* are there to define non-sexual space and create halakhic boundaries. One could view this *halakhah* in a more positive light as an expression of exquisite mindfulness, rather than as a deterrent to the male *yetzer*. It takes the mundane act of passing, which is normally utterly insignificant in any and every other prohibited relationship, into something that makes the couple mindful of the non-sexual space

Behavior When the Couple is Prohibited by Laws of Niddah

they have chosen to create through halakhic observance. Multiple times a day, it can serve as a reminder for the couple that they are committed to changing the dynamic between them, using different love languages and investing in other forms of connection.[36]

That said, couples should use common sense in this regard. If an object is too heavy to carry alone or an infant is sleeping and there is no one around to help, they are permitted to carry something together or hand an item from one to the other, provided, of course, that they take care not to touch deliberately.

There are two interesting *responsa* that, to my mind, reflect the modern discourse on the application of *harkhakot* in public. Rabbi Moshe Feinstein was asked about easing the restriction on passing objects in a public space since there should be no concern for "breaching of safeguards," i.e., getting carried away in public, and second, to avoid embarrassment, specifically to the woman, if it become obvious to everyone around that she is a *niddah*. Rabbi Feinstein answered strongly in the negative, emphasizing that since women regularly menstruate, there is no reason for this to cause any embarrassment, and the opposite should be true. The couple should feel proud to make it known that they are keeping these *halakhot*.

In contrast, 40 years later, Rabbi Yuval Cherlow of Israel was asked the same question.[37] His answer is far more nuanced than that of Rav Moshe. After having spoken to women about this specific issue, Rabbi Cherlow shows a sensitive awareness of women's feelings in this regard. He cites rabbinic authorities who were lenient about passing things both in public and in the presence of the couple's children. He also validates the discomfort women feel when their bodies are scrutinized and wonders about the immodesty in granting others the

---

36. Once there are children, particularly infants and small children, using common sense becomes paramount. Never put the baby on the floor of a bus or hood of a car as an alternative to passing from hand to hand! Various *responsa* have been written about passing the baby safely, and it should be clear to all that the baby's safety takes precedence over the law prohibiting passing things from one to another, which is a rabbinic fence.

37. http://shut.moreshet.co.il/shut2.asp?id=6735

knowledge that a couple is prohibited or permitted. Furthermore, he notes that while in the past there were places where it was customary for menstruating women to wear different clothing while prohibited, which marked their status publicly, today this is not the case, and women are deliberately private about such matters. Finally, he notes that if halakhic authorities are too stringent in this matter, it could potentially have more serious consequences. Couples who mock or disregard this particular *halakhah* may eventually reject the other more significant safeguards in this area of *halakhah*. This is an inverse application of the fear of the "slippery slope," which normally leads halakhic authorities to more stringency.

Finding the Right Balance

Halakhah is an intricate religious structure that directs and governs our days, weeks, months, and years by interpreting the will of the Divine into human behavioral practice. Just as *kashrut* governs what we eat, the weekly Sabbath and Jewish holidays govern our time, and multiple laws govern our interaction with one another, the laws of *niddah* govern and have the potential to transform one of the most important aspects – that of sexuality.

However, when I teach and counsel couples, I never promise them that such physical separation will automatically be beneficial for a relationship. As with other aspects of marriage, communication, consideration, and patience, along with goal setting and constant reflection, can help the couple integrate this in a positive way. Still, it is a process that takes time and effort.

Many of the couples tell me that they are planning to keep the *niddah* laws in some capacity but have decided against full compliance for a variety of personal and emotional reasons. It is interesting that while halakhically these laws are seen as no less important than Shabbat and *kashrut*, there are many observant couples who make non-halakhic choices with regard to the *niddah* laws despite simultaneously leading a fully halakhic lifestyle in every other way.

Some couples remain very conflicted about this behavior, feeling a sense of guilt, or worse, shame and failure, over their inability to

Behavior When the Couple is Prohibited by Laws of Niddah

uphold *halakhah* properly. This is particularly acute when the couple's level of observance in other areas suggests scrupulous adherence. Others are less conflicted and seek to incorporate those laws that empower their relationship while rejecting restrictions that might cause conflict or distance.

During my sessions, I emphasize the element of choice. Especially with regard to our bodies and sexuality, it is imperative for people to feel that they have agency over what they do and what is being done to them. Those who choose to keep these laws – out of belief and commitment to religious law and tradition – must strive to find a sense of control in this area of their life, especially when *halakhah* challenges them. My overarching aim is to help people think thoughtfully and considerately about these choices and talk openly about how they will manage their relationship as it fluctuates between different types of interaction at different times and stages in their marriage.

To this end, it is important for each of the partners to engage in candid conversations with one another even before marriage, and certainly throughout their marriage, about the impact *niddah* laws have on their interactions in and out of the bedroom. Greater sensitivity to their respective individual needs will help them have a greater appreciation for their different "love languages" and how their similarity or diversity will affect them as they transition from being sexually permitted to prohibited and back again.

When a woman menstruates, it marks the onset of mandated, prolonged non-sexual space. This may come as a relief to one or both spouses if there are intimacy issues or an imbalance in the sexual relationship. On the other hand, this transition may require greater emotional resources. If the couple is careful to remove all touch from the relationship, this decision can trigger feelings of loneliness as the husband and wife embark on almost two weeks of constant physical separation.

On the other end of this cycle is *mikvah* night, when the couple is meant to engage in sexual relations to express their yearning for one another. However, *mikvah* night is not an automatic panacea ensuring sexual satisfaction and emotional intimacy. While it can work as an aphrodisiac for some marriages, it does not always work that way for others. There are those for whom the night is rife with tension over the logistics of the woman going to the *mikvah*, the experience itself (which not all women enjoy, and for some, impacts their ability to engage sexually upon arriving home), and the expectations over resuming relations. It is not uncommon for couples to chafe, privately or openly, against the expectation that they move from nothing to everything. Some complain that sexuality is not an on and off switch. I have heard both men and women express frustration over the assumption that sexual relations will be automatically resumed. For this reason, we must make room for couples to be honest about the lived experience of the laws restricting and renewing sexuality so that we can normalize their experiences and help them gain traction over the process.

When thinking about the shift into sexual space, communicating expectations and incorporating some transitional behavior such as a romantic dinner, quality time, and small gifts can help the couple reconnect in a positive and gradual way. A new trend I have observed is the husband immersing in the morning in a *mikvah*. This can be important for couples searching for something more egalitarian as they observe these laws.

Over the last decade of teaching *niddah* in different forums and working with couples before and during marriage, I have found that many people are looking to infuse their sexuality with meaning. These laws hold potential for some in achieving that goal. Nonetheless, therapists, rabbis, counselors, and educators who work in this area must show awareness of the complex interplay between halakhic requirements and individual need, and develop strategies and language to respond adequately to the many-layered issues that arise for couples encountering these laws for the first time or after many years of marriage as issues around sexual desire shift and evolve.

Chapter Nine

Premarital Relationships

Introduction

According to halakhic norms, touch between the sexes outside the context of marriage is prohibited under nearly all circumstances. A person who abides by this code of conduct is referred to as *shomer negiah*, literally "one who observes [the prohibition of] touching." I am often asked where the mandate to be *shomer negiah* is found in the Torah. It isn't although the answer is more complicated, as will be explained below. This pseudo-halakhic term was coined in the twentieth century in the wake of vast changes in society that included increasingly casual interaction between males and females and the growing exposure of Orthodox young people to the expectations in secular culture that they be sexually active. Thus, *shomer negiah* became a useful (if somewhat vague) umbrella term meant to encapsulate all that Orthodox Judaism wishes to impart regarding physical interaction between men and women before marriage. It is meant to describe a Torah lifestyle that demands abstinence before marriage as an essential tenet of religious morality and commitment to *halakhah*. While it sends a very clear and concise message, *shomer negiah* also tends to shut down any deeper conversation on the topic of sexuality, particularly for those who are in need of rabbinic counsel and halakhic direction. Rarely is an actual textual source cited when the subject is addressed.

As we will see, the *halakhot* of non-marital sexual contact have a degree of nuance which is rarely taught. However, even if they are not taught, the reality of unmarried couples and their religious educational needs demand more than simply the assertion of a blanket prohibition. We need to address:

a. Complexities that religious adults encounter in the often long years before, or sometimes after, marriage (e.g., divorce or death of a spouse).

b. The reality that many people fail to live up to this standard.

Much of the chapter is directed at a Modern Orthodox community for whom years of casual socializing and/or a long courtship often precede the decision to marry. Nonetheless, I am increasingly becoming aware of expectations for premarital touch among people dating in the more right-wing yeshiva world, especially among older singles and previously married men and women. Many complain that it is hard to find sensitive rabbinic authorities willing to acknowledge the realities of what some of them – men and women – are confronting, particularly for those who remain single for a considerable period of time.

Forbidden Touch[1]

Do Not Come Near

While the *shomer negiah* rhetoric conflates all touch into a single prohibition, there are significant halakhic differences between sexual, emotional, and casual types of touch that should be made clear to those in a relationship with the potential for physical contact. The prohibition of physical touch between unmarried men and women rests on the *niddah* status of women from the onset of their first menstruation as was analyzed in the previous chapter. A very concise summary of that discussion will be presented here nonetheless. All rabbinic authorities agree that sexual touch is prohibited when the

---

1. The next few paragraphs are excerpted from Chapter Eight Part Two. For a longer analysis of the source material, see there.

Premarital Relationships

woman is a *niddah*, meaning she has not completed seven clean days after menstruation and immersed in the *mikvah*.[2] However, there is disagreement in the early rabbinic sources as to whether sexual touch is prohibited on a *d'orayta* (biblical) or a rabbinic level based on the interpretation of the relevant verses in the Torah. The main source for the prohibition is the following verse in Leviticus:

Leviticus 18:19	ויקרא פרק יח
Do not come near a woman during her period of uncleanness to uncover her nakedness.	יט וְאֶל אִשָּׁה בְּנִדַּת טֻמְאָתָהּ לֹא תִקְרַב לְגַלּוֹת עֶרְוָתָהּ.

Based on early rabbinic interpretation of this verse, Maimonides prohibited sexual touch as violating *d'orayta* (biblical) law in both *Sefer Hamitzvot* and *Mishneh Torah*. He explicitly writes that any sort of sexual contact between a man and a prohibited woman (including his wife when she is *niddah*) is a violation of a biblical prohibition. Subsequently, this became the dominant halakhic position and the one that is almost exclusively cited.

Other early post-Talmudic authorities took issue with Maimonides on this subject, the most well-known being Nahmanides, who understood that sexually touching a prohibited woman violated rabbinic law and only the "uncovering of nakedness" (the biblical euphemism for intercourse) violates a biblical commandment. He concluded that the rabbinical prohibition against sexual touch served as a "fence," a safeguard against transgressing the biblical law, in order to prevent a situation that might ultimately lead to sexual relations.

In line with Maimonides, Shulhan Arukh codified the prohibition of sexual touch as a *d'orayta* (biblical) prohibition. Rabbi Shabtai HaCohen, known as the *Shakh* (an acronym of the title of his

---

2. The focus will be on a woman who is *niddah*, but the same methodology applies to all sexually forbidden relationships. For a detailed analysis of this prohibition and the halakhic requirements see the previous chapter.

seventeenth-century commentary on the *Shulhan Arukh*, *Siftei Kohen*), noted in his commentary that even according to Maimonides, only sexual touch is prohibited by Torah law and that touch that is not explicitly sexual is rabbinically prohibited:

Shach: Yoreah Deah 195:10	שך: יורה דעה קצ"ה: י
Maimonides' view seems correct (that intimacy for pleasure's sake carries the force of a Torah prohibition). He, himself, was only referring to the sort of hugging and kissing associated with intercourse for we find in several places in the Talmud that the Amoraim would hug and kiss their daughters and sisters.	ומכל מקום משמע דאף הרמב"ם לא קאמר אלא כשעושה חיבוק ונישוק דרך חיבת ביאה שהרי מצינו בש"ס בכמה דוכתי שהאמוראים היו מחבקים ומנשקים לבנותיהם ואחיותיהם....אלמא דאינו לוקה אלא בדרך תאוה וחיבת ביאה...

This does not imply that Nahmanides or the *Shakh* would be casually permissive about non-sexual touch, but this distinction has significant halakhic implications for couples who are trying to create sexual boundaries with an awareness of the different gradations of prohibition with regard to touch in *halakhah*.

Emotional Touch

In the previous chapter, source analysis is brought regarding different kinds of touch in the context of married couples when they are prohibited from touching and the possible leniencies in the cases of physical illness, mental anguish, and acute emotional need. While the majority of halakhic authorities remain stringent on all but the most extreme situations, there has been growing awareness of the role affectionate touch plays during mental and physical distress (not life-threatening), and there are rabbinic authorities who have begun to respond with nuanced and moderate halakhic direction for couples seeking guidance (see there).

As noted previously, affectionate or emotional touch does not fall into a clear halakhic category. Where does it stand in the discourse between the explicitly sexual and the casual/professional? Since *halakhah* seeks clarity particularly in the area of sexuality, it has been easier to eliminate all touch as potentially sexual. Few halakhic sources show concern for mental or emotional well-being even in the legitimate context of a marital sexual relationship. Certainly outside of marriage there are no halakhic sources that countenance leniency for any kind of touch. Yet the absolute ban on touch stands in stark contrast to the very human need for physical contact that many people seek in order to feel an emotional connection to someone else. While this does not justify violating *halakhah* outright, single adults who find themselves in need of physical touch while dating seriously either for emotional support or to foster intimacy, could rely on some of the distinctions cited in the previous chapter that distinguish between sexual touch and touch to alleviate mental/emotional distress (during childbirth, acute anxiety, depression, etc.).

THE HALAKHIC PROHIBITIONS RELATING TO NON-MARITAL SEXUAL RELATIONS

Kadesh/Kadeshah

In this section, the halakhic differences between promiscuous and committed non-marital sexual relations will be considered. Interestingly, there is no outright prohibition in the Torah against engaging in consensual sexual relations when a woman is unmarried (if she is not *niddah*). There is, however, a specific Torah prohibition against sexual promiscuity that can be found in Deuteronomy 23:18:

Deuteronomy 23:18	דברים פרק כג פסוק יח
No Israelite woman shall be a cult prostitute [*kadeshah*], nor shall any Israelite man be a cult prostitute [*kadesh*].	לֹא־תִהְיֶה קְדֵשָׁה מִבְּנוֹת יִשְׂרָאֵל וְלֹא־יִהְיֶה קָדֵשׁ מִבְּנֵי יִשְׂרָאֵל׃

Who are the *kadeshah* and the *kadesh* according to the *halakhah*? It is interesting to note that the words *kadesh* and *kadeshah* come from the Hebrew root *k.d.sh* meaning holy, reflecting the ancient practice of sexual rituals as a form of worship in other religions.[3] Maimonides, however, takes the unequivocal position that the *kadeshah* refers to all sexual relations outside of *kiddushin*:

Maimonides Mishneh Torah Laws of Marriage Chapter 1:4	רמב"ם משנה תורה הלכות אישות פרק א הלכה ד
Before the Torah was given, a man would meet a woman in the marketplace and if both he and she desired, he could give her payment, engage in relations with her wherever and then depart. Such a woman is referred to as a harlot. When the Torah was given, relations with a *kadeshah* became forbidden as it is stated, "There shall not be *kadeshah* among the daughters of Israel." Therefore, a person who has sexual relations with a woman for fornication, without matrimony, receives lashes as prescribed by the Torah, because he had relations with a *kadeshah*.	קודם מתן תורה היה אדם פוגע אשה בשוק אם רצה הוא והיא נותן לה שכרה ובועל אותה על אם הדרך והולך לו, וזו היא הנקראת קדשה, משנתנה התורה נאסרה הקדשה שנאמר +דברים כ"ג+ לא תהיה קדשה מבנות ישראל, לפיכך כל הבועל אשה לשם זנות בלא קידושין לוקה מן התורה מפני שבעל קדשה.

---

3. BDB Dictionary, p. 873.

Premarital Relationships

Comment of Raavad:	השגת הראב"ד:
A woman does not become a *kadeshah* unless she is dedicated [to promiscuity, i.e.,] she abandons herself to everyone. However, if she designates herself for one man, she does not incur lashes nor is there a prohibition and she is the concubine that is described in the scripture.	א"א אין קדשה אלא מזומנת והיא המופקרת לכל אדם אבל המיוחדת עצמה לאיש אחד אין בה לא מלקות ולא איסור לאו והיא הפילגש הכתובה.

While Maimonides takes a hard line against all sexual relations outside of marriage, anchoring his position in the prohibition of *kadeshah*, the medieval commentator on Maimonides' Mishneh Torah, Rabbi Abraham son of David known as Raavad, disagrees. He argues that only a promiscuous woman who is available to any man is a *kadeshah*. If the woman is monogamous, designating herself to one man, there is no prohibition, even if they are not formally married. He identifies this type of relationship as that of a man with a concubine which he believes is permitted. According to Maimonides, in contrast, only kings are allowed to take concubines.[4] This argument between Maimonides and Raavad had no practical consequence for most people for many hundreds of years. It is remarkable to note that in the eighteenth century, Rabbi Jacob Emden sought to reintroduce the institution of the concubine in response to the sexual immorality of his own day. In a very long responsum, he analyzes many of the sources brought earlier in this chapter and concluded that there is room to permit a man to take a woman as a concubine in order to avoid greater promiscuity with many women! Among other things, he insisted that a couple committing to this non-marital framework observe the laws of *mikvah*, practice monogamy for the duration of the relationship, and act in consultation with a rabbi.[5]

---

4. See Mishneh Torah Law of Kings Chapter 4:4.

5. She'elat Yaavetz Pt. 2 No. 15.

While Emden's suggestion was rejected by both rabbis and communities alike, his approach is thought-provoking in light of the current dating culture. Emden felt it better for people who engage in sexual activity to have some degree of religious sanction rather than the totally forbidden activity that they were engaging in anyway. Although such a sexual relationship could not be equated with marital sexuality, at least it could infuse their sexuality with some form of commitment and meaningful intention. In a similar vein, Professor Zvi Zohar tried to revive the idea of concubine as a halakhic framework for monogamous non-marital sexuality in an article he published in 2006.[6] His article was summarily dismissed by rabbinic authorities and Orthodox laypeople alike, although it led to much lively discussion around many Shabbat tables!

The *Niddah* Prohibition and Single Women Using the *Mikvah*

It did not escape the notice of Jewish men already 700 years ago that if (Jewish) women, even prostitutes, immersed in the *mikvah* 7 days after menstrual bleeding stopped, they would no longer be considered *niddah*. Rabbi Isaac ben Sheshet Perfet, known as Rivash, a Spanish Talmudic authority in the fourteenth century, was asked by the men of his community whether Jewish prostitutes in town should immerse in order to prevent men who used their services from transgressing the laws of *niddah*. Furthermore, they stated, perhaps it would be better for all single women to immerse themselves since it is known that sometimes people transgress. Having single women immerse themselves in a *mikvah* after menstruating would prevent those who had relations with them (and the women themselves) from receiving *karet*.

In a thunderous response, Rivash unequivocally rejected any such policy. First, he clarified that prostitution is prohibited whether the women are *niddah* or not. Second, he affirmed the practice of unmarried women not going to the *mikvah* as a means of protecting

---

6. Zvi Zohar, *Living Together as a Couple without Huppah and Kiddushin* (Hebrew), Aqdamot, 2006.

Premarital Relationships

the daughters of Israel; if unmarried women are always in a state of *niddah*, the threat of *karet*, he argued, is an important deterrent to sin:

Responsa Rivash 425[7]	שו"ת הריב"ש סימן תכה
Question: You asked me to explain to you that which is written in the Torah: "And to a menstruating woman do not come near to uncover her nakedness," is it said about every menstruating woman, be it his wife or be it an unmarried woman? And if so, how was this not mentioned in all the laws of *niddah* discussed in Rashba in the book *Torat HaBayit* and not by Raavad in the book *Baalei HaNefesh*? For according to their words, they only talked about married women; and how is that everyone says that an unmarried woman is permitted? And our Sages, how did they allow any prostitutes to remain in the world as they presumably do not purify themselves? And how did they not make a decree, some corrective or restriction for the purity of single women so that the many not falter as anyone who has relations with her [the unmarried woman who has not gone to the *mikvah*] is punished with *karet*, and one who touches the little finger of a *niddah* incurs lashes? And if the Torah was talking only about one's wife when she is a *niddah*, there is difficulty with the language of Maimonides in many places since it is apparent from his	שאלת: לבאר לך, מה שכתוב בתורה: ואל אשה בנדת טומאתה, לא תקרב לגלות ערותה. אם נאמר על כל אשה נדה: בין באשתו, בין בפנויה? ואם הוא כן, איך לא הזכירו דבר זה, הרשב"א ז"ל בספר תורת הבית; ולא הראב"ד ז"ל בספר בעלי נפש? כי לפי לשונם, לעולם לא דברו: אלא באשתו של אדם; ואיך מורגל בפי כל אדם: פלונית פנויה מותרת? וחכמים ז"ל, איך הניחו שום קדשה בעולם? כי מסתמא, אינן מטהרות עצמן. ואיך לא תקנו: שום תקון, או שום גדר של טהרה, בפנוי'; כדי שלא יכשלו בה רבים, אחר שהבא עליה ענוש כרת, והנוגע בה באצבע קטנה, חייב מלקות? ואם באשתו בלבד הכתוב מדבר, הוקשה לך לשון הרמב"ם ז"ל, בהרבה מקומות.

---

7. Thanks to Dr. Jennie Rosenfeld for help with the translation.

words that the prohibition of a *niddah* applies both to one's wife and to an unmarried woman.
Responsum: It is clear that the prohibition of relations with a *niddah* is not only with one's wife; rather, whether she be one's wife, or another's wife, or an unmarried woman… and this is a simple matter. And no-one ever doubted it. And even speaking about it is unnecessary. The verse also said simply "To a menstruating woman do not come near." And it made no distinction between one's wife and an unmarried woman for it did not say "to your wife"…..
And that which you asked: how did our Sages allow any prostitutes to remain in the world as they do not purify themselves [through immersion]. Heaven forbid that our Sages would allow prostitution, and make her permitted! And even if they immersed [to purify themselves] from *niddah*! For the verse proclaims: "There should not be a prostitute from the daughters of Israel." ….Come let us reprimand our generation which is not behaving properly. And the leaders of our generation hide their eyes [and pretend not to notice the Jewish prostitutes], lest the promiscuous Jewish men falter with non-Jewish women, fire will be ignited, and find brambles and the grain pile will be consumed [i.e., it will lead to even worse consequences]. And the prostitutes that existed in the time of the Sages were against their wishes.… And that which you wondered: How did they not establish immersion for the

שנראה מדבריו: שאסור הנדה: בין באשתו בין בפנויה.
תשובה: דבר ברור הוא: שאסור ביאת הנדה; לא באשתו בלבד, אלא: בין באשתו, בין באשת חברו, בין בפנויה... וזה דבר פשוט. ולא נסתפק בו אדם מעולם. והדבור בו מותר. גם הכתוב אמר סתם: ואל אשה בנדת טומאתה. ולא חלק: בין אשתו, לפנויה. שהרי לא אמר: ואל אשתך....
ומה שהוקשה לך: איך חז"ל הניחו שום קדשה בעולם, שהרי אינן מטהרות עצמן. חלילה שחז"ל יניחו קדשה, ויתירוה! ואף אם תהיינה טובלות לנדותן. והכתוב צווח:
לא תהיה קדשה מבנות ישראל... באו ונצווח על דורנו, שאין דומה יפה. וגדולי הדור, העלם יעלימו את עיניהם, פן יכשלו בני פריצי עמנו, בנכריות, ותצא אש, ומצאה קוצים, ונאכל גדיש. והקדשות שהיו בימי חז"ל, שלא ברצון חכמים היו....

| unmarried woman, so that people not falter with her? There is no room for wonder. Since the unmarried woman is prohibited as we explained, it is the opposite! For if she would immerse then she would truly be a stumbling block for then people would be lenient about the prohibition [of pre-marital sex], since the prohibition is only rabbinic [and not liable for *karet*]… | ומה שנפלאת: איך לא תקנו טבילה לפנויה, כדי שלא יכשלו בה רבים? ואין כאן מקום תמה! שהרי כיון שהפנויה אסורה, כמש"כ. אדרבה! אם היתה טובלת, היה בה מכשול: שהיו מקילין באסורה; כיון שאין אסורה, אלא מדרבנן. |

Rivash cites Maimonides that sex outside of marriage is a biblical prohibition; furthermore, even those who disagree with Maimonides (i.e., Raavad) agree that non-marital relations with a woman who is not *niddah* violate rabbinic law.[8] Nonetheless, the fact that such relations were not subject to *karet* and perhaps not a biblical prohibition at all contributed to the policy of preventing single women from immersing in the *mikvah*, ensuring they would remain in a state of *niddut* until their marriage. Rivash recognized that if single women were allowed to go to the *mikvah*, it would be easy for people to justify outright promiscuity to themselves. The societal, religious, and halakhic norms of traditional Jewish society in place both before and after Rivash's responsum precluded single women from using the *mikvah*, and his position on the matter essentially became the only one that is cited thereafter in *Tur* and *Shulhan Arukh*. By aggressively enforcing a ban on *mikvah* use before marriage, the severity of the threat of *karet* acted (and continues to act) as a deterrent.

Interestingly, the issue of single women using *mikvah* has reemerged in the last 25 years but with a major difference: instead of men wishing all women immersed in order to have non-commital sexual relations without risking *karet*, women are seeking to immerse as a

---

8. This statement is not completely accurate since according to Raavad and his school of thought, when a man designates a woman as his concubine, sexual relations are permitted.

way of rendering their sexual activity more in tune with *halakhah*. They usually come to the decision to go to the *mikvah* together with their partner, rarely in consultation with halakhic authorities since they perceive that rabbinic authorities will disapprove.

There are a variety of rabbinic opinions about whether single women should immerse in a *mikvah* when they are sexually active, but these are all passed around in an oral rather than written manner. Most often, counsel, if sought, will be given, appropriately on a case-to-case basis. Some reason halakhically that at least *karet* is avoided and perhaps the couple's engagement with *mikvah* raises the chances of their maintaining a level of commitment to observance and to monogamy. Others align with Rivash and argue that it is impossible to sanction non-marital relations even with *mikvah* immersion. Allowing women to immerse would give these relations a veneer of permissibility. These rabbis contend that couples *should* feel guilt over their transgressive behavior.

To summarize, the practice of single women using the *mikvah* is unique to a halakhically observant, educated demographic. While it is rarely rabbinically sanctioned, engaging in sexual relations after the woman has immersed in a *mikvah* is still within the bounds of their observant lifestyle.[9] They know they are violating the religious mandate to remain celibate until marriage but are also aware that the severe biblical prohibition of relations with/while a *niddah* (i.e., liability to incur *karet*) is neutralized by the woman's immersion in a *mikvah*. Many of those I teach are completely unaware of Maimonides'

---

9. In the early twenty-first century, this practice came to be a part of public discourse in Israel when questions were raised about state control of who was eligible to immerse in publicly funded *mikvaot*. It was common practice for *mikvah* attendants to inquire as to the marital status of women. If a woman hesitated or answered honestly that she was single, she was denied entry and forcibly removed. Many argued, and continue to argue, that a publicly funded space should be accessible to all women. After many years of prolonged litigation that eventually made its way to Israel's High Court, a "don't ask, don't tell" policy was agreed upon – explicitly single women would not be allowed to immerse, however, *mikvah* attendants were no longer permitted to ask the marital status of the immersing women.

prohibition on all non-marital sexual relations regardless of *mikvah* immersion.

This is one of the ways these couples navigate the conflict inherent in the reality of their lived experience as both Orthodox Jews and sexually active singles.[10] Not surprisingly, this practice is most prevalent in cities where there are large clusters of religious singles; cities allow more anonymity around *mikvah* use than in in the past when the community could monitor closely who was using the *mikvah*.

Summary of Opinions about Non-Marital Sexual Relations

- Non-marital sexual relations defined as penetrative sex (anal or vaginal) carry the greatest degree of halakhic consequence if the woman is *niddah* since the punishment for such relations is *karet*.

- If one has relations with an unmarried woman who is not *niddah*, it still violates a biblical transgression of *kadeshah* according to Maimonides although Raavad disagrees (as analyzed above). It is difficult to find public rabbinic sanction for a committed, monogamous sexual relationship between unmarried people, although there are individuals throughout halakhic history who have ruled like Raavad (notably Rabbi Emden) and acknowledged that such a relationship, if monogamous and the woman immerses in the *mikvah*, does not violate any explicit prohibitions.

OTHER ASPECTS OF NON-MARITAL SEXUALITY

Expectations of Virginity

There are several other aspects to consider when thinking about non-marital sexuality that are quasi-halakhic and nonetheless prevalent

---

10. It should be noted that not all couples who define as Orthodox use *mikvah* even when sexually active. I have encountered couples who deliberately decided to wait to use the *mikvah* until marriage in order to distinguish non-marital from marital sexual relations; in this model, *mikvah* becomes a frame for their commitment to a Jewish marriage.

in the discourse in the Modern Orthodox community. Virginity, particularly for women, is a religious expectation that is expressed in the Jewish marriage contract (*ketubah*). Specifically, the *halakhah* mandates that the minimal *ketubah* of a virgin is twice as much as that of a non-virgin. The language of the *ketubah* of a previously unmarried woman refers to the bride as a virgin. One of the educational tactics used in religious education is to tell young women that the public reading of the *ketubah* at her wedding is a declaration of her chastity and if she is not a virgin, the *ketubah* will be adjusted to reflect her promiscuity. This is more a scare tactic than a true threat since the *ketubah* is a contract between husband and wife. If the husband does not object, the information in it about the woman's virginity does not have to be factual and her prior sexual experience need not be a matter of public record.[11] Since many young women are ignorant of this halakhic possibility, the threat of being exposed in the *ketubah* is a real one.[12]

Fear of *Mamzerut*

There is a popular misconception that if a woman becomes pregnant out of wedlock, the child will be stigmatized as a *mamzer*, inaccurately translated as "bastard," which in English does mean a child born out of wedlock. The threat of one's child being *mamzer* is significant since a child categorized as such is *halakhically* permitted to marry only other *mamzers*, and the children of that marriage will also be *mamzers* with the same strictures, ensuring that the status is forever

---

11. *Igrot Moshe Orah Haim* 4: 118. Regarding the writing of the *ketubah*, you need not tell the rabbi who is officiating. By signing the *ketubah*, the groom is agreeing to the use of the term "virgin" – and there is no further concern. He is thereby legally bound to the terms of a virgin's *ketubah*, even if in truth the bride is not, so long as she did not mislead him.

12. This misconception has also led to situations where religious couples choose to engage in oral and anal sexual relations to preserve the woman's virginity out of fear that her *ketubah* be compromised, or because they believe that by refraining from vaginal intercourse they escape the punishment of *karet*, unknowing that anal intercourse incurs the same punishment.

passed on. However, in *halakhah*, this tragic status is limited to the child of an adulterous[13] or incestuous sexual relationship. The child born from a non-marital relationship or to a woman who has sexual relations when *niddah*, is not a *mamzer*, and the aforementioned fear is unfounded. Nonetheless, the possibility of giving birth to a *mamzer*, since it is vaguely associated with all illicit sexual relations, adds to the stigma around non-marital sex.

Masturbation

It should be clear from all that was written above that sexual relations between two individuals outside of marriage is prohibited. What about self-stimulation which only involves the person with their own body? Here too there is no sanctioned outlet, particularly for men. Male masturbation is indisputably prohibited. In fact, a man who deliberately stimulates himself for sexual pleasure culminating in ejaculation is described as wasting seed, a sin equated with spilling blood in some kabbalistic sources. While the primary source material for this prohibition is vague,[14] in some later religious texts the avoidance of masturbation is called *shmirat habrit* or *guarding the covenant*, which is meant to reflect a man's commitment to his covenant with God as expressed through the central rite of circumcision, symbolizing sexual self-control. It is beyond the scope of this book to present an analysis of sources on the topic. Suffice to say that the Zohar's extreme position, equating masturbation with a transgression worse than all others, has had a tremendous impact on attitudes toward male sexuality and masturbation.

Female masturbation is barely mentioned in rabbinic sources. There is a difference of opinion in the *rishonim* regarding whether

---

13. Adultery is defined as a married woman having sexual relations with a Jewish man who is not her husband.

14. There is a range of opinions among halakhic authorities on the question of male masturbation. Some view it as a Torah prohibition and others argue that it is a rabbinic prohibition. There are lenient opinions that argue that a married couple may engage in non-penetrative sexual intercourse for the sake of sexual pleasure, even though the man ejaculates outside of the woman's vagina.

it is permitted. It is not mentioned at all in Shulhan Arukh. The majority opinion is that since a woman experiencing sexual pleasure does not waste seed, female masturbation is not explicitly prohibited. Nonetheless, there is an air of disapproving silence on the topic, reinforcing the attitude that sexual self-gratification is to be avoided even if not overtly forbidden. It is certainly never normalized or directly addressed as a legitimate outlet.

Unsanctioned Sexual Urges

Stories about unsanctioned and illicit sexual urges appear throughout rabbinic literature. Often, the protagonist shows heroic discipline in refraining from sin. However, in the text below, an outlet is suggested for a man who is overcome by his desire:

B. Talmud Kiddushin 40a	תלמוד בבלי מסכת קידושין דף מ עמוד א
Rabbi Abahu said in the name of Rabbi Hanina: It is preferable that a person transgress in private rather than desecrate God's name in public as it is written.... Rabbi Ilai the Elder says: If a person sees that his evil inclination is overcoming him, he should go to a place where he is not known and wear black clothes, and he should cover himself in simple black garments, and he should do as his heart desires, but he should not desecrate the name of Heaven in public.	אמר רבי אבהו משום רבי חנינא: נוח לו לאדם שיעבור עבירה בסתר ואל יחלל שם שמים בפרהסיא, שנאמר: ואתם בית ישראל כה אמר ה'... איש גילוליו לכו עבדו [ואחר] אם אינכם שומעים אלי ואת שם קדשי לא תחללו. אמר רבי אלעאי הזקן: אם רואה אדם שיצרו מתגבר עליו, ילך למקום שאין מכירין אותו, וילבש שחורים ויתכסה שחורים ויעשה כמו שלבו חפץ, ואל יחלל שם שמים בפרהסיא.

Premarital Relationships

The passage begins with a mandate to transgress discreetly rather than publicly in order to protect God's name. In the anecdote that follows the opening statement, Rabb Ilai considers a man who is overcome by his sexual nature. He presents the lesser of the evils in allowing a person to discreetly find a way to surrender to his illicit sexual urges without blatantly and publicly flaunting the religious values and practices of the religious community.

In the next source, despite the risk to a man's life, the rabbis forbid any outlet for his illicit sexual desire:

B. Talmud Sanhedrin 75a	תלמוד בבלי מסכת סנהדרין עה
Rav Yehuda says that Rav says: There was an incident involving a certain man who set his eyes upon a certain woman and passion rose in his heart, to the point that he became deathly ill. And they came and asked doctors. And the doctors said: He will have no cure until she engages in sexual intercourse with him. The Sages said: Let him die; she may not engage in sexual intercourse with him. May she stand naked before him? Let him die; she may not stand naked before him. May she converse with him behind a fence? Let him die and not converse with him behind a fence. Rabbi Ya'akov bar Idi and Rabbi Shmuel bar Naḥmani disagreed about this issue. One of them says: The woman in question was a married woman, and the other one says: She was unmarried.	תלמוד בבלי מסכת סנהדרין דף עה עמוד א אמר רב יהודה אמר רב: מעשה באדם אחד שנתן עיניו באשה אחת, והעלה לבו טינא. ובאו ושאלו לרופאים, ואמרו: אין לו תקנה עד שתבעל. אמרו חכמים: ימות, ואל תבעל לו. - תעמוד לפניו ערומה? - ימות ואל תעמוד לפניו ערומה. - תספר עמו מאחורי הגדר? - ימות ולא תספר עמו מאחורי הגדר. פליגי בה רבי יעקב בר אידי ורבי שמואל בר נחמני. חד אמר: אשת איש היתה, וחד אמר: פנויה היתה.

373

| This makes sense according to the one who says that she was a married woman. But according to the one who says that she was unmarried, what is the reason for all this? Rav Pappa says: Because of a flaw on the family, [i.e., harm to the family's reputation]. Rav Aḥa, son of Rav Ika, says: So that the daughters of Israel should not be promiscuous with regard to forbidden sexual relations. | בשלמא למאן דאמר אשת איש היתה - שפיר. אלא למאן דאמר פנויה היתה מאי כולי האי? - רב פפא אמר: משום פגם משפחה. רב אחא בריה דרב איקא אמר: כדי שלא יהו בנות ישראל פרוצות בעריות. |

In the scenario described in this text, a man has developed an unnatural desire for a specific woman. The rabbis forbid him to have sexual relations with her, see her naked, or even converse with her behind a fence to assuage this desire, although it may lead to the loss of his life.

In the Talmudic discussion, Rav Pappa and Rav Aḥa try to understand why such stringency would be necessary for an unmarried woman given that no severe sexual prohibition exists when it comes to an unmarried woman (as compared to adultery or incest). Since most prohibitions are overridden for the sake of saving a life, why is that not the case here? Rav Pappa suggests the concern is for her family's honor. Rav Aḥa takes the discussion in a different direction: the concern is for the moral character of the daughters of Israel. Read through a modern lens, his response suggests that if we begin asking women to perform sexual acts for men outside of marriage, it would result in women losing their moral compass regarding sexuality.

I would add to this that the premise of the story, allowing a man to objectify a woman for his own sexual needs without any consideration for her as a partner (not to mention without consideration for her consent!), is antithetical to the moral, social, and religious fabric of a Torah-based society. Regardless of how one reads the story, we see evidence that sexual morality within the rabbinic discourse goes beyond the letter of the law.

Premarital Relationships

Taken together, the stories seem to be polar opposites, but in fact, I believe they can be read in synergy with one another. In the Rabbi Ilai text, a man's inability to overcome his evil inclination is acknowledged, and he is counseled to find a sexual outlet in the most discreet way possible. Rabbi Ilai's advice is for him to act outside his regular society in order not to threaten societal norms or desecrate God's name. In contrast, the text in Sanhedrin describes a case in which there is no tolerance for illicit desire. In this story, the woman is known to both the man and the rabbis. She is a daughter and a sister. Any action on his part will take place publicly and within society. Protecting sexual morality in this situation is paramount, at least for the family's sake and for the protection of all of the sisters and daughters of Israel in our communities. Together, it seems that the stories can be read as reflecting the complexity of evaluating individual situations that have a potential impact on the fabric of religious society.

Concerning the broader "*shomer negiah*/non-marital sexuality" conversation, providing private guidance to many religious men and women who are engaging in sexual activity of one sort or another is a necessity. However, religious society can and should publicly reinforce its sexual values that are expressed by *halakhah*. In a similar vein, perhaps it is time to tone down the harsh rhetoric about male masturbation and rethink its severity compared to other forms of sexual release. Acknowledging the often overpowering nature of sexual urges opens the possibility of candidly acknowledging that masturbation may be a preferable alternative to sexual experimentation between two people. It certainly avoids causing harm to another person. This is not without precedent. Sefer Hassidim in the thirteenth century writes:

Sefer Hassidim 176	ספר חסידים קעו
A person once asked about one who is overcome by desire and lest he sin and have sex with a married woman or	מעשה באחד ששאל מי שיצרו מתגבר עליו וירא פן יחטא לישכב עם אשת איש

with his *niddah* wife or any of the other sexual prohibitions which are forbidden to him. Can he masturbate so that he does not sin? He answered him at that time he should masturbate since if [the alternative is sex with] a married woman, it is preferable to masturbate and not sin with a woman. However, he needs atonement and should sit in ice during the winter or he should fast for forty days during the summer.	או עם אשתו נדה או שאר עריות האסורות לו אם יכול להוציא זרעו כדי שלא יחטא והשיב לו באותה שעה יש לו להוציא שאם אשת איש מוטב שיוציא שכבת זרע ואל יחטא באשה. אבל צריך כפרה ישב בקרח בימי החורף או יתענה ארבעים יום בימי החמה.

Sefer Hassidim did not want his readers to become casual about masturbation; the demand that he perform a penance reinforces the *de facto* nature of the suggestion. Nonetheless, the question and answer presented are fascinating and reflect a thoughtful awareness of the need for a sexual outlet for men facing enforced abstinence, even in the case of a *niddah* wife where the prohibited period will eventually end!

To conclude this section, the question of how to direct men and women engaging in sexual behavior before marriage is a complicated one. Nonetheless, as we have seen above, there are "action items" that could certainly minimize harm and degree of transgression. In the manner of Rabbi Ilai who showed a willingness to confront and respond to one individual's imperfect reality outside of the mainstream framework and values of the greater religious community, rabbis and educators should be prepared and willing to pastorally support, with whatever degree of halakhic guidance is relevant, those among us who are living their own imperfect realities while striving for commitment to Torah and *mitzvot*.

Premarital Relationships

SEX EDUCATION

Crossing the *Shomer Negiah* Threshold

The space in which sexual behavior and religious observance intersect is a fractious one. People who perceive themselves as careful with halakhic observance but nonetheless begin to sexually experiment will often deny to themselves that such behavior is taking place. The power of desire overpowers judgment which is then greatly exacerbated by the guilt due to the "sinfulness" of the encounter. Subsequent shame over illicit behavior can then potentially contribute to a harmful sense of disassociation from the sexual experience along with the inability to take responsibility or acknowledge what is happening, which can lead to true objectification or dehumanization of the other person during or after the interaction. In certain circles, intense sexual feelings are too often coupled with drinking, social expectations, and an inability to discuss or set boundaries. This is not unique to religious couples who are sexually exploring. However, once the *shomer negiah* threshold is crossed, there is no direction or framework for thinking about other halakhically important guideposts when touching, or possibly sexually using, another person.

Much of the focus in *negiah*-based conversations is almost entirely preoccupied with the concern that touch can, and perhaps almost inevitably will, become sexual. This is certainly a greater concern today than in the past as secular society no longer attaches any stigma to non-marital and casual sexual relations. On the contrary, sexual relations before marriage is the norm, and sexual experimentation is regarded as healthy.

One of the only books written about *shomer negiah* is Gila Manolson's popular book, *The Magic Touch*, published in the 1980s.[15] It promotes the notion that refraining from all touch before marriage promises something magical. Manolson reiterates over and over the potency of touch and the ease with which it can be abused, cheapened, or trivialized. The book, primarily directed at an audience of young

---

15. Gila Manolson, *The Magic Touch*, Feldheim, 1992.

people in high school and college, aims to discourage them from using one another for purely physical release, encouraging readers to date and marry young and to avoid sexual experimentation, saving the sanctity of touch for marriage.

Manolson is on point in recognizing that the promiscuity of secular culture puts pressure on young men and women to engage in sexual contact that is forbidden by the *halakhah*. Moreover, I believe she is correct that such meaningless sexuality can ultimately stunt the ability to develop deep intimacy. The alternative she promotes, to save all touch until marriage, has been adopted by many men and women who exert enormous efforts to remain steadfastly committed to *halakhah* while dating. They accept that physical intimacy will begin only after marriage. In many cases, this commitment to avoiding sexual impropriety and the inevitable sexual tension that results spur them more quickly toward marriage.[16]

More recently, Dr. Yocheved Debow, in her excellent book, *Talking About Intimacy and Sexuality*,[17] writes, "Our children are generally ignorant of Judaism's nuanced and positive approach to sexuality and are deeply entrenched in the images and beliefs of the approach of general society, which often presents a casual and rather shallow perspective…Judaism's approach…is a resounding "yes." The laws that restrict [premarital sexual activity] are formed ultimately to make intimacy in marriage more successful and enjoyable."[18]

In this way, Debow encourages parents to simultaneously normalize sexual development and the struggles that challenge our

---

16. It should be obvious that while the religious dating culture exerts pressure to date and marry quickly to avoid any touch before marriage, it neither guarantees a happy marriage nor pleasurable sexual intimacy. In some cases it pushes people to marry badly, before they really can ascertain character and compatibility. However, given that people who date for longer periods of time and even live together also are not guaranteed a happy marriage or pleasurable sexual intimacy, it is fair to conclude that every model for dating and marriage comes with its strengths and weaknesses.

17. Yocheved Debow, *Talking About Intimacy and Sexuality: A Guide for Orthodox Jewish Parents*, Ktav, 2021.

18. Debow, p. 205.

young adults while encouraging halakhic observance as the ideal. Throughout her chapter on this topic, she balances normalization of emerging sexuality and sexual feelings with the expectations and obligations of those committed to halakhic observance. However, given her target Orthodox audience, Debow strongly emphasizes the potential benefit that halakhic observance offers to meaningful sexuality.

The reality of modern relationships, however, does not always correspond to the ideal presented in either book. Sometimes the lack of touch represses intimacy, acting as an impediment rather than an impetus to move quickly toward marriage.[19] The book does not address the reality that touch is frequently expected or inevitable as a relationship unfolds and deepens, across the religious spectrum depending on age and stage of life. For couples embarking on dating following divorce or the death of a spouse the absolute ban on touch before marriage may raise other difficulties unique to this demographic. For instance, if their previous sexual relationship was unfulfilling or dysfunctional, lack of physical intimacy may act as a significant deterrent to their willingness to embark on a committed relationship a second time.

Formulating a Jewish Sexual Ethic?

While casual non-relational sex does not reflect holiness (and is *halakhically* forbidden), it does not absolve those engaging in such sexual relations from ethical or even religiously motivated considerations. Especially in such spaces (of casual sexual interaction), there is a need to encourage people to think about crafting a Jewish sexual ethic that they can call upon during such encounters. At the very least, people should be proactive in invoking other Jewish values and commandments: to respect a fellow human being, to avoid causing harm to oneself or one's partner, and to protect oneself and

---

19. This can happen in marriage as well where couples experience alienation and distance during the days on which touch is prohibited. See Chapter Eight - Part Two for reference to *niddah's* impact on the marital relationship.

one's partner. Being honest and intentional about sexual decision-making, especially where it runs counter to religious practice, can help people implement other ethical practices and other Jewish values.

Even within the context of a relationship, I have seen how cognitive dissonance between the perception of religious observance levels and prohibited sexual behavior can inhibit emotional closeness that might be formed through the physical intimacy which is happening anyway. Shame over sexual exploration becomes detrimental, hindering the possibility of touch serving as a conduit for emotional growth and an impetus to move toward marriage.

To give an example, which is really a composite of many stories I have heard over the years: a young woman described a situation in which she and her boyfriend, both *halakhically* observant and committed to *shomer negiah* behavior, were careful not to be alone with one another indoors. Yet, they repeatedly found themselves in compromising situations in outdoor spaces hoping not to get caught! Marriage was not a possibility for at least a year given their ages (eventually they did marry). The rabbi's wife she went to for counsel was kind yet failed to give guidance beyond encouraging the couple to continuously recommit to *halakhah*. The sense of constant failure was crippling the couple's ability to gain control over the situation. Here, the cognitive dissonance created around *shomer negiah* was leading to more extreme sexual behavior rather than toward no touch. I suggested that they create safer and more realistic boundaries by acknowledging their behavior, infusing it with mutual respect for one another, and being clear about what role physical touch was playing in their relationship in terms of bringing them toward greater emotional intimacy. In other words, they needed to create a Jewish sexual ethic to contain their "non-halakhic" behavior.

An Imperfect World: How Should We Be Educating?
To reinforce religious values, some form of religious sex education is imperative.

As noted above, what is concerning from a sexual education standpoint is that all that exists is a legalistic halakhic discourse (as outlined above) in which the degree of transgression is the only factor considered. We must be able to engage in a value-based conversation about consent, intimacy, and the give-and-take inherent in sexual activity. Rarely is there any honest discussion about healthy sexual outlets. Since everything is prohibited, the possibility of being intentional about setting practical limits is unavailable to those finding themselves sexually experimenting.[20]

While seeking to stay true to our commitment to *halakhah* is paramount in religious communities, it is also the responsibility of parents and educators to ensure that conversations are held about agency and consent, which must be articulated in even the most religious of spaces, if only to warn against predators or the dangers of drinking in coed environments. Especially in the younger years, it is vital that religious education be accompanied by clear information about sexual development and the normality of sexual desire and attraction, for both heterosexual and LGBTQ students.[21]. Only then can people take ownership and make room for clear decision-making with religious values and/or halakhic commitment as guiding factors.

As a religion, we are committed to protecting life. Evading discussions about safe sex can lead to dangerous encounters that can result in pregnancy and abortion or possibly life-threatening,

---

20. This last piece is not unique to Orthodox Judaism. Secular society, with all of its openness, has the same problem in reverse. There is no permission to set limits because everything is permitted. There is an urgent need in secular society as well to be mindful about limits, consent, pleasure, desire, and respect.

21. The topic of religious men and women who are LGBTQ and struggling to define their sexual identity within the framework of religious observance is complex. However, it is impossible to completely ignore a reality that almost every religious community and attendant institutions is confronting. For religious men and women who are LGBTQ there is even less conversation around sexuality. Beyond the halakhically mandated abstinence only position, I believe we need to help LGBTQ members of our community reconcile their sexual identity without completely abandoning the hope of meaningful and committed relationships. Furthermore, halakhic authorities, religious educators, and parents must provide guidelines and direction based on values from within *halakhah* as well as defining more clearly gradations of halakhic observance for these members.

sexually transmitted diseases. Similarly, failure to provide clear definitions of consent concerning touch and sexual behavior runs the distinct risk of non-consensual interactions when such engagement occurs. If we do not infuse these nuanced conversations about sexual behavior outside of marriage with other Jewish values, like loving/respecting one's partner, along with values of righteousness, justice, and human dignity, all of which are part of a Jewish sexual ethic within marriage, there is a grave danger that no sexual ethic will be implemented.

This is not to suggest that we halakhically permit the prohibited. However, halakhic sources reveal that there are significant and nuanced distinctions in the degree of transgression incurred between different kinds of touch and types of sexual behavior. Not everything fits into the same prohibitive basket of sin. It is certainly within the purview of religious parents, educators, and rabbis to provide resources and offer advice beyond the boundaries of Jewish law. The Sages of the Talmud repeatedly recognized that sometimes in matters of sexuality guidance is mandated, particularly outside of the mainstream framework.

In my years of teaching and lecturing, I find that many religious single men and women are desperately looking to build a Jewish sexual ethic and infuse their sexuality with meaning even while acknowledging the non-halakhic nature of the behavior. It is here, at this most critical area of their lives, they find themselves without any sort of pastoral guidance from educators, rabbis, and mentors. In order to create an authentic religious response, we must intentionally and fully think about the values and vocabulary we can use in a Jewish context outside of a justification framework. This too is Torah and we need to teach it well.

Appendix

A Rupture of Her Own
Nechama Goldman Barash
Reprinted with permission, with minor updates, from Tradition 51:4 (Fall 2019)

In the late 1980s, I was part of a small group of young women at Stern College interested in studying Talmud seriously. I had never studied Talmud before. There was both a feminist agenda and an intellectual challenge that propelled me towards the study: If boys could do it, then so would I! Gradually, I began to recognize it as my personal spiritual heritage. It was fortunate that as I reached early adulthood, courses of study began opening up to provide women like myself with the ability to bridge the gap in their Talmud skills. As learning programs for women opened up, I took part. First at Stern College and then, from the early '90s onward, in Jerusalem, I spent years studying Talmud at Matan before going on to study *halakhah* in Nishmat's Yoatzot Halacha program and then in Matan's Hilkhata program. The evolution of halakhic thought and application fascinated me spiritually and intellectually and gave rise to a longing to be part of the chain of transmission and education.

As I pored over the texts, I also began to recognize that the voices were of men talking about women but not represented by women. One early example comes to mind. We were studying the eighth chapter of *Sanhedrin*, specifically the topic of killing a would-be perpetrator to save him from a greater sin, such as murder or adultery, in effect taking justice into one's own hands and saving the victim. A third party is permitted to kill a man trying to rape a married woman since biblically adultery is a capital crime. However, he is not permitted to do so for an unmarried woman since sexual relations with her is not punishable by death. This was morally complicated for me. Rape is a heinous violent crime. That sexual violence against an unmarried virgin was not serious enough to warrant the same measure of extreme intervention as was warranted to save a married woman was incomprehensible. To further the incredulity, the Torah fines the rapist by obligating him to marry his victim and pay a fine to her father. It is often explained as being in the interest of the woman, so that she would not remain humiliated and abandoned. The (former) virgin was considered blameless and guaranteed the status and rights of a married woman and her father would receive monetary compensation, and after this, all is presumed well! This was difficult to reconcile as a young, modern woman new to Talmudic discourse. It called into question conflicts between tradition, text, interpretation and morality. Our teacher, at the time a young and very serious Talmud scholar and congregational rabbi, seemed utterly surprised at how contentious a topic this was for the class of Stern students.

What was completely missing from the discussion of rape in rabbinic literature both there and elsewhere was women's actual experiences of such a violation. This absence of women's voices from the endless texts about women's bodies, signs of virginity, detailed discussions about menstrual flow, sexual permissibility, and breast development is jarring. Once uncovered from the shroud of traditional male-authored exegesis, many unsettling questions about female identity and agency emerge. And yet, it is also a window into a world that has direct impact on halakhic practice and Jewish ritual.

The challenge that came with learning text was seeing the words through a lens it had never been held up to – the lens of women's perceptions, thoughts, and considerations. Hand in hand with slowly gaining mastery over the language and skills necessary to study and understand Talmudic texts and codes of law, came the growing recognition that I was reading these texts differently than the men who were teaching me or my male counterparts who were studying the same thing. While most men are able to delve into the legal conversations in an impersonal way, my experience from the world of a women's beit midrash is that one cannot remain indifferent to statements that objectify women in a way that is no longer acceptable in modern society.

The initial rush which came with the privilege of Talmud study morphed into a life-long experience of ongoing connection. Studying Talmud allows me to access the most seminal Jewish text after the Torah. It connects me to my past and illuminates my present and future. There is a sense of awe in listening to the voices learning and interpreting the Torah as they have for thousands of years. No topic is too small or mundane and the many stories and narratives give insight into personal and theological struggles. It is an intellectual challenge and a spiritual anchor. Moving from the Talmud into the vast world of halakhic codification, I better understand how I am meant to live my life in a constant encounter with the divine. Torah study has a vibrancy and passion that invites connection through questioning and exploring and provides the guidelines and boundaries I need for this ongoing journey.

However, in my pursuit of knowledge and understanding, there is also a sense of alienation. I cannot ignore that the world of Talmud is a world of hierarchy. In that hierarchy men have more *mitzvot* and obligation in the private and public sphere, serve as witnesses and judges on rabbinic courts, acquire women in marriage, and have exclusive control over divorce, all of which translate into more stature and worth. This is best exemplified in a classic Talmudic discussion: if a man and woman are drowning and only one can be saved, the man takes precedence because his life is worth more as a result of his greater obligations to Torah and *mitzvot*.

Not surprisingly, I am most drawn to the texts that are the most challenging—and most directly relevant—for me. There is something ineluctably fascinating in reading about yourself through the eyes of another. Over and over again I return to the tractates of *Ketubot*, *Kiddushin,* and *Gittin* as well as the tractate of *Nidda*, circling the texts and re-immersing, searching for my voice in a sea of men's voices about women's bodies, women's experiences, and women's most intimate moments.

The situation becomes more acute when women seek written proof that the codes of dress and behavior mandated by religious society are justified. Dress style has always been mimetic, based on society's expectations and standards. In the Talmud, this is expressed in a series of short *sugyot* around the code called *dat yehudit* or Jewish practice which is concerned with the behavior and dress of (married) Jewish women in an attempt to prevent acculturation. Religious women today actually want to acculturate in their dress and are heavily influenced by fashion styles that largely fall far short of the modesty standards required by religious communities.

When my students unpack the sources and engage in text analysis on this topic, they are underwhelmed by how unrelatable and insufficient the sources seem. The Talmudic and post-Talmudic discussions on the topic are androcentric and are almost exclusively concerned with men's obligation to not lose focus due to a women's partial bodily exposure during ritual practice. There are no fully parallel restrictions on men or is there any mention of female sexual arousal that occurs with the interaction between the genders.[1] While inevitable in modern Jewish institutions, text study on matters of dress, hair covering, and women's singing voices can lead to a complete delegitimization of the topic. This is largely as a result of the absolute emphasis placed on the written word as the repository for finding truth. There has been a reframing of these issues, in part by women who talk about modest dress in terms of female empowerment and self-respect which injects a positive vocabulary into the discourse. However, this falls short of explaining why a certain skirt or sleeve length or skirts versus pants are the necessary criteria to mirror those important values.

The buttressed fortress of *halakhah* as a monolithic institution passed down from Sinai is at times eroded when text study brings to light the spectrum of interpretation and the various external influences

---

1. Tzohar published an article by R. David Stav noting this imbalance and imposing laws of dress and conduct on men in parallel.

that infiltrates rabbinic decision-making. My experience has been that in today's source-based learning environment, the "touchstone of religious authenticity," as it were, invites new challenges to the foundations of religious life. Often, rigorous text study, especially on women's issues, but not only, can lead to disillusionment. The demystification of halakhic sources unmasks the fragility of the entire construct which at times can be shattering. There is a growing sense that in this generation the entire system of *halakhah* is on trial! I spend many hours discussing and defending its integrity, value, and truth with students after teaching contemporary halakhic issues. For some, text study liberates, providing tools to grapple with and reconcile our tradition and lending context to the structure. This, however, does not always lead to stricter devotion. Often students feel at liberty, because of the learning, to pick and choose what speaks to them. For others, there remains an unsettling sense of the arbitrary, and meta-questions of faith and belief hover implacably in the background.

I believe that we are at a seminal time in Jewish history. The walls of the academy might be tilting forward and backward to regain equilibrium, but the inner core is solid and strong and will withstand. The challenge is to find more nuanced and authentic ways to teach the sources but simultaneously admit that not everything is text-based and the values and traditions that have been passed on through the generations are as much at the core of our Jewish identity and observance as the text itself.

Bibliography

Adler, Rachel. *Engendering Judaism: An Inclusive Theology and Ethics.* Philadelphia: The Jewish Publication Society, 1998.

Alexander, Elizabeth Shanks. *Gender and Timebound Commandments in Judaism.* New York: Cambridge University Press, 2013.

Berkovits, Rahel. *A Daughter's Recitation of Mourner's Kaddish.* New York: JOFA, 2011.

Biale, David. *Eros and the Jews: From Biblical Israel to Contemporary America.* Los Angeles: University of California Press, 2015.

Biale, Rachel. *Women and Jewish Law.* New York: Schocken Books, 1984.

Boyarin, Daniel. *Carnal Israel, Reading Sex in Talmudic Culture.* Los Angeles: University of California Press, 1993.

Cohen, Pinchas. *A Practical Guide to the Laws of Niddah and Taharat Mishpacha.* Jerusalem: Targum Publishers, 2022.

Cohen, Seymour. *The Holy Letter: A Study in Jewish Sexual Morality.* New Jersey: Jason Aaronson, Inc., 1993.

Cohen, Shaye J.D. *The Beginnings of Jewishness: Boundaries, Varieties, Uncertainties.* Los Angeles: University of California Press, 1999.

Collins, Kenneth, Samuel Kottek, and Fred Rosner. *Moses Maimonides and His Practice of Medicine.* Haifa: Maimonides Research Institute, 2013.

Debow, Yocheved. *Talking About Intimacy and Sexuality: A Guide For Orthodox Jewish Parents.* New Jersey: Ktav, 2012.

Bibliography

Ellinson, Getsel. *Woman & the Mitzvot, Vol. 1: Serving the Creator.* The World Zionist Organization, 1986.

Ellinson, Getsel. *Woman & the Mitzvot, Vol. 2: The Modest Way.* The World Zionist Organization, 1986.

Farley, Margaret A. *Just Love: A Framework for Christian Sexual Ethics.* New York: Continuum Publishing Group, 2006.

Fonrobert, Charlotte Elisheva. *Menstrual Purity: Rabbinic and Christian Reconstructions of Biblical Gender.* Stanford: Stanford University Press, 2000.

Gold, Michael. *Does God Belong in the Bedroom?* Philadelphia: The Jewish Publication Society, 1992.

Golinkin, David. *The Status of Women in Jewish Law: Responsa.* Jerusalem: The Schechter Institute, 2012.

Grossman, Avraham. *Pious and Rebellious: Jewish Women in Medieval Europe.* New England: Brandeis University Press, 2004.

Halpern, Micah D., and Chana Safrai, eds. *Jewish Legal Writings by Women.* Jerusalem: Urim Publications, 1998.

Hauptman, Judith. *Rereading the Rabbis: A Woman's Voice.* Colorado: Westview Press, 1998.

Henkin, Chana, and Yehuda Herzl Henkin, eds. *Nishmat Ha-Bayit: Contemporary Questions on Women's Reproductive Health.* Jerusalem: Maggid Books, 2021.

Henkin, Yehuda. *Equality Lost: Essays in Torah Commentary, Halacha, and Jewish Thought.* Jerusalem: Urim Publications, 1999.

Henkin, Yehuda. *Understanding Tzniut: Modern Controversies in the Jewish Community.* Jerusalem: Urim Publications, 2008.

Kaufman, Debra Renee. *Rachel's Daughters: Newly Orthodox Jewish Women.* New Jersey: Rutgers University Press, 1993.

Knohl, Elyashiv. *The Marriage Covenant: A Guide to Jewish Marriage*. Ein Tzurim: Yeshivat Kibbutz Ha-Dati, 2008.

Koltun, Elizabeth, ed. *The Jewish Woman: New Perspectives*. New York: Schocken Books, 1976.

Kwall, Roberta Rosenthal. *The Myth of the Cultural Jew*. New York: Oxford University Press, 2015.

Manekin, Rachel. *The Rebellion of the Daughters: Jewish Women Runaways in Habsburg Galicia*. Princeton, New Jersey: Princeton University Press, 2020.

Meiselman, Moshe. *Jewish Woman in Jewish Law*. New York: Ktav Publishing House, 1978.

Mevorach, Oriya. *What Are You Asking?* (Hebrew). Jerusalem: Maggid, 2020.

Morozow, Sara, and Rivkah Slonim. *Holy Intimacy: The Heart and Soul of Jewish Marriage*. Cambridge, MA: Shikey Press, 2023.

Nacson, Yonatan. *A Summary of the Laws of Niddah*. Adir Press, 2018.

Ner-David, Haviva. *Life on the Fringes: A Feminist Journey Toward Traditional Rabbinic Ordination*. Needham, MA: JFL Books, 2000.

Orenstein, Peggy. *Boys & Sex*. New York: Harper Collins, 2020.

Orenstein, Peggy. *Girls & Sex*. New York: Harper Collins, 2016.

Plaskow, Judith. *Standing Again at Sinai: Judaism From a Feminist Perspective*. San Francisco: Harper, 1991.

Ribner, David S., and Talli Y. Rosenbaum. *I Am For My Beloved*. Jerusalem: Urim Publications, 2020.

Rosensweig, Yonatan, and Shmuel Harris. *Nafshi Bishe'elati: The Halakhot of Mental Health* (Hebrew). Jerusalem: Maggid, 2022.

Safrai, Shmuel, Ze'ev Safrai, and Chana Safrai. *Mishnat Eretz Israel, Tractate Ketubot A and B*. Jerusalem: E.M. Lipshitz Publishing House College, 2013.

Bibliography

Saiman, Chaim N. *Halakhah: The Rabbinic Idea of Law*. New Jersey: Princeton University Press, 2018.

Seidman, Naomi. *Sarah Schenirer and the Bais Yaakov Movement*. Liverpool: Liverpool University Press, 2019.

Shalit, Wendy. *A Return to Modesty: Discovering the Lost Virtue*. New York: The Free Press, 1999.

Shapiro, Yaakov. *Halachic Positions: What Judaism Really Says About Passion in the Marital Bed*. Jonathan Shapiro, 2017.

Smart, Michal, and Barbara Ashkenas, eds. *Kaddish: Women's Voices*. Jerusalem: Urim Publications, 2013.

Snyder, Stephen, M.D. *Love Worth Making: How to Have Ridiculously Great Sex in a Long-Lasting Relationship*. New York: St. Martin's Press, 2018.

Sobolofsky, Zvi. *The Laws and Concepts of Niddah*. Jerusalem: Maggid, 2010.

Sperber, Daniel. *On Changes in Jewish Liturgy: Options and Limitations*. Jerusalem: Urim Publications, 2010.

Sperber, Daniel. *Rabba, Maharat, Rabbanit, Rebbetzin: Women With Leadership Authority According to Halachah*. Jerusalem: Urim Publications, 2020.

Tucker, Ethan, and Micha'el Rosenberg. *Gender Equality and Prayer in Jewish Law*. New York: Ktav Publishing, 2017.

Wasserfall, Rahel R., ed. *Women and Water: Menstruation in Jewish Life and Law*. Brandeis University Press, 1999.

Weiss, Avraham. *Women at Prayer: A Halakhic Analysis of Women's Prayer Groups*. New Jersey: Ktav Publishing House, 1990.

Zimmerman, Deena R. *A Lifetime Companion to the Laws of Jewish Family Life*. Jerusalem: Urim Publications, 2011.

About the Author

Rabbanit Nechama Goldman Barash teaches contemporary *halakhah* and Talmud at Matan, Midreshet Torah V'Avodah (MTVA), and the Pardes Institute in Jerusalem. She also lectures on sexuality and *halakhah* through the Eden Center, an Israeli organization dedicated to enabling all women to have a personally meaningful and welcoming experience in the *mikvah* (ritual bath). Privately, she teaches and advises couples of different religious backgrounds on how to integrate *mikvah* practice into their marital intimacy.

Nechama moved to Israel in 1991 after graduating with a BA from Stern College in New York. She holds a master's degree in Talmud from Bar-Ilan University. She is an alumna of Matan's Advanced Talmud Institute and a graduate of Nishmat's Yoatzot Halacha program, which certifies her to serve as an advisor to individuals with halakhic questions around marital intimacy. She also studied at Matan's Hilkhata – Advanced Institute for Halakhic Studies for three years which gave her a broader exposure to classic halakhic texts around Shabbat and *kashrut*. Nechama is an active member of the rabbinic organization Beit Hillel and participates in interfaith dialogue with Roots, an organization based in Gush Etzion where she lives. This is her first book.